Second Edition

DOING JUSTICE, DOING GENDER

Susan Martin dedicates this book to her late mother, Harriette Ehrlich, and to her grandchildren, Jacob, Rose, Oliver, and Nicole.

Nancy Jurik dedicates this book to her mother, Carolyn Nekuza Jurik.

Second Edition

DOING JUSTICE, DOING GENDER

Women in Legal
and
Criminal Justice
Occupations

Susan Ehrlich Martin
Chevy Chase, Maryland

Nancy C. Jurik
Arizona State University

SAGE Publications
Thousand Oaks ▪ London ▪ New Delhi

For information:

Sage Publications, Inc.
2455 Teller Road
Thousand Oaks, California 91320
E-mail: order@sagepub.com

Sage Publications Ltd.
1 Oliver's Yard
55 City Road
London EC1Y 1SP
United Kingdom

Sage Publications India Pvt. Ltd.
B-42, Panchsheel Enclave
Post Box 4109
New Delhi 110 017 India

Printed in the United States of America

Library of Congress Cataloging-in-Publication Data

Martin, Susan Ehrlich.
Doing justice, doing gender : women in legal and criminal justice occupations / Susan Ehrlich Martin, Nancy C. Jurik.—2nd ed.
       p. cm.
Includes bibliographical references and index.
ISBN 1-4129-2720-X or 978-1-4129-2720-8 (cloth)—ISBN 1-4129-2721-8 or 978-1-4129-2721-5 (pbk.)
    1. Sex discrimination in criminal justice administration—United States.
2. Policewomen—United States. 3. Women correctional personnel—United States.
4. Women lawyers—United States. I. Jurik, Nancy C. II. Title.

HV9950.M3 2007
364.973082—dc22   2006015203

This book is printed on acid-free paper.

06   07   08   09   10   10 9 8 7 6 5 4 3 2 1

Acquisitions Editor:	Jerry Westby
Editorial Assistant:	Kim Suarez
Production Editor:	Laureen A. Shea
Copy Editor:	Jennifer Withers
Typesetter:	C&M Digitals (P) Ltd.
Proofreader:	Kevin Gleason
Indexer:	Will Ragsdale
Cover Designer:	Candice Harman

Contents

List of Tables

Acknowledgments

This revised version of *Doing Justice, Doing Gender* is the outcome of the equal collaboration of the authors who undertook this revision at the urging of Sage editor Jerry Westby. Our goal, as in the initial version, is to produce a readable but thorough and theoretically grounded examination of the changes that have occurred in the criminal justice organizations, occupations, and women's work in them both over the past 40 years and, in this edition, in the past decade. As our readers will discover, there is both good news and bad news. The numbers of women in policing, legal careers, and corrections work have grown, and more women are moving up the career ladder to become supervisors and partners in law firms. Nevertheless, discrimination and informal barriers to women's achievements in these occupations continue. In this edition, we have maintained our theoretical perspective and the organizational structure of the earlier book. We have updated the material by discussing new trends in each of the occupations and how these affect women, and we have included new research findings and statistical material. In addition, given growing globalization and the presence of women in justice occupations worldwide, we have included some materials on women in each occupation from an international perspective.

We wish to thank the six Sage reviewers whose comments helped guide our revision: Polly F. Radosh, Phoebe Morgan, Becky L. Tatum, Rebecca S. Katz, Jessie Krienert, and Lori Elis. We also wish to thank Belinda Herrera for help with the references and comments on Chapter 2 and Madelaine Adelman for suggestions on Chapter 9. Gray Cavender reviewed and edited several of the chapters and made helpful suggestions and provided strong intellectual and moral support. Malcolm Martin gave continuous support from the initiation through the completion of the revision.

CHAPTER 1

Introduction

Changes in Criminal Justice, Occupations, and Women in the Workplace

Before 1972, the number of women employed in the justice system as police officers, lawyers, judges, and correctional officers (COs) was minuscule; those women were excluded from most jobs that entailed the exercise of authority over men. Women worked only as "specialists," drawing on qualities and skills associated with their gender. For example, policewomen supervised women and juvenile arrestees and performed secretarial work. Women lawyers were concentrated in specialties deemed "appropriate" for women, such as domestic relations; they rarely litigated cases or became judges. Women COs worked in prisons for women or in juvenile institutions where their capacity for "mothering" was considered beneficial for rehabilitating delinquent youth.

As part of a larger societal trend, women have entered the workplace in increasing numbers and moved into occupations traditionally filled by men only. Since the late 1970s, a growing number of women work in all parts of the justice system. In the criminal justice system (CJS), police agencies hire women as patrol officers, and probation and parole departments assign mixed-gender caseloads to women. Local jails, state correctional systems, and the Federal Bureau of Prisons hire women to guard men inmates. Women lawyers handle civil and criminal cases as private or governmental attorneys and serve as judges and magistrates. Women also comprise a growing proportion of the professors in law schools and departments of criminal justice, criminology, and sociology, where they educate the next generation of CJS personnel. Women are also advancing in justice fields; more women have been promoted and hold visible leadership positions. To some extent, the presence of women in these realms is now taken for granted.

Despite these inroads, individual and organizational resistance to women in justice fields continues, and women are often still treated as second-class citizens in the station house, courtroom, and prison. The obstacles faced by women justice workers are part of organizational and societal arrangements that construct and reinforce women's subordination to men. Women in fields numerically dominated by men face many barriers: exclusion from informal work cultures; hostility expressed in social interactions; organizational policies that permit gender segregation, differential assignments, sexual harassment; and the marginalization of women with family responsibilities. The confluence of these barriers often produces fewer recruits, lower pay, slower advancement, and in some cases, higher dropout rates for the women in these fields.

Resistance to women may be associated with the social control functions of justice occupations. Criminologist Frances Heidensohn (1992, p. 99) has argued that social control is a "profoundly gender-linked concept." Women have always helped to maintain social order, initially only informally in the family. Later, women were given institutional authority over children and other women but had to operate within control systems dominated by men; they rarely were granted formal authority over men.

> The view that men "own" order and have sole rights to preserve it, seems to be at the core of much of the equality debates. (Heidensohn, 1992, p. 215)

This book examines the organization of justice occupations along gender lines. In investigating these occupations, we note that they involve more than a set of tasks or the source of a paycheck. An occupation provides social and emotional rewards and affects many aspects of life and identity. It influences the manner in which a person is treated by others, even outside of work. It also defines social status and shapes income, lifestyle, and children's life chances. In industrial societies, what one does is a primary source of who one is (R. H. Hall, 1994, pp. 6–9).

We examine the justice system occupations of policing, law, and corrections. We focus broadly on the field of law, both civil and criminal, and more narrowly on municipal policing and correctional security in men's prisons. Our choices reflect both the limited literature available on other aspects of justice work and the intense gender-based resistance to women who enter these three fields.[1] This book addresses the following questions:

1. Historically how have the roles of women working in the justice system changed, and how are such changes connected to larger societal and occupational transformations?

2. What barriers have women in justice occupations encountered at the interpersonal, organizational, occupational, and societal levels?

3. How have women performed in their expanded duties and how have they responded to work-related barriers?

4. What effects have women had on the justice system, victims, offenders, coworkers, and the public?

5. What barriers and challenges are women in the CJS likely to face in the future?

The answers to these questions combine three divergent areas of inquiry: work and occupations, the justice system, and gender studies and changes in each area. We are especially interested in how gender differences are constructed, maintained, challenged, and reconstructed in the workplace.

Gendered divisions of labor in the justice system and elsewhere are part of larger ongoing processes of differentiation in society. Social differentiation, or the practice of distinguishing categories based on some attribute or set of attributes, is a fundamental social process and the basis for differential evaluations and unequal rewards. Differentiation assumes, magnifies, and even creates behavioral and psychological differences to ensure that the subordinate group differs from the dominant one. It presumes that differences are "natural" and desirable. Social differentiation based on gender is found in virtually every society (West & Zimmerman, 1987). Gender differences are produced simultaneously with differentiation along a variety of dimensions, including class, race, ethnicity, religion, and sexual orientation. We will argue that the social accomplishment of such differences occurs simultaneously and is integrally linked with the production of social inequality, shaping the social location of individuals and the social institutions in which they work, live, and interact (Burgess-Proctor, 2006; Fenstermaker & West, 2002). The production of difference is also influenced by the perception and control of human bodies, and we will attend to the ways in which bodies figure in to policing, law, and correctional work.

The next section of this chapter provides a brief overview of the CJS mission. It is followed by discussions of the history of women in justice occupations, and socioeconomic conditions that led to expanding opportunities for women workers.

The CJS: Mission, Processes, and Workforce

The mission of the CJS is to control conduct that violates the criminal laws of the state. The components of the CJS include law enforcement, courts, and corrections; they are responsible for the prevention and detection of crime, and the apprehension, adjudication, sentencing, punishment, and rehabilitation of criminals. Critics argue that the term "criminal justice system" is a misnomer for several reasons. First, although components are linked in the processing of criminal offenses, coordination across agencies often is lacking. Agencies are characterized by internal and interorganizational conflicts over goals, resources, and authority that are complicated because these agencies work at different levels of government and often have overlapping jurisdictions. Second, critics argue that the CJS does not promote justice (Belknap, 2001; Clear, Cole, & Reisig, 2006). The U.S. CJS is large and costly, and its funding often comes at the expense of vital social service and educational programs. Third, the CJS disproportionately focuses on "street crimes" to the exclusion of crimes by corporate executives and other societal elites. This leads to a fourth and related critique: the overrepresentation of poor men of color as offenders convinces many analysts that, across all stages, the CJS not only replicates but magnifies racism (Christie, 2000; Parenti, 1999). Critics also argue that the CJS reinforces class and gender inequalities that characterize the larger social context (Belknap, 2001; A. Y. Davis, 2003).

Total expenditures for the CJS in 2001 were more than $167 billion dollars, about half of which were spent on salaries for the nearly 2.3 million CJS employees (Bauer & Owens, 2004). That year, more than a million persons (or about 46 percent of CJS employees) worked for law enforcement agencies, mostly in 18,000 local police and sheriff's departments, and about 488,000 people (21 percent of CJS employees) worked for local, state, and federal courts. Corrections has several subsystems: local jails; state and federal prisons; community corrections, including probation, parole, and community residential centers; and juvenile corrections. By 2001, these agencies employed 747,000 people (more than double the nearly 300,000 corrections employees in 1982; Bauer & Owens, 2004).

The CJS has undergone significant expansion and transition since women first became involved in the mid-19th century. These changes have been associated with women's expanding roles as CJS workers.

Historical Context of Women in Justice Occupations

The ratio of men to women in occupations, in the justice system and elsewhere, is seldom static. Internal pressures within work organizations and in larger social and economic arenas produce changes. To understand women's situation today, we must consider their CJS work history, and the role of the women's movement in promoting expanding work opportunities for women.

Throughout the 19th century, U.S. justice and crime control were inefficient and corrupt; reforms were sporadic and ineffectual. In both the United States and the United Kingdom, women entered the public sector through participation in moral improvement campaigns to end slavery, adopt prohibition, and establish social welfare institutions such as the juvenile court. A first-wave feminist movement fought for women's right to vote, obtain an education, and own property. Women's groups also addressed a wide range of other social issues, including the identification of economic deprivation and men's moral depravity as causes of poverty, out-of-wedlock pregnancy, and criminality among women. Reformers attacked public indifference to the poor and moral double standards for men and women. By caring for "fallen women," they hoped to bring about a moral reordering of society (Heidensohn, 1992; Schulz, 2004).

At first, women worked through volunteer social services. However, as they succeeded in getting the state to assist and extend social control over the poor, many women sought formal positions in public institutions. They presented themselves as specialists in working with women and children (Rafter, 1990). They argued for police matrons to "save wayward youth and helpless women from the evils of industrialism, alcohol, and other abuses" (S. E. Martin, 1980, p. 22). They demanded that prisons hire matrons to work with incarcerated women and children and that they be housed in facilities separate from men's prisons (Freedman, 1981).

In their efforts to protect women from men and from their own worst instincts, reformers became part of social control systems dominated by men. Ironically, as reformers tried to curb vice and crime, they simultaneously participated in the oppressive "protection" of their own sex, especially targeting impoverished or working-class women and girls (Chesney-Lind & Pasko, 2004). Although they carved out new forms of women's work, early CJS professionals reinforced gender stereotypes that subsequently limited women's career possibilities for more than half a century (Schulz, 2004).

Early in the 20th century, immigration, urban migration, the failure of prohibition, and the rise of organized crime compounded CJS problems and made periodic reform efforts short-lived. In 1931, the National Commission on Law Observance and Enforcement (appointed two years earlier by President Hoover to conduct a national study of the American CJS and known as the Wickersham Commission) detailed the lawlessness of the police and shortcomings of the U.S. justice system. However, the Depression and World War II impeded implementation of the suggested reforms. During this period, women's CJS work opportunities stagnated. From the 1930s to the 1970s, women's numbers diminished, and restrictions on their duties continued.

However, a series of social and economic changes that began with World War II culminated in the expansion of women's work roles. Almost three decades of economic prosperity after this war obscured the seeds of disaffection and rebellion that exploded in the 1960s and 1970s. Precipitating conditions included the middle-class exodus to the suburbs, cultural values focused on consumption, deteriorating inner cities, rising urban crime rates, political corruption, racism, poverty, and gender subordination (Davey, 1995; Echols, 1989). These social tensions converged with CJS problems that had been ignored since the 1920s. The result was a turbulent decade that included the Civil Rights and antiwar movements, urban riots, political assassinations, the women's movement, and lesbian/gay rights movement.

A second wave of feminism was stimulated by women's participation in civil rights and antiwar activities, especially when women were denied leadership positions in these movements (Freedman, 2002). Once set in motion, the women's movement created a dynamic pattern in which legal changes altered social attitudes and led to further demands for change, culminating in greatly expanded work opportunities for women in the CJS and elsewhere. The movement was fueled by increases in women's education and massive entry into paid work that were largely unnoticed in the 1950s and 1960s. These changes stimulated middle class women's frustration with the "feminine mystique" (Friedan, 1963) and contributed to the formation of groups such as the National Organization for Women (NOW). NOW supported the anti–sex-discrimination provisions of the 1964 Civil Rights Act and Equal Pay Act of 1963, the Equal Rights Amendment (ERA), and the expansion of abortion rights (Freedman, 2002).

Much of the initial energy of a unified women's movement was dissipated by the mid-1970s through factionalism and by the unsuccessful battle over the ERA. Nevertheless, congressional passage of the ERA and the 1973 Supreme Court decision in *Roe v. Wade* that made abortion a legal option for women meant that feminism was taken more seriously. Feminist goals, such as women's rights to paid employment, equal pay for equal work, and jobs in all occupations without limitations imposed by sex discrimination, became more socially accepted. The women's movement became more institutionalized during the 1980s and won many legal victories related to antidiscrimination laws, sexual harassment, and the passage of the Violence Against Women Act of 1994, which was renewed in 1998 and 2005.

By the 1980s, however, women of color and lesbians attacked the second-wave women's movement for centering on the experiences of white middle class women in framing feminist agendas (Moraga & Anzaldua, 1983). The movement was also criticized for ignoring the experiences of poor women and women with children in its initial program for change. These critiques have led to a broader feminist agenda designed to address the needs of these formerly excluded groups. Expanded feminist approaches stressed multiple sites of inequality and dominance that included race, class, and sexual orientation as well as gender discrimination. This "intersectional" model examines gender "through the lens of difference while at the same time acknowledging the instrumental role of power in shaping gender relations" (Burgess-Proctor, 2006, p. 35).

The social activism of the 1950s through 1970s stimulated a variety of changes in the legal system and in the CJS. These legal shifts converged with economic trends to increase the demand for and supply of women workers in justice occupations.

Legal Changes

During the 1960s and 1970s, legislation extended civil rights and equal employment opportunities to formerly excluded social groups, including women. Interpretation of these laws by courts has shaped both the implementation and effectiveness of this legislation in three areas critical to working women: equal employment opportunity, sexual harassment, and the treatment of pregnancy and maternity leave.

Equal Employment Opportunity Law

Equal employment opportunity law rests on Title VII of the Civil Rights Act of 1964 and the Equal Employment Opportunity Act of 1972, which expanded coverage of Title VII to most private and public employers, including state and local governments. Title VII prohibits discrimination on the basis of race, religion, creed, color, sex, or national origin with regard to hiring, compensation, terms, conditions, and privileges of employment. Employers may not refuse to hire, segregate, or classify employees so as to deprive them of employment opportunities because of sex. An exception is permitted only if it can be proven that sex is "a *bona fide* occupational qualification (BFOQ) reasonably necessary for the normal operation of that particular business or enterprise." This interpretation is warranted only "where it is necessary for the purpose of authenticity or genuineness," such as in hiring an actor or actress. The law prohibits an employer from refusing to hire a woman because of assumptions about the comparative employment characteristics of women in general (e.g., they are not as strong as men), because of gender stereotypes (e.g., that women are less capable of aggressive "salesmanship"), or because of the preferences of coworkers, employers, clients, or customers (Federal Register, 1965, p. 14927). Title VII also established the Equal Employment Opportunity Commission (EEOC) to enforce its provisions.

In the early 1970s, several cases challenged sex-based classifications that had limited women's work opportunities. In *Griggs v. Duke Power Co.* (1971), the Supreme Court made it easier to win discrimination cases by ruling that the plaintiff does not have to prove that the employer intended to discriminate. Once a plaintiff shows that job qualifications disproportionately exclude a group or class, the burden falls on the employer to prove that the requirements are BFOQs and that no other selection mechanisms can be substituted. Application of this standard (i.e., discriminatory impact regardless of intent) invalidated minimum height and weight requirements that had excluded women from police and corrections work.

In 1965, "affirmative action" began with Presidential Executive Order 11246, which required all federal contractors to develop written affirmative action policies to redress past discrimination by increasing recruitment, promotion, retention, and on-the-job training for women and minorities. During the 1970s, courts and the EEOC gradually interpreted *Griggs* as requiring other employers to establish equal employment opportunity (EEO) plans, such as numerical goals for the hiring and promotion of protected race and sex groups. Some affirmative action programs were instituted by consent decrees (i.e., judicially enforceable settlements that were entered into by both sides) that resulted from successful lawsuits charging race and sex discrimination. Other programs were initiated by employers anxious to avoid court involvement in their personnel practices.

These legal changes were highly significant in expanding women's work opportunities. However, the courts did not always rule in women's favor. For example, some courts permitted exceptions to the prohibitions on BFOQs. In *Dothard v. Rawlinson* (1977), the Court agreed that height and weight requirements for COs in Alabama's maximum security prisons violated Title VII but still ruled that the ban on women working in contact positions was justifiable given that this prison was unsafe for women. The court decisions that followed *Dothard* were less likely to accept BFOQs. However, court decisions in EEO cases have not generally exhibited a consistently linear pattern of progress for either white women or men and women of color.

In the 1980s, the Supreme Court began to limit affirmative action programs and narrow the grounds on which plaintiffs could win discrimination suits. For example, in *City of Richmond v. Croson* (1989), the Supreme Court ruled that in state and local contracting, affirmative action was a "highly suspect tool," and subjected affirmative action plans to "strict scrutiny," holding that they were unconstitutional unless racial discrimination could be proven to be "widespread throughout a particular industry." In addition, the Court mandated that "the means chosen 'fit' this compelling goal so closely that there is little or no possibility that the motive for the classification was illegitimate racial prejudice or stereotype." Such an instance arose in the case of *United States v. Paradise* (1987). The Court upheld the use of racial quotas as a remedy for the systematic racial discrimination in the Alabama Department of Public Safety (state police), which, after 12 years of litigation and court decrees, had failed to end "pervasive, systematic, and obstinate discriminatory exclusion of blacks." It upheld the lower court order to promote one black officer for every white officer promoted to sergeant. In the lone Supreme Court decision specifically involving affirmation for women, *Johnson v. Transportation Agency, Santa Clara County* (1987), the Court upheld a county affirmative action program that set goals for achieving a workforce in which women, minorities, and people with disabilities would be represented in proportion to their population in the county's labor force.

Despite court rulings that began to narrow affirmative action in the 1980s, in 1990 Congress passed one of the most sweeping pieces of civil rights legislation since the Civil Rights Act of 1964: the Americans With Disabilities Act (ADA). A federal statutory provision (Section 504 of the Rehabilitation Act of 1973) prohibited discrimination against qualified but disabled individuals in programs that received federal funds. However, the ADA goes beyond Section 504 to include entities (e.g., public services, private employers) that do not receive federal funds (Almanac of Policy Issues, 2006). The term "disability" refers to an individual who (1) has a physical or mental impairment that substantially limits one or more major life activities, (2) has a record of such an impairment, or (3) is regarded as having such an impairment. It requires the covered entity (e.g., employer or public facility) to provide "reasonable accommodation" for "qualified individuals with a disability" unless the accommodation poses an "undue hardship" on that entity. A "qualified" individual is one who is able to perform the essential functions of employment. "Reasonable accommodation" refers to job restructuring (i.e., part-time or modified work schedules, acquisition or modification of equipment or devices, provision of qualified interpreters, or other similar accommodations) or making existing facilities accessible to and usable by individuals with disabilities. "Undue hardship" refers to accommodations that require significant difficulty or expense (relative to the overall financial resources and type of operation).

The accommodation provision of the ADA has been a useful legal device in affirmative action claims because it recognizes the need for organizations to accommodate the situations of diverse individuals rather than requiring them to assimilate into organizations designed for some "nondisabled" majority. The concept of "reasonable accommodation" has been used as a mechanism for resolving inmate privacy concerns and the opportunity for women COs to work in men's prisons as well as for lactating women seeking accommodations in order to pump breast milk. However, what constitutes a recognized disability and reasonable accommodation under the ADA continues to be a legally unresolved matter, as the body of law interpreting the ADA is still emerging. A number of recent cases have limited the rights of employees (Almanac of Policy Issues, 2006).

In the 1990s, affirmative action was further narrowed but was still permitted in certain circumstances. In *Adarand Constructors, Inc. v. Pena* (1995), the Supreme Court reaffirmed the ruling in *Croson* (1989) and extended the standard established in that case to federal contracting. The Court again required "strict scrutiny" of affirmative action programs, arguing that they must fulfill a "compelling government interest" and be "narrowly tailored" to fit the particular situation. A month later, President Clinton noted that the Court's decision set stricter standards but reaffirmed a continuing need for affirmative action. He issued guidelines that called for eliminating any program that created quotas, preferences for unqualified individuals, or reverse discrimination or whose purpose had been served. Nevertheless, many employers have continued to implement voluntary affirmative action policies.

More recent cases involve the status of affirmative action in higher education. In *Grutter v. Bollinger* (2003), the Supreme Court ruled (5–4) to uphold the University of Michigan Law School's policy permitting race to be one of many factors considered by colleges in selecting students because that selection policy furthered a compelling interest in diversity but was individualized in its approach. At the same time, it ruled (*Gratz v. Bollinger*, 2003) that the university's formulaic approach used in its undergraduate admissions procedure was not permissible. How much affirmative action will be permitted in the future is uncertain given the continued narrowing of its uses and the replacement of Justices O'Connor (who wrote the *Grutter* majority decision) and Rehnquist by more conservative Justices Roberts and Alito on the high court.

Sexual Harassment Law

Sexual harassment is another important legal issue affecting working women. Sexual harassment, a term that came into use in 1976 (MacKinnon, 1978), is recognized as a form of sex discrimination prohibited under Title VII of the Civil Rights Act of 1964. Two general types of sexual harassment have been addressed by the courts: "*quid pro quo*" and "the hostile work environment." First, *quid pro quo* harassment involves an explicit exchange: there is a sexual advance or proposition with which the woman must comply, or forfeit an employment or educational benefit. Second, hostile environment sexual harassment occurs "when an employer encourages or tolerates the existence in its workplace of an environment fraught with sexual innuendo and intimidation or other forms of harassing conduct sufficiently severe or pervasive to alter the terms and conditions of a woman's employment" (Gregory, 2003, p. 125). It includes a variety of overtly sexual behaviors such as touching, teasing, and making comments about a woman's appearance or sexuality that require no response on the woman's part but establish a pattern that makes her work environment unpleasant or hostile. "Gender harassment" that is unrelated to sex but includes derogatory comments or behavior directed toward a woman solely because of her gender may also meet the legal criteria of a hostile work environment (Gregory, 2003, p. 150).

At first, courts refused to view sexual harassment as sex discrimination under Title VII (*Barnes v. Train*, 1974). However, by 1977, several lower courts ruled that *quid pro quo* sexual harassment was a form of sex discrimination (Gregory, 2003, p. 122). The courts first recognized hostile environment harassment in *Bundy v. Jackson* (1981), a case involving a woman prison counselor. Bundy claimed that she had been harassed by several supervisors and that her rejection of their overtures had blocked and delayed her job advancement. The court reasoned that whether or not the complaining employee lost tangible benefits (i.e., *quid pro quo* harassment), the employer had condoned a hostile and discriminatory work environment that violated Title VII. Unless employers are prohibited from maintaining a "discriminatory environment," a woman employee could be sexually harassed with impunity as long as the action stopped short of firing or taking other formal action against her when she resisted.

In *Meritor Savings Bank FSB v. Vinson* (1986), the Supreme Court, in its first ruling related to sexual harassment, unanimously affirmed that both *quid pro quo* and hostile environment sexual harassment are prohibited by Title VII and that employers may be held liable for acts of sexual harassment committed by their employees. According to the facts presented, the plaintiff, Michelle Vinson, had acquiesced to sexual relations with her immediate superior out of fear of losing her job, but neither reported the problem nor used the bank's complaint procedure. The alleged harasser denied all allegations of sexual misbehavior; the bank claimed that because it did not know of the situation, it could not be held responsible. The Court held that in hostile environment cases, the victim does not have to demonstrate economic harm, but for sexual harassment to be actionable, it must be so severe or pervasive that it alters the conditions of the victim's employment.

In 1991, the U.S. Senate hearings for Clarence Thomas's confirmation to the U.S. Supreme Court, and Anita Hill's testimony against his confirmation, more than any single act, brought sexual harassment "out of the closet" as a legitimate harm. This controversy also pitted the woman's perception of harassment against the viewpoint claimed by her harasser. In *Ellison v. Brady* (1991), the Ninth Circuit Federal Appellate Court developed the "reasonable woman" standard stating that this, rather than the traditional legal standard (i.e., the "reasonable man" or "reasonable person"), should prevail in determining whether conduct is "sufficiently severe or pervasive to alter the conditions of employment and create an abusive working environment."

During that same year, Congress amended Title VII of the Civil Rights Act to provide victims an opportunity to seek damage awards in sexual harassment cases. Prior to that time, although Title VII made employers liable for sexual harassment in their agencies, it included no provision for damages, and relief was purely equitable (i.e., victims were eligible only for back pay awards). Acknowledging that employers require more than an injunctive order and the likelihood of having to pay a meager back pay award to encourage them to do the right thing, Congress amended the title so that sex discrimination would come at a price. It mandated that defendants recompense women for their injuries by providing for punitive damages when the employer's behavior was particularly egregious, but it left unclear just what that situation required. The goal of this initiative was to combat sex discrimination as well as recompense the victims.[2]

In *Harris v. Forklift Systems, Inc.* (1993), the Court clarified this standard, ruling that for a work environment to be abusive, the harassing conduct does not have to "seriously affect [an employee's] psychological well being" or lead her to "suffer injury." The Court adopted what it termed "a middle path" between conduct that is "merely offensive" and that which causes psychological injury. Determination of what is sufficiently severe and pervasive to be actionable is based on the totality of the circumstances and depends on such factors as its frequency, its severity, and whether it physically threatens or humiliates or unreasonably interferes with the employee's work.

In 1998, two cases clarified the extent of employer liability. The Supreme Court ruled that employers are held to a standard of strict liability for unlawful harassment that "culminates in a tangible employment action such as discharge, demotion or undesirable assignment" by supervisors (*Faragher v. City of Boca Raton*, 1998). When there has been no tangible employment action, an employer may raise an affirmative defense to liability by proving that (1) it exercised reasonable care to prevent and correct sexually harassing behavior and (2) the employee unreasonably failed to take advantage of any preventive or corrective opportunities to avoid harm (*Burlington Industries v. Ellerath*, 1998). Simply having a policy is not enough; the employer must take reasonable steps to prevent sexual harassment and stop it when it occurs. This includes a duty to distribute its policy to employees, train managers in dealing with complaints, create multiple reporting channels once harassment starts, and have follow-up procedures in place. While the law is still evolving, these cases have established that an affirmative defense is not available when the supervisory harassment involves a tangible job benefit like a promotion, nor is it available to shield employers from liability where the employing organization's response is ineffective or unreasonable. Antiharassment policies must be effectively implemented and enforced, provide multiple reporting channels, and protect the victim against retaliation.

Pregnancy and Family Leave

A third important area of law that affects women workers is pregnancy and maternity leave. In two decisions, *Geduldig v. Aiello* (1974) and *General Electric Co. v. Gilbert* (1976), the Supreme Court held that exclusion of pregnancy-related disabilities from an insurance plan was not sex discrimination. When existing benefits or opportunities are offered equally to men and women, it was not discrimination to withhold additional benefits that might be particularly valuable to one sex. The basic principle of the *Gilbert* decision is that Title VII protections did not cover pregnant women because the act protected only against discrimination based on gender. According to the Court, failure to provide disability benefits for pregnancy made a distinction between two groups of women—the pregnant and nonpregnant—rather than a distinction between women and men. Thus, it was not discrimination.

In 1978, Congress rejected the Court's view and amended Title VII with the Pregnancy Discrimination Act (PDA). The PDA prohibits discrimination on the basis of pregnancy, childbirth, or related medical conditions and requires employers who provide employment benefits to treat pregnancy like any other temporary disability. The law assures women of at least the same minimum benefits offered men; it permits, but does not require, an employer to provide additional protection for pregnant workers.

In *Newport News Shipbuilding and Dry Dock Co. v. EEOC* (1983), the Supreme Court specifically acknowledged that Congress overturned the holding in *Gilbert* with the PDA. Women now are bringing and winning class action cases regarding pregnancy discrimination in benefits, as well as in hiring and promotion decisions. For example, in 2002 the EEOC settled a class action pregnancy discrimination case against Verizon charging that its predecessor companies discriminated against women on maternity leave by denying them service credit for the time they were on leave. The number of pregnancy discrimination claims filed with EEOC between 1992 and 2000 increased by nearly 25 percent (Gregory, 2003, p. 96).

As with other forms of antidiscrimination law, pregnancy discrimination law has both expanded and restricted women's employment opportunities. Even when pregnant women are treated badly by their employers, they do not necessarily have a "lawful" claim of employment discrimination. According to the PDA, such discrimination exists only in situations where pregnant women are treated less favorably than nonpregnant employees with temporary disabilities who work in similar circumstances. Moreover, employers have also become more savvy about hiding pregnancy discrimination practices in order to protect themselves from legal claims (Gregory, 2003). The scope of the PDA is still a matter of contention. While all Circuit Courts recognize that it covers pregnancy, some Circuit Court decisions still apply the PDA narrowly to pregnancy but not to claims based on related situations that only women face, such as breastfeeding, contraception, and infertility treatments; others include these conditions within its scope (Eldredge, 2005).

In an effort to provide additional time off for employees who need to care for their families, the U.S. Congress passed the Family and Medical Leave Act in 1993. This law states that "covered" employers must grant an "eligible" employee up to a total of 12 work weeks of unpaid leave during any 12-month period for one of more of the following reasons: (1) birth and care of the employee's newborn child, (2) placement with the employee of a son or daughter for adoption or foster care, (3) care for an immediate family member with a serious health condition, or (4) medical leave when the employee is unable to work because of a serious health condition. Among the list of requirements for eligibility under this act are specifications that the employee must work at least 24 hours per week for an employer who has 50 or more employees (U.S. Department of Labor, 2006). Individuals whose employment situation does not meet these criteria are not eligible for family leave. Those who do take leave time must be able to cover the pay loss that they will experience. In contrast to the United States, workers in many European countries are guaranteed more lengthy and paid family leave options (Freedman, 2002).

Despite inconsistencies, legal decisions have advanced the employment opportunities of white women and men and women of color. Social movement and legal activism and economic trends have also promoted changes within the justice system, and such changes have further transformed women's work roles in policing, corrections, and law.

Systemic Reforms and Expanded Opportunities for Women

Efforts to reform and professionalize justice system staff and to expand legal education have increased women's employment opportunities in justice fields. Social activism contributed to the creation of new law schools and their burgeoning enrollments. Eliminating gender barriers in admission to law schools, as well as the opening of a number of new law schools, has led to a major shift in law school enrollments. The proportion of women law students has increased, and women also comprise a growing proportion of lawyers working in the civil and criminal justice systems.

The occupation of law has traditionally been viewed as a prototypical profession. Definitions of a profession vary, but the recognition of any occupation as such depends on the power of those in the field to persuade lawmakers and the public that they are a profession and deserve that status on the basis of possession of unique expertise and the ability to apply this knowledge (R. H. Hall, 1994, pp. 44–53). Often, a group seeks such recognition to gain the higher salaries, greater social standing, and increased autonomy associated with the label (Seron & Ferris, 1995).[3] In contrast to law, CJS occupations have not traditionally been viewed as professions.

As civil rights law and related court interpretations opened many educational and employment opportunities previously closed to persons of color and white women, the CJS was expanding and facing pressures to reform and professionalize its staff. During the 1960s, discontent with the CJS and its inability to respond to growing urban problems led to a simultaneous emphasis on "law and order" and rational planning and reform. The former was a shorthand expression for a general fear not only of street crime, but of the violence and demonstrations surrounding the Civil Rights and antiwar movements. However, it was also a critique of the violent methods used by CJS officials in responding to these matters. In 1965, President Johnson expanded the federal government's role in criminal justice processes. He appointed the President's Commission on Law Enforcement and the Administration of Justice (the President's Crime Commission) to analyze the nature and origins of crime in the United States and to make policy recommendations. The Commission recommended that criminal justice agencies be shaped to form an integrated "system," with better coordination among police, courts, and corrections. It called for upgrading CJS personnel by recruiting white women and people of color, widening women's assignments, raising selection standards, and providing more rigorous training to all system personnel.

To implement these recommendations, Congress passed the Omnibus Crime Control and Safe Streets Act of 1968. The Act created the Law Enforcement Assistance Administration (LEAA), which supplied funds to states for criminal justice planning, innovative programs, and personnel training. LEAA funds and higher educational qualifications led to expanded community college and university programs in criminology and criminal justice in the 1970s. Although Congress abolished the LEAA in the 1980s, the program's growth, combined with EEO regulations, generated many women graduates from associate's and bachelor's degree programs in criminal justice and related fields. (Today, more than half of the students in such programs are women.) The equalization of educational opportunities in general and the expansion of criminology graduate programs in particular also allowed many women to earn graduate degrees and become the researchers and professors who educate future CJS practitioners (Wilson & Moyer, 2004). These trends produced a growing pool of white women and of men and women of color to fill concomitant CJS demands for more highly educated workers.

As further impetus for expansion and reform, prison riots during the 1970s and 1980s forced federal and state officials to address crowded and squalid living conditions in prisons and inmates' demand for rights (Goldstone & Useem, 1999). These riots occurred in a context of expanding legal services for the poor and growing civil rights for racial and ethnic minority groups who were disproportionately incarcerated (Hawkins & Alpert, 1989). Court-ordered racial integration of prisons heightened tensions in overcrowded facilities. Courts intervened to protect inmates' constitutional rights. Commissions formed to deal with the prison riot crisis recommended solutions similar to those of the President's Crime Commission: increased rationalization, centralization, and staff professionalization (Clear et al., 2006). Even as these reform efforts were emerging, competing movements advocated the end of rehabilitation as a goal for prisons. Whether or not rehabilitation had been seriously attempted, it was abandoned and replaced with mandatory sentencing and other get-tough sentencing policies (Cavender, 2004).

Changes in CJS personnel practices combined with EEO regulations removed many arbitrary and culturally biased personnel practices, such as selection criteria and assignments based on friendship or on attributes unrelated to job performance. Administrators' control over officers' personal lives, from hair length to living arrangements, has been increasingly challenged by new generations of officers. Universalistic standards produced more opportunities for people with particular skills regardless of how well they "fit" into the informal group and, thus, have created more diverse CJS staffs with respect to gender, race, ethnicity, and sexuality.

CJS reforms entailed discourses that challenged the arbitrary use of force in policing and corrections. In this context, discourses refer not just to language but to frameworks for understanding, frameworks that may include texts to guide actions. In the case of CJS reform efforts, detailed rules were written to govern the use of force by police and COs, making it a means of last resort. Police and correctional administrators believed that professionalizing their personnel by raising training and educational requirements would reduce unlawful acts of violence and abuse by staff, and protect CJS agencies from external control by courts and community boards (Jurik & Musheno, 1986).

Well-trained professional officers were to rely on interpersonal skills, exercise restraint, and avoid relying on brute force. Since women have not generally been associated with the use of physical strength to attain their ends, this attempt to undermine the centrality of force in police and corrections has served to bolster the position of women workers (Britton, 2003; National Center for Women & Policing, 2002b). Emphasis on communication skills and teamwork also supported arguments that women could work in the CJS even in formerly all-male positions. Reform discourses also suggested that white women and men and women of color would be more likely to empathize with citizens, arrestees, and offenders and less likely to engage in brutal and arbitrary treatment.

These arguments alone might not have been sufficient to expand CJS jobs to women had it not been for the 1973 Crime Control Act, which amended the 1968 Omnibus Crime Control and Safe Streets Act. The Crime Control Act prohibited discrimination against women in the employment practices of any agencies that received LEAA funds. LEAA Equal Employment Opportunity guidelines required agencies to assess their recruiting and hiring practices, analyze promotion and training procedures, formulate an EEO program, and file it with the state planning agency through which most of its funds were disbursed. Other guidelines prohibited hiring standards (e.g., minimum height requirements) that discriminated against women and were not associated with successful police job performance. LEAA threatened to withhold payments to grant recipients who failed to comply with these regulations. Loss of LEAA monies was a serious threat to law enforcement agencies (Feinman, 1986). Gradual enforcement of the EEOC guidelines caused a ripple effect throughout the CJS, so that by the late 1970s, departments had begun to hire more white women and people of color (U.S. Department of Justice, 1981; Walker, 1985).

In addition to reform and legal rationales, women provided an important pool of workers for justice system expansion. Economic recession and industrial restructuring of the 1970s and 1980s strained middle- and working-class families, forcing more married women, including those with young children, into the paid workplace. Rising divorce rates increased the number of single mothers in search of decent-paying jobs. These conditions converged with increased educational opportunities to produce a labor pool of high school– and college-educated women available for professionalizing CJS jobs. During the same period, demographic factors led to a shortage of qualified white men willing to work for CJS wages (Jurik & Martin, 2001).

Men staff and supervisors did not always welcome reform and professionalization strategies or the increased presence of women within their ranks. Many complained that these changes feminized their occupation and gave them less power than before. Staff resentment was fueled by the tendency of police and correctional professionalization efforts to focus on individuals without accompanying organizational changes (Jurik & Musheno, 1986). Many reform advocates hoped that professionalization would promote gender neutrality, fairness, efficiency, and respect for the CJS and its workers (National Research Council, 2004), but many officers also believed that they lost the autonomy needed to do their jobs (Hogan, Lambert, Jenkins, & Wambold, 2006). In the case of corrections, reforms have done little to alleviate images of COs as performing society's dirty work (Tracy & Scott, 2006). Some men police officers have also protested reform efforts and community policing methods for feminizing their work (S. L. Miller, 1999).

Despite men's resistance, the CJS continued to expand, and women provided an important source of the labor for its monumental growth. Ronald Reagan's election as President of the United States in 1980 accelerated the political shift to the right that began in the 1970s. Reagan launched a war on drugs that increased penalties for consumption as well as sale of drugs. He also promoted more punitive determinate sentencing policies and appointed judges likely to agree with judicial interpretations that would erode defendant rights. These policies added still greater numbers to the populations of persons who were arrested, tried, convicted, and incarcerated and, in so doing, further stimulated the demand for CJS personnel.

Thus, social movements, legal activism, economic shifts, and changes in the CJS have prompted the expansion of women's work roles in policing, law, and corrections that we described at the beginning of this chapter. Women have indeed made tremendous progress in these fields, but this progress is not always linear. There are setbacks and continuing barriers. The path toward equality with men in the workplace will entail understanding and challenging the barriers that we begin to describe in the following section.

Women and Today's Justice Occupations

In this book, we argue that women's experiences in justice occupations must be examined in relation to prevailing social conditions and the ways that those forces shape the climate of justice work organizations. In part, continuing opposition to women in justice occupations is related to the structure of work organizations in today's society and its mismatch with women's disproportionate responsibilities for family care work.

Since the 1980s, the growing public sense of economic insecurity and fears of crime have continually encouraged the growth of the CJS and demands for CJS workers. These conditions have expanded the opportunities for white women and men and women of color in the United States. However, this social climate has also reinforced barriers to women by promoting seemingly gender-neutral organizational conditions that differentiate and subordinate women who work in these fields.

There has been a societal backlash against civil rights and feminist activism and renewed support for a tough stance on street crime (Davey, 1995; Faludi, 1991). The implementation of antidiscrimination laws and expanded feminist political agendas have been slowed by the rise of political and social conservatism in the United States along with increased social and economic inequalities. Conservative politicians have challenged the gains of the Civil Rights Movement by exploiting public fears (Davey, 1995). Social conservatives in the "pro-life" movement have threatened to roll back women's control over their own bodies by criminalizing abortion. Dominant societal images of women's proper roles shape workplace experiences, but visions of the proper role of the CJS in society are also influential in framing the opportunities available to women workers in justice fields.

Although police and correctional administrators have tried to "professionalize" personnel and implement equal opportunity hiring and promotional policies, their efforts have not necessarily improved the respectability and working conditions of CJS personnel or brought about full equality for all workers. These efforts have been met with resistance by men staff who fear "reverse discrimination" and the feminization of their work. Moreover, the image of "professionalized" police and correctional officers may disadvantage as well as benefit women. Images of the professional are linked closely with images of masculinity, such as objectivity and universalism in making decisions; images of women, in contrast, portray them as too emotional and attached to others to make impartial judgments.

These components of a professional image have provided numerous rationales for the exclusion of women from the legal profession. Ironically, law, which has traditionally been seen as a model profession, appears to be "deprofessionalizing" or, to use Kritzer's (1999) term, entering into a "postprofessional phase" that combines three elements: lawyers' loss of exclusivity, increased segmentation in applying abstract knowledge due to greater specialization, and the growth of technology that has made their specialized knowledge widely available. Other service providers (e.g., accountants and paralegals) are encroaching on the work that was previously the exclusive preserve of lawyers; their major clients (large corporations) are seeking ways to limit and monitor the costs of their services; and the independent practitioners who once dominated the profession are being replaced by salaried employees. Most lawyers now work in large bureaucratic firms, corporations, or government organizations, including prosecutors' offices (Carson, 2004), where they experience a significant loss of autonomy. Increased competition between law firms has meant increased monitoring of partner and associate attorney billable hours and a reduction of the sometimes more meaningful pro bono work for social causes. Establishment of non-partnership career tracks in many large firms is another manifestation of changing professional status, if not deprofessionalization, of lawyers. There is a danger that women may be disproportionately relegated to such positions (Reichman & Sterling, 2002).

Ironically, recent social trends have both promoted and undermined the position of women in justice occupations. Get-tough-on-crime discourses have remained popular for more than three decades. The war on drugs has continued apace, and get-tough policies now include more stringent enforcement of immigration laws. The terrorist destruction of the World Trade Center on September 11, 2001, has led to a war on terrorism that entails increased detention of undocumented immigrants and citizens of Middle Eastern descent. The political rhetoric and increasingly punitive practices that accompany it have now effected huge increases in the numbers of those arrested and convicted and the mass imprisonment of men and women, particularly men and women of color (Christie, 2000).

This milieu has resulted in the mushrooming of CJS expenditures and personnel. For example, total expenditures grew 366 percent, from about $36 billion in 1982 to $167 billion in 2001, an increase of 165 percent in constant dollars (Bauer & Owens, 2004). Although serious crime fell substantially in the 1990s to levels not seen since the 1960s, get-tough programs have continued to thrive. For example, President Bill Clinton succeeded in getting funding (distributed through the U.S. Justice Department's Office of Community Oriented Policing Services) to hire 100,000 new officers and establish community policing programs.

Since the mid-1980s, there has been a strong movement in policing away from a centralized command-and-control model and toward a community policing model that develops partnerships with neighborhood residents and gives rank-and-file officers more discretionary power to deal with particular situations. Community policing discourses have been supportive of the growing diversity among sworn personnel in terms of race, ethnicity, gender, and sexual orientation, but the extent of implementation and the effects of these new models are unclear.

The emphasis on crime control has been accompanied by other political movements to dismantle the welfare state (Davey, 1995). The war on terrorism and continuing high rates of unemployment and underemployment continue to heighten public fears and promote state fiscal crises. These conditions have led to decreased spending for welfare, social services including mental and physical health care, and other social investments such as education and physical infrastructure. Budget cuts have increased the proportion of the population in need and, at the same time, reinforced public demands for "law and order." The CJS must now deal with higher proportions of individuals who are learning disabled, mentally ill, noncitizens, drug addicts, victims of natural disasters and terrorism, and persons with chronic health problems. Agencies must do this without adequate expenditures for treatment programs and other relevant social services (Clear et al., 2006). These special-needs populations combined with system overcrowding promote uncertainty and danger for those processed by and working in the system.

Budget limitations in the face of growing CJS responsibilities have encouraged governments at all levels to search for ways to promote efficiency and reduced costs for policing courts and corrections. There have been many efforts to promote greater interagency coordination for surveillance activities. Subcontracting and full-scale privatization of government CJS functions have greatly expanded (Hallett, 2002; Useem & Goldstone, 2002).

Even non-privatized policing and correctional agencies are affected by a "new managerialism" that mandates that government agencies are organized and function more like businesses. Such agencies are expected to be more cost-effective, treat clientele as customers, and vest greater responsibility for quality and cost-effective product in frontline staff (Jurik, 2004). Along these lines, police rely on greater numbers of non-sworn, or civilian employees, who are not entitled to the same union representation, hiring and retention rules, and benefit packages as regular police. Law firms and legal departments both in the corporate world and in government also are larger and more bureaucratic; the nature of attorneys' practice has expanded to new areas of law (e.g., environmental issues), has become more specialized, and increasingly involves corporate rather than individual clients. Finally, lawyers and CJS workers face greater pressures and demands for longer hours that leave workers less time for leisure and family life (Reichman & Sterling, 2002). These characteristics are becoming a standard component of work not only in justice fields, but in the American workforce more generally.

These justice system trends have important implications for workers, especially women. The ever-growing demands on the CJS, the sheer numbers of people processed in it, and the budgetary limitations on the funding of programs and services mean that justice workers are increasingly overburdened, work in overcrowded and dangerous situations, and perform lots of routine and unpleasant tasks. Inadequate programs and services plus dangerous working conditions fuel stress and resistance to women. Opponents claim that women are neither physically nor emotionally strong enough to meet the challenges of contemporary justice work. The pressures of new managerialism reinforce demands for constant availability, while inflexible work schedules may be more difficult for women, given their still relatively greater family responsibilities. Despite any resistance generated by these conditions, however, women are still a vital source of labor for this expanding system. Their presence in it is likely only to increase in years to come.

Contents of the Second Edition of This Book

The following chapters provide a conceptual framework for understanding gender differentiation in the workplace, look more closely at women's experiences and contributions in our three focal justice occupations, and then identify themes across occupations. Chapter 2 begins with a review of alternative perspectives on the barriers to women in traditionally men's occupations. It elaborates our framework for examining the social production of gender differences along with those related to race, ethnicity, and sexual orientation and explores the subordination of women in policing, law, and corrections work. Chapters 3 through 8 form the heart of our analysis. We divide the discussion of each occupation into two chapters: police in Chapters in 3 and 4, law in Chapters 5 and 6, and corrections in Chapters 7 and 8. For each occupation, the initial chapter deals with the historical and contemporary situation of women and the barriers that they face in everyday work situations. The second chapter for each occupation connects these everyday barriers to their larger organizational and societal milieu. Chapter 9 integrates these issues by comparing barriers, problems, and achievements of women across justice occupations. It examines women's effects on the occupation, work organization, and clients by addressing the question, "Do women make a difference?" It also looks toward the future, changes we regard as likely, and policies and practices needed to promote progress.

The analysis illuminates the gendering of justice organizations and occupations. It demonstrates that these jobs are not gender-neutral, "empty" positions waiting to be filled by the "best qualified" candidate (Acker, 1990). It reveals how these work organizations operate according to ideologies, customs, and practices that produce and reproduce gender inequality (P. Y. Martin, 1991, p. 208). Labor markets, occupations, organizational hierarchies, supervisory practices, procedures for hiring and advancement, work groups, and work activities are all infused with gendered images and consequences.

In this revised edition of *Doing Justice, Doing Gender*, we have maintained our overall theoretical framework but have incorporated into it the growing literature on the simultaneous production of gender, race, class, and sexual orientation in social interaction and social organizations, sometimes referred to as "doing difference" (Fenstermaker & West, 2002). We have updated statistical material and have incorporated material related to the changes that have occurred in each of the occupations in the past decade as well as in laws and policies shaping organizational practices. We have also incorporated more discussion of how the body both frames and is framed by work experiences in justice fields. Also new is an international dimension. While our primary focus is on the United States, we have incorporated some materials and many citations for those who want to explore further the status of women employed in justice occupations worldwide.

A Note on Perspective and Terminology

Recent scholarship about gender and racial equality has criticized traditional social science notions of objectivity and universality, claiming that what one writes or chooses to study is influenced by the writer's social location. Critics assert that claims of objective knowledge are based on elite, white, heterosexual, European-orientated, man-centered perspectives. They suggest that writers identify themselves in terms of gender, race, sexual orientation, social class, and any other relevant biographical information to enable readers to better evaluate the truth of claims attached to the knowledge that is being presented (P. H. Collins, 2000).

With this in mind, both authors are white, heterosexual, and middle class. Susan Martin grew up in suburbia and has lived with her husband in the Washington,

D.C., area for 35 years. She has two grown sons and four grandchildren. Nancy Jurik was raised on a small farm in the southwestern United States during the 1950s and 1960s, and now lives in the Phoenix area with her husband and colleague Gray Cavender. She is a professor in the School of Justice & Social Inquiry at Arizona State University.

Our book follows a feminist approach: it places women at the center of inquiry in building a base of knowledge and an understanding of gender as it intersects with race, class, and sexual orientation and is featured in all aspects of human culture and relationships (Andersen, 2005). Feminism is not treated as a single theory; it embraces a world view and movement for social change; it includes a diverse set of perspectives identifying and representing women's interests; it holds distinct agendas for ending women's oppression that vary according to the specific structures and situations confronting women of various races, ethnicities, socioeconomic statuses, and sexualities.

One aspect of our feminist commitment is to avoid sexism and racism in language. This is no easy matter; it has resulted in phrases that sound awkward because they do not conform to customary language usage.

Historically, the term "sex" referred to biological categories of individuals—men or women—determined by hormones, anatomy, and physiology. Since the 1960s, the term "gender" has come to refer to the aspect of human identity that is socially learned—masculinity or femininity. With the gradual recognition that biological and cultural processes are more interrelated than previously assumed, conceptualizations of sex or gender as unchanging attributes of individuals have yielded to recognition of the importance of interaction in constructing each. We follow the usage and definitions of Candace West and Don Zimmerman (1987), who distinguish among three separate concepts: sex, sex category, and gender. Sex is the application of socially agreed on biological criteria for classifying people as men or women, usually based on chromosomal typing or genitalia. In everyday life, people are placed or proclaim their membership in a sex category based upon visible indicators such as clothing and hair style. Gender refers not simply to what one "is" but something one "does" or enacts on an ongoing basis. Hence, the book's title includes the phrase "doing gender," which will be more fully explained in Chapter 2 (West & Zimmerman, 1987).

We use the terms "women of color," "men of color," or "people of color" to refer collectively to racial and ethnic groups that are not of white-European origin. The terms "African-American" and "black" are used interchangeably to refer to Americans with African heritage. In the absence of more detailed racial-ethnic breakdowns, the undifferentiated term "Hispanic" refers to individuals who are of Puerto Rican, Mexican-American, or other Latin-American heritage. For the same reasons, the undifferentiated terms "Asian-Americans" and "American Indians" are employed.

Despite our determination to present data addressing gender and race, often this was impossible because data on CJS workers rarely are compiled along both gender as well as racial and ethnic lines, and there are very limited data about variations in the CJS work experiences of women from different racial or ethnic groups. Even when race-gender breakdowns exist, they often are grouped into distinctions of "white" and the undifferentiated category "nonwhite." Nevertheless, whenever possible, we describe the experiences of women justice workers from various racial and ethnic groups. Likewise, the presumption of heterosexuality and continuing "closeted" status of many homosexuals have led to limited research on the experiences of gays and lesbians in the workplace. We discuss the available research and analyze the ways in which the heterosexual presumption is used to control women justice workers.

Endnotes

1. We would have liked to have focused on women's activities in the practice of criminal law. Apart from several studies comparing sentencing by men and women judges, there simply are no studies available on women in criminal law per se.

2. Although the law gives victims the opportunity to recover damages, the process of damage determination in sexual harassment litigation exacts a cost for the plaintiffs in terms of humiliation (Fitzgerald, 2003). To prove that the damage inflicted harm and that the defendant organization was responsible usually means the woman must undergo a psychological evaluation by a clinician determined by the defendant. This often results in victim-blaming and additional emotional distress.

3. Most definitions of the concept of profession include (1) a theoretical body of knowledge based on lengthy study and not possessed by outsiders; (2) formal organization of members; (3) occupational self-regulation through control of recruitment and training, and performance standards based on a code of ethics; (4) a service orientation toward clients and the community; and (5) a distinctive occupational culture (Trice, 1993). Seron and Ferris (1995) emphasize autonomy or authority to control their work as the key element.

CHAPTER 2

Explanations for Gender Inequality in the Workplace

The history of women's work needs to be retold . . . as part of the story of the creation of a gendered workforce. In the 19th century, . . . certain conceptualizations of male skill rested on a contrast with female labor (by definition unskilled).

(Scott, 1990, p. 144)

The subordination of women in law and criminal justice occupations reflects larger inequalities that permeate social life. Jobs and tasks are assigned according to the worker's sex category. Women's paid work is usually accompanied by lower levels of income and status than men's. The segregation of jobs within occupations and industries according to sex category and the devaluing of women's work explain much of the wage differentials between men and women (Padavic & Reskin, 2002).

Paid work is also divided along the lines of race and class. In the Western world, whites tend to hold better-paying and higher-status jobs (Amott & Matthaei, 1996). More advantaged socioeconomic groups gain access to more desirable jobs. Social relations of race, class, and gender converge to shape the nature and distribution of work. Historically, African-American women have performed low-paid domestic work, and elite, white men have headed major institutions (Amott & Matthaei, 1996).

When women enter occupations numerically dominated by men, they encounter much resistance from clients, coworkers, and supervisors. The women who remain in these occupations often are restricted to assignments and tasks designated for women.

Over the past few decades, women workers have made significant advancements in the workplace, and many signs of overt resistance to women workers have diminished. But women have not yet attained parity with men in numbers, pay, or rank. Workers and researchers seeking to document the continuing barriers to working women have described what they refer to as "second generation discrimination," a form that is more covert and embedded in interactions and organizations (Sturm, 2001). These gender differentiation processes continue to highlight presumed natural differences between men and women, and create them where no real differences exist (Padavic & Reskin, 2002; Reskin, 1988; West & Zimmerman, 1987, p. 137). Differentiation legitimates the unequal treatment of women and men workers.

Since the late 1980s, social scientists have moved away from viewing gender as an attribute of individuals. Most predominant approaches use "gender" as a verb to describe the organizational and interactional processes that differentiate men and women (Acker, 1990, p. 146). For example, they describe how different cultural and organizational practices "gender" work.

This usage is consistent with the theoretical approach that we adapt in this book. The use of gender as a verb emphasizes the emergent and socially constructed nature of gender differences and gender subordination. Although gender references concrete bodily and material characteristics and circumstances, perceptions and understandings of it are neither unified nor consistent, but are actually emerging and changing social constructions. Although we focus on gender differentiation in the workforce, it will be clear throughout this book that gender differences must always be considered with the social construction of other dimensions of human identities such as race, ethnicity, class, and sexual orientation. These dimensions of human identities vary in salience from one situation to the next and often converge with other features of human identities such as age, education, and ableism or disability to frame women's workplace experiences. Thus, human identities are ongoing and situated constructions, but they are always constructions that are framed by their larger social historical context.

This chapter begins with a brief overview of past debates about the nature of gender and sources of gender differentiation and women's subordination. Then it details our social construction approach for studying the struggles of women working in legal and criminal justice organizations (Lorber & Farrell, 1991).

Categorical Approaches to Gender Inequality at Work

A variety of approaches have been used to explain gender inequality in the workplace. Up through the 1980s, most feminist perspectives posited that sex comprised two categories, male and female, and that gender behavior consisted of two corresponding categories, masculine and feminine. Such treatments often ignored the wide historical, cultural, individual, and situational variations *within* as well as *between* categories of so-called masculine and feminine behavior (Scott, 1990).

Many cultures construct femininity and masculinity in opposition to each other: femininity represents what masculinity is not (de Beauvoir, 1974). Other dimensions of social relations such as race, ethnicity, sexual orientation, and class are also viewed categorically. Such theoretical treatment of gender is consistent with general societal practices of categorizing and dichotomizing social phenomena (I. M. Young, 1990). This cultural habit stems from a general tendency in Western philosophical thought to conceptualize reality in terms of sets of mutually exclusive and opposing categories (Cixous, 1971; Scott, 1990; I. M. Young, 1990).[1]

Feminist movements emerged at the turn of the 19th to 20th century (first-wave feminism) and again in the middle of the 20th century (second-wave feminism) to dispute popular and scientific beliefs about the essential nature of men and women (Freedman, 2002). Second-wave feminists challenged popular beliefs and biological theories that the differences between men and women were rooted in universal and immutable physiological sex differences given at birth (Lorber, 2001). They popularized a distinction between sex as the biological differences between male and female, and gender as socially learned differences between boys and girls and men and women (Garfinkel, 1967; Freedman, 2002). As more research was conducted, increasing amounts of the so-called "natural differences" between men and women were shown to be an outcome of social learning (Lorber, 2001). This led many feminists to assert that men and women were fundamentally the same, and that childhood socialization and cultural pressures, not biology, were the source of gender differentiation.

Feminists also argued that the cultural sources of women's subordination to men emanated from the creation of separate spheres of activity and influence for men and women. Traditionally, women were relegated to the private sphere of home and family and were excluded from the public domains of politics and paid work. Feminists advocated policies to better incorporate women into the public sphere of social life and to permit women to attain the same work-related skills and opportunities as men (Freeman, 1989; Friedan, 1963).

Women and Men as Essentially the Same: Gender Roles and Gender-Neutral Organizations

Although some popular and scientific communities continued to argue that biology was destiny, this emphasis on nurture rather than nature as the source of gender differences became widely accepted during the second half of the 20th century. Many of the arguments about the importance of culture and environment in shaping identity are stated in gender role theory and its many applications to workplace gender inequality. Gender role theory posits that childhood learning processes (i.e., gender role socialization) instill different occupational aspirations and capabilities in men and women. Boys are encouraged to develop traits associated with competence, instrumentality, and achievement. Girls' socialization emphasizes their future family roles and encourages the development of nurturance, emotional expressiveness, and physical attractiveness (Nieva & Gutek, 1981; Parsons & Bales, 1955). This perspective complements microeconomic human capital theory, which argues that women's wages are lower because, relative to men, they invest less time and money on their education, job training, and continuous labor force participation (Mincer & Polachek, 1974). Male coworkers and managers also may be socialized to resent women's encroachment into "their" spheres. They learn to prefer working with men as peers or supervisors (Nieva & Gutek, 1981).

Critics challenged gender role theory for assuming that personalities are largely fixed after childhood. They also argued that a focus on gender role characteristics ignores the myriad other influences that affect individuals in general and workers in particular.

Rosabeth Moss Kanter (1977) has argued that job and organizational characteristics, not gender role learning, produce apparent male-female differences and produce women's subordination at work. In her gender-neutral organizational theory, Kanter (1977) identified opportunity, distribution of power, and proportional representation as key organizational determinants of workers' experiences, attitudes, and job performance. *Power* consists of the resources to get things done, the formal and informal ability to make and enforce decisions. *Opportunity* means the chance for upward mobility; only upper-echelon jobs have real power to make decisions that affect organizational policies. *Proportional representation* refers to the organizational representation of individuals from various social groups (e.g., gender, race, ethnicity, class, physical disability, and sexual orientation). Those whose social type constitutes a numerical minority (less than 15 percent) in their job or work organization are more visible, experience performance pressure, and often are excluded by dominant social groups. These "tokens" are pressured to conform to stereotyped images of their social type (Kanter, 1977).

Equality as Sameness

Many popular analyses of working women view "feminine" behavior as problematic in the workplace (e.g., Evans, 2000; Frankel, 2004; Kanter, 1977). Many of these arguments suggest that to be successful, women should behave in ways that correspond to images of men workers (i.e., aggressive, confident, rational, and unemotional).

A recurrent theme in the most popular feminist perspectives of the 1960s and 1970s was that women's essential nature was the same as men's. Gender role theories suggested that similar socialization practices will make women behave more like men. Gender-neutral organization theory emphasized that women and men behave similarly when they have equal power, opportunity, and numbers (Kanter, 1977).

Drawing on gender role theory and gender-neutral organization theory, many feminists called for policies that would guarantee the equal treatment of women and men. The notion of equal treatment has gradually gained popularity with much of the general public. However, the meaning of equal treatment in practice continues to be a matter of much debate. For example, some feminists have argued for gender-neutral socialization practices for children, and the elimination of discrimination in education and jobs through equal employment opportunity laws (Bird & Briller, 1969; Friedan, 1963). They have advocated policies that provide women access to a full range of jobs and treat women the same as men are treated.

Feminists also advocated affirmative action policies to ensure that women have equal opportunities to educational programs, jobs, and promotions (Freeman, 1989). Such programs promised to increase the numbers of women and other minority social types and to reduce resistance to these organizational newcomers. Additionally, feminists have argued for sexual harassment prohibitions, pregnancy leave policies, and more flexible work arrangements to assist women in their efforts to promote equal opportunities for women in the workplace and educational spheres. Pay equity or comparable worth policies were proposed to evaluate the qualifications and pay level of all jobs according to a gender-neutral schema so that the inequality in pay due to the gender segregation of occupations could be addressed. For example, one pay equity evaluation determined that despite performing similar sorts of job duties and possessing similar sorts of skills, women employed in social work positions made only a third of the money of men working in probation occupations (Freedman, 2002, pp. 182–183).

Many countries outside the United States adopted antidiscrimination policies to redress past gender, racial, ethnic, and religious discrimination. In southern African nations, affirmative action has helped incorporate black Africans into jobs once monopolized by whites. Northern Ireland has tried to assist Catholic workers who experienced discrimination. Sri Lanka, Malaysia, and several European Union countries implemented various forms of affirmative action programs (Freedman, 2002).

Despite the spread of antidiscrimination laws and policies around the world, opposition to them has grown in the United States. Public advocates of equality as sameness-type policies argue that affirmative action and other women- and minority-friendly policies treat women, racial minorities, and other protected groups of individuals (e.g., ethnic or religious minorities, the disabled) differently from able-bodied white men. They refer to such practices as "reverse discrimination." Affirmative action opponents argue that most overt discrimination has disappeared and that equality means gender- and race-blind hiring, promotion, and school admission decisions (Gregory, 2003; Omi & Winant, 1994). During the 1990s, several successful campaigns overturned affirmative action policies in universities, and court decisions narrowed the scope of continuing programs.

Gender-neutral organization approaches try to overcome the issue of "special treatment" for women by suggesting policies to change work organizational structure in ways that would benefit all. Kanter (1977) has advocated flattening organizational hierarchies and extending greater opportunity and power to workers at all levels. Some feminists have argued that the problems with these debates about what constitutes equality stem from the emphasis on gender sameness.

Men and Women as Different: Equality as Difference

The sameness approach has been criticized for using men's behavior as the standard for evaluating women. Some feminists have viewed the domination of masculine cultures of power and privilege as the root cause of all forms of inequality. They argued that inclusion in male-dominated institutions and the right to work on the same terms as men would not end gender subordination (MacKinnon, 1989). Some feminists went so far as to identify distinctive elements of a "feminine" culture and call for the fundamental redesign of social organizations so that feminine characteristics could be more fully appreciated.

Beginning in the late 1960s, groups referred to as cultural feminists distinguished what they viewed to be key differences in the cultures of men and women (Echols, 1989). Carol Gilligan's (1982) research on moral development suggested that men focus on abstract concepts of rules and rights, an abstract ethic of justice. Women are concerned with relationship and responsibility, an "ethic of care." Gilligan (1982) concluded that the moral domain should include both care and justice, but because caring is associated with femininity, it has been defined as morally immature. Gilligan's "different voice" construct led feminist legal scholars and social scientists (e.g., Brush, 1992; Menkel-Meadow, 1986) to conclude that guiding images in law and the workplace were masculine. Some cultural feminists argued that women's physiology produces a culture that is different from and superior to men's (Daly, 1984); others attributed such differences to childhood socialization and suggested that each "culture" could benefit from traits associated with the other (Chodorow, 1978).

Regardless of the source of gender differences, cultural feminists argued that a feminine ethic of care could help transform public life for the benefit of all (e.g., Echols, 1989). They predicted that displacing masculine with feminine culture would reduce violence and workplace hierarchy and increase consensual decision-making and concern for clients, as well as promote organizational arrangements for reducing family and work life conflicts. Along these lines, some researchers suggested that women who move into traditionally men's occupations may bring "special abilities" to the workplace that include unique insights into organizational problems, conflict diffusion, improved communication, and greater sensitivity and rapport with clients. However, the success of women in transforming their work organization depends in large part on the degree to which traditionally man-centered work cultures value or discourage their influence (Kissel & Katsampes, 1980; S. L. Miller, 1999).

Calls for Radical Economic and Cultural Change

In response to early feminist calls for the incorporation of more women into existing work, educational, and political spheres, some feminists argued that major systemic changes were necessary for promoting equality. They called for changes to address not only gender subordination, but also class and racial subordination.

In the 1960s, socialist feminists argued that both capitalism and patriarchy fuel social inequality (I. M. Young, 1981). They highlighted the economic dimensions of men's resistance to women workers and sexist ideologies that bound women to the home and legitimated their exclusion from higher-paying men's jobs. Patriarchal ideologies and exclusionary practices produce pools of women who provide free housework and child care as well as cheap, flexible paid labor (Hartmann, 1979). Socialist feminists also identified the historical economic conditions that promote change in labor market demands for women (Milkman, 1976), and historical cases in which management used gender, race, and ethnic antagonisms to divide workers and prevent them from successfully gaining better wages and working conditions (Hossfeld, 1990).

More recent critiques of capitalism have examined the international division of labor that draws on women and men from developing countries as a source of low-paid workers for labor-intensive manufacturing and service jobs both in their own countries and as immigrant workers in industrialized countries (Amott & Matthaei, 1996; Mies, 1998; Sassen, 1998). Even these exploitative jobs are stratified along gender lines whereby women workers are subordinated to male managers and particular types of jobs are designed with women in mind and with pay and conditions commensurate with the cultural devaluing of women workers. For example, the reliance on immigrant women, often women of color, as a source of cheap child care and housework permits predominantly white and middle-class women to advance in workplaces that are organized around the presumption that someone is at home to take care of the family (Romero, 2002). Cheap domestic labor permits work organizations designed around this male breadwinner model (with a wife at home) to continue functioning, and it stratifies women workers along class and often racial lines (Hondagneu-Sotelo, 2001; Hurtado, 1989).

Socialist feminists have avoided debates about women's sameness and difference, focusing instead on widespread economic and cultural changes to dismantle both capitalism and patriarchy. They would extend equal work opportunities to men and women workers and also institute policies to alleviate women's double workday by increasing child care/family leave programs and increasing men's involvement in domestic work. Although their framework promised to incorporate other forms of exploitation such as racism, ageism, and heterosexism (Jurik, 1999), the experiences of white, first-world women typically informed the core of the theory (e.g., their view of the home as a source of women's oppression). Moreover, their analysis of the contradictions and changes in patriarchy over time often failed to reflect the diversity of women's experiences around the globe (Jurik, 1999).

Moreover, historical and comparative research has documented significant variations in patriarchal forms as well as in culturally dominant conceptions of masculinity and femininity over time and cross-culturally (Kessler & McKenna, 1978). Even within a single society, individuals hold different and sometimes conflicting notions of what behavior constitutes socially appropriate masculinity and femininity. Gender-appropriate behavior also varies from one situation to the next. Conceptualizations of gender as a fixed attribute of individuals do not adequately convey the fluidity of gender across social contexts.

Challenging Gender Dichotomies: Gender as Process

Several groups of theorists have challenged the conceptualization of gender as two opposite categories. Postmodernists (Cixous, 1971; Scott, 1990), critical race feminism (P. H. Collins, 2000; A. Y. Davis, 1981), cross-cultural research (Mohanty, 2003), queer theory (Beemyn & Eliason, 1996), and gender constructionist perspectives (Connell, 1987; Messerschmidt, 1993; West & Fenstermaker, 1995) criticize categorical models of gender as static, ethnocentric, and ahistorical. They challenge notions of equality that focus on whether women as a group are the same as or different from men as a group; they also dispute the existence of a unified and essential nature for either men or women. They examine gender as an ongoing and contradictory historical and interactional process, not as an attribute of individuals.

Postmodernists criticize tendencies to universalize women's experience and to view sex categories as natural dichotomies (Cixous, 1971; Scott, 1990). For example, Judith Butler (1990) rejects the binary system of gender categorization (i.e., male versus female). She questions the category "woman," arguing that it implies a natural, essential, and unified identity for all women. She argues that notions of gender as a fixed attribute are culturally constituted. She describes gender as an ongoing performance by individuals through gender stylizations of the body (e.g., modes of walking, talking, and dressing). This stylization permits individuals to resist dominant cultural conceptions (e.g., as with drag queens), but more often they conform to culturally prescribed versions of gender.

Empirical research reveals reasons that many women of color and women in developing nations do not relate well to feminist issues and theories in industrialized nations. Women's experiences of social class, work, and family vary across racial, ethnic, and national origin groups (A. Y. Davis, 1981; Glenn, 1992). Critical race feminists have identified important race and ethnic variations in women's experience of oppression and the manner in which gender and race identities converge to create unique forms of oppression for women of color in the workplace (Romero, 2002). For example, up until the 1960s, most black women were forced to work initially by slavery and later because of household poverty, even though the pervasive discourse was that women belonged in the home. Thus, many black women found respite from exploitative paid labor arrangements through domestic and child care labor in their own homes and for their own families. These experiences challenged many white middle-class feminist portraits of home and family life as a source of women's oppression and of paid labor as a source of women's liberation (P. H. Collins, 2000).

International and cross-cultural analyses have also identified differences in women's experiences and in feminist concerns across national boundaries (Naples & Desai, 2002). Women's groups in many developing and Eastern European nations have approached their rights more from the standpoint of their role as mothers seeking to safeguard the present and future for their children; in so doing, they eschew many of the concerns of middle-class feminists in industrialized nations (Freedman, 2002; Mohanty, 2003). For example, long faced with the double workday of paid work and domestic responsibilities, women in former Soviet bloc nations do not see paid labor as liberating (Kiczkova & Farkasova, 1993; Siklova, 1993).

Research documenting the experiences of lesbian, gay, bisexual, and transgender (LGBT) feminists have drawn attention to the centrality of sexuality in understanding gender inequality and oppression (Lorber, 2001). LGBT perspectives uncovered oppressions that LGBT women confronted not just from men but from their straight "sisters" (Freedman, 2002). Feminist movements of the 1960s and 1970s largely repressed, ignored, and rejected the issues raised by LGBT women, but even feminist perspectives that sought to be more accepting failed to come to grips with sexuality as an organizing feature of social life (Rich, 1980). For example, queer theory highlights the ways in which assumptions of heterosexuality construct and constrain human identities (Beemyn & Eliason, 1996). Heterosexism is the presumed norm for human conduct, and images of LGBT behavior are assumed to be deviant and subordinate. Consistent with some of the work in postmodern theories, queer theory seeks to deconstruct (i.e., identify and challenge) taken-for-granted and often oppressive assumptions in human life. Queering can also be used as a verb that refers to challenging other presumed arrangements in social life (Valocchi, 2005). For example, one might "queer" assumptions about family life that treat single-parent or gay families as deviant or problematic. "Queering" work schedules might lead to an analysis of how inflexible work schedules assume that there is someone at home to care for children and do household chores (i.e., a stay-at-home wife; M. Bernstein and Reimann, 2001; Sedgwick, 1993).

Over the past two decades, new generations of feminists have also begun to challenge images of "proper feminist behavior" and views of the body prescribed by the second-wave feminists who preceded them (e.g., issues about dress, makeup, music, and family life; Else-Mitchell & Flutter, 1998; Labaton & Martin, 2004). New feminist perspectives on the body address the dynamic interplay of nature and nurture forming human experiences (Lorber, 2001). These gender-as-embodied approaches argue that gender imagery is significant in shaping human bodies (e.g., through dieting, physical activity, and conditioning). For example, Kathy Davis (1997) links the cultural formation of women's bodies to issues of power. "From the sexualization of the female body in advertising to the mass rape of women in wartime, women's bodies have been subjected to processes of exploitation, inferiorization, exclusion, control, and violence" (K. Davis, 1997, pp. 10–15).

These new approaches emphatically oppose the taken-for-granted view that men and women have essential natures, and move beyond earlier feminist arguments about whether women are essentially the same as or different from men (Messerschmidt, 2004). For example, biologist Anne Fausto-Sterling (2000) emphasizes the changeability of human bodies over the lifetime. She argues that because genitalia come in many sizes and shapes and because the physiology of sex changes over the course of the lifetime, sex should be regarded as a continuum rather than as a static category fixed at birth.

In our analysis of women working in justice occupations, we conceptualize gender as an embodied social process. We refer to this model as the social construction of gender and describe how it applies to women and the workplace in the next sections.

Our Approach: The Social Construction of Gender in the Workplace

Our approach is to analyze gender in the justice workplace as an ongoing social construction that is interwoven with other dimensions of social relations, including race, class, and sexual orientation (West & Fenstermaker, 1995). We refer to gender as an emergent property of social practice and not as a fixed attribute of individuals. We use the term social practice to refer to both everyday social interactions and the larger historical and institutional contexts in which those interactions are located (Giddens, 1976). In developing our framework, we draw on analyses of gender and other forms of social differentiation (e.g., race, sexual orientation) as interactional accomplishments (Fenstermaker & West, 2002; West & Fenstermaker, 1995; West & Zimmerman, 1987), and on understandings of how historical events and social structures such as divisions of labor, power, and culture (Connell, 1987; Messerschmidt, 1993; I. M. Young, 1990) and institutions such as the family, state, and work organizations (Acker, 1990, 1992; Kelly, 1991) frame the interactions that produce gender. We also understand that the production of gender is an embodied social process that may exhibit continuities but nevertheless also varies significantly across individuals, situations, time, and social groups (Messerschmidt, 2004; K. Davis, 1997).

Doing Gender: Gender as a Routine Interactional Accomplishment[2]

Sociologists Candace West and Don Zimmerman (1987) argue that although gender is presumed to be the reflection of natural differences rooted in biology, these differences are accomplished by individuals in routine interactions with others. In Western industrialized societies, infants are assigned to one of two sex categories based on chromosome type before birth, or genitalia after birth (Kessler & McKenna, 1978). Throughout life, we identify and categorize people according to their sex and categorize ourselves in relation to others (West & Zimmerman, 1987). Of course, in most daily social interactions, people cannot see these physiological criteria. Instead, they rely on social signs of sex category, such as hairstyle, dress, voice, and physical appearance (Goffman, 1976). Individuals take up the project of establishing their gender identity as boy or girl and, later, as man or woman (Connell, 2002).

Once individuals are categorized, their behavior is viewed as a "natural" reflection of their "innate" sex category, and their behavior serves as evidence of the natural differences between men and women, or boys and girls. In industrialized societies, gender self-attribution is typically viewed as a permanent identity (Kessler & McKenna, 1978). This assumption gives one's gender project a sense of unity and coherence over time and space. The observer's role in defining the person and his or her behavior as masculine or feminine is forgotten (Messner, 2000; West & Zimmerman, 1987).

Individuals are held accountable for their gender performances (Fenstermaker & West, 2002). That is, the production of gender involves the activity of managing conduct in light of social perceptions regarding "conceptions, attitudes, and activities appropriate to one's sex category" (West & Zimmerman, 1987, p. 127). As they manage these social signs of gender identity, individual actors are aware of their bodies—how their bodies feel and how their bodies are viewed by others. Accordingly, they understand the world from their embodied place in it (Messerschmidt, 2004).

Yet, despite popular assumptions about the permanence of sex and gender categories, the actual accomplishment of masculinities and femininities varies across situations and over time because gender is continuously renegotiated through social interaction, and one's identity includes contradictions and diversity in gender-related strategies and practice (Fenstermaker & West, 2002; Messerschmidt, 2004). The consistencies and contradictions of gender construction stem from the confluence of pervasive and conflicting societal expectations (e.g., peer group versus parental views), the variety of social situations (e.g., work, home, religious events, sport activities), and the diversity and agency of individuals (age variations, cultural variation, degrees of individual awareness).

Gender as Structured Interaction

Clearly, the accomplishment of gender does not occur in a vacuum. Individuals are not simply free to perform gender in any way they desire; they know that others have expectations and may call them to account for their behavior. Thus, they configure and orchestrate their actions in anticipation of others' interpretation in that situation:

> Marking or displaying gender must be finely fitted to situations and modified or transformed as the occasion demands. Doing gender consists of managing such occasions so that . . . the outcome is seen and seeable in context as gender-appropriate or purposefully gender-inappropriate. (West & Zimmerman, 1987, p. 132)

An important part of the social accomplishment of gender entails bodily accountability. In part, how one does gender is shaped by the experience of one's body, and the management of one's body is also part of the doing gender process. Accordingly, Messerschmidt (2004) has described the production of gender as an *embodied* social practice. He argues that the mind and body are inextricably linked. "The body is a sensuous being—it perceives, it touches, and it feels, it is a lived body. And given that consciousness consists of perceptual sensations, it is therefore part of the body and not a separate substance" (Messerschmidt, 2004, p. 45; also see I. M. Young, 1990, pp. 147–148). This view of the body is quite different from a biological determinist perspective because it emphasizes the mutual influence of physical material existence and the culture in which bodies are located. As human beings, we understand the world from our embodied place in it, and social discourse mediates our experience of our bodies (Lorber, 2001). Adolescents provide a straightforward example of socially mediated perceptions and concerns about bodies and the ensuing struggles to manage bodies and concomitantly do gender in ways that win peer approval or challenge oppressive peer and parental expectations. Unfortunately, such gendered and sexualized concerns about the body do not disappear with age; they only change form.

Even though contemporary scholars have worked the body back into their formulations, they maintain that physiology is not fixed and does not determine gender. Bodies and gender are convergent and emergent features of social interaction. Accordingly, femininity and masculinity are neither settled beforehand nor fixed for life. They are *accomplished* in everyday social interactions. The expression "doing gender" refers to the embodied and situated accomplishment of gender difference (West & Zimmerman, 1987).

Sarah Fenstermaker and Candace West (2002) argue that in addition to doing gender, we also accomplish other "categories" around which we allocate social goods and opportunities. They use the term "doing difference" to describe the simultaneous accomplishment of gender, race, class, and other forms of differentiation where "relations of power are at work to produce the accountably weak, unworthy, deni-grated, and the justified practices surrounding them" (p. xvi).

We stress that individuals cannot do gender and other forms of social difference in just any way that they desire because the construction of social identities is "structured"; that is, individuals know they will be socially accountable for their actions. It is through accountability that social structure enters the picture. Social structures help form our preconceptions and expectations about the "nature" and behavior of ourselves and those with whom we interact. Social structures are regu-lar patterns of interactions that have emerged over time; they frame, constrain, and channel behavior (Giddens, 1976, p. 127; Messerschmidt, 1993, p. 63). For people to even engage in social interaction, they must have some understanding of social structure; they must know about social patterns (Connell, 1987, p. 94). Robert Connell (1987), Iris Young (1990), and James Messerschmidt (1993) have identified three interconnected social structures that are relevant for studying women's expe-riences in the workplace: gendered divisions of labor, power, and culture.[3]

The division of labor includes the distribution of tasks, occupations, and work-ing conditions. Fundamental to the division of labor in Western industrialized societies are distinctions between the planning of tasks and their execution, and between paid and unpaid labor (Braverman, 1974; Hochschild, 1989; I. M. Young, 1990). The division of labor is also organized along the lines of race, ethnicity, class, and national origins (Amott & Matthaei, 1996). Historically, elite white men have been associated with planning and conceptualizing work, and working- and lower-class white men and men of color have been associated with task execution or man-ual labor. Women have been associated with the unpaid planning and execution of domestic work for their families. Women's family responsibilities are replicated in the paid workplace, where they are responsible for the paid execution and support of men's plans or for tending to the bodily needs of others. Women of color and recent immigrant women are disproportionately relegated to paid domestic labor for white families or to other forms of paid manual labor (e.g., factory work; Amott & Matthaei, 1996). International divisions of labor also consign workers in devel-oping countries to lower paid jobs with working conditions inferior to those of workers in industrialized countries. Disproportionately, workers in developing nations are located in low-paid factory and service-sector jobs (Mies, 1998).

Associated with the division of labor are corresponding levels of power, a second dimension of social structure. Power refers to the ability to set up the rules and pro-cedures whereby decisions will be made, and the access to material resources and decision-making positions (I. M. Young, 1990, pp. 22–23). Power relations among men and women have been constructed historically along the lines of race, ethnic-ity, class, and sexual orientation. The gendered division of labor means that women are typically located in jobs with less decision-making power than those dispropor-tionately occupied by upper-class, white men (Connell, 1987; P. Y. Martin, 1991). However, power is not an absolute structure, and power relations vary depending on the social and historical context (Connell & Messerschmidt, 2005). Race, eth-nicity, class, and sexual orientation converge with gender and situational context to structure power relations. For example, in one situation, a male factory worker may experience power over his family, but at work, he may be subordinated to factory managers. In another case, a white woman may be subordinated to her husband at home, but she may simultaneously exert authority over her child care worker, who may be an immigrant from Mexico. Although fluid, power relations reflect persistent patterns of gender inequality; men still disproportionately control the large-scale economic, religious, political, and military institutions of authority in society.

Culture, our third dimension of social structure, refers to recurrent social practices including "symbols, images, meanings, habitual comportment, stories, and so on, through which people express their experience and communicate" (I. M. Young, 1990, p. 23). Within any society, there are varied, competing, and conflicting cultural views, but some cultural notions predominate over others. Cultural images of gender and sexuality provide two central examples. Connell (2002) emphasizes the existence of multiple cultural images of masculinity and femininity, but he notes that some are more dominant than others. Images of masculinity and femininity associated with white, middle-class, and heterosexual men and women are those more likely to be ideologically dominant. Connell (1993) uses the term *hegemonic masculinity* to characterize the culturally idealized forms of masculinity in a given historical and social setting. Throughout past and contemporary history, it entails maintaining the dominance of men over women. Hegemonic masculinities are those most culturally honored, glorified, and extolled in the media and in major societal institutions (political, educational, religious, and others). *Emphasized femininity* is the culturally idealized form of femininity in a given historical and social setting. It complements hegemonic masculinity because it orients toward accommodating the interests and desires of men.

Connell and Messerschmidt (2005) distinguish between hegemonic masculinity and other forms, such as "complicit masculinity" (those that benefit but are not major proponents of hegemonic forms) and "subordinated" (exhibiting less popular forms of masculinity) and "oppositional" forms (actively opposing hegemonic masculinity, e.g., pro-feminist men). Similarly, multiple and sometimes conflicting versions of femininity exist in society, with some images being more widely accepted and valued than others at any one point in time. In practice, however, gender may be "done" in ways that simultaneously support some aspects of hegemonic masculinity and emphasized femininity and in other ways oppose them. Some self-conscious efforts by individuals to challenge culturally dominant views of gender may actually end up bolstering them. Moreover, individuals may also do gender in ways that unconsciously promote dominance, such as when men bond through sexual joking or sports talk that excludes the women present. Patricia Yancey Martin (2001) refers to such practices as "mobilizing masculinities." Examination of the real-world experiences of men and women and girls and boys demonstrate the complexity of doing gender (J. Miller, 2002; C. L. Williams, 1995).

Hegemonic masculinity has been associated with paid employment, heterosexism, uncontrollable sexuality, authority, control, and aggressiveness, while traits such as sociability, fragility, compliance with men's desire for ego-stroking, sexual receptivity, marriage, housework, and child care have been associated with emphasized femininity (Connell, 1987). However, in more recent work, Connell & Messerschmidt (2005) caution against defining hegemonic masculinity or emphasized femininity through trait inventories because these convey an inaccurate sense of stability. Societally prescribed ideals of gender vary over time and across situations and social groups, and "ideals" may not be manifest in the actual lives of any particular individual or groups of individuals. In other words, doing gender is an ongoing and relational process that references but does not necessarily conform to cultural images and ideals. Ideals of gender also vary and conflict across racial, ethnic, class, sexual orientation, and age groups, as well as across local, regional, and global levels. Behavior interpreted as conforming to hegemonic masculinity, emphasized femininity, or any other vision of gender is open to reinterpretation in each new social situation. Although ideals of masculinity as aggressive, dispassionate, and competitive and of femininity as passive, nurturing, and emotional may be culturally dominant in one region, opposing visions of masculinity and femininity may coexist in the same society and sometimes within the same individual (Connell & Messerschmidt, 2005).

There are also cultural images of more and less desirable forms of sexuality. Sexuality, which includes sexual desire, behavior, and identity, is also socially constructed (Burrell & Hearn, 1989, p. 18). Cultural images define a hierarchy of more or less acceptable forms of sexuality with married heterosexual parents at the top (Messerschmidt, 1993).[4] Single women and men continue to report pressures to be married, especially as they grow older. In some cultures, sex out of wedlock may still result in the murder of women who violate these norms. However, as with cultural images of exemplary gender, ideals about sexuality are neither fixed nor uniform. Hegemonic sexuality is highly contested in contemporary society. Debates over gay and lesbian marriages and gay and lesbian adoptions illustrate two areas in which legal and cultural ideals are being challenged (M. Bernstein & Reimann, 2001; Dalton & Fenstermaker, 2002). In addition, the rights of openly gay and lesbian police officers to serve on municipal police forces are now officially supported in some cities (S. L. Miller, Forest, & Jurik, 2003).

Although social structures are important in shaping gendered, racialized, classed, sexualized, and embodied social interactions, they are neither absolute determinants of, nor external to, social interactions. They are realized only through social action, but these actions are always shaped by patterns and expectations that have emerged from interactions of the past (Messerschmidt, 1993, p. 63; also see Giddens, 1976, p. 127).

Doing Gender in Work Organizations

The workplace is an important site for doing gender and other dimensions of social difference. Workplace interactions simultaneously arise from, reproduce, and sometimes challenge the social structural divisions of labor, power, and culture hierarchies discussed in the preceding section. Joan Acker (1992) stresses that despite the appearance of gender neutrality, gender is a pervasive feature of every aspect of organizational life. Patricia Yancey Martin (2003) uses the term "gendering practices" to illustrate the link between social structures and actual behavior. She argues that within society and work organizations, there are a range of styles and strategies for doing gender with which people are familiar. These are gendering practices. People consciously or unconsciously choose from among these practices as they do gender in specific interactions (P. Y. Martin, 2003).

Over the past four decades, women have made significant advancements in the world of paid work. They have increased their numbers, entered jobs traditionally off-limits to them, gained more leadership positions, and successfully argued for pay commensurate with their education, skills, and job performance. Nevertheless, gendered divisions of labor and power continue to permeate work organizations. Acker (1990) identifies cultural images, interactions, identities, and policies that produce and sustain gendered divisions of labor and power. These practices are linked to the inequalities in the social institutions of family, state, and labor markets and frame the production of gender in work organizations.

Links Between the Family and the Workplace

Western industrial societies treat home and work as naturally separate spheres, but this separation was not true of preindustrial societies. Nor is it really an accurate characterization of work and family life today. Then and now, family and work are integrally related to one another.

In preindustrial, agrarian societies, the household was the center of economic production. Beginning in England in the mid-1800s, industrialization moved production out of the home. Men, women, and children went to work in factories. However, men assumed the highest-skilled, best-paying jobs (Hartmann, 1979). Work has also been historically segmented along the lines of race, ethnicity, and immigration status. In the 1840s, upper-class reformers and men's labor unions called for restrictions on the labor of children and women. Women were accused of deserting their children to steal men's jobs (Seccombe, 1986). Eventually a "family wage" was developed that paid enough to the upper layers of British working-class men so that their wives could stay at home. A similar system for "preserving the family" developed in the United States (Messerschmidt, 1993; Zaretsky, 1978). Although many families, especially those of color, did not receive the family wage, it had the symbolic effect of designating men as breadwinners, and women as homemakers or as working for "pin money" at the margins of economic activity (I. M. Young, 1981). Despite continuing restrictions on women's workforce participation, increasing demands for cheap labor and the need for increased income to support families drew women in the United States, Britain, and Western Europe into the workforce in increasing numbers during the 1800s. In the 1900s, as the need for industrial labor spread, young women in more nations began to move from the countryside to city work in factories. Other women worked at home as pieceworkers to earn money for essential family needs (Beneria & Roldan, 1986).

Today, data from the United Nations (2000) indicate that more than half of mothers of infants (and more than 60 percent of all women) in the United States are in the paid labor force. Other developed countries report figures of around 49 to 55 percent of women who engage in economically gainful activity (i.e., formal or informal employment or business activities). In recent decades, women throughout the world have increased their income-producing activities ranging from a low of 29 percent in Northern Africa to a high of 62 percent in sub-Saharan Africa (United Nations, 2000).

Despite their increased participation in income generation, women continue to bear a disproportionate share of unpaid domestic responsibilities. After their first shift of paid work, women perform a "second shift" of child care and housework (Hochschild, 1989). In the 1970s and 1980s, as women increased their paid employment activities, men took on a greater share of unpaid domestic labor, but increases in men's domestic labor stalled during the 1990s even though women's paid labor force participation continued to climb (Bianchi, Milkie, Sayer, & Robinson, 2002). Women's domestic and paid work responsibilities also overlap more than do men's in both time and space (e.g., while at work getting calls from sick children, leaving work to take a child to an after-school program). These disproportionate domestic responsibilities foster cultural images that devalue women's worth in the workplace. There is a dialectical relationship between gender subordination in domestic life and gender subordination in the paid workplace. A woman's domestic identity makes her a less desirable worker to employers. Her low income and subordination in the paid work world diminish her power in the family and increase her economic dependence on a man, or on state welfare.

Women's historical relegation to criminal justice jobs as clerical support or specialists in the needs of women and children illustrates the spillover of domestic responsibilities into justice work organizations. Even today, as women have assumed more traditionally male jobs in legal and criminal justice occupations, expectations that they will be those primarily responsible for child care often remove them from fast tracks for managerial and administrative-level positions (Epstein, Seron, Oglensky, & Saute, 1999).

Women face difficulties balancing paid work and domestic responsibilities worldwide. Even in affluent Scandinavian countries with progressive family leave programs, women continue to bear a disproportionate share of household responsibilities (Freedman, 2002). In many developing countries, husbands are unable to find gainful employment and are forced either to remain unemployed or to migrate to other nations to find work. Women also migrate to industrialized countries in search of employment opportunities. They often find paid domestic positions caring for the families of middle-class women who work. These paid domestic positions in other countries mean many women must mother their children long-distance and leave them in the day-to-day care of other family members (Ehrenreich & Hochschild, 2003). Faced with a husband's underemployment, unemployment, or abandonment, some women begin small, informal ventures called microenterprises to support their families (Jurik, 2005). Although widely touted as a source of liberation for poor women in developing countries, these increased economic responsibilities come as an addition to the already challenging demands that women face caring for families in poor, nonindustrialized societies (Poster & Salime, 2002).

Labor is simultaneously divided according to national origin, class, race, and gender. Evelyn Glenn (1992) describes historical divisions of domestic labor along these lines. In the 19th century, middle-class white women accepted gender-based divisions of labor and the "domestic code" but sloughed off more burdensome domestic tasks onto women of color. This "delegation" of household labor to women of color freed white women for supervisory tasks in the home and for cultural and volunteer activities. Racial division of domestic labor benefits white men by insulating them from dirty work and from those who do it at home and in the workplace (Glenn, 1992; Romero, 2002). By the middle of the 20th century, much domestic work formerly done in the home became paid work in public settings, but gender and racial divisions of labor persist today. Women of color still are disproportionately employed in dirty work (e.g., cooking food, cleaning or caring for the elderly and ill), while white women in the same settings are disproportionately employed as lower-level professionals (e.g., receptionists, nurses) or supervisors (Amott & Matthaei, 1996). Accordingly, divisions of labor simultaneously construct race and gender and overlap both paid and unpaid worlds of work. However, efforts to challenge gender and racial disadvantage in the workplace have resulted in greater work opportunities for women of color. In legal and criminal justice occupations, women of color are assuming increasing numbers of posts but still face barriers to advancement.

The Gendered State

The state, which includes both political and legal institutions, long has presented many barriers to women in the workplace. Historically, it has facilitated domination by white men workers in many ways (Connell, 1987; Messerschmidt, 1993). Despite struggles to increase their representation in lawmaking and regulatory bodies, women still comprise a minority in major lawmaking and regulatory bodies.

Until 1971, a woman's rights and responsibilities were essentially determined by her position in the family, and laws that classified according to sex were constitutional (Minow, 1988; Schultz, 1991). Laws have limited women's access to paid employment, upheld racially and sexually discriminatory hiring practices, criminalized forms of fertility control (e.g., abortion and some contraceptive devices), regulated marriage and divorce, prohibited women's ownership of property or businesses, supported unequal education, and restricted women's immigration from some countries (Amott & Matthaei, 1996).

During the second half of the 20th century, political struggles challenged sex, race, and other forms of discrimination in the workplace. Civil rights and women's movements questioned white men's "birthright" to the most desirable jobs. Demonstrations by various disadvantaged groups (e.g., African-Americans, American Indians, Asian-Americans, Chicanos/as, senior citizens, gay/lesbian coalitions, the physically challenged) stimulated legislative attempts to eliminate discrimination in many areas of social life. In the 1970s, mounting public opposition led some employers to end overt discriminatory hiring and promotional preferences for young, white, nondisabled men (Padavic & Reskin, 2002).

As we discussed in Chapter 1, the law has not been unified in its position on gender equality. Although the legal situation has improved somewhat in terms of fairness, most laws continue to be rooted in the experiences of heterosexual, white, and nondisabled men workers. Those who are not similarly situated to this ideal worker may be disadvantaged (MacKinnon, 1989; Minow, 1988). For example, maternity leave policies and practices in many justice work organizations continue to disadvantage women. Women are often penalized informally when they take maternity leaves or take advantage of policies that permit flexible and part-time work schedules

(Epstein et al., 1999; Sugden, 2005). Some seek mother-friendly—and typically lower status and pay—work environments (Reichman & Sterling, 2002).

As we will elaborate, there are many inconsistencies in the experiences of women workers in justice occupations. For example, federal laws requiring equal employment opportunity helped women advance in corrections, but at the same time, federal court rulings about inmate privacy restricted women's work assignments in men's prisons (Maschke, 1996). In recent years, federal courts have been much more supportive of women's work opportunities in men's prisons. However, mandatory sentencing and tougher penalties for immigration violations, drug crimes, and other get-tough policies have increased prison populations in the United States and around the world (Christie, 2000). Although these policies were intended to be neutral with regard to gender, they decreased funding for rehabilitation programs, exacerbated prison overcrowding and danger, and by so doing indirectly fueled challenges to women's equal work opportunities in men's prisons (Jurik & Martin, 2001).

Gendered Labor Markets

Barbara Reskin and Patricia Roos (1990) have conceptualized the gender, racial, and ethnic composition of occupations as a queueing process: there are gendered and racialized *labor queues* in which employers rank waiting workers, and *job queues* in which workers rank job opportunities. Changes in the gender (or race) composition of occupations occur when employers change their ordering of workers in the labor queue or, alternatively, when workers reorder their valuations of jobs.

A variety of social forces, including political, legal, economic, and demographic changes, shape employer and worker preferences and, accordingly, job and labor queues. For example, social policies (e.g., hospital policies requiring that all nurses be RNs) may increase the educational requirements for an occupation. Social and economic factors also may increase the proportions of college-educated workers for existing labor queues. If educational requirements increase but salary levels do not, a shortage of qualified white men applicants may develop. Qualified white women and both men and women of color may then be hired to make up the deficit in workers of the desired social type. This pattern was important in encouraging the entry of women into what were traditionally men's justice jobs.

Political and legal struggles may also alter employers' hiring practices. Legal changes such as the prohibition of discriminatory educational admission practices, and affirmative action hiring processes can change employment opportunities for women workers (Kelly, 1991, pp. 10–12). Other political changes can result in shortages of men workers and an increase in the hiring of women workers (e.g., as in World Wars I and II).

Virtually all changes in the social, political, and economic spheres of society affect the demand for workers and for jobs. Labor market queueing processes reveal the gendered consequences of ostensibly gender-neutral macro social and economic changes. In the 1970s and 1980s, the first large-scale movement of women into predominantly men's occupations occurred. This movement was encouraged by the expansion of several gender-integrated occupations (e.g., sales) and the shrinkage of several highly gender-segregated ones (e.g., automobile factory work).

Women also began to enter several traditionally male occupations (e.g., bank management, bartending) due to changing societal attitudes and legal regulations that fostered more equal employment opportunities (Reskin, 2002).

These issues of labor and job queues are very relevant to the justice system. In Chapter 1, we discussed the historical conditions that increased the demand for women workers in the criminal justice system. Perceived increases in crime rates, social movements, and state legislative and policy directives increased the size of the criminal justice system and pressures for agency reforms. Reforms converged with demographic changes, economic forces, and equal employment and educational opportunity laws to increase the demand for, and availability of, women workers for men's justice occupations. Explosive growth in policing and correctional occupations fueled increased demands for workers regardless of gender. However, the working conditions in these organizations often deteriorated due to declining budgets for support staff, equipment, and training and heightened danger due to prison overcrowding and gang-related violence on the streets and in prison (Clear, Cole, & Reisig, 2006).

Despite increased entry of women into a variety of traditionally male occupations over the past three decades, significant barriers to women's equal opportunities remain, and there is much progress needed to attain parity with men. Even in occupations where women have increased their proportional representation, there is still gender stratification within occupations according to job titles (Bielby & Baron, 1986). No doubt such "resegregation" helps explain the persistence of gender wage gaps within occupations. Also, women's progress into the ranks of organizational leadership positions has been very slow (Britton & Williams, 2000; Ferree & Purkayastha, 2000). Researchers argue that understanding the reasons for this stalled progress requires a greater understanding of the internal workings of organizations (Reskin, 2002; Sturm, 2001).

Gendered Work Organizations

Gender relations in the family, state, and labor market are inextricably connected to the production of gender in work organizations. Analysis of gendered work organizations considers how "advantage and disadvantage, exploitation and control, action and emotion, meaning and identity are patterned in terms of a distinction between male and female, masculine and feminine" (Acker, 1990, p. 140). The analytically distinct but connected dimensions of gendered organizations are discussed in the following sections.

Division of Labor in Work Organizations

Organizations include interactions that control, segregate, exclude, and construct hierarchies of workers based on gender, race, and class (Acker, 1992). Throughout work organizations, jobs are segregated along these lines.

Women have made disproportionate gains in some male-dominated fields, but women workers continue to be heavily concentrated in a smaller range of occupations than are men (Padavic & Reskin, 2002). Initially, most of these gains were made by educated white women, but over the past two decades, women of color have also made advances such that occupational segregation and pay gaps between white women and black women have declined. Nevertheless, gaps between women as a group and white men, and between white men and men of color remain large.

Changes in levels of occupational integration mask other tendencies toward gender inequality. Within occupations, industries, and firms, there is pervasive internal stratification: men and women perform different tasks (Padavic & Reskin, 2002).[5] Jobs become informally identified as "men's" or "women's" work, but these informal distinctions are associated with pay differentials and unequal promotional prospects (Bielby & Baron, 1986). Gender segregation in the workplace is a complex and multifaceted phenomenon that requires consideration not only of occupation, but also of industry, job title, employment situation (public versus private firm), and job status (full-time, part-time, self-employed; M. Charles & Grusky, 2004). Gender segregation is a persistent worldwide issue for industrialized as well as developing countries (Padavic & Reskin, 2002). However, the exact patterns of gender segregation vary across countries, especially when comparing industrialized and developing countries (M. Charles & Grusky, 2004).

Understanding gender segregation and women's disadvantage requires knowledge of routine practices within workplace organizations (Reskin, 2002). Men gatekeepers (owners, managers) often seek to exclude women from occupations, organizations, or jobs if they perceive women as a threat to men's material or symbolic status (Cockburn, 1991). Supervisors hinder women's advancement by reserving better assignments for men. Higher pay, greater social status, and power accompany "men's jobs" (C. L. Williams, 1995). Differences persist even when women and men perform the same tasks (Bielby & Baron, 1986). In the criminal justice system, work assignments of women and men often result in disparate access to power structures. Higher-profile work assignments are more often given to men since men supervisors are more comfortable interacting with them and assume that they will be more effective and dedicated workers (Reichman & Sterling, 2002).

Culture and Sexuality in Work Organizations

Gendered organizations are also sites for the construction and display of cultural images, and images surrounding gender, race, and sexuality are especially pervasive. Culture includes symbols and ideologies that legitimate and, on occasion, challenge divisions of labor and power hierarchies. They help us make sense of the world by creating shared meanings and frameworks to understand life (Trice, 1993). Cultures create a sense of "we-ness" by drawing boundaries between members and others. They are constructed through verbal and nonverbal communication, including dress and demeanor.

Workers develop informal occupational and organizational cultures. Work cultures are informal because they do not always correspond to the formal rules of the organization. Informal work cultures may operate outside of organized occupational groups such as professional associations and unions. Yet, work cultures are influenced by mandates of formal work organizations and occupational associations. Work cultures also are shaped by cultural hierarchies outside work organizations.

A work culture is not monolithic. There may be multiple or competing work cultures within a work organization or occupation. Researchers have described competing occupational cultures within policing, with "management cops" and "street cops" each having their own distinctive ideologies and cultural forms (Reuss-Ianni, 1983). More recently, with the introduction of community policing models, policy makers and administrators have sought to change police culture by increasing the emphasis on better communication with community members and crime prevention strategies. However, many officers have resisted such changes and associated many community policing models with soft, feminine strategies (J. M. Brown & Heidensohn, 2000; S. L. Miller, 1999).

Work cultures also may converge with the organizational climate of particular work settings. Correctional officer cultures are shaped by the distinctive character of the prison physical structure and organization in which they are located (e.g., minimum versus maximum security prison; Britton, 2003; Useem & Goldstone, 2002).

Work groups draw on larger cultural ideals to develop their own ideals of masculinity and femininity. Consistent with Connell's (1987, 2002) arguments about hegemonic masculinity and emphasized femininity in society and Acker's (1990) view of gendered jobs, workplace research has identified the existence of multiple and often conflicting idealized and gendered images of workers. Images of masculinity and femininity associated with white, heterosexual men and women are those more likely to be ideologically dominant in many workplace settings (e.g., Britton, 2003; C. L. Williams, 1995).

In predominantly men's occupations, dominant work culture images often associate effective job performance with culturally dominant ideals of masculinity that are relevant for the sex category and social class of job incumbents. Although its exact forms vary, the suppression of emotions appears to characterize masculinity across social classes in Western industrial societies. Physicians and lawyers are expected to conform to dominant notions of middle-class masculinity that include the rational manipulation and control of ideas but avoidance of emotional displays. Men's working-class occupations often expose workers to physical demands and danger. Consequently, in these occupations, competence becomes associated with culturally dominant notions of working-class masculinity that call for displays of physical strength, courage, and aggressiveness (C. L. Williams, 1989). Men in occupations such as mining and policing often equate fearlessness with masculinity (Hunt, 1984). Such masculine images are constructed as opposites of culturally emphasized femininity, which is seen as weak, emotional, and incompetent (S. E. Martin, 1999; C. L. Williams, 1995). Accordingly, jobs become resources for doing masculinity (Messerschmidt, 1993), and the exact content of the culturally dominant image of gender and competence varies to some extent within each work organization and situation.

Work cultures may advance unsavory images of women and other cultural subordinates. For example, a work group composed predominantly of white heterosexual men might argue that women are too physically weak, or that gay men might try to seduce them. White workers might hold images of black workers as lazy. Workers who are members of culturally dominant groups may propagate such stereotyped images and respond negatively to subordinates accordingly. Such cultural images help construct and justify existing gendered divisions of labor (Acker, 1990). However, the acceptance of these images varies across work settings, as well as across workers who might differ in race, class, sexual orientation, and age.

The confluence or intersection of various dimensions of socially constructed identities gives rise to diverse work experiences and challenges to culturally hegemonic images of competent workers in each setting. For example, some gay men and lesbian police officers argue that their marginalized social status as homosexuals gives them keener insights and skills to better police other socially marginalized groups. Organizational mandates of equal opportunities for gay and lesbian officers may support the construction of positive workplace identities that include both "out" homosexual and competent police officer (S. L. Miller et al., 2003). Still, subordinating images of cultural "others" abound in work organizations.

Kanter (1977) has identified four cultural images used to subordinate women in the workplace: the "little sister," who is dependent and incompetent; the "seductress," who is incompetent and flirts with men at work; the "iron maiden," who is competent but is cold and harsh; and the "mother," who takes care of men's emotions but is sometimes "nagging."[6] These images are applied to women workers in the justice system.

Subordinating images may be simultaneously racialized, sexualized, and age-specific as well as gendered. Angela Y. Davis (1981) and Patricia Hill Collins (2000) discuss subordinating images of black women. "Mules" do the dirty work for which white women are too delicate; "Jezebels" are sexually promiscuous, and aggressive; "Mammies" are deferential and "know their place"; "Matriarchs" are aggressive and controlling; and "Uppity" black women do not "know their place" and expect to be treated as though they were equal to white women or to white men.

Sexuality is an important dimension of workplace culture and is often a means of promoting gender subordination. Enforced heterosexuality is a primary mechanism for subordinating women at home and on the job (Cockburn, 1991; Rich, 1980). As in other occupations, heterosexuality is a central aspect of masculine dominance among criminal justice system workers. If men or women workers fail to meet the expectations of informal work groups, they may be labeled homosexuals as a means for devaluing them. Women may be labeled lesbians when they perform their jobs as well as a man, or if they refuse men's sexual advances. Men who show support for women or display emotions at work may be labeled as "sissies" or homosexuals.

Workplace Interactions and Identities

Men and women workers actively produce gender and other forms of social differences in workplace interactions. These interactions simultaneously produce and reproduce the work organization and other institutions in society. There is considerable interplay between wider cultural imagery and competing constructions of masculinity and femininity in the workplace. Workers' everyday practices are accountable to these cultural images but may not necessarily correspond to them. For example, unless she works in a hip record store, a woman who chooses to shave her head bald will likely have to account for this style when she goes to work at an office the next day. If she is not fired or teased too badly, this style may become an available model for other women who work with her. In this way, workers construct varieties of femininities and masculinities through specific practices (Connell & Messerschmidt, 2005).

Interactions between men and women in traditionally men's occupations are gendered and sexualized (C. L. Williams, 1995). Even today, some men coworkers and superiors are overtly hostile, but typically use more subtle interactional techniques to undermine women workers. They can exert performance pressure by constantly questioning or scrutinizing women's performance. They also use boundary maintenance techniques to separate women from men socially or physically (Kanter, 1977). Superiors may give women gender-typed assignments (e.g., clerical chores). Correctional managers may assign women to areas that are physically isolated from men coworkers and inmates (Britton, 2003).

Boundary maintenance techniques include verbal cues such as commenting on women's appearance, performance, or sexual relationships, as well as nonverbal cues such as stares or "playful" touching (Kanter, 1977; S. E. Martin, 1978). Men can also emphasize their difference from women by exaggerating displays of masculinity (e.g., telling of sexual exploits).

Exclusionary tactics help maintain boundaries. Historically, women were not admitted to law schools, a necessary prerequisite for practice. In occupations such as policing and corrections where essential training is conducted informally on the job, coworkers may exclude women from training interactions or sabotage them, even to the point of jeopardizing women's physical safety. Friendships off the job are important sources of information and informal influence. In some occupations (e.g., banking, law), the golf course or social club may be as important as the office for making influential contacts and trading information. If they are excluded from these organizations, women are deprived of the benefits of informal information exchange and lose opportunities for mentoring (Huffman & Torres, 2002).

Paternalism refers to situations in which men extract submission and even gratitude from women in exchange for excusing them from difficult jobs. Because men's protection of women appears to be helpful, women may welcome relief from hard assignments, but paternalism denies women the chance to demonstrate their abilities and creates resentment among other workers (Swerdlow, 1989).

Other interactional devices for constructing men's dominance include undermining and invalidating women. Men invalidate women by refusing to accept their authority, denigrating their work products, and magnifying their failures. When women complain about discrimination, men may respond that women's disadvantage is simply a "handicap that nature imposed on them." Men's achievements are attributed to skill, but they often imply or even seek legal redress by claiming that a woman's promotion or other accomplishments are the result of sexual favors or reverse discrimination (Bagilhole, 2002; Cockburn, 1991).

The production and reproduction of work organizations is inextricably associated with sexuality, as well as with gender (Burrell & Hearn, 1989, p. 2). Sexualization may occur through subtle avenues of dress, demeanor, and behavior. Sexualization also includes sexual harassment—overtly sexual talk, unwanted contact, and physical advances (Cockburn, 1991).

Sexual harassment is a problem faced by women, minority, and LGBT workers around the globe (Gruber & Morgan, 2005). For example, sexual harassment that is specifically homophobic is a tactic that is commonly applied by military men. Labeling women lesbian affects all women regardless of their sexual orientation and can be used to end a woman's career even if the allegations are false (Embser-Herbert, 2005). Sexual harassment has been recognized as a problem in many countries but is strongly denied in others (Siklova, 1993). Sexual harassment assumes patterns that reinforce gender, race, and class subordination. Power differentials, gender ratios, race, ethnicity, and age significantly affect the likelihood of being sexually harassed (MacKinnon, 1978; Schneider, 1991). However, even women in supervisory positions are harassed by men subordinates (Gruber & Morgan, 2005).

Organizational policies regarding sexuality are often inconsistent within and across work organizations: employers use women's sexuality in advertising and client relations to increase profits but try to limit its expression in employee interactions. Waitresses may be expected to wear short skirts and to flirt with men customers (E. J. Hall, 1993). In contrast, women correctional and police officers may be expected to wear uniforms that disguise breasts or other physiological signs of sex category (Sugden, 2005; L. E. Zimmer, 1986). Finally, although managers may regard relationships among workers as problematic for the organization, men managers' exercise of the "sexual prerogative" with women subordinates may be informally condoned.

Responsibility for sexualization is usually attributed to women. Men's heterosexuality is not problematic in the workplace, but women must be asexual. If women return men's sexual humor or "flirt," they are labeled negatively. "What is funny coming from a man is obscene coming from a woman" (Cockburn, 1991, p. 156). It is usually women who are blamed, demoted, transferred, or fired for "sexuality problems" arising at work. Women who ignore or reject men's advances are labeled prudes or lesbians. This "lesbian threat" enforces heterosexual dominance and undermines women's efforts to bond with each other for political and friendship purposes (Cockburn, 1991).

Despite the widespread resistance to women in traditionally men's fields, men's responses are not uniform. For example, some men in corrections have supported women's entry into formerly men's jobs and allied themselves more closely with women coworkers than with sexist men coworkers and superiors (Jurik, 1985). Other men denigrate supportive men as "mama's boys" or "women" and question their masculinity (Cockburn, 1991).

There are significant differences in the experiences and behavior of women workers according to race, ethnicity, and sexual orientation. Women of color sometimes feel that white women coworkers are no more sensitive to issues of racism than are white men. They sometimes bond more closely with men of their own race than with white women coworkers (Owen, 1988). They also tend to be less willing than are white women to file claims of sexual harassment. If the harasser is a white man, they fear that they will not be believed; if he is a man of their own race, they feel disloyal (Belknap, 1991; P. Y. Martin, 1991). In contrast, lesbians appear more willing than are straight women to use the label sexual harassment in describing unwanted sexual approaches from men in the workplace (Schneider, 1982). Yet, heterosexual women may distance themselves from lesbians in the workplace, thus preventing effective organization to combat sexism in the workplace (S. L. Miller et al., 2003).

Research indicates that women's work styles vary according to age, education, rank, and tenure (McElhinny, 1993). Sometimes, women succumb to the pressures of men-dominated work cultures. They acquiesce to men's protection and accept restricted work assignments. They reproduce cultural notions of emphasized femininity as passive, supportive, and emotional (S. E. Martin, 1980). In other cases, women emulate culturally dominant forms of masculine work behavior. They refuse protection or special duties and struggle to demonstrate their equality to men coworkers by engaging in "masculine" behavior (L. E. Zimmer, 1986). Women who display qualities associated with masculinity are criticized even when they exercise appropriately assertive behavior: coworkers describe them as "mannish." This label becomes "a stick with which to threaten other women" (Cockburn, 1991, p. 69). Women who adopt less authoritarian approaches are met with resistance since they are seen as "weak" and, thus, ineffective leaders.

The construction of gender is not solely a reflection of culturally dominant images of masculinity, femininity, and competence. Individuals may do gender in ways that oppose dominant cultural and organizational images. Some women have challenged work culture imagery that equates competence with dominant notions of masculinity. They claim that "feminine qualities" such as caring, communication, and conflict-diffusion skills enhance work performance, and they argue that femininity and competence are not mutually exclusive categories.

Other women have tried to substitute more androgynous or "gender-neutral" professional images that emphasize rational-formal, rule-oriented behavior and oppose aggressive, macho behavior (Brush, 1992; Stojkovic, Pogrebin, & Poole, 2000). However, the professional ideal still fails to challenge institutionalized images of workers as men devoid of family responsibilities. Iris Young (1990, pp. 139–140) describes other cultural biases in the professional ideal:

> Professional behavior . . . signifies rationality and authoritativeness, [and] requires specific ways of sitting, standing, walking and speaking, namely without undue expression. . . . One should speak firmly, without hesitation or ambiguity, and slang, dialect and accent should be absent from one's speech.

For these reasons, working-class police officers may ridicule professional modes of speaking and handling cases as too formal and feminized (Jurik & Martin, 2001; Schulz, 1995). In some research, citizens described the middle-class, professional, objective styles of police talk to be cold and unfeeling to them as crime victims (McElhinny, 1993).

Models of professionalism are associated with elite, white men (Cavender & Jurik, 2004). Connell (1993) suggests that culturally dominant forms of masculinity are changing from an interpersonally and physically aggressive (read: working-class) style to one that is more professional and technocratic. The professional is a detached manager, an expert, and a bureaucrat. Managers and technocrats are not openly hostile toward women; they "do not directly confront feminist programs, but instead, under-fund or shrink them in the name of efficiency and voluntarism" (Connell, 1993, p. 615). The ideal professional aims for organizational universalism, rather than emotional connections to others or "special rights" for women or other social groups (McElhinny, 1993).

Gendered Organizational Logic

Organizational rules and regulations often intentionally and unintentionally disadvantage women. As women have become viewed as a more permanent part of the workforce and as gender and racial equality discourses have become more widely adopted, overt displays of sexism and racism have diminished to some extent. However, gendered, racialized, and sexualized practices remain embedded in most work organizations. Such second-generation discrimination includes covert or unconscious structural disadvantage and is difficult to identify and document without in-depth empirical analyses of work organizations and careers over time. Gender as well as other forms of inequality remain implicit in the logic of organizations through written work rules and the practices (formal and informal) surrounding training, work assignments, and promotions (Wilkins & Gulati, 1996).

Research on women in nontraditional occupations reveals the ways in which organizational logic is gendered. Employers' and employees' devaluing of work characteristically performed by women is institutionalized through formal organizational rules and procedures. Acker (1990, pp. 148–149) describes the gendered character of task valuation:

> Organizational logic assumes a congruence between responsibility, job complexity, and hierarchical position. . . . Lower-level positions, the . . . jobs filled predominantly by women, must have equally low levels of complexity and responsibility. Complexity and responsibility are defined in terms of managerial and professional tasks.

In most work organizations, supervisors rely on ostensibly objective training, assignment, and assessment procedures that incorporate social constructions of competence. Generally, work qualifications have been developed based on notions of heterosexual masculine competence, but now frame the assessments of working women and men (Morash & Greene, 1986). For example, training in policing and corrections emphasizes physical criteria that may have little relevance for effective job performance, but that nonetheless disadvantage women. Conversely, qualities such as negotiation and mediation skills typically attributed to women lawyers often are not included among formal evaluation criteria (Menkel-Meadow, 1986). The gendered organizational logic of law firm work hours and around-the-clock availability to clients shapes the implementation of affirmative action, family leave, and sexual harassment policies (Cockburn, 1991; Reichman & Sterling, 2002).

Organizations change over time, and shifts in organizational discourses are rarely gender neutral. We will elaborate how organizational reform and professionalization in policing and corrections advanced the arguments of women seeking to enter occupations in those fields. Another example of the unintended gender effects of organizational change can be found in state and federal government movements to privatize many public services and manage remaining government agencies in ways that more closely resemble the methods of private businesses. Because government at all levels has historically been an important source of jobs that provide good pay, benefits, and security as well as advancement opportunities for white women and persons of color, privatization may disproportionately disadvantage these groups of workers. The less rigorous enforcement of equal opportunity standards in hiring and promotion that characterize private business have typically made it more difficult for women and minorities to advance in those arenas (Dantico & Jurik, 1986; Perrucci & Wysong, 1999).

In addition, government agencies are now undergoing a new phase or second wave of privatization. This "new privatization" means the redesign of government agencies so that they operate more like our cultural ideal of a private business (Jurik, 2004). Many labels have been used that identify how new privatization is accomplished: audit culture, leaderless organizations, new entrepreneurialism, and the term we will use, new managerialism. This new managerialism emphasizes idealized forms of private sector efficiency in government agencies and includes downsizing managerial staff, flattening organizational hierarchies, and devolving management responsibilities to line-level staff. These "new managerial" philosophies mean that in theory, everybody becomes a manager (Silvestri, 2003). In some settings, these organizational discourses promote increased workplace democracy and flexibility that might support the advancement of women. At the same time, there are organization contradictions because new managerialism fosters an ethos of increased competitiveness, entrepreneurial conduct, and aggressiveness that may be hostile to women in the workplace. Many governmental work organizations are now less open to flexible work arrangements for employees, especially among those who assume the limited number of remaining management positions. The loss of workplace flexibility and increased work intensity make it difficult for women with families to advance in government sector organizations (Hull & Nelson, 2000; Meuser, 2003).

Summary

Many analyses of women's subordination in the workplace have conceptualized gender as an individual attribute that is socially and biologically determined. From this perspective, gender is a preemployment attribute of workers who enter ostensibly gender-neutral work organizations. Gender differences at work are regarded either as the result of inherent worker differences or as not really gender differences at all. These views ignore the changes in gender across history, cultures, and situations and the ways in which work dynamics help to shape emerging gender identities.

We rely, instead, on a view of gender as a process that emerges through social practice. Accumulated patterns of social interaction throughout history generate structured societies—divisions of labor, power, and culture. These practices simultaneously construct gender, race, and class and other dimensions of identities and social inequality. Social constraints shape the forms of femininity, race, ethnicity, class and sexual orientation that are available, encouraged, and permitted in the work-place and elsewhere. Thus, as individuals construct their identities, they simultaneously reflect, reproduce, and sometimes challenge existing social structural arrangements. Individuals do gender and other dimensions of identity with differing degrees of awareness and intentionality. Even when they do not intend or are unaware of it, their conduct may still reflect, add to, or challenge culturally dominant ideas.

We highlight gender as an integral accomplishment of life in social institutions. We have outlined a framework to analyze the social construction of gender in work organizations through divisions of labor, work cultures, interactions, and organizational logic. The construction of gender within work organizations is also shaped by dynamics in social institutions—family, state, and labor market. As these institutional processes produce gender, they produce race, class, sexual orientation, age, and other forms of social differentiation (Frankenberg, 1993). Gender is never done in isolation from other social relations, but each of these features may vary in salience from one situation to the next.

Drawing on the framework outlined here, the following chapters analyze the social production of gender in justice work organizations. For the occupations of policing, law, and correctional security, we examine (1) *changing labor queues* produced by wider changes in institutions such as the state, family, and labor market; (2) *gendered work cultures* and their link to the nature of the occupation and wider cultural images; (3) *men doing gender* in their interactions with women entrants to justice organizations; (4) *the gendered logic* of justice organizations; and (5) *women doing gender* in responding to gender subordination. A concluding chapter compares the forms of gender subordination across justice occupations and considers the significance of changing gender ratios for justice fields.

Endnotes

1. Each category is treated as a distinct and consistent whole: similarities among members are emphasized. Describing the unified group is easiest when contrasting it with some other opposite group (e.g., man/woman, white/black). Then, individual cases are neatly located in the appropriate category. Overlaps between and differences within categories are de-emphasized. The first category is more highly valued than the second, which threatens to disrupt the unity of the first. Historically, men have been viewed as rational and objective; women have been viewed as less than men since they are regarded as emotional and ruled by their bodies (I. M. Young, 1990).

2. West and Zimmerman (1987) developed the term "doing gender."

3. Connell (1987) defines power, division of labor, and cathexis as key structures of gender subordination. Messerschmidt (1993) uses "sexuality" instead of cathexis. We chose I. M. Young's (1990) formulation of "culture," which seems to be more inclusive of race, ethnic, and class subordination.

4. Less desirable options include married but childless heterosexuals, single heterosexuals, celibates, monogamous homosexuals, and so forth (Messerschmidt, 1993, p. 74).

5. "Segregation" and "ghettoization" are commonly used terms in the literature, but by using the term segregation, we do not intend to equate women's experiences with those of oppressed race and ethnic groups (Reskin & Roos, 1990).

6. We viewed Kanter's (1977) term "role stereotypes" as too static for our conceptualization of gender as a process.

CHAPTER 3

The Nature of Police Work and Women's Entry Into Law Enforcement

B efore the 1970s, nearly all police officers in the United States were white men; women comprised less than 2 percent of sworn personnel, and "policewomen" served in specialized positions. Racial and ethnic minorities also were greatly underrepresented in policing. Common language, job titles, and media presented images of police that were both gendered and linked to white working-class culture. In the past 30 years, the image of a police officer as a white man has been weakened, and both the number and proportion of women in policing have grown. By October 2003, women comprised 11.3 percent of sworn personnel (U.S. Department of Justice, 2005) and could be found in all specialized assignments and ranks, including chief. Nonetheless, women police in the United States still are underrepresented, regarded with suspicion by many men officers, and face discriminatory practices within the informal police culture and the formal organization. The limited numbers and similar barriers have been documented for women police officers in Europe (J. M. Brown & Heidensohn, 2000), Australia (Prenzler & Hayes, 2000; Sugden, 2005), the former Soviet bloc nations, and former colonial nations of Asia and Africa (J. M. Brown & Heidensohn, 2000; Natarajan, 2001, 2003).

Legislation, executive action, and judicial decisions have altered eligibility criteria, selection standards, and assignment and promotion practices that discriminated against women. The open and organized harassment encountered by the first women on patrol has largely disappeared. Yet, women officers still must cope with gendered organizational policies and practices, hostile work environments, and an occupational culture whose "cult of masculinity" glamorizes violence and denigrates women (M. Young, 1991, p. 192).

This chapter explores the history of women in policing, their broadened occupational roles since the 1970s, and the ways the work and police occupational culture contribute to the continuing resistance to women officers. Although the focus is on the United States, data we present on women in policing in England, Canada, and Australia as well as Europe and the rest of the world make clear that around the globe, women officers encounter similar challenges and barriers resulting from "the stereotypic cultural values of the police that may be seen as an almost pure form of 'hegemonic masculinity'" (Fielding, 1994, p. 47).

An Historical Overview: From Matron to Chief

Preliminary Phase: 1840–1910

Women first entered the criminal justice workplace in the early 19th century in the United States and England as prison matrons exclusively for women and girls. The next step was to go from prison matron to jail matron working with women and girls in police lockups, initially in the New York Police Department and subsequently in other large city agencies. Gradually, they extended their responsibilities beyond strictly custodial work but continued in work that reinforced their traditional role as caregivers to other women while simultaneously ensuring careers for these upper-middle-class women (Schulz, 2004).

The Specialist Phase: 1910–1972

In 1910, Alice Stebbins Wells became the first sworn woman officer in the United States. From then until the mid-1970s, "policewomen" were restricted in number, paid less than men, selected by different criteria from men officers, and assigned to work primarily with women and children. Wells sought an appointment as a sworn officer in the Los Angeles Police Department, convinced she could be more effective in preventive and protective work with women and children if she had police powers.

The early policewomen's movement had several sources. First, women of the "social purity" reform movement in the late 19th and early 20th centuries sought social change and staked out work roles that were extensions of women's domestic roles and their feminine characteristics. Many of the early policewomen were upper-middle-class women "eager to act as municipal mothers to those whose lifestyles they believed needed discipline," namely poor women (Schulz, 2004, p. 486). The few African-American policewomen hired worked in large city departments with African-American women and girls. They shared many of the educational and elite characteristics of their white sisters (Schulz, 2004).

Second, women's early successes in establishing a place for themselves in policing stemmed from the confluence of their aims with those of some progressive police reformers. Both sought to free policing from corrupting politics, upgrade personnel, and professionalize police work. In the 1920s, reform efforts were characterized by competition between two models of reform: a crime control or efficiency/managerial model and a social service/crime prevention model (Appier, 1998). The latter claimed that scientific police work could prevent crime by discovering and eliminating its causes. Wells and other women reformers espoused "crime prevention . . . as a recognized and growing part of police duty" (A. S. Wells, 1932, p. 15). Few reform-oriented men, however, mentioned the association of crime prevention or professionalism with policewomen. Rather, the policewomen's presence caused a dilemma: if preventing crime was the primary duty of the police, and if women were better at it than the men, then men would assume second-rate status within police departments.

Many leaders of the policewomen's movement understood the threat they posed to men and sought to reduce it. They created Women's Bureaus that were separated administratively, and sometimes physically, from the rest of the department. They avoided wearing uniforms and carrying guns, and often were required to have a college education, but encountered lower physical standards than the men. When their upper-middle-class backgrounds, higher levels of education, and sense of superiority resulted in tension and opposition from the mostly working-class men, policewomen often sought a peripheral role. Consequently, they were "kept at arm's length from the main organization and, perhaps, a little despised by the remainder of the force" (Hutzel, 1933, p. 3). At the same time, the Women's Bureaus and policewomen's insistence that they be in charge of them enabled them to create a mechanism for a few women to rise in rank (Schulz, 2004).

Women's inroads into policing came to a halt during the 1930s. Hiring was frozen during that decade. Moreover, the crime control model of police work, which viewed officers primarily as soldiers in a war against crime, almost totally eclipsed the crime prevention model. The crime control model, fostered by J. Edgar Hoover and the FBI at the national level, centralized control and adopted a military-style command structure to address police corruption. The crime control model also firmly reinforced male, working-class culture and values in police departments and reaffirmed the superiority of the masculine virtues of the fearless crime fighter who is able to overcome resistance (Walker & Katz, 2005).

For the next 40 years, a few policewomen gained assignments to detective, vice, and crime lab units, but the vast majority were assigned to juvenile work or secretarial duties. Their recruitment, training, salary, and promotion remained limited. In 1960, there were only 5,617 women in policing and security work in the United States (Census figures cited in Heidensohn, 1992, p. 55), and they comprised less than 1 percent of sworn personnel. Nevertheless, the women who entered policing after World War II were middle-class careerists, not upper-class feminists and "child-savers," and were increasingly dissatisfied with restriction to the "women's sphere" (Schulz, 2004).

In Europe and Australia, the early history of women in policing closely parallels that of the United States. In 1903, the first woman officer was sworn in in Stuttgart, Germany. By 1915, at least 35 German cities employed policewomen, and women officers had been hired in Denmark, Great Britain, Holland, Hungary, Latvia, Norway, Poland, Siam, Sweden, Switzerland (Schulz, 1998, p. 72), and Australia (Prenzler, 1998). During World War I, women were used to guard their nation's morals as women became controllers of other women's sexual conduct across the European continent. The factors affecting the hiring of women and the limitations on their duties and numbers found in the United States also were characteristic of these other nations. They too were influenced by broader movements such as international feminism and the human rights movement (J. M. Brown & Heidensohn, 1996).

Nevertheless, local and regional conditions affected the pace and nature of the changing conditions for women in policing (e.g., Prenzler, 1998).

Between World Wars I and II, in Europe and Australia, policewomen's work continued to revolve around women and children. World War II saw women again charged with the guardianship of the nation's morals as they were expected to exert a restraining influence on women's sexual behavior.

From "Policewoman" to Chief: Changes Since 1972

Change for women in policing began in the 1960s and accelerated in the 1970s and 1980s in the United States. In the past decade, progress has continued, albeit at a glacial pace. In England and Australia, the integration of women began about a decade later but has paralleled trends in the United States. Women's integration in the former Soviet nations and those in Africa and Asia has been slower.[1] In 1961, a policewoman won a lawsuit against New York City and gained the right to compete in a promotional process not limited to women. Four years later, Felicia Schpritzer became the city's first woman sergeant (Bell, 1982). In 1968, the Indianapolis Police Department assigned two women to patrol duties; in 1972, the Metropolitan Police Department of Washington, D.C., became the first municipal agency to put a significant number of women on patrol (initially as an "experiment"). Since then, the representation of women in all types of departments has increased, and women have been integrated into patrol and virtually all other police activities.

Women's transformation from specialist "policewoman" to generalist patrol officer is related both to the police crisis of the 1960s and to social and economic changes in the status of women during that decade (discussed more fully in Chapter 1). Each reform movement contributed to a new role for women in policing by changing their place in the labor queues.

Police Crisis of the 1960s

In the 1960s, police faced a series of challenges. Violent crime rates rose. Low salaries and the retirement of World War II veterans resulted in "manpower" shortages. There were urban riots stemming from the civil rights movement and the police response to it, and rising economic and social expectations, but continuing poverty. The police encountered growing public frustration with "police brutality." Officers had to adapt to new procedures for protecting citizen's rights to due process resulting from several Supreme Court decisions.

In reviewing criminal justice system problems, two presidential commissions called for sweeping changes, with particular emphasis on the police. Their recommendations included higher personnel standards, improved management, greater use of science and technology, a reexamination of the meaning of police professionalism, and attention to police-community relations. They also called for subordination of strength and aggressiveness to the qualities of emotional stability and intelligence; greater sensitivity to minority problems in recruitment of personnel; elimination of discriminatory selection criteria; and hiring more officers who were college educated, persons of color, and women.

The Women's Movement

The women's movement contributed to expanding the recruitment pool of women officers by changing gender stereotypes and values, and altering traditional concepts of masculinity and femininity. Although the women's movement did not assure equal opportunities for female officers, it stimulated a new social climate within police departments. Social norms and practices, ranging from standards of sexual behavior, appearance, and grooming to women's educational options and career choices, were challenged and changed during the 1960s and 1970s, fostered by and supporting challenges to the legal status quo.

Legal Changes: Legislation and Judicial Interpretation

Antidiscrimination laws contributed to the influx of women into police work. Before passage of the Equal Opportunity Act of 1972, many local laws and ordinances prohibited women from patrol assignments and promotions in rank. The 1972 Act extended to local police agencies provisions of the Civil Rights Act of 1964 and expanded the powers of the Equal Employment Opportunity Commission to enforce Title VII. The Crime Control Act of 1973 required police departments with 50 or more employees that received $25,000 or more in federal grants to implement equal employment opportunity programs for women or face withdrawal of funds (Bell, 1982).

In the 1970s, many police agencies were sued for discriminating on the basis of gender, race, or both. Lawsuits contested departments' entrance requirements related to education, age, height, weight, and arrest records; their selection criteria, including written examinations, agility tests, and veterans' preference; and discriminatory assignment and promotion procedures (Potts, 1983; Sulton & Townsey, 1981). Many of these cases resulted in court orders or consent decrees that established affirmative action programs, including quotas and timetables for hiring and promoting women and persons of color. Other decisions supported plaintiffs' challenges to height and weight standards and to agility tests that were neither sufficiently job related nor adequately validated (Hale & Menniti, 1993).

To comply with emerging case law, police agencies modified recruitment practices, eligibility requirements, and selection criteria. Almost all agencies eliminated or altered height and weight requirements and modified physical agility tests that disproportionately eliminated women and Hispanic and Asian men.[2] Some agencies also replaced agility tests that emphasized upper body strength with physical performance tests that assess health and fitness. The new tests measure cardiovascular function, body composition, flexibility, and dynamic and absolute strength, and have performance norms adjusted for age and sex.

Police departments also revised written entrance examinations that adversely affected persons of color, and standardized oral screening procedures for both selection and promotion. Personal interviews were standardized, with a single set of questions administered by trained interviewers including white women and men and women of color. These newer procedures leave less room for arbitrary decisions, but candidates still tend to be judged on qualities, standards, or attributes associated with masculinity (e.g., self-confidence and assertiveness).

The affirmative action policies adopted by many police departments significantly affected the representation of white women and men and women of color through-out policing and in supervisory positions (S. E. Martin, 1991). During the 1980s, the Supreme Court's reinterpretation of Title VII limited the use of affirmative action programs but did not eliminate them. By 1987, more than half of police agencies serving populations larger than 50,000 had implemented affirmative action plans. Recently, however, the court-ordered plans implemented in major cities 20 years ago have expired and have not been renewed at a comparable rate. The 2001 annual survey of police departments conducted by the National Center for Women & Policing reported that of the 247 agencies with more than 100 officers that responded to the survey, 40 had been under a consent decree at some time, but only 22 of those remained in effect. During the decade of the 1990s, only six departments reported being subject to new decrees (National Center for Women & Policing, 2002a).

This decline in court-mandated affirmative action increases the likelihood of diminished recruitment, retention, and promotion for women and persons of color in the coming decade. The impact of the implementation and termination of a consent decree is illustrated by personnel changes in the Pittsburgh Police Department, which was under a court order from 1975 to 1991. The order mandated that for every white man hired, the department was to hire one white woman, one African-American man, and one African-American woman. When the court order was imposed, only 1 percent of all officers in the Pittsburgh police were women. By 1990, the department had 27.2 percent women officers, the highest woman officer representation in the country. Following the lifting of the court order, the proportion of women hired dropped to 8.5 percent from the 50 percent rate mandated under the order. As of 2001, women's representation had dropped to 22 percent of the department's sworn personnel (National Center for Women & Policing, 2002a).

In addition to the effects of civil rights laws passed in the 1960s and early 1970 that altered police personnel practices, other Supreme Court decisions in those decades also radically altered traditional concepts of law enforcement. The "due process revolution" required police agencies to alter street justice practices such as arbitrary arrests, random searches and seizures, and other violations of civil liberties. The "tough cop" tactics characteristic of the crime control model of policing had become more restrained as the pendulum swung back toward a crime prevention model.

The Impact of Research

Because the initial assignment of women to patrol in large numbers in 1972 was regarded as an experiment, nine evaluations of women's performance were conducted to determine whether women could perform adequately on street patrol in diverse jurisdictions. These included Washington, D.C. (Bloch & Anderson, 1974), St. Louis (Sherman, 1975), New York City (Sichel, Friedman, Quint, & Smith, 1977), Denver (Bartlett & Rosenblum, 1977), Newton, Massachusetts (Kizziah & Morris, 1977), Philadelphia (Bartell Associates, 1978), California (California Highway Patrol, 1976), and Pennsylvania (Pennsylvania State Police, 1974).

Although some gender differences were found, all the studies but the second phase of the Philadelphia evaluation concluded that men and women are equally capable of police patrol work. Some of the studies found women to be less proficient in the use of firearms and to have more accidents in comparison to men (St. Louis, Washington, D.C., and New York City); others reported that women have a "less aggressive" policing style, evidenced by fewer arrests (Washington, D.C.) and fewer citizen complaints (Denver). Morash and Greene (1986) identified a number of areas in which these evaluations were gender biased.[3] Nevertheless, the evaluation findings meant that sex could no longer be considered a bona fide occupational qualification for the job of patrol officer and that women had to be given an opportunity to serve on street patrol.

The Increasing Representation of Women in Police Work

These changes in policing and in the larger social and legal environment led to women's assignment to patrol duties in most large municipal, state, and federal law enforcement agencies by the end of the 1970s. From 1980 through the present, women's representation and responsibilities have steadily expanded despite resistance from most of the men. For example, in 1975, women constituted 2.2 percent of the sworn personnel in municipal departments (Martin, 1980). They comprised 3.8 percent of municipal officers in 1980, 8.3 percent in 1990, 10.9 percent in 2000, and 11.3 percent in 2004, as shown in Table 3.1. The table also indicates that women have consistently had greater representation in the large departments (where they comprise 16.4 percent of personnel) than in those that are smaller in size and that the gap has not diminished over the past 24 years. In addition, the decline in women's representation in the largest agencies between 2000 and 2004 suggests that to move beyond token numbers, more aggressive recruiting and retention efforts will be necessary.

Increases in the representation of women in law enforcement have occurred in agencies of differing types and have included women of color. Comparing data for 1990 and 2000 across agency types, as shown in Table 3.2, the proportion of women continues to be greatest in sheriff's departments. However, the table also indicates a decrease in women's representation from 15.4 percent of all deputies in 1990 to 12.4 percent in 2000. State police agencies lag behind municipal and sheriffs' agencies in hiring women. In 1990, women comprised only 4.6 percent of the sworn personnel; in 2000, that proportion had risen only to 5.9 percent.

Table 3.3 shows that by 2000, municipal and sheriff's departments that previously were almost exclusively white and male have become much more diverse. Among local agencies, nearly 12 percent of officers are African-American, including 9 percent of the men and 2.7 percent of the women; similarly, Hispanic officers have made gains. Hispanics comprise 8.3 percent, including 7.2 percent of men officers but only 1.1 percent of women officers. American Indians, Asian-Americans, and other groups comprise 2.4 percent of officers, almost all of whom (2.4 percent) are men. The proportion of officers of color in municipal policing (30 percent)

Table 3.1   Women Officers in Municipal Policing by Agency Size: 1980–2004

	Large[a]		Medium[b]		Smaller[c]		Small[d]		Total	
	Number	%	Number	%	Number	%	Number	%	Number	%
1980	5,131	4.6	1,242	4.2	1,010	3.1	3,615	3.0	11,179	3.8
1990	15,673	12.6	2,851	8.2	2,363	6.2	7,494	5.2	28,335	8.3
2000	25,305	16.2	4,841	10.2	3,825	8.3	12,443	7.0	46,414	10.9
2004	23,989	16.4	5,191	11.0	4,230	8.9	10,497	7.9	49,837	11.3

Source: U.S. Department of Justice (1981, 1991, 2001, 2005).

a. Cities with populations greater than 250,000. In 1980, included 57 cities; in 1990, 62 cities; in 2000, 68 cities; in 2004, 69 cities.

b. Cities with populations between 100,000 and 249,000. In 1980, included 108 cities; in 1990, 127 cities; in 2000, 161 cities; in 2004, 174 cities.

c. Cities with populations between 50,000 and 99,000. In 1980, included 273 cities; in 1990, 321 cities; in 2000, 376 cities; in 2004, 391 cities.

d. Cities with populations less than 50,000. In 1990, included 8,997 cities; in 2000, 9,781 cities; in 2004, 10,028 cities.

Table 3.2   Full-Time Sworn Local Police, Sheriff's Deputies, and State Police in 1990 and 2000 by Gender

	Local Police		Sheriff's Departments		State Police	
	1990[a]	2000[b]	1990[a]	2000[c]	1990[a]	2000[d]
Number of officers	363,061	449,200	141,418	164,711	52,372	56,346
Percent men	91.9	89.4	84.6	87.5	95.4	93.4
Percent women	8.1	10.6	15.4	12.5	4.5	6.6

a. U.S. Department of Justice, Bureau of Justice Statistics (1992, p. 3, Table 3; and p. 11, Table 28).

b. Hickman and Reaves (2003a, p. 4, Table 7).

c. Hickman and Reaves (2003b, p. 4, Table 7).

d. Reaves and Hickman (2002).

approaches their representation in the U.S. population, although across ethnic groups women continue to be greatly underrepresented. However, nearly a quarter (23 percent) of black officers are women, whereas white, Hispanic, and other (i.e., Asian-American and American Indian) women comprise 8, 13, and 11 percent of the officers of their racial/ethnic groups, respectively.

Several factors may contribute to the large proportion of black women among women in municipal policing. First, black women may view law enforcement as an attractive option compared to the narrow range of jobs traditionally open to them. Second, black women have long been activists and leaders in the black community. Becoming a police officer enables a black woman to wield authority in the African-American community and to work to alter an organization often viewed as oppressive.

Table 3.3   Full-Time Sworn Local Police and Sheriff's Deputies
in 2000 by Gender, Race, and Ethnicity

Number of Officers	Local[a] 449,200[c]		Sheriff's Departments[b] 164,711[c]	
	% Men	% Women	% Men	% Women
White	70.9	6.5	73.7	9.1
Black	9.0	2.7	7.0	2.3
Hispanic	7.2	1.1	5.3	0.8
Other	2.4	0.3	1.4	0.2
Total	89.4	10.6	87.5	12.5

a. Hickman and Reaves (2003a, p. 4, Table 7).

b. Hickman and Reaves (2003b, p. 4, Table 7).

c. Reaves and Hickman (2002).

Third, affirmative action recruiting messages aimed at African-American communities reach both women and men.

Women also have made inroads as officers in federal law enforcement agencies, although their representation varies widely. In 2002, for example, women comprised 28 percent of Internal Revenue Service law enforcement agents, 12.1 percent of the agents in the Immigration and Naturalization Service (which is the largest federal law enforcement agency), and only 8.6 percent of Drug Enforcement Administration sworn agents (Reaves & Bauer, 2003). Data from the FBI illustrate the growth in women's presence. In that agency, which had no women agents prior to 1972, women comprised 14.5 percent of the special agents by June 1996 and 18 percent in June 2002 (Reaves, 1997; Reaves & Bauer, 2003).

Women are slowly being promoted into supervisory ranks but continue to be underrepresented, particularly in the highest ranks. In 1978, women comprised less than 1 percent of the personnel above the officer rank in municipal agencies serving populations of more than 50,000 (Sulton & Townsey, 1981); by the end of 1986, women still made up only 3.3 percent of supervisory personnel in those agencies and were found mostly at the lower ranks (e.g., 3.7 percent of the sergeants but only 1.4 percent of supervisory personnel of a higher rank; S. E. Martin, 1990). Newer data from a survey conducted by the National Center for Women & Policing (2002a) that included responses from 247 agencies with more than 100 officers indicate that as of 2001, in large police agencies women comprised 13.5 percent of the personnel in line operation positions, 9.6 percent of supervisory personnel, and only 7.3 percent of top command positions. Comparing the distributions of women and men, 85.4 percent of the women are in line operations, 13.2 percent are in supervisory positions, and 1.5 percent are in top command, whereas 79.4 percent of the men are in line operations, 17.8 percent are in supervisory positions, and 2.8 percent are in top command.

In most law enforcement agencies, women of color also are underrepresented. They hold 4.8 percent of sworn positions and only 1.6 percent of top command positions, while they comprise 8.2 percent of the overall labor force over age 16 (National Center for Women & Policing, 2002a). More than half (60 percent) of the large police agencies surveyed reported no women in top command positions, and the vast majority (88 percent) reported no women of color in their highest ranks (National Center for Women & Policing, 2002a).

In small and rural police agencies (i.e., those with less than 100 sworn officers and in counties with populations less than 50,000), the underrepresentation of women is greater. Women hold only 3.4 percent of all top command positions, 4.5 percent of supervisory positions, and 5.3 percent of line positions.

In 1990, a breakthrough occurred when Elizabeth Watson became chief of the Houston Police Department, the sixth largest municipal agency in the United States. She served in that position until 1992, when a newly elected mayor selected a new chief. Between November 2003 and April 2004, five women were appointed chief in major police agencies in the United States: those in Detroit, San Francisco, Milwaukee, Boston, and Fairfax County, Virginia (a suburb of Washington, D.C.; Leinwand, 2004). While these promotions indicate that some women have finally risen to the top, women are chiefs in only 175 of the nation's approximately 18,000 police departments—or about 1 percent of agencies. Most of the women chiefs lead college and university police forces, three oversee transportation agency departments, and two head Native American tribal polices. The vast majority of women chiefs are located in small communities (Schulz, 2004).

Women's underrepresentation among supervisors, particularly in command staff positions, reflects the extent to which police management remains a gendered occupation. In fact, given the retreat from affirmative action, the National Center for Women & Policing (2002a) suggests that even the current number of women supervisors may represent the peak of women's achievement rather than the front of a new wave. The continued underrepresentation of women in police work generally and in supervisory positions is particularly disappointing in light of the 18 percent growth in the number of sworn police personnel between 1992 and 2000, which also opened opportunities for a substantial increase in new supervisory personnel.

The growth in the representation of women in police agencies in other countries is generally parallel to that of the United States. For example, according to Pru Goward (2002), Federal Sex Discrimination Commissioner, in Australia, women comprised 13.5 percent of various police forces in 1995 and 18.9 percent of sworn personnel in 2001 but continue to be concentrated at the lower ranks. In June 2001, women comprised 34.0 percent of the probationary constables, 28.7 percent of constables, 16.5 percent of senior constables, 7.2 percent of sergeants, 5.1 percent of senior sergeants, and 2.9 of senior executives (Goward, 2002). Although the first women officers were not employed in New Zealand until 1941, by 1984 their representation had increased to 5.2 percent, and by 2000 women officers represented 15 percent of the national force, although there were no women among the 15 members of the sworn executive staff (E. K. Butler, Winfree, & Newbold, 2003). In England, women make up about 17 percent of police personnel and have a limited share of senior rank. On the European continent, average percentages of women police range from 4 percent in Portugal and Belgium to 6 percent in Denmark,

8 percent in Germany and Hungary, 12 percent in the Netherlands, and 13 percent in Sweden. Thus, women experience only token presence within most police organizations, particularly at the senior rank. There are no women in the highest police grades in Denmark, Ireland, or Portugal. Only Sweden and the United Kingdom have women at the chief officer rank (J. M. Brown & Heidensohn, 2000). In 1997, in France, women represented 7.7 percent of constables, 9.2 percent of inspectors, and 10 percent of superintendents (Maniloff, 1998).

The Nature of Policing: Scope of Work and Occupational Culture

Nature of the Work

Police officers are the gatekeepers of the criminal justice system, enforcing the law and arresting offenders. In addition, officers are expected to prevent crime, protect life and property, maintain peace and public order, and provide a wide range of services to citizens 24 hours a day. A common thread unifying these diverse activities is the potential for violence and the right to use coercive means to enforce the officer's definition of the situation to establish social control at that moment (Bittner, 1970). Policing has traditionally been regarded as "men's work" because it is associated with crime, danger, and coercion, yet people frequently fail to question the logical shifts in the statement that "coercion requires force which implies physique and hence policing by men" (Heidensohn, 1992, p. 73).

Crime fighting is the aspect of the job that for many years has been regarded by both officers and the public as "real" police work. It is visible, publicly valued, and the most satisfying part of the work for most officers. Detectives focus on investigating crimes and making arrests, are relieved of service or order maintenance tasks, and get more pay, prestige, and personal autonomy. The association of catching criminals with danger and bravery marks police work as a "man's job."

The daily reality of policing is far less glamorous. Most police calls involve requests for service and order maintenance tasks. One study of police activity in three California departments found that only 31 percent of all incidents involved officers in crime-related activities (i.e., apprehending felons or investigating and suppressing crime; M. K. Brown, 1981). Violence, even verbal aggression, is a relatively rare occurrence (Garner & Maxwell, 2002). Rather, policing involves officers with people at their worst—when they have been victimized, are injured or helpless, or are guilty and seeking escape. To be effective, officers must restore order in volatile situations and use interpersonal skills to gain compliance rather than bravado.

The Police Officer's "Working Personality"

The combination of danger related to unpredictable physical violence, authority to exercise force, and organizational pressures for efficiency has resulted in a unique set of behaviors and attitudes termed the officer's "working personality" (Skolnick,

1994). Faced with danger, officers become suspicious. Because they have discretion to decide when and whether to use morally dirty means to handle problems, they are feared by and isolated from citizens. Isolation leads them to close ranks against outsiders and view themselves as a "thin blue line" between anarchy and order.

In an effort to inhibit the abuses of power and corruption historically associated with urban policing, administrators have adopted a quasi-military organizational structure and have imposed numerous rules on officers. Despite the elaboration of rule books, discretion is an essential part of the job. Street patrol requires situational decision making; rigid rules have little value in fluid and sometimes volatile situations. Consequently, most officers routinely violate or circumvent rules.

To protect themselves from supervisors who may punish rule infractions and from a citizenry viewed as hostile, officers have created a unique, cohesive occupational culture. Cops rely on fellow officers for physical protection, support, solidarity, and social identity. Their job becomes a way of life, and the occupational culture provides both an alternative morality and an identity (Fielding, 1994; Manning, 1997; Skolnick, 1994; Westley, 1970).

Occupational Culture

The informal work culture of street patrol officers has several "rules." Officers are expected to remain silent about other officers' illicit behavior, to provide physical backup to fellow officers, and to mete out street justice to persons who display disrespect for the police. Officers who fail to abide by these rules are not trusted by others and face ostracism, the silent treatment, and outright rejection as a partner (Westley, 1970). Other characterizations of the police ethos include the need to "show balls" (Reuss-Ianni, 1983) or display bravery (Kappeler, Sluder, & Alpert, 1998) and the norm of emotional self-management. An officer who displays too much anger, sympathy, or other emotion in dealing with job situations is not viewed as someone able to deal with the pressures of police work (Pogrebin & Poole, 1995).

Until the 1970s, police assured group solidarity by recruiting and selecting a homogeneous group of working-class white men. "Outsiders" were eliminated by physical requirements (women) and written tests and/or educational requirements (blacks and other people of color). Background investigations and personal interviews eliminated the remaining candidates who failed to express "correct" masculine attitudes, including toughness, conventional middle-class norms, and hegemonic heterosexuality (Messerschmidt, 1993).

Women continue to be disproportionately excluded by preemployment physical fitness tests that reinforce the masculine model of policing by maintaining the association of strength and physicality with the notion of the ideal police officer (Sugden, 2005). In the United States, the great majority (89 percent) of 62 large agencies that responded to a 2001 survey indicated that they use some form of physical agility testing prior to entry-level selection. However, there was little standardization regarding the physical capabilities that should be tested, the actual tests, and the criteria used to identify successful performance (National Center for

Women & Policing, 2003). The study also found that departments that do not have preemployment physical agility tests have 45 percent more sworn women than those with such tests. The negative impact of these tests on women in light of the failure of agencies to require officers to pass physical testing or maintain fitness standards once they leave the academy, however, led the National Center for Women & Policing (2003, p. 2) to speculate that the purpose of the testing is "to screen out female applicants across the board."[4]

How much the culture has changed in response to external demands and internal pressure to employ women, persons of color, and gay and lesbian police in the past quarter century is unclear. Despite many examinations of such reforms as professionalization and community-oriented policing (COP), researchers have not adequately assessed the effect of increased diversity on the police culture in light of other changes in policing. Some studies have found that black and Hispanic officers have more positive attitudes toward community policing and are critical of their departments' handling cases involving excessive use of force. However, as Walker and Katz (2005, p. 162) observe, "the relationship between race and ethnicity, of attitudes, and actual job performance is extremely complex." Similarly, a National Research Council review found little evidence that African-American and Hispanic officers perform differently from whites in their interactions with citizens. In sum, the change in the composition of rank and file in police departments suggests that the homogeneous police culture has been weakened but has far from disappeared.

Recent Trends in Policing and Their Implications for Women and Persons of Color

For more than half a century, efforts to reform the police have focused on changing street practices to eliminate three categories of recurrent problems: corruption, police brutality, and alienation from the community (G. Sykes, 1985). In the 1970s, these issues were addressed primarily by "professionalizing" policing in a way that was narrow in scope and conceptually inaccurate. Professionalization included efforts to increase organizational efficiency and productivity by expanding top-down control, improving recruitment and training, hiring more white women and persons of color, and adding technology and resources. This contributed to tension between the traditional "street cop" and "management cop" cultures (Reuss-Ianni, 1983). It also has resulted in a policing style characterized as the "emotionally-guarded interactional 'style-without-a-smile'" (McElhinny, 1993, p. 310). Despite facing such emotionally wrenching situations as injury, death, and deranged persons, the "professional" officer is expected to avoided emotional displays.

Since the 1980s, police organizations have embraced a number of organizational changes and approaches to policing. In addition to increased diversity (including recruitment of gay and lesbian officers), these changes include adoption of COP, civilianization and privatization of law enforcement, greater use of emerging technologies, and, most recently, adaptations to address terrorism and other disasters. Each of these changes and their impact on women and other groups will be briefly discussed.

Community-Oriented Policing

In the 1980s, community-oriented policing (COP) became the watchword for gaining public support by linking the officer to the community, neighborhood, and citizens in the "co-production" of crime control and public safety services and closing the communication gap between police and the communities they served (Skolnick & Bayley, 1986). However, COP has a variety of definitions. For some agencies, it has meant instituting particular tactics and strategies (e.g., foot patrol and storefront offices) or community relations programs (e.g., Neighborhood Watch and DARE). Others regard it as an innovation that transforms the professional model of policing to one that is "more focused, proactive and community sensitive" (Greene, 2000, p. 301), by reshaping the social and formal organization of police departments and their relationships with other organizations. Another group regards COP as a new philosophy or "set of ideas that can transform the structure, activities, operations, and even the culture of police departments" (National Research Council, 2004, p. 85). They expect COP to shift the emphasis away from an exclusive focus on crime control to one of crime prevention, community problem solving, and citizen empowerment.

COP requires police organizations to reconceptualize what is "real" police work. It shifts the focus from dealing with individual "crimes" after the fact to having officers seek to address recurrent problems affecting order and public services. Such an approach demands a loosening of the grip of traditional control-centered management to allow more officer discretion and autonomy (Greene, 2000). It calls for officers who have good interpersonal skills and are trained in problem identification, analysis, and solutions (Jurik & Martin, 2001).

The extent to which COP as implemented goes beyond rhetoric and actually redefines the police role, expands reciprocity in police-community relations, and decentralizes police services and command structures varies across agencies and still is unclear. A 1999 survey of local departments found that 64 percent reported having one or more full-time community police officer (Hickman & Reaves, 2001). However, these data may suggest that rather than transforming patrol officer behavior, a small percentage of officers are assigned to COP roles, while the majority of patrol officers to continue to serve as reactive "crime fighters."

Three recent studies support such a conclusion, whereas an extensive review of the research on COP to date found that while police are using a variety of tactics under the COP strategy, there is not yet enough evidence to determine whether community policing is a success (National Research Council, 2004). Zhao, He, and Lovrich (2003) compared survey responses from more than 200 municipal police agencies in both 1990 and 2000 regarding their prioritization of police "core functions." They found that rather than decreasing the emphasis on crime fighting, COP represents a comprehensive effort by local police simultaneously to control crime, reduce social disorder, and provide services to citizens. Pelfrey (2004) compared the attitudes and behavior of COP and traditional patrol officers. He found that COP officers are more likely to support problem-oriented and community-oriented concepts but are no less likely than traditional patrol officers to support traditional patrol concepts. Additionally, COP officers are more likely to engage in community policing tasks but also conduct traditional policing activities at similar levels as traditional officers. Both groups share a foundation of belief in the traditional practices of law enforcement. COP officers have simply augmented traditional attitudes and beliefs with largely favorable perceptions of community policing practices and tasks while traditional officers have negative views of COP.

S. L. Miller (1999) focused on the relationship of gender to community policing. Using interviews and observational data, she explored how men and women officers reconcile incompatible images of masculinity and femininity in enacting the COP role. She observed that community policing offers the prospect of a shift toward greater emphasis on and rewards for community service, crime prevention, and problem solving and a de-emphasis on crime fighting. However, its emphasis on activities that demand formerly feminine-labeled skills such as caring, informality, empathy, and communication also may be seen as "feminizing" the management of social control. For that reason, COP arouses opposition from men officers who see it as another effort to feminize policing and are likely to resist or undermine it. Thus, the success of COP rests on recasting such attributes into gender-neutral terms to gain support by a male-dominated police force (Fielding, 1994; S. L. Miller, 1999). To succeed, it requires recruiting a new breed of officers, training them in new skills, developing ways to more effectively measure their success, and avoiding officer burnout. Additionally, it requires neutralizing the negative attitudes toward COP of more senior field training officers (Haarr, 2001). Once an officer has worked as a COP officer, however, it appears to have a lasting effect in expanding the use of interpersonal skills and addressing community problems in the officer's subsequent assignments (S. L. Miller, 1999; Pelfrey, 2004).

Terrorism and Other Disasters

The attack on the World Trade Center on September 11, 2001, has made clear the need for the police to change to better address terrorism; similarly, Hurricane Katrina demonstrated the importance of responding to natural disasters more effectively. Terrorism is defined by the FBI as "the unlawful use of force or violence against persons or property to intimidate or coerce a government, the civilian population, or any segment thereof in furtherance of political or social objectives." It includes both domestic and foreign terrorism. The former is carried out by Americans on American soil, which accounted for about 80 percent of terrorist incidents and 90 percent of deaths before September 11 (Walker & Katz, 2005). Nor was the September 11 attack the first involving foreign terrorists. In 1993, the World Trade Center was bombed; in 1998, embassies in Kenya and Tanzania were bombed.

A decade before the September 11 attack, a survey had found that many departments were concerned about and taking some actions related to terrorism but that only 12 percent of respondents regarded their agencies as well or very well prepared for such an attack (Riley & Hoffman, 1995). Despite the creation of the Department of Homeland Security and pledges of billions of dollars to pay for training, equipment, and planning by first responders, a nationwide survey of local agencies suggests that only 19 percent have made extensive changes in preparation for a terrorist attack. Most have made modest changes (47 percent) or no change at all (9 percent; National Crime Prevention Council, 2002). Thus, law enforcement agencies remain poorly equipped to deal with large-scale disasters. They tend to devote limited resources to emergency planning and do so in isolation from other community organizations. The chaos that occurred before and immediately after Hurricane Katrina (including the inability of the police to stop looting and the flight of many police from New Orleans) illustrates the inadequacies of planning for and communication among police agencies in response to a disaster (albeit a domestic natural one).

Nevertheless, efforts to address the threat of terrorism have led to a variety of new demands on police agencies and officers. They now must respond to suspicious situations; provide extra security for buildings, critical infrastructure, and events; investigate terrorist networks; and improve planning and coordination among agencies, including law enforcement, public health, medical organizations, and the military. Many agencies (particularly large urban departments) have reassigned personnel to regional task forces and special units. They also are assessing local security risks, increasing planning and policy development, dealing with staff shortages due to deployments of National Guard and reserve military units, learning how to safeguard their own employees from new chemical and biological risks, and seeking ways to maintain open communication with the communities they serve while gathering new information and intelligence. These changes appear to have had limited effect on routine police work except to increase the proportion of sworn officers with special, non-patrol assignments.

The likely impact of terrorism or other disasters on women officers in policing is uncertain. Some suggest that the response has led to increased militarization of the local police and sales of new military technologies to local agencies (National Research Council, 2004). This would suggest a shift toward a more macho style of policing. However, others point to the importance of COP in developing inter-agency plans and intelligence gathering and foresee a new, more androgynous and innovative blend of policing in response to new threats. Thus, the impact of terrorism for women in policing is uncertain.

Civilianization and Privatization

Other structural changes in the police workforce and police organizations include shifting responsibilities for various functions away from the traditional sworn officer to civilian (non-sworn) employees of the police (i.e., civilianization) and to private police who are employed by commercial security companies (i.e., privatization). These, along with COP, are part of the rethinking of the ways that police deal with community-level crime issues and the effort to reevaluate the structure and functioning of police agencies. Both civilianization and privatization may have an impact on women officers' role and opportunities in public law enforcement. While each of these trends has been the focus of several reviews and studies (e.g., Bayley & Shearing, 2004; Forst, 2000; Kostelac, 2004), none addresses the implications for women.

The proportion of civilian police employees has grown from about 8 percent in 1950 to 18 percent in 1977, 27 percent in 1994, and 30 percent as of 2003 (Kostelac,

2004). These workers, who are predominantly women, are paid less than sworn officers (or have positions as contract workers without job security and benefits) for carrying out a broad range of functions. Their jobs include those previously conducted by sworn officers (e.g., dispatching) as well as more technical positions in computer technology, forensics, research and analysis, and human resources (Forst, 2000).

Privatization is another response to the inability of public police to meet all social needs in terms of security and protection. Policing is increasingly privatized as commercial companies take over functions long held by public police institutions. These for-profit organizations are focused more on crime prevention because their job is to make crimes less likely to occur. With the growth of large private facilities like airports and malls that are used for primarily public activities, the role of private security in monitoring activities has grown. This may have a greater impact on women and racial/ethnic minorities since these groups are lower in the job queue and likely to be hired by private policing employers who offer lower pay and fewer benefits as well as limited mobility opportunities.

How these employees relate to sworn officers and whether there are gender differences in their assignments and their interactions with sworn officers are unknown. Does the growing opportunity to go into police work without the dangers and difficulties of being a sworn officer draw potentially qualified female recruits into civilian or private security positions, thereby reducing the pool of women for sworn positions, or are the recruitment pools separate? Do women civilians encounter the discrimination and sexual harassment that sworn women face, and do departments address these in similar ways? Is there cooperation between these two groups of women, or does increased civilianization threaten women officers and limit their growing numbers? Each of these is an unanswered question with a likely impact on women officers.

The Police Culture and Men's Opposition to Women Officers

Few occupations have been as fully defined as "masculine" or resistant to the integration of women as policing. Despite changes in both the nature of policing and the status of women, many men officers continue to believe that women cannot handle the job physically or emotionally and, therefore, should not be allowed to exercise the moral authority of the state or be integrated into policing. This hostile attitude has been characterized as "a huge if shadowy presence which hangs like a miasma" over women officers (Heidensohn, 1992, p. 65). Beyond the sexist attitudes of individual men, the work culture is characterized by heavy drinking, crude jokes, racism, and homophobia and demands that women who enter it "subsume 'male characteristics' to achieve even a limited social acceptability" (Young, 1991, p. 193).

Men's most vocal concerns about women as police usually are stated in terms of physical capabilities, but the scope of opposition to female officers is far broader and deeper. More than a quarter century ago, S. E. Martin (1980, p. 79) argued that the integration of women into police patrol work as coworkers threatens to compromise the work, the way of life, the social status, and the self image of the men.

Resistance to women's integration is related to the nature of the work, the occupational culture, and the manner in which these are used as resources for doing gender, and continues today, although in a less overt manner.

The Logic of Sexism and Women's Threat to Police Work

Jennifer Hunt (1984, p. 294) observed that "the policeman's world constitutes a symbolic universe permeated with gender meanings" that explain much of their behavior. "The logic of sexism" rests on their dualistic worldview that associates gender-stereotyped oppositions (i.e., masculinity/femininity) with various organizational symbols (e.g., street/station house), occupational themes and work activities (e.g., crime fighting/service and order maintenance), and situational meanings (e.g., public/domestic, dirty/clean). In each of the gender-stereotyped opposites, the item associated with the feminine is undervalued (Hunt, 1990).

From this dualistic perspective, men create an idealized image of policing as action oriented, violent, and uncertain. They define themselves through these images that are closely associated with the "masculine" side of contrasting pairs of gender-linked symbols and then use their work as a resource for doing masculinity. Thus, officers associate "real police work" with crime fighting that takes place on the street, often involves collusion in "dirty knowledge" of illicit activity, celebrates physical prowess and involvement in fights, demands emotional control in the face of danger, and evades formal rules. This viewpoint has been characterized as "street cop culture" (Reuss-Ianni, 1983). In contrast, supervisory, station house, and police academy assignments are associated with "feminine labor" involving "inside work" and women's skills. These are associated with the "management cop" culture disdained and resisted by "street cops" (Hunt, 1990).

Women threaten these working-class men's cultural norms, group solidarity, and definition of policing as "men's work" and themselves as masculine. Thus, the integration of women into street patrol has evoked strong opposition that men generally explain in terms of the physical differences between themselves and women, who tend to be smaller and weaker. While men assert that women's physical characteristics are the primary reason that women are less able to perform the job, their assignment to patrol poses a dilemma. In one of the few remaining occupations in which strength and physical ability occasionally are useful, women's presence implies either that the men's unique asset—physical strength—is irrelevant, or that a man who works with a woman will be at a disadvantage in a confrontation.

Three other less frequently articulated concerns also support men's resistance to women: the belief that women are "mentally weaker," the view that women are unable to command public respect as officers, and the concern that "moral" women will break the code of silence and expose the men's illicit activities. Besides providing less "muscle" to a partner, men regard women as "too emotional" and, therefore, unreliable in the face of danger. If women cannot be trusted to aid their partners in physical confrontations or to react to fearful or emotionally charged situations in unemotional and "objective" ways, they threaten the basic norms of police work. Many men assert that they patrol in a more cautious (and, in their view, less effective) way with a female partner.

Women's Threat to the Public Image and Citizen "Respect"

Women officers are perceived to threaten the rule that the police should maintain respect on the street. In some instances, the uniform and badge are insufficient; the officer's personal authority and manner of conveying it are needed to gain citizen compliance. Men in this society are accustomed to viewing women as objects to be dominated rather than authority figures to be feared and obeyed. Conversely, women are unused to exercising authority over men. Men officers, therefore, fear that citizens will deny or resist women officers' efforts to exercise police authority and that this challenge to authority will be generalized to the police. Yet the alternative scenario, a woman exercising authority over men, is also threatening to men officers' identities (Martin, 1980).

Women also threaten to expose the "police myth," which hides the demeaning nature of the work and sustains the public image as a successful crime fighter. They remind the men that

> they can only achieve illusory manhood by denying and repressing the essential feminine dimension of police work, which involves social relations, paper work, and housekeeping in the public domain. (Hunt, 1984, p. 294)

Women's Threat to Group Solidarity and Men's Identity

Women's presence also undermines the solidarity of the men's group by changing the informal rules by which officers relate to and compete with each other. The world of the men's locker room is filled with talk focused on sports, women's bodies, and sexuality that fosters men's bonds based on normative heterosexuality. Men officers virulently oppose homosexuality among police as a threat to group solidarity, police control of "deviant" behavior, and the hierarchy of sexualities. As the objects of much of the men's talk, women cannot participate in it on equal terms. Their integration raises the specter of sexual intimacy between officers. Such sexual ties compete with the demands of loyalty to the group that is essential in work involving danger. Despite the possibility of homosexual relationships, when all police were men, the department treated their sexuality as unproblematic as long as it was heterosexual. The fear of heterosexual competition among the men, however, causes organizations to try to eliminate sexuality and emotion from organizational functioning (Acker, 1992).

Women officers also threaten to disturb the informal distribution of rewards because officers no longer compete on equal terms. The "rules of chivalry" (i.e., code of gender interaction by which a "gentleman" relates to a "lady"), as well as the potential for the abuse of power to coerce sexual favors (in violation of the rules of chivalry), often come into play in a gender-integrated police force. In such cases, gender is invoked as some men offer, and some women accept, exemptions and "favorable" assignments by taking "unfair advantage" of their sex. Because within the men's status order, sexual dalliances are viewed as power perks, women who accept sexual bargains are targets of officers' resentment, but male supervisors who permit such inequality to arise among officers are not. Women who reject the "bargain" and sexual advances are punished with the label "dyke" or "lesbian" regardless of their sexuality; women who are open lesbians pose additional problems for the men since they are unavailable as sexual targets and untroubled by the lesbian label.

Men's opposition to the integration of women also reflects a "deeper concern about who has a right to manage law and order" (Heidensohn, 1992, p. 215). In fact, Heidensohn asserts, the view that "men 'own' order and have sole rights to preserve it" is the real but unstated issue underlying their arguments that women are unsuitable and will shatter men's solidarity. Men's resistance to women on patrol is better understood as emanating from a struggle over the ownership of social control.

Women's integration challenges men's use of police work as a means of doing masculinity. Men strengthen their gendered identities through doing work that is labeled "masculine" and by fostering the image of their jobs as "men's work." Gender segregation in the workplace, therefore, enables them to heighten the distinction between masculinity and femininity (C. L. Williams, 1989, p. 133). Preserving job activities labeled "for men only" simultaneously reinforces the association between masculinity and social control. If a man relies on another man, it is defined as "male bonding" or "camaraderie"; his reliance on a woman is viewed as a sign of weakness and, therefore, unmanly. The presence of women poses a bind for a man who wants to depend on his partner but does not want to depend on a woman. For many men, the simplest solution is to exclude women from patrol work. Since that is not possible except in very small departments, the most vigorous opponents of women deal with their presence by avoidance; the rest appear to view "good" women cops as "exceptions" but treat women as a group as outsiders.

Men police fear that women on patrol will threaten the public image of the cops since large segments of the population share the men's stereotypes of women as more emotional and less physically aggressive than men (Grant, 2000). The inclusion of gay and lesbian officers adds to the image concerns of the male officers about being "men's men."

In sum, the combination of danger and power over the mechanisms of social control has resulted in a close association between policing and masculinity. The men have opposed women's integration into their ranks as a threat to their definition of the work, occupational culture, social status, and self-image as men's men, which is a psychological "fringe benefit" of the job.

Barriers to Women Officers: Interaction, Ideology, and Images

Men express their opposition to women officers through interaction patterns that marginalize and exclude them. Women's social isolation denies them mobility opportunities by limiting information, mentors, informal training, and a sense of comfort on the job. They also face conflicting expectations and double standards regarding their performance. On the one hand, their visibility leads to higher performance standards than men confront; on the other hand, they encounter paternalistic treatment where little is expected of them. Sexual and gender harassment also are common occurrences. Each of these barriers is shaped by race-ethnicity and sexual orientation as well as by gender.

The resistance faced by the first women on patrol was blatant, malicious, widespread, organized, and sometimes life threatening (Bloch & Anderson, 1974; Hunt, 1984; S. E. Martin, 1980). Initially, many men refused to teach these women skills routinely imparted to new men; they failed to respond quickly or assist women seeking backup. Often, supervisors assigned women to dangerous foot beats alone (while men worked in pairs), overzealously enforced rules, depressed women's performance evaluations, sexually harassed them, and ignored women's mistreatment by fellow officers.

There were a few men who favored the integration of women into patrol and who assisted women. However, they did so at the risk of being ostracized by fellow street cops, and their actions on behalf of women tended to be viewed by other men as directed toward particular individuals rather than efforts to benefit women as a group (S. E. Martin, 1980). Today, the proportion of men who are comfortable working with women partners has grown substantially, but such men still rarely overtly resist the dominant attitudes.

Discrimination and hostility are less openly tolerated now but continue to permeate police organizations. A recent study found a consensus among experienced women officers that "policing has changed with the times [and] that the discrimination of the past is not present in the same form today" (Gossett & Williams, 1998, p. 68). Nevertheless, two thirds of the women perceived continued discrimination by colleagues, supervisors, and citizens in less overt form, including derogatory comments, inappropriate behaviors, and failure to take the women seriously. In the station house, frequent pranks, jokes, and comments that call attention to women's sexuality make it clear to women that they are "outsiders." For women of color and lesbians, harassment amplifies their outsider status. For example, lesbian women may be assumed to be masculine and therefore more competent than heterosexual women on the street, but are harassed due to their gender and heterosexual male officers' curiosity and hostility (S. L. Miller, Forest, & Jurik, 2004). By sexualizing the workplace, men superimpose their gender superiority on women's claims to work-based equality.

Interactional Dilemmas

Because women comprise only a small proportion of officers, they also suffer the consequences of tokenism (Kanter, 1977). Their visibility as tokens leads to little margin for error. At the same time, women are treated paternalistically, expected to do less than the men, extravagantly praised for doing an average job, denied opportunities to take initiative, and/or criticized for doing so (i.e., acting "like a man").

They are also pressured to conform to gendered stereotypes as "mother," "little sister," or "seductress." The errors of an individual woman are exaggerated and generalized to all women as a class. Conversely, positive efforts to organize a women's association or advance an individual woman, regardless of her accomplishments, raises concerns about "favored treatment."

Both the physical and the social environment provide a variety of cues that reflect and maintain women's subordinate status. Physical arrangements make clear that both the street and the police station are "male turf." Locker room and lavatory facilities for women are limited; sexually oriented magazines "accidentally" left in the station still are common sights.

Double standards also persist regarding language, sexuality, appearance, and demeanor. Women face "language dilemmas" in deciding whether to curse (and use "male" language) or not (and give up the opportunity to make "strong" statements), whether to tolerate men's use of gross language, and how to deal with being called "hon" or "sweetheart" by colleagues. Women supervisors also must deal with refusal of male subordinates to acknowledge their rank. In fact, Haarr and Morash (2005) found that language harassment (defined as offensive use of profanity) remains a significant source of stress for women. Describing the work environment and double standards that women encounter, a woman sergeant in Susan Martin's (1990, p. 153) study summarized the situation this way:

> There's a certain finesse a woman has to have, a certain feminine grace. If you tell it like it is and don't watch your figure or fix yourself up or have what the men expect, you won't be given quite the preference. . . . For example, they let a capable woman go [from a detective assignment] because she's fat . . . yet they'll give breaks to the biggest male toad with a foul mouth.

Off-duty socializing also poses interactional dilemmas for female officers. The men often drink together after work and participate in team sports or other shared recreational activities. Women's limited participation in this informal socializing deprives them of an important source of information and feedback and the opportunity to make contacts, cultivate sponsors, and build alliances that contribute to occupational success (S. E. Martin, 1980). Although the "stag party" atmosphere of off-duty partying has diminished, women are only partially integrated into the informal activities and influence structure. Some women choose not to socialize outside of work due to family responsibilities or concern with gossip. Although it protects their reputations, this social withdrawal isolates women. Other women participate in social activities, but at the risk of sexual rumor and innuendo.

The Sexualized Workplace

Men maintain women's status as "outsiders" by sexualizing the workplace (Cockburn, 1991; Swerdlow, 1989). Women experience sexual propositions and threats as well as sexual harassment as a condition of work, including unwanted touching, comments that call attention to their sexuality or express antiwoman sentiment, and a variety of pranks and jokes (Hunt, 1984; S. E. Martin, 1980; Sugden,

2005; M. Young, 1991). Women still find sex magazines, dildos, and vibrators in their lockers and mailboxes, and encounter betting pools on who will be the first to have sex with a new woman officer. Sugden (2005, p. 17) argues, "women are desexualised, hyper-sexualized and defeminised by male police officers as a means to confirm and stabilize the masculinity and heterosexism of policing."

Most women officers have experienced sexual harassment on the job. In one study, Susan Martin (1990) found that 63 percent of 72 women officers interviewed in five large urban departments recounted instances of sexual harassment on the job, including 25 percent who had experienced *quid pro quo* harassment. According to a 1990 Michigan State University study of 26 urban and rural departments, 12 percent of the women officers said they had been touched by supervisors in an offensive way in the past year; 4 percent said their bosses had tried to force them to have intercourse (cited in Cooper, 1992, p. A-10).

Studies conducted outside the United States also document high rates of sexual harassment of women officers in many nations. Jennifer Brown's (1998) survey of police personnel in England and Wales found that 70 percent of women officers experienced some form of sexual harassment directed at them personally in the six months prior to responding to the questionnaire, and 44 percent had experienced harassment often. Sutton (1996) reported even higher rates in Australia. J. M. Brown and Heidensohn (2000) cite similar studies finding sexual harassment in Belgium, Denmark, and Holland.

Regardless of how they react, such harassment is problematic for women. It is an important source of stress (J. M. Brown & Grover, 1997; Haarr & Morash, 2005; Texeira, 2002; Wexler & Logan, 1983); it isolates women from men colleagues and divides women. Although many women officers experience sexual harassment, they have not united or taken coordinated action to press for change. Instead, women tend to reproach other women, asserting that those who get sexually harassed "ask for it" through their demeanor or behavior. Such victim blaming makes the woman rather than her harasser the target of criticism.

The Intersections of Race, Ethnicity, Sexual Orientation, and Gender

The simultaneous effects of race-ethnicity and gender for women in policing rarely have been examined. Although sociologist Diana Pike (1992, pp. 275–276) observed that "being black as opposed to being female generates a very different organizational adaptation and response" because "black men do not challenge the quintessential police officer role in the same way women do," she ignored the unique situation of black women officers.

Men's initial resistance to the presence of women on patrol led to hostile treatment regardless of race. Nevertheless, men's different reactions to and treatment of black and white women reflect differences in cultural images and attitudes (Belknap & Shelley, 1992; S. E. Martin, 1994; B. R. Price, Sokoloff, & Kuleshnyka, 1992; Texeira, 2002; Worden, 1993). Because cultural images or stereotypes of white and black women differ, black women often are treated according to separate norms and images. They are less frequently "put on the pedestal" or treated as "ladies" or "little sisters" to be protected by white men. Rather, they are treated as "jezebels" (sexually aggressive women) or "welfare mothers" (i.e., seen as likely to get pregnant and take advantage of "light duty"; P. H. Collins, 2000).

S. E. Martin (1990) found that white women, particularly those who were physically attractive, were more likely than black women to get inside assignments and protection on street patrol. A number of black women observed that white men backed them up when they had a white partner but not when they had a black one. Belknap and Shelley (1992, p. 63) found that black women were less likely than white women to believe that fellow officers recognized when they had done a good job. Black women also report encountering racist stereotypes (e.g., that they are stupid) and outright racial harassment. Texeira (2002) observed that black women in law enforcement experience "racialized sexual harassment" and believe that they are being harassed *because* they are African-American women. As one black woman commented on the combination of race and gender problems she encountered (S. E. Martin, 1994, p. 393),

> Sometimes I couldn't tell if what I faced was racial or sexual or both. The black female is the last one on the totem pole in the department.

Lesbian officers confront additional problems due to the hegemonic masculinity and homophobic attitudes of many of the male officers. The first issue gay women encounter is whether to hide their sexual orientation (and, by staying "in the closet," hide an important part of their identity and life) or to "come out" and risk possible physical or verbal abuse and withdrawal of support from fellow officers. For many, the decision rests on both individual characteristics such as ethnicity and the organizational climate of the department (S. L. Miller et al., 2004). In addition, lesbian cops adapt to work demands by making an extra effort to prove themselves as competent officers. A survey comparing gay and straight women officers with gay men and white heterosexual men found that on a measure of gender-related attitudes toward policing, the gay women "out machoed" the white men, while the gay men scored no differently than heterosexual men officers. The authors (Myers, Forest, & Miller, 2004) suggest that nontraditional police officers still feel like outsiders who must prove they are tough enough to qualify for the job. In interviews conducted as part of the same study, many of the lesbians sought to gain acceptance as officers by separating themselves from "typical" female officers by hard work and proving themselves as "tough crime fighters."

Summary

This chapter has examined the work of patrol officers, the historical and current role of women in police work, and the sources of men's resistance to women's presence. Initially, women entered policing as specialists, doing work that was an extension of their domestic roles. Women's integration into police patrol in the United States was fostered by a number of factors related to both changes in the nature and organization of police work following urban unrest and changes in the social status of women, particularly legal changes following the 1972 Amendments to the 1964 Civil Rights Act.

The number of women officers has grown in the past three decades both in the United States and around the world. Currently, women represent only about 12 percent of sworn personnel in the United States and about 9 percent of supervisors. Similarly, they comprise about 15 percent of officers but a smaller proportion of supervisors in England, New Zealand, and Australia. Despite their increased representation, policing remains associated with masculinity, and the informal work culture continues to be strongly resistant to women because their presence threatens men's definition of their work and themselves. Women are perceived as a threat to the men's physical safety, group solidarity, and occupational identity as "macho" crime fighters. In addition, their presence undermines the close association of their work with masculinity and men's control over social order.

The increased emphasis on community-oriented policing in the past two decades has fostered a change in police ideology and a greater emphasis on communication with citizens, service to communities, and crime prevention. These characteristics are associated with femininity. Although one might expect this to have led to an increase in the representation and promotion of women, there is little evidence of such a change. Instead, police administrators' emphasis on changing the way the police do the job has resulted in resentment and resistance by many rank-and-file officers who are concerned about the feminization of policing. For COP to gain acceptance, the skills and activities must be defined in ways that are more gender neutral. The effects on women of other changes in policing, including civilianization, privatization, and responses to terrorism and natural disasters, are still unclear.

What is clear is that women officers encounter interactional barriers and gendered images that establish them as outsiders, sexual objects, targets of men's resentment, and competitors who threaten to change the rules of officer interaction. Compounding these stresses, black women officers face dilemmas arising from racist stereotypes, and lesbians encounter homophobia.

In addition to an informal work culture that marginalizes and excludes them, women enter a police organization with rules, policies, and practices that are far from gender neutral. These organizational barriers and on-the-street dilemmas for women and the manner in which they have responded to and overcome them are the subject of the next chapter.

Endnotes

1. For more data on the history of women in policing in the United States, see Appier (1998), Feinman (1986), and Schulz (2004). For studies of women police in Britain, see Heidensohn (1992), S. Jones (1986), and M. Young (1991); for those focused on Australia, see Prenzler (1994, 1998), Prenzler and Hayes (2000), and Sugden (2005); for women in New Zealand, see E. K. Butler et al. (2003); for studies on women police in India, see Natarajan (2001, 2003). For an international comparative perspective, see J. M. Brown (1997) and J. M. Brown and Heidensohn (2000).

2. Fyfe's (1987) survey found that by 1986, fewer than 4 percent of municipal agencies still had minimum height and weight standards as entry criteria.

3. Morash and Greene (1986) point out several biases. The evaluations emphasized situations and characteristics associated with male stereotypes (e.g., aggressive patrol). They assumed that observed differences resulted from personal or psychological peculiarities of the women rather than as responses to negative experiences once in the department. They failed to measure the accomplishment of specific police behaviors. They lacked clear standards for weighing frequent policing tasks relative to atypical but critical events and for determining "good" police performance. They overemphasized gender stereotypes. Fewer than half of the items in the evaluations related to specific behaviors; many assessed whether officers met such male stereotypes as forceful and decisive. Common but unpopular tasks were de-emphasized in favor of items involving violence.

4. The Cooper Institute for Aerobics Research developed the most widely used age- and gender-normed physical performance tests that were adopted by a number of agencies in the 1980s. According to the Web site of the Cooper Institute for Aerobics Research (2004),

> These standards are no longer acceptable for mandatory programs since the 1991 Civil Rights Act asserts that separate standards are against the law. The principle is expressed as **Same Job = Same Standard.** Consequently, in our opinion, age and gender standards are in conflict with this law if applied as mandatory standards for selection (academy entrance), completion of training (academy exit) or maintenance programs (for incumbents).

The Institute recognizes that the absolute standards it recommends will have a disparate impact on women but maintains that they are validated as job related.

CHAPTER 4

Women Officers Encountering the Gendered Police Organization

Departmental policies and informal practices gender police work in ways that disadvantage women officers. These processes begin with recruitment and selection, are reinforced through training and assignments, and permeate encounters with citizens. Although departments have opened the doors to the station house, they have resisted changes to ease women's integration. Standards for evaluating performance, behavior, and appearance are designed for men, from preemployment physical tests and displays of physical bravado to the tailoring of uniforms and lack of policies regarding light duty during pregnancy. Women face dilemmas because the men do not want the women to behave like men or to accept women who "act mannish" as equals. Women who act "feminine" are regarded as incompetent officers, and those who have children are viewed as inadequate both as officers and as mothers. These dilemmas and barriers affect women officers' work lives and identities by shaping occupational opportunities, creating unique stresses, increasing turnover rates, and leading to several adaptive strategies for survival and success in policing.

Gendered Organizational Logic: Policies and Practices

Gender and Selection

As noted in Chapter 3, selection procedures that deliberately screened out women and ethnic minorities were changed in the 1970s as a result of lawsuits.

Nevertheless, women are disproportionately disqualified early in the selection process by their higher failure rate on preemployment physical tests that are used by the great majority of departments in the United States (National Center for Women & Policing, 2003) and in Australia (Prenzler, 1996). Women fail at a higher rate than men due to tests specifically related to upper body strength and size, despite the absence of evidence that these relate to policing duties. Sugden (2005) suggests that the tests are geared to the muscular physique found among males; perpetuate the association of the masculine image of policing with force, strength, and control; and serve primarily to reinforce the masculine model of policing as well as reducing the number of women recruits.

Gender and Training

Police training includes several phases. Recruits receive brief (about four months) but intensive academy training, followed by several months of on-the-job training, patrolling under the supervision of an experienced officer. They remain subject to summary dismissal throughout their probationary year.

The Training Academy

At the training academy, new recruits learn law and legal procedures, first aid, and policing skills, as well as the importance of group solidarity and paramilitary discipline. In addition to the formal curriculum, there is a "hidden curriculum" that, according to sociologists Anastasia Prokos and Irene Padavic (2002, p. 454), teaches students

> that it is acceptable to exclude women, that women are naturally very different from men and thus can be treated differently, that denigrating and objectifying women is commonplace and expected, and that they can disregard women in authority. For each of these lessons, male recruits learned accompanying strategies for excluding and antagonizing women.

The formal curriculum and the manner in which it is taught are gendered in a number of ways, all designed to strengthen "the male macho image" (Pike, 1992, p. 262). The curriculum emphasizes the development of physical and technical skills in which men are likely to have an initial advantage, over interpersonal skills in which women are more likely to excel. It devotes "an inordinate amount of attention" to the dangers of police work and how to respond to danger (Kappeler, Sluder, & Alpert, 1998, p. 91), including ample time focused on firearms skills, dangerous calls, and officer survival. As a result, officers come to view citizens as potential sources of violence and "symbolic assailants" rather than as potential sources of information and support, reinforcing a "we/they" worldview. Instructors' frequent "war stories" also emphasize the physical aspects of policing and danger on patrol, reiterating women's "outsider" status.

Although many policy manuals have eliminated gendered language, instructional methods and content also exemplify the gendered nature of the academy and police organization into which recruits must fit. Classroom characterizations of women highlight their difference from men and their inappropriateness for patrol through humor and stereotyped images (Pike, 1992). Women appear as sex objects in jokes and training films, denigrating women and heightening gender boundaries. Recruits are told that women victims and suspects pose unique problems for officers related to women's sexiness (Pike, 1992). Women officers are portrayed as having stereotypic interpersonal skills but as disadvantaged by their lack of physical strength and aggressiveness, which are given greater weight as occupational ideals. When men students disparage women, the instructors ignore their comments, making clear to the women that such behavior is condoned in policing. Men students also resist women instructors' institutional power by openly questioning their authority. For example, they talked among themselves during female instructors' lectures and showed them less courtesy and respect (Prokos & Padavic, 2002).

Gender differences also are fostered by teasing and flirting. All recruits get teased as a rite of initiation "to see if they can take it," but women's teasing highlights the fact that they are regarded as sex objects (Pike, 1992). Similarly, flirting reinforces the response to women as sex objects, the occupational working definition of police officers as macho and masculine, and the gendered nature of the organization by highlighting women's visibility and difference from men.

Dealing with the physical differences between men and women has posed dilemmas for police departments and recruits. Officers must gain control of others, occasionally by use of physical force. Academy training includes self-defense techniques as well as fitness, flexibility, and strength training, although the extent to which strength and fitness are necessary on patrol is unclear. Men enter the academy with a physical advantage. They are usually larger and stronger than women and are more likely to have had previous athletic and bodybuilding experiences. Men also are more likely to have played contact sports that introduced them to important elements in the police culture, including controlled use of violence, teamwork and group loyalty, uniform behavior, tolerance of physical pain, and a willingness to inflict pain on others (Gray, 1975). The adoption of all-around wellness standards with norms adjusted by age and gender has stimulated officer resistance. As one man administrator observed, "The idea that [a woman] must do the same number of push-ups as me is hokus pokus but it's been bred into many officers including the women" (S. E. Martin, 1990, p. 65).

Academy training also may foster inequality by permitting or encouraging women to seek exemptions, particularly from physical training standards. Some women are passed on, permitted to "whine" or claim a medical exemption, by instructors who "let them slide." This treatment identifies those women as different from officers who learn to "suffer in silence," increases men's resentment of the presence of all women, and heightens the concern about female colleagues' ability to carry out patrol duties. It also divides women into those who seek exemptions and those who play by the rules and feel obliged to prove that the exemption seekers are not typical (S. E. Martin, 1980).

Prokos and Padavic (2002) observed similar physical training dilemmas for women. The women who were strong were identified as exceptions; other women were picked on in physical training or were ignored by instructors. Men students treated the women as if they were fragile. While they may have thought they were being helpful, their behavior reified the idea of women's weakness and taught the women that they would be treated differently from men academy recruits and that they were viewed as less capable.

Field Training and Patrol: Cycles of Success and Failure

Following academy training, rookies usually undergo supervised field training for several months. During this period of on-the-job training, they learn the "tricks of the trade," including the informal rules of the street cop culture. Subsequently, rookies are certified to patrol alone, although supervisors tend to assign them as "floaters" to cover for officers on leave or off duty. As openings occur, they obtain permanent beat or scout car assignments.

The rookie's field training assignment and initial behavior on patrol are the basis of both self-confidence and a career-long reputation that affects opportunities. All rookies face "reality shock" when they begin street patrol. Both overprotection and under-instruction retard development of patrol skills. Gender-based differences in interaction compounded by gendered patterns of socialization in the academy and expectations of women's patrol performance influence rookies' responses, creating self-fulfilling prophecies for many women officers (S. E. Martin, 1980).

These patterns were most evident for the first generation of women who faced organized efforts to drive them out, including insufficient instruction, coworker hostility, and the "silent treatment" (that "made eight hours seem like eight days"); close and punitive supervision; exposure to danger and lack of backup; and paternalistic overprotection. As S. E. Martin (1944, p. 141) observed, one woman recounted, "I was at the precinct 10 days before I knew I had a partner 'cause . . . [the men] called in sick and I was put in the station." Another stated,

> My first day on the North side, the assignment officer looked up and said, 'oh shit, another fucking female.' . . . My sergeant called me in and said the training officer doesn't want to ride with you but I've given him a direct order to work with you. (p. 141)

While such overt expressions of hostility are less frequent today, supervisors still tend to keep new women from the busiest beats, and partners tend to protectively seize the initiative. Women who object to such treatment often are labeled "bitches" or "dykes." This pattern results in the following cycle of protection, incompetence, and de-motivation (S. E. Martin, 1980, p. 129):

> (Rookie) officers . . . face unfamiliar and unpredictable situations on the street. In successfully taking action and overcoming their fears, most officers gain confidence as they develop policing skills. The ability to cope with the paperwork, the law, the courts, and most importantly, the citizens they encounter all bolster confidence. . . . The officer who does not have or take the opportunity to develop street patrol skills as a result of limiting assignments, inadequate instruction, or overprotection is likely to act hesitantly or fail to act

in a confrontation. Because an incompetent officer is regarded by colleagues as a potential danger to themselves as well as the officer in question, they are anxious to get such an officer off the street or minimize his or her street activities, thus perpetuating the cycle of incompetence on patrol.

This paternalistic pattern creates a catch-22 for women. They are protected and not really expected to behave like the men on patrol, and then blamed for failing to meet performance standards. This cycle also leads to pressure on women to leave street patrol "before anyone gets hurt," thus depriving some individuals of opportunities to become effective patrol officers. Women as a group also are affected. They are divided into those who seek paternalistic protection and those who reject it and criticize the protected women. Women supervisors also face a bind: they incur some women's anger when they fail to give protected women special treatment but encounter hostility from the men for "protecting" less competent women. Paternalistic treatment of some women increases men's resentment of all women, whom they blame for playing by different rules from men, despite the fact that these "breaks" are created by male supervisors and supported by their own behavior. Both the "pushes" of the cycle of protection and the "pulls" of opportunities opened by diversity efforts to assign women to all units has steadily channeled women out of patrol and into more "feminine" positions.

Gendered Assignment Patterns

Within police precincts, there are quiet and active beats, permanent and rotating patrol assignments, and other assignments (e.g., to a vice unit or station house duties). Most precinct officers are assigned to a permanent scout car or foot beat that they may have for many years. Statistical data on day-to-day assignments by officer gender in the United States are virtually nonexistent. But interview data suggest that the first generation of women were slower to get permanent scout cars and were assigned to quieter beats and to the station house more often than men with similar seniority (S. E. Martin, 1980, 1990). A recent examination of discriminatory patterns of police assignments in England and Wales finds that both women and men perceive women to be deployed more frequently than men to station duty, safe beats, and dealing with sex offense victims and less frequently to dealing with violent offenders (J. M. Brown, 1998).

Over the course of a policing career, most officers obtain temporary or permanent assignments to non-patrol duties. Some are promoted. The most coveted assignments offer higher organizational status, opportunities for additional pay (often through overtime), greater autonomy, and less continuous supervision. These characteristics describe the work of detectives and tactical unit officers, who do not have to respond to calls for service or wear a uniform but who have crime fighting assignments associated with masculinity. Support staff assignments to the training academy or administrative units and community policing positions, including DARE officers, offer better working conditions, including regular daytime hours, but are less esteemed due to their association with management and feminine labor (Hunt, 1984).

The limited existing statistical data on assignment patterns suggest wide variation across law enforcement agencies in the extent and nature of the division of labor but unsurprising gender and race-ethnic variation in their distribution. Sulton and Townsey's (1981) survey indicated that white men were overrepresented in investigative and traffic units; women and men of color were overrepresented in juvenile and technical units, including dispatcher assignments. These variations reflect prevailing patterns prior to women's assignment to patrol, men's greater seniority (a criterion for distributing desirable assignments), and a gendered organizational logic.

Susan Martin's (1990) survey of municipal departments serving populations of more than 50,000 found that by 1987, women were slightly underrepresented in detective and vice units and overrepresented in administrative and other units. Case studies conducted in five of those departments identified consistent patterns of gender differences with respect to the number and types of prior assignments and the current assignments of officers. In three of the four departments for which assignment data were available, the number of different assignments an officer had over a career was significantly greater for women than for men of similar race-ethnicity, rank, and length of police service. This difference may indicate that women had more opportunities and greater mobility than the men because many were members of the first cohort to benefit from affirmative action policies. Alternatively, it may be that women tended to transfer out of assignments when they met hostility and harassment. Both factors probably operated simultaneously.

Consistent differences between the assignments of men and women at the time the data were collected also were found. When assignments were divided into three groups—patrol, other line units (i.e., traffic, investigation, vice, and other patrol support), and administrative and staff support—women in all four agencies were more likely than men to be in staff support units. In three of the four, they also were less likely to be assigned to patrol, while the pattern for investigation and patrol-support assignments was inconsistent. These data suggest that rather than being integrated into police work, women are being re-ghettoized into an enlarged pool of assignments considered appropriate for women. For example, women have become evidence technicians and administrative sergeants who are the powerful but "paper-pushing" assistants to shift commanders.

Newer data on changes in these patterns of assignment are very limited. Data from the San Francisco Police Department on women's assignments to special units in 1995 suggest that stereotyped assignments continue. Women comprised 33 percent of the 18 officers on the academy staff, 22 percent of the 9 officers in the sex crimes unit, and 19 percent of the 31-person juvenile unit. However, there were no women among the 6 officers in canine, the 12 in homicide, the 14 in the robbery, or the 63 working solo motorcycles (Ness & Gordon, 1995, p. A11).

An international review of women's deployment patterns (Boni, 1998) also found that women tended to be overrepresented in routine patrol, communications, and support assignments (including training and community relations units) and underrepresented in such specialized duties as traffic, dog handling, and investigations. This suggests that men continue to believe that women are unsuited for certain jobs and that women self-select out of certain assignments and into others.

Other practices that undermine gender integration in all specialized units appear to include department managers' unenthusiastic commitment to equal opportunity philosophies, weak implementation of those policies, and resistance to flexible employment practices (J. M. Brown, 1997; Prenzler & Wimshurst, 1997). This led Boni (1998, p. 23) to observe, "formal EEO [equal employment opportunity] legislation and policies seem to have been insufficient to ensure the integration of females into all spheres of policing."

Performance Evaluations

Performance evaluations often are a mechanism for preserving gender and racial-ethnic power structures. Supervisors in most departments evaluate individual officers, usually on an annual basis. Vague criteria for measuring "good" police work permit evaluations to reflect seniority and the informal status system of the agency, to include gender-biased categories for evaluation, and to rest on the gendered subjective judgments of supervisors, most of whom are men. Nevertheless, these ratings have profound effects on an officer's career. In many departments, the supervisor's evaluation is an important component in the promotion process. It also may influence transfer decisions and the officer's occupational self-image.

Both officer performance rating systems and their outcomes are gendered in several ways. Often, evaluation forms use sexist language (i.e., the masculine pronoun to define traits and characteristics). Vague evaluation criteria such as "personal relations" and "quantity of work" that appear to be gender neutral in fact may be based on performance standards for men. For example, instructions for the Chicago Police Department's rating forms suggest that in assessing "the quantity of work," raters consider only arrest activity, traffic enforcement, court attendance (which stems from the prior two), and award history. Public service, crime prevention, and other types of activities receive no notice. Similarly, in rating "personal relations," supervisors are instructed to consider the employee's ability to cooperate in team efforts and whether the employee is "someone with whom most other members are able to work comfortably" (S. E. Martin, 1990). Under this system, women are doubly penalized. If men are not comfortable working with a woman or overprotect her, it is she who is negatively evaluated for "inadequate" personal relations. In addition, a woman's crime prevention activities are not rewarded in the same way as arrests in the measure of "quantity of work" but only are recognized as reflecting a presumably positive "attitude toward service to the public."

Instead of viewing women's performance as a negative deviation from the norm of street cop culture that emphasizes crime fighting, variations in policing styles might be viewed as potential sources of alternative definitions of social control. The insistence on assessing women's performance "by the male standard" obscures the fact that the crime fighting model embraced by "a predominantly male-oriented police system has failed to prevent, deter, or resolve crimes that have been brought to its attention" (Bell, 1982, pp. 119–120).

Despite the advent of community policing in the past two decades, Walker and Katz (2005) maintain that performance evaluations continue to have very limited procedures for identifying and rewarding good behavior in non–law-enforcement situations that comprise the bulk of police work. And, within community policing units that have an expanded view of policing goals and values, women do not necessarily get fairer evaluations. As S. L. Miller (1999, p. 220) observed in evaluating community policing, "given traditional gender role expectations in many community policing situations, women do not get any or enough credit and men get too much." As a consequence, "unfair standards of evaluation are manifested in the assumptions made about gender roles and about who is 'working' versus who is 'doing what comes naturally.'"

Gendered Organizational Logic and Women's Occupational Mobility

Women and men officers in the same agency actually work in very different environments as "internal and external factors combine to create a highly differentiated, engendered structure of employment" (Holdaway & Parker, 1998, p. 53). External factors include family ties; internal factors include pressures on women to be more aggressive to be seen as doing the job, to work harder and constantly prove themselves, and to avoid mistakes that get magnified, while at the same time, their performance is underrated and they get little support from fellow officers.

Both formal rules and informal practices affect career opportunities and gender differentiation in police agencies. Organizational factors affecting mobility include the number and types of assignments and promotions available, rules regarding transfers and promotions, the availability and distribution of training opportunities, and equal employment opportunity policies. But, as Silvestri (2003) noted, equal employment opportunity policies emphasizing gender neutrality obscure the underlying gender structure of the organization and the definition of the police role as masculine. Thus, the actual distribution of opportunities is shaped by the informal work culture, sponsorship by influential individuals, and apparent "fit" with others in the unit and larger organization, which itself is gendered.

Both formal rules and informal practices hinder women's careers in policing by pressing them into certain assignments and expecting them to perform in ways that conform to popular cultural images of femininity. Women learn that they do not fit in the gendered organization through the division of space (e.g., limited locker room and bathroom facilities and informally segregated seating at roll call), images and symbols (e.g., offensive sexual reading matter in the station), rules regarding appearance (e.g., standards for fingernails and jewelry), uniforms that are designed for men's bodies, and lack of provisions for pregnancy and motherhood (e.g., the absence of formalized "light-duty" policies and the limited availability of such assignments, and lack of part-time work).

Women officers are overrepresented in staff assignments and underrepresented in patrol support positions for reasons related to the "logic of sexism" (Hunt, 1990). First, in elite tactical units such as gang squads and swat teams, the work involves handling heavy equipment (e.g., battering rams), there is fierce competition for assignments, and the few women who attain them often feel isolated and transfer out (S. E. Martin, 1990; Price, Sokoloff, & Kuleshnyka, 1992). In contrast, prevailing images of women assume that they have office skills and that "inside" work is feminized and not real policing. Many of the men encourage women officers to reduce the burdens of tokenism encountered on patrol by transferring to assignments viewed as gender appropriate. Staff assignments tend to provide a more comfortable work environment, with fixed daytime hours that are attractive to many of the women with primary child care and other family responsibilities. Sometimes supervisors make assignments or transfers based on stereotypes of women's skills without consulting the woman who finds herself assigned to sex crimes or juvenile units (Holdaway & Parker, 1998). These assignments have long-term effects on women's upward mobility.

Women's promotion and transfer opportunities also are affected by departmental rules and bargaining agreements as well as informal sponsorship ties and departmental leadership. While seniority rules handicapped the earlier cohorts of women, the negative impact of these rules has diminished but not disappeared because women have less seniority due to their higher turnover rates. Women continue to lack sponsors, mentors, or "rabbis" whose support is essential for special assignments and promotions. Although some departments have implemented formal mentoring programs, there is little evidence that they are effective; in addition, in some instances they have generated backlash at the "special treatment" afforded women and persons of color for whom the programs were designed. The commitment of the chief and command staff to full integration and diversity also can broaden the opportunities for women, racial and ethnic minorities, and homosexual officers (S. E. Martin, 1990; S. L. Miller, Forest, & Jurik, 2004). Too often, however, administrators hold the same negative attitudes toward these groups as the rank and file and tolerate discriminatory practices.

The advent of community-oriented policing has opened new assignment opportunities as well as a challenging dilemma for police leadership. The skills most compatible with community policing, while ideally gender neutral, emphasize incorporating such attributes as care, empathy, and informality, which often are labeled "feminine." This has resulted in a "subterranean effect of gendered expectations and task divisions" in community policing. Men avoid such assignments as "women's work," which they see as "antithetical to their masculinist self-image as aggressive crime fighters" (S. L. Miller & Hodge, 2004).

To move toward community policing while reinforcing the professional/ masculinist model, some agencies embrace alternative models. For example, in implementing its community policing program, the New York City police leadership challenged the stereotype that it is "women's work" by using terms such as "re-engineering" and "strategic crime fighting" to sell the new paradigm of policing to male officers and the public. Nevertheless, in most agencies the first generation of community police officers (CPOs) was disproportionately women and racial and ethnic minorities. A high rate of promotions among the first generation of CPOs has resulted in more men seeking community policing assignments as a way to increase their likelihood for upward mobility but also has contributed to continuing resistance to community policing and resentment among patrol officers (S. L. Miller, 1999).

How community-oriented policing is implemented varies by neighborhood, the resources available to the officers, departmental policies, and the officers' own approach to the assignment. S. L. Miller (1999) identified striking gender differences in men and women CPOs' priorities and neighborhood activities (although both believed CPOs were invisible to and needed closer cooperation with and support from patrol officers). Male CPOs avoided being seen as doing "women's work" by emphasizing the connection to law enforcement. They sought assignment to high-crime neighborhoods in which they initially established order and authority. They showed up on the "front lines" at night and encouraged patrol officers to walk with them in the neighborhood. They focused on building sports programs but kept residents from getting too close. Women CPOs tended to build nurturing bonds with community members and leaders. For example, they forged links with local health care providers and sought to improve coordination between parents and schools. Even when they produced similar results in terms of community mobilization and crime reduction, the men and women CPOs were also perceived in gender-stereotypic ways. The men CPOs tended to be hailed as "supermen" for carrying out particular activities (e.g., working with children), whereas the women were regarded as simply completing traditional female tasks and practicing a nonaggressive style of policing.

Susan L. Miller (1999; S. L. Miller & Hodge, 2004) believes that the success of community policing rests on police departments' finding ways to gender neutralize it by redefining the traits often associated with "feminine behavior" so that they no longer are stigmatized as "just social work." At the same time, agencies must address the gendered assumptions that devalue women's contributions by viewing women community officers' successes as arising from "doing what comes naturally" while giving high praise, greater credit, and likely promotions to men who produce the same results.

Moving Up: Women and Promotion

In contrast to the "cult of masculinity" that characterizes the police culture of men in the rank and file, women who are promoted into police management encounter a gendered environment in which "managerial masculinity" dominates. This new managerial culture in policing is preoccupied with meeting performance indicators and targets. It encourages a form of competitive masculinity so that the manager's success is linked to decisive action, productivity, and risk taking. In one of the few studies focused on women in police management, Marisa Silvestri (2003, p. 42) observed, "The police leader of the 21st century is a tough and forceful leader, symbolized by aggressive, competitive and performance traits." In the words of one of the women managers she interviewed, "You have to have an element of ruthlessness, selfishness, drive and determination." In the 1990s, policing in England and the United States moved to a new managerial order focused on improving the quality of service delivery. Agencies in both countries also have sought to reduce the number of ranks and flatten the managerial hierarchy, pushing managerial responsibility downward to lower grades without conferring greater authority or recognition. This has resulted in increased rivalry and competitiveness between men and women over the reduced number of higher-level management jobs. These changes have had a negative effect on women. Flatter organizations usually mean more work, more pressure to work longer hours, and a "workaholic 'macho' ethos which increasingly associates managerial competence with masculinity" (Silvestri, 2003, p. 65).

Additionally, men tend to view their own careers and career aspirations as more important than those of women and, in an environment of limited opportunity, compete more fiercely.

All police begin at the lowest rank; those who become managers must work their way from the bottom through the ranks. Factors that enhance the likelihood of promotion include a strong educational profile, attendance at Bramshill in England and at the FBI Academy in the United States, informal mentoring, and the "right" assignments. While experience in a variety of assignments is desirable, not all assignments are considered equal. Jobs labeled "for women" (e.g., training) often are career "dead zones," while operational experience, which allows an officer to demonstrate credibility, is essential. Often, women are given assignments that they did not seek; usually these are not operational and hinder their careers. Without operational experience, women do not feel competent or confident to take promotional exams to command positions. Getting to the top also requires achieving an identity cultivated through a long and uninterrupted career pattern. Family commitments remain a major stumbling block in women's career promotion because it is difficult to reconcile the work, career, and promotion requirements of the organization with demands of family life, even for women without children. Holdaway and Parker (1998) found that 17 percent of women versus 5 percent of men report work-family conflict as reason not to seek promotion.

Even those women who rise in rank are not necessarily accepted in the senior managers' "club," whose rituals and behavioral norms rest on male networks of both professional and social ties of many years based on homosociality. To succeed in police management culture, women must accept the competitive traits that govern it by adopting male models of identity and behavior. They also must work harder and longer to justify their elevation to the position of being "honorary men." They must learn how to communicate messages of power and authority through presence and voice, how to be hard and unemotional, and how to avoid being seen as weak. Thus, success rests on adapting to the gendered patterns and masculine culture of the organization by adopting individualistic strategies, without being critical of the structural arrangements of the organization that allow the male model to flourish. Those women who are able to penetrate police upper management despite contradictions, conflicts, and dilemmas succeed in doing leadership as "active gendering agents" who do both masculinity and femininity to achieve their goals.

Family-Related Policies and Practices

The gendered nature of policing is made clear by police department policies that tend to ignore or exacerbate the strains between home and work life. In many departments, patrol officers have rotating shifts, uncertain demands for overtime related to arrests, and unexpected call-ups for emergencies. These practices, as well as the stressful nature of the work, put strains on family life for all officers. Since women still bear the greater share of responsibility for household maintenance and child care, however, these strains fall more heavily on women officers. Some have questioned whether these policies and the related open-ended expectations of officer availability are necessary. For example, Dick and Jankowicz (2001) challenge the myth that frontline policing is demanding, unpredictable, and dangerous and that it requires rotating shifts and extended hours that make it incompatible with motherhood. Rather, they assert that these expectations serve to reproduce and maintain certain values and practices that are legitimized, such as the subordination of home to work. Similarly, Jennifer M. Brown (2002, p. 8) observed that the new police managerialism has led to new "ritual arguments" against women officers, one of which asserts, "good coppers put the job before anything else, women put children first, ergo women with children do not make good coppers."[1]

Because police officers risk physical injury, most departments allow or require pregnant officers to leave patrol assignments once their pregnancy becomes known. At the end of 1986, however, only 25 percent of municipal agencies had policies related to pregnancy, and only 74 percent of these routinely reassigned pregnant officers to a light-duty position. In 14 percent of the departments, a woman was forced to go on extended leave when she was unable to continue her normal assignment, and 12 percent of the departments had not had to deal with a pregnant officer (S. E. Martin, 1990). Smaller departments were more likely not to have a light-duty option than large ones. Many women forced to leave policing for six to eight months in order to have a child resign from police work.

A more recent Canadian study found that more than half of the departments surveyed in British Columbia lacked formal policy surrounding pregnancy and maternity leave issues and the use of light duty for pregnant officers (Powolek, 1996). While several of the British Columbia departments have adopted job sharing as part of their collective bargaining (union) agreements, to date, job sharing in fact has been quite limited because there is wide recognition that departmental commitment is lukewarm and even temporary use of this option is likely to have a long-term negative impact on the officer's career.

In Canada, Australia, and England, police agency policies include not only job sharing but part-time work and more generous maternity leave policies than police departments in the United States. Nevertheless, across nations, these policies are not consistently implemented. The absence or infrequent use of family-friendly policies impacts both women and men. Nevertheless, the effects are often seen as "women's problems" and a reason that women do not belong in police work, thus hampering women's careers and contributing to their higher turnover rates. It is unclear whether existing organizational practices are really necessary for effective policing or are both the product and the producer of the power relations that exist in the organization.

Uniforms and Appearance: Formalizing Gendered Images

Messerschmidt (2004, p. 48) observed that the body is an essential part of gender construction. We fashion appearance and actions to create properly situationally adorned and performed gendered bodies in doing gender. Police uniforms distinguish officers from other citizens and are symbolically important to both the public and officers as the embodied ideal image of police. Officers stand for "inspection" as part of roll call and may be disciplined for infractions like wearing shoes that are not polished. Uniforms also affect performance. An officer who cannot move freely cannot perform the job effectively. The first cohort of women assigned to patrol wore skirts and carried their guns in pocketbooks. Although uniforms were soon changed, a new and largely symbolic debate arose: should women's gear be identical to that of men or designed for women? Regardless of how departments resolved the issue, it made clear the gendered nature of how an officer should look (i.e., like a man). Until rules regarding hair length were changed in response to protests from the men in the 1970s, women were required to have hair as short as the men or tuck long hair under their hat. While the stated reason was that long hair posed a potential danger to the officer, the effect was to exert control over women's bodies and their feminine appearance. Similarly, jewelry and makeup rules have generated debates related to the extent to which women officers may be permitted to appear different (i.e., feminine) and still be accepted as police. In England, debates about hair and jewelry prevailed into the 1990s (M. Young, 1991); they continue currently in Australia (Sugden, 2005).

As Sugden (2005) observes, the uniform contributes to the regulation and control of women officers and their bodies but also is a site for their resistance. For example, women are required to wear the belt that carries equipment on their hips, bruises them, and contorts the female body. The uniform and belt change the walking style of women who move their bodies in new (masculine) ways. While the uniform hides the women officer's female body, some women wear makeup and jewelry as a form of resistance. Nevertheless, their appearance and behavior is continually subjected to "the scrutinizing male gaze" that dictates gender-appropriate behavior on the job and subsequently becomes internalized by the woman.

Equipment too affects the officer's performance, and when it is ill-fitting, it may convey to women that they are disregarded. For a number of years, the body armor made available to women was designed for men and did not fit women's bodies. Women generally have weaker grip strength and less familiarity with firearms than their male counterparts when they enter the academy. A study of recruits without prior firearms experience found that women's grip strength and marksmanship scores improved significantly during training but remained significantly lower than men's scores. This difference, however, was due primarily to their lower grip strength (M. T. Charles & Copay, 2001). Since this difference in marksmanship is an important one for officers, departments can and should adopt one of two ways to eliminate it: increasing their grip strength through additional training for any officer below a certain score or issuing a weapon that is suited for their grip strength and hand size. Ignoring such differences sustains the gendered assumptions of the organization.

Doing Gender on the Street: Dilemmas of Police-Citizen Encounters

Gender and Police Work

When women workers enter men's turf, they usually are required implicitly to accept men's definitions of that work and the behavioral scripts designed by and for men workers. Thus, even when women do police patrol, job tasks and service styles remain gendered. A central element of policing across situations and tasks is the need to gain control and maintain respect for police authority. Although both men and women officers may perform policing tasks, the meanings of such activities remain associated with manhood and must be addressed as the officers do masculine dominance. For women in policing, this means finding ways to deal with citizens' perceptions, interactions, and occasional challenges to authority.

In police-citizen interactions, the officer seeks to take control but faces uncertainties arising from incomplete information about the citizen and the situation. Citizens often are reluctant to talk to an officer or may behave in inappropriate ways. They may seek to disrupt normal interaction by disavowing the officer's identity as a member of the police and the authority associated with it and relate "person to person," refocusing the interaction on irrelevant statuses, such as gender or race-ethnicity to gain an advantage (Goffman, 1961).

Citizens generally defer to police officers, who tend to have higher status than most citizens they encounter. At any time, however, reference to an officer's lower "irrelevant" characteristics may reverse the flow of deference and threaten the officer's control of the situation. Such interruptions are more prevalent for officers with devalued race-ethnic and/or gender statuses. Thus, how officers and citizens do gender in these situations depends on the sex categories of the participants, the specific circumstances, and the meaning of gender in the situational context. A woman cop may be called "officer" but still is judged in terms of gender stereotypes and pressured to prove that she is "an 'essentially' feminine being, despite appearances to the contrary" (West & Zimmerman, 1987, p. 140). Her sex category may be used to discredit her engaging in certain patrol activities, while her involvement in law enforcement may be used to discredit her performance as a wife and mother.

Because police work has been so closely associated with men and masculinity, the ways that men officers do gender as they do dominance have been treated as natural and thus have been virtually invisible. The close association of authority and control with masculinity, however, makes certain types of interactions with citizens more problematic for women cops, who must find ways to limit attention to their sex category, or take advantage of it.

Work organizations do gender by constructing and legitimating a gendered image of workers and by calling for enactment of scripted behavior (i.e., stereotypic sequences of actions for familiar or recurring situations); men and women workers do gender by differentially enacting these gendered scripts (E. J. Hall, 1993). In policing work, roles are engendered both by police departments and by individual officers, and the concept of "good service" varies across situations and interactions. Good police work, however, involves taking control of whatever situation arises.

The traditional script for police-citizen encounters calls for masculine behavior (i.e., dominance or control), particularly in dealing with criminal offenders, most of whom are men or boys. However, it also may require providing service or emotional support to victims and their families, which may be viewed as feminine, and so, devalued (DeJong, 2004; Hunt, 1990; Jurik & Martin, 2001; S. L. Miller, 1999). Thus, gendered scripts in policing relate to the definition of the encounter as "crime fighting" or "providing service" and of the citizen as a suspect who requires control or a victim who merits support.

The interpersonal resources available to officers and citizens' expectations of culturally dominant images of "masculine" behavior tend to put women at a disadvantage on street patrol. Women patrol officers, in order to gain and maintain credibility as officers, must avoid smiling and appearing friendly (except, of course, as "Officer Friendly," a title that explicitly reverses the stereotype of police for the sake of "community relations"). They must demand deference rather than deferring to others.

Scripts in police work also are based on race, sexuality, and class. Many officers dislike working in upper-class precincts, which have less crime but also are characterized by different patterns of police-citizen interactions. Although there is greater civility, officers' blue-collar social status is lower than that of most citizens they encounter, and the officers resent these citizens' frequent demands for service as well as their reversal of the flow of deference owed to the officer. Similarly, lesbian officers may seek assignments to neighborhoods with large homosexual populations because they believe they can bring a greater degree of empathy and sensitivity to their interactions with citizens (Myers, Forest, & Miller, 2004).

Doing Gender in Patrol Work

In police-citizen encounters, four possible combinations of gender and social category may arise: men officers with men or women citizens, and women officers with men or women citizens. Each combination has different expectations and management problems, as police relate to citizens by "doing gender" while "doing dominance" or otherwise enact the police role.

When men officers interact with men citizens, their shared manhood can be effectively used as an interpersonal resource in some situations by men officers. Generally, this is to the citizen's advantage since it says, in effect, "act like a man (read: exercise self-control) and I won't have to exert my authority as an officer to overpower you." It also benefits the officer by minimizing the necessity of using force and enables him to act as a "good guy," giving a little to gain compliance. When suspects or offenders attempt to define the situation in terms of shared manhood, however, officers may view the interaction as a denial of the deference owed to their office. When a man officer relies too heavily on the authority of the badge or rejects a man citizen's effort to be treated as a man, the result is a "duel of manhood" with a high probability of a verbal or physical confrontation since the man who backs down first fails the "test of masculinity" (J. Price, 1996). The officer, by dispensing "street justice," reflects a failure to maintain his emotional self-control but displays police authority.

Men officers' double status superiority over women citizens generally leads to few problems arising in such interactions except those related to sexuality. Men officers may use the authority of their office to control or gain compliance from women who may have gotten "shrill" by calling on them to "act like a lady" (read: behave in a calm, dignified manner) to gain chivalrous treatment. If invoking the rules of chivalry works, the officer has maintained control while enhancing his sense of manly generosity. If it fails, he still may treat the woman as a wayward "girl" on whom he will not waste his time or will use force.

A "flirting" script or sexual flattery may be used by man officers, particularly with prostitutes, who may be manipulated to become informants in exchange for leniency. This "patriarchal bargain" reinforces gender power relations. However, in interactions with female victims, which often require displays of empathy, male officers face emotional demands that most seek to avoid. The men's discomfort arises both due to the emotional hardness developed in police work and to the norms of emotional reserve included in their definition of masculinity (S. E. Martin, 1999).

Interactions between women officers and men citizens are problematic because police expect to take control of situations and be shown deference by citizens; men may defer to the office but resist being controlled by or deferential to a woman. Thus, expectations regarding how a man relates to a woman and to a police officer generally differ and often conflict. In fact, women officers generally are given deference, either out of gender-blind respect for the uniform or because doing so does not challenge a man citizen's manhood if he chivalrously complies. Conversely, fighting a woman (particularly when men are witnesses) may cause a man citizen loss of status, whether he wins or loses the physical encounter.

The problem for a woman officer, however, is that men may revoke their deference, particularly if she is "unladylike" and acts "like a cop." Since women are often at a physical disadvantage, they may have to rely on the deference of male citizens as a control strategy. Although women officers generally try to minimize rather than activate their gender status, they recognize that men seek to redefine situations so as to affirm men's status superiority.

When women officers encounter sexist or sexual comments that intrude on but do not alter the outcome of an interaction, they generally ignore them, as is expected of officers in the face of a variety of citizen verbal abuse. In dealing with offenders, some women draw on citizens' stereotypes that women are "trigger happy" or are emotional in the face of danger. Some draw on familial roles or social stereotypes such as "matriarch" or "aggressive bitch" in asserting authority.

Other strategies by which women officers gain situational control involve use of various verbal and nonverbal cues to convey through voice, appearance, facial expression, and body postures that they are to be taken seriously regardless of their physical stature. Learning to transmit these messages, however, often requires changing such habits as smiling and literally learning how to stand up to people.

In dealing with women citizens, women officers get both greater cooperation and more resistance than do men. For example, a study involving structured observation of new patrol officers found that women citizens were both more positive and more negative in interactions with women officers in general, and similarly had stronger positive and negative reactions to advice and assistance provided by women than by men (Bloch & Anderson, 1974). Similarly, S. L. Miller (1999) reports that women community-oriented policing officers relate easily to women citizens, drawing on shared parental roles and neighborhood concerns to bridge differences with citizens and break barriers of mistrust through the common ground of parenting.

The dynamics of police-citizen interactions are affected not only by the gender of the participants (including witnesses) but their age, race-ethnicity, class, and sexual orientation. Thus, black officers, who historically were prohibited from arresting white citizens, may draw on racial bonds in dealing with black citizens but may have to overlook racial slurs or condescension in gaining white citizens' compliance, as well as some black citizens' epithets like "traitor."

Using Gender

Effective police officers of both genders are flexible, able to use both the "crime fighter" script (associated with masculinity) and the "service" script (associated with femininity) according to situational demands. They draw on all the interpersonal resources available to them and appeal to "gender-appropriate behavior" as well as citizens' respect for police authority to gain cooperation. They use citizens' expectations and values to their advantage, doing gender in a way that diminishes social distance and maintains control at the same time. They rely on the authority of the badge and tools of policing only when necessary and may interact with citizens by invoking gendered familial authority roles (i.e., mother, big brother). This more informal and androgynous style of policing has been fostered by community-oriented policing (S. L. Miller, 1999).

Ineffective officers may either too rigidly rely on their formal authority and enact only the crime fighting aspects of their role or, alternatively, emphasize only the community service script and fail to maintain control of interactions when they are challenged. The former shortcoming is more characteristic of men officers; the latter is more characteristic of women officers. Thus, ineffective men tend to provoke fights and generate citizen complaints that might have been avoided by a less bullying attitude; they demand deference, equating doing masculinity with doing police dominance. Ineffective women, in contrast, cannot overcome the handicaps women face in seeking to control men. On patrol, they fail to take control or assert the authority of their office as cops in situations that require it.

Women's Response: Adaptations, Costs, and Survival Strategies

Women have responded to barriers to their integration into police work in several ways. In dealing with work-related stresses, some have left policing, others have sought assignments that are more comfortable than patrol, and another group has used other coping strategies. Although all women officers must deal with conflicting expectations as both women and officers, their policing styles and mechanisms of adaptation vary. Most have responded by adopting work-related attitudes similar to those of the men of their race-ethnic group. Identifying with the perspective of dominants is a mechanism often used by subordinates for coping with discrimination. Nevertheless, their behavioral responses to harassment and discrimination are more varied.

Attitudes Toward Police Work and On-the-Job Behavior

Both men hostile to the entry of women and women's advocates have assumed that women officers would behave differently from men on patrol. Men feared they would not respond aggressively; advocates anticipated that women would have greater commitment to public service, more calming demeanors, and more empathetic and less violent encounters with citizens. These assumptions were based on extrapolations from the work of Gilligan (1982) and cultural feminists on differing socialization experiences and perspectives on morality and justice. The limited data comparing job-related attitudes of men and women officers have neither supported the belief that women view their occupational role differently from men nor refuted the possibility of some differences (e.g., Wimshurst, 1995; Worden, 1993).

Worden's (1993) study comparing the attitudes of men and women in 24 departments found few gender differences in officers' perceptions of the public, their occupational roles, their colleagues, and their departments. Based on data collected in 1977, the study found that women were as ambivalent as men about restrictions on their autonomy on the job. They were mildly but equally positive in their views of the public, and as length of police experience increased, women's views of citizens converged with those of the men. Unexpectedly, white women were as complimentary about their colleagues and as positive about their departments as places to work as white men. Both black women and men shared less positive views of their colleagues as officers than did white officers. Worden (1993) interprets the absence of gender differences in perceptions of the workplace as telling less about women's objective experiences in policing as about their experiences with hostile working environments in other occupations and their willingness to adopt male definitions of the work.

In a study of community policing, Engel and Worden (2003) observed that officers' and supervisors' gender affects the time officers spend conducting problem-solving activities. The percentage of a shift spent in problem solving was 1.6 times higher for female officers and 1.4 times higher for officers with a woman supervisor. The women officers were significantly less likely than the men officers to report problem solving as a priority (12.1 percent compared to 27.8 percent, respectively). There were no gender differences in supervisors' priorities for problem solving or their ability to communicate their priorities. The gender difference in officers' activities arose because the women officers were better at accurately interpreting their supervisors' priorities for problem solving (correlations were 0.24 for female officers but −0.01 for male officers).

A study in one English police agency found that women aspire to promotion as much as or more than men. However, women had lower expectations of promotion than men, and fewer took the promotional exam (Holdaway & Parker, 1998). Factors that appear to inhibit them include a lack of organizational or supervisory support, the negative effect of the gendered work environment on their self-confidence as officers, and their reluctance to face isolation and performance pressure as supervisors. In addition, they were much more likely to cite conflict with family commitments (identified by 17 percent of the women and 5 percent of the men) as reasons not to take the exam.

Despite frequent claims that women and men patrol differently, this difference rarely has been systematically measured in the past two decades. Two recent reports based on structured observation data from the Project on Policing Neighborhoods study conducted in Indianapolis and St. Petersburg provide new evidence that refutes two traditional stereotypes about police work and women. The stereotypes assume that women are insufficiently authoritative and unwilling or unable to display their coercive authority and that women are more nurturing and thus more effective in comforting victims and agitated citizens. The findings of these studies suggest that it is the specific situation rather than the officer's gender that affects police behavior.

Christina DeJong (2004) reported minimal difference between men and women in providing support or comfort to citizens. Officers of both sexes were most likely to display comforting behavior in situations in which citizens were injured, were depressed, or had been victimized. Other significant situational factors that affected the likelihood of giving comfort were the presence of other citizens (which increases the likelihood) and the presence of other officers on the scene (which reduces the likelihood). Looking at the joint effect of sex and race, DeJong found nonwhite female officers were less likely than other officers to provide comfort to citizens.

Similarly, Paoline and Terrill (2004) found minimal support for hypothesized gender differences in the use of physical and verbal coercion in dealing with citizens. They defined coercion as an act that threatens or actually inflicts physical harm on citizens. It was measured as being absent, verbal, or physical in each call. There was no measure of whether it was "excessive." Men and women officers used coercion in similar proportions of calls for service, and both tended to employ verbal force much more frequently than physical force. Use of coercion by both men and women officers was most likely when the suspect was arrested, resistant, drug/alcohol impaired, and younger. The only statistically significant gender difference was the greater likelihood for male officers to use higher levels of force against male suspects; the level of force used by women officers was independent of suspect gender. These two studies indicate few gender differences in both use of coercion and provision of support in dealing with citizens. The minor differences that were found arose as a consequence of the gendered interactions of officers with citizens and fellow officers that reinforce women officers' identities as they do gender on the job.

A study of the use of excessive force and citizen complaints, however, found that women officers "are substantially less likely than their male counterparts to be involved in problems of excessive force" (National Center for Women & Policing, 2002b, p. 2). The study used three measures: excessive force payouts, sustained allegations of excessive force, and citizen complaints. In each instance, women were underrepresented relative to their representation in policing. For example, between 1990 and 1999, judgments or settlements in civil liability lawsuits involving excessive force by an officer on the Los Angeles Police Department indicate that the ratio of payouts involving excessive force used by men officers was greater than those by women officers by 23:1 (National Center for Women & Policing, 2002b, p. 3). Similarly, data on sustained allegations of excessive force indicate that although women represented 17 percent of department personnel, only 2 percent of the sustained allegations involved women officers. Additionally, women were under-represented in citizen complaints of excessive use of force based on data from the San Jose and San Francisco police departments. In sum, while the research to date suggests no difference in use of routine coercion, women are significantly less likely than their male colleagues to use excessive force.

Police Work, Discrimination, and Stress

Occupational stress has been linked to dissatisfaction, absenteeism, burnout, performance problems, physical illness (Haarr & Morash, 2005; Wright & Saylor, 1991), and emotional distress (He, Zhao, & Archbold, 2002; He, Zhao, & Ren, 2005). Several studies of police agencies (Morash & Haarr, 1995; Wexler & Logan, 1983; S. E. White & Marino, 1983) have found that both levels of stress and the primary stressors of men and women police are similar. Both men and women experience stress from relations within the organization (e.g., problems with supervisors), organizational climate (e.g., lack of management support), job circumstances (e.g., too much or too little work), ambiguities built into the occupational role, and career advancement issues. For example, sociologists Merry Morash and Robin Haarr (1995) found that the strongest predictors of stress for both men and women were the lack of influence over day-to-day operations, overestimates of physical abilities, inadequate equipment and uniforms, and lack of advancement opportunity.

Ni He and associates (2002, 2005) found no gender differences in officers' physical illness in response to work-related stress but higher levels of emotional stress in women than in men officers. They also found that women officers respond more frequently to stresses with constructive coping (e.g., talking to a spouse or friend about the problem; taking action to address it) than the men and are significantly less likely than the men to turn to destructive coping mechanisms (e.g., yelling or shouting at spouses or other family members; increased smoking, drinking, and/or gambling). For both men and women officers, the spillover of work-family conflict and use of destructive coping strategies also significantly contribute to stress.

Additionally, women officers face stressors specifically associated with being a woman, including the lack of acceptance as officers and the denial of information, sponsorship, and protection (Wexler & Logan, 1983). Morash and Haarr (1995) observed that two sources of stress, sexual harassment and "language harassment" (i.e., deliberate exposure to profanity and sexual jokes), were significantly correlated with workplace problems for women. In contrast, the strongest predictors of men's stress were being "set up" in dangerous situations and ridiculed by coworkers. The circumstances related to gender-specific work stresses differed, but each represented a gender-related challenge to the individual's self-definition as masculine or feminine (in terms of hegemonic masculinity and emphasized femininity), respectively.

Haarr and Morash (2005) conducted a follow-up of their 1990 survey in 2003 to examine changes in workplace problems, stress levels, and coping strategies by gender and race. As shown in Table 4.1, in 2003 men reported a significant reduction in a variety of workplace problems, including the overestimation or underestimation of their physical abilities, language harassment, bias, and stigmatization due to

Table 4.1   Workplace Problems and Stress Means for 1990 and 2003 by Gender

Scales	Time 1 1990 Men	Time 2 2003 Men	Male F Test	Time 1 1990 Women	Time 2 2003 Women	Female F Test	Time 2 F Test Men vs. Women
Workplace problems							
Physical ability overestimated	5.03	4.81	6.2**	4.56	4.81	3.1	.0
Physical ability underestimated	5.51	5.20	7.9*	5.78	5.50	3.2	4.9**
Lack of advancement opportunity	8.52	7.66	20.8*	7.23	7.30	.1	2.9
Ridicule and setups	9.77	9.77	.0	9.61	10.03	1.7	1.4
Lack of influence	12.86	12.61	.9	12.65	13.00	.9	2.1
Invisible	14.09	13.40	8.5*	13.35	13.79	1.1	1.8
Sexual harassment	12.72	12.39	3.1	13.53	13.32	.2	14.1*
Bias	13.70	11.88	46.9*	14.88	13.55	7.9*	29.1*
Language harassment	4.17	3.81	6.9*	5.46	4.49	11.3*	17.7*
Stigma, appearance	4.84	4.55	5.7**	4.99	4.74	1.3	1.9
Stress	11.50	10.31	26.3*	11.17	11.34	.2	14.6*

Source: Haarr and Morash (2005).

*$p \leq .01$.

**$p \leq .05$.

appearance. These reductions cumulatively seem to explain the significant reduction in men's stress. In contrast, there was no decrease in women's stress or in sexual harassment (i.e., offensive romantic advances, threats or attacks, exposure to pornography and comments about homosexuality). The only significant changes in workplace problems reported by women officers were with respect to a decrease in bias (i.e., a measure of their perception of being treated prejudicially because of gender and spending considerable energy in response) and language harassment (i.e., offensive profanity and jokes about sex), which at both times were experienced by significantly more women than men officers. In 2003, women were significantly more likely than men to report that their physical abilities were underestimated, that they experienced sexual and language harassment and bias, and that they were experiencing job-related stress. Thus, women did not benefit from the same significant reduction in workplace problems as the men.

Both men and women officers between 1990 and 2003 became more active in their response to stress and increased the use of various coping strategies. In 2003, women were more likely than men to verbalize their feelings to coworkers and to use informal coping approaches involving interaction with other officers and forming bonds within their racial and ethnic group, but were no more likely to use formal action than the men. In short, women did not benefit as much as men in reduction of workplace problems; they continued to experience language and sexual harassment and bias at a level that is higher than that of men. This may explain their higher levels of stress, although there were significant reductions in two "female-related stressors," bias and language harassment. The authors conclude (Haarr & Morash, 2005, p. 15),

> Women working alongside men in the same police department do not neces-sarily live in the same work world, because female officers are confronted with unique organizational and structural barriers, in the form of higher levels of harassment and discrimination, hostility, and other negative social interactions on the job.

Discrimination and harassment are among the problems experienced by women officers in a wide variety of nations. J. M. Brown and Heidensohn (1996) collected data from women officers attending two international conferences of policewomen as well as from women in a large number of forces within the British Isles. While the sample is far from representative of women police, it comes from more than 700 women serving in 34 countries who have an average of 12 years of experience in their respective forces. Most work as patrol officers; 51 percent are at the officer/constable rank. As Table 4.2 indicates, the women reported that they were most likely to experience discrimination in terms of deployment/assignment (56 percent), training opportunities (33 percent), and promotion (30 percent). Only 20 percent said they had never experienced sexual harassment from a male colleague or supervisor. The survey also indicated that officers from the United States and Canada were most likely to report being the subject of discriminatory treatment or harassing behavior. Scandinavian women police were least likely to experience discrimination. It is unclear whether these differences are attributable to cultural variation or disparities in policies and procedures or, alternatively, are the result of perceptual differences and stem from variation in women's tolerances. What the authors conclude is that sexual harassment is a "ubiquitous phenomenon" and that women are a marginalized minority across police jurisdictions.

J. M. Brown and Heidensohn (2000, p. 80) also tested the effects of numbers or token status on the levels of harassment that women experience. They found that harassment did not vary across units or by women's representation in various units. For example, the levels of harassment that women experienced in canine and traffic units (where they comprise less than 5 percent of personnel) were the same as those experienced by women in patrol (where they make up about 15 percent of officers) and in headquarters (where they comprise nearly a third of personnel).

Turnover: Adapting by Leaving

One study of diverse occupations found that women are entering male-dominated occupations more easily than might have been expected. However, they also are leaving those jobs quickly. This led J. Jacobs (1989) to conclude that women's employment is less a permanent achievement than a temporary pass through a "revolving door." Prenzler and Hayes (2000, p. 35) similarly observed that there is a "partial revolving door" among women police in Australia who are resigning primarily due to the incompatibility of police work with women's family commitments.

Table 4.2   Percentages of Women Police Reporting Discrimination or Sexual Harassment

Country/ Region	Number	Promotion (%)	Assignment (%)	Training (%)	Overtime (%)	Harassment[a] (%)
Africa	27	33	57	33	33	24/36
Australia	204	23	56	27	16	38/79
Benelux	36	30	34	20	6	27/36
British Isles	171	19	59	29	21	36/79
Canada	32	40	69	45	13	58/81
Eastern Europe	19	25	67	33	20	15/31
Mediterranean	8	50	50	50	20	0/20
Scandinavia	25	29	21	21	12	36/64
United States	159	46	62	45	13	59/81
TOTAL	707	30	56	33	18	78

Source: J. M. Brown and Heidensohn (1996).

a. The first percentage represents those who responded that harassment occurred "sometimes" or "often." The second percentage also includes the response that harassment occurs "rarely."

Policing is "structured to accommodate a male chronology of continuous and uninterrupted employment" (Silvestri, 2003, p. 80). Officers are expected to serve full-time and have unbroken career patterns to demonstrate their commitment and credibility. Women are considered unable to separate home and work, are constructed as unreliable and unsuitable in an organizational environment, and are expected to drop out when they start a family.

Data on gender differences in turnover rates in policing are limited and inconsistent. An early study by Sulton and Townsey (1981) found similar turnover rates for men and women in U.S. municipal police departments. In contrast, women's turnover rates were found to be significantly higher than men's in a California sheriff's department (Fry, 1983), in three Canadian urban agencies from which women resigned at rates approximately three times greater than men (Seagram & Stark-Adamec, 1992), and in municipal and state police departments in the United States (S. E. Martin, 1990). Susan Martin's (1990) study found that women had higher turnover rates than men in both municipal and state police departments but that the gender difference was substantially larger in the latter. For example, in 1986 in municipal departments, 4.6 percent of the men and 6.3 percent of the women separated for reasons other than retirement. In state police agencies, only 2.9 percent of the men but 8.9 percent of the women left their departments. Thus, women's turnover rate in state police agencies was nearly three times that of men.

An examination of 11 municipal police agencies commissioned by the British Columbia Police Commission (Polowek, 1996) identified dissatisfaction with promotional policies, transfer policies and opportunities, management style and practices, and the cost of housing as common reasons that men and women consider leaving police work. Women officers raised two additional sets of problems: meshing work and family (including the lack of policies related to pregnancy, maternity and parental leave, lack of department support of child care, and limitations on job sharing), and pressures associated with being a woman in a male-dominated environment (including sexual harassment and problems arising from tokenism). Haarr (2005, p. 450) also identified gender discrimination as "woven into women's resignation decisions" during their first 16 months in police work.

A study of resignations in 10 police forces in England and Wales found women resigning at higher rates than men, although they did so later in their careers (C. Cooper & Ingram, 2004). The data suggest that their resignations are related to having children since more than a quarter of the women who resigned (but none of the men) left to look after the household or family. Sadly, few of these women recommended reduced hours or help with child care as ways of retaining them. It appears that either they do not believe policing can or should be made a better place to work for people with domestic responsibilities, or they believe that accommodations for families are not employer responsibilities. Policies assuring equality of opportunity do not adequately address the unique problems women face in a gendered organizational environment that makes very little accommodation for family life.

Quitting may be appropriate for some officers and appears to be the only way to solve problems or eliminate stresses for others. However, it has three negative effects for women as a group. First, it diminishes efforts to increase women's representation. Second, it means that women accumulate seniority more slowly than men. This may reduce competition for "women's jobs" and enhance individual women's mobility opportunities, but it reduces the likelihood of women increasing their representation in specialized assignments and supervisory positions. Third, quitting is a form of acquiescence to the status quo of the gendered organization and a perpetuation of its myths.

Coping Strategies, Adaptations, and Work Styles

Faced with openly discriminatory treatment and the burdens of performance pressures, group boundary heightening, and encapsulation in stereotyped roles (Kanter, 1977), women actively develop coping strategies. For example, S. E. Martin (1978, 1980) identified two opposite ideal types or patterns of behavioral adaptations used by female officers that she characterized as POLICEwomen and policeWOMEN. Because most policewomen, in fact, seek to embody characteristics of each pattern and reject either extreme, few can be neatly categorized as fully embracing or typifying either coping strategy. The typology, nonetheless, highlights the nature of the dilemmas women assigned to patrol face in being accepted as both officers and women.

S. E. Martin (1980) characterized as POLICEwomen those who identify with the police work culture and seek to gain acceptance by being more professional, aggressive, loyal, street oriented, and macho than the men. In resisting traditional gender-based stereotypes, acting like men, and even outproducing them, however, POLICEwomen face the negative stereotypic labels of "dyke" or "bitch," which imply that they are "defeminized" and thus not "real women." They crave acceptance but never can quite become "one of the boys"; those who are sexually active are labeled "easy," which makes clear the persistence of the double standard by which men control women's sexuality.

PoliceWOMEN, conversely, are deprofessionalized and unable or unwilling to fully enact the street patrol role. They tend to be uncomfortable on patrol, fearful of physical injury, and reluctant to assert authority and take control of situations. Often feeling helpless, uncomfortable with men's crude language, and trying to remain "ladies," they accept the paternalistic bargain. They welcome or tolerate men's protection and often conform to such gender stereotypes as seductress, mother, pet, and helpless maiden in interactions with men officers (Kanter, 1977). Unable to prove themselves "exceptions" among the women, many policeWOMEN embrace the service aspects of policing, display little crime fighting initiative, and seek non-patrol assignments and personal acceptance as "feminine" women (S. E. Martin, 1980). Despite more than a quarter century of being "integrated" into police work, which itself has changed, as Sugden (2005, p. 168) observed, "women police continue to be either de-professionalised or de-feminised" and have problems in constructing their gender identity on the job.

Most women officers cope with the gendered work organization and its sexism by tending toward enacting one of these two broad patterns. Nevertheless, many are not consistent and respond with elements of each pattern at various times. In addition, they actively seek to resist traditional gender arrangements and stereotypes. As Sugden (2005, p. 168) explains, women continue to monitor themselves and decide whether feminine or masculine behavior should be displayed, constantly negotiating and performing expressions of gender-appropriate behavior. Sometimes they broaden the meaning of a female identity by acting tough and assertive and following the scripts of masculinity considered inherent to policing. While their work behavior displays disdain for feminine traits, through hair, makeup, and jewelry they negotiate a more feminine appearance and thus "discretely reconfigure the policing identity so that it includes both masculinity and femininity." Such efforts have contributed to the modification of definitions of femininity and masculinity and to the emergence of new cultural patterns and occupational role identities. Some women have successfully combined valued attributes associated with both masculinity and femininity in their behavioral repertoire and have developed self-definitions perceived to be "feminine, trustworthy, and professionally competent" (Hunt, 1990, p. 26). M. Young (1991, p. 240) characterized these "new police-women" as

> self-contained, self-consciously feminine women, unwilling to play the traditional role of home-maker, wife, and mother or become the butch "burglar's dog" taking the part of a surrogate male. Many . . . remain overtly feminine, yet operate in the macho world of policing without inhibition. They are professional, competent, and attractive and in consequence are feared and revered, for they have upturned the prescribed homogeneity of the male ideology which assigns women a clearly defined place on the margins and which they are expected to fill gratefully.

Many women have achieved this new status by "striking a balance" between traditional feminine stereotypes into which men press them and the "opposite but equally negative gender stereotype" (Jurik, 1988, p. 292). As one Australian woman officer stated (Sugden, 2005, p. 152),

> You have to find the line (in balancing masculinity and femininity) without becoming too much like a man. At the same time, you can't be prissy.

Balancing strategies include projecting a professional image, demonstrating unique skills, emphasizing a team approach, using humor to develop camaraderie and thwart unwelcome advances, and gaining sponsorship to enhance positive visibility (Jurik, 1988). Community-oriented policing has facilitated building new skills and balancing role enactments through a more androgynous style (displayed by men as well as women COs; S. L. Miller, 1999).

Women in policing demonstrate professionalism primarily by displaying physical courage, being willing to use physical force in threatening situations, remaining on patrol, and playing by the rules. While adhering to this masculine "street cop" model of police behavior, women have expanded the definition of "professionalism" to include improving their skills (e.g., by learning new languages and getting other specialized training), treating the public well, emphasizing close links with the community, and working very hard (J. M. Brown, 1998; J. M. Brown & Heidensohn, 2000).

In addition, women have withstood or faced down sexual harassers, often demonstrating a sense of humor in the process. In reacting to the sexualized environment, many women have relied on witty rejoinders rather than "feminine" responses or complaints when they were the butt of jokes or teasing. Yet in "giving it back," they have had to avoid acting or appearing to act in a sexual or flirtatious way, since "a woman cannot operate by men's rules and get away with it" (Cockburn, 1991, p. 156). Others have laughed at the men's "jokes" or suffered in silence, trying to fit in and avoid making waves, and "thinking of the larger picture." But, as Sugden (2005) notes, although ignoring sexual harassment may serve an individual, it harms women as a group because it may be interpreted as consent, validates such harassment as normative behavior, and allows it to continue.

Most have dealt with sexual propositions informally. Solutions have ranged from drawing their gun on a wayward scout car partner to threatening to call the offender's spouse, relying on support from a trusted friend or partner, silently regarding this treatment as the cost of doing the job, seeking transfers away from tormenters, and resigning. Some have acquiesced, gaining a degree of protection and support. A few have brought formal complaints and lawsuits. Although retaliation is illegal, such complaints sometimes set off retaliatory waves that drive out women. A growing number of suits, however, have resulted in large settlements for women (S. C. Collins & Vaughn, 2004).[2] Sponsorship by a supervisor or peer often leads to greater acceptance and decreases the likelihood of harassment for individual women officers. However, sponsorship based on what officers perceive as a sexual bargain can result in ostracism and limit long-term career success.

Women rarely have adopted a unified or organized response. Several factors have prevented formation of strong women's organizations within or across agencies.

These include divergent occupational and gender role perspectives across racial lines, mistrust and racism, and men's success in using a "divide and conquer" strategy to keep women competing with each other and relying on individualistic strategies to gain acceptance.

For both black and white women, acceptance by men of the same race is more important than support of other women, for work-related and social reasons. Men have more policing experience and more "muscle," and are available in greater numbers than women officers. Since women on patrol must depend on them for backup, their support may be a matter of life and death. In addition, social activities, including dating and marriages, occur along racial lines. Men of both races control "their" women's on-duty behavior by threatening them with social isolation both on and off the job (S. E. Martin, 1994) or categorizing them as lesbians.

In Australia and Europe, there are stronger and more active networks of women officers than are found in the United States (e.g., the European Network of Policewomen). However, Australian women, like their American counterparts, tend to feel uncomfortable with the association between policewomen's groups and feminism and are fearful that it will lead the male officers to see an "us-versus-them" effort (Sugden, 2005).

Meshing Personal and Occupational Lives

As in other occupations, women in policing face strains that their jobs put on family life. These problems are exacerbated by departmental policies and informal norms that expect officers to put the job first, with little leeway for personal or family commitments and constraints. Since women still bear the greater share of family responsibilities, this puts heavy strains on women officers, particularly those with children. In a study in one department in England, 7 percent of the men and 19 percent of the women without children but 23 percent of the men with children and 39 percent of the women with children reported that work often interferes with home life (Holdaway & Parker, 1998). Compounding women's problem is the men's "unfit mother attitude," which is part of the police culture (J. M. Brown & Heidensohn, 2000).

Some women cope by avoiding any allusion to issues related to child care commitments and difficulties working overtime or particular shifts since their colleagues would interpret this as evidence that they are unsuitable for police work (Holdaway & Parker, 1998). Similarly, Sugden (2005, p. 115) found the persistent view among Australian women officers that successful women "had chosen to dedicate themselves exclusively to their career and had prioritized their work lives above all else." Women who pursue the part-time work option face considerable resistance and are subject to such negative stereotypes as "half a copper."

Pregnancy also compounds women officers' problems. Light-duty assignments are limited and often available only at the discretion of supervisors. Women who get light-duty jobs find that they are put in isolated and often boring positions since management does not know how to use pregnant women officers' skills effectively. Nevertheless, many women accept the gendered organizational norms and values that hold that policing is incompatible with pregnancy and motherhood. They resign once they have a family and the agencies make it difficult for them to work part-time or return after taking leave without loss of seniority. In sum, organizational policies related to parenthood are far from gender neutral; women but not men may have to choose between having a child and a police career.

Summary

Women entering policing encounter a strongly gendered organization. Policies related to training, assignments, and performance evaluations are far from gender neutral. Women also are disadvantaged by overprotection and under-instruction and double standards regarding appearance and performance.

In the informal social world of the police, women remain outsiders, excluded from activities, sponsorship, and information networks important for career advancement. Unable to become "one of the boys," they encounter a sexualized workplace in which they are the object of men's sexual initiatives and innuendos.

Patterns of gender differences begin during training, continue in field training, and lead to differences in mobility. Women are more likely than men to leave street patrol, and when they transfer, they tend to go into community service and staff support positions, while men tend to transfer into more prestigious line units. A higher proportion of men than women also get promoted to supervisory positions.

Women officers' work attitudes do not differ substantially from those of men officers, and their job performance is equally competent. Nevertheless, their experiences on the job are different because as women they must negotiate a way through gendered organizational processes for distributing assignments and power, gendered interactions with colleagues and citizens, and a gendered work culture. They must deal with sexual and language harassment, uncertain backup, social isolation, and dilemmas regarding appearance and demeanor. Such behavioral choices reproduce cultural images of a gendered work organization and gender identities of men and women cops.

To deal with work-related stress and dilemmas, two primary coping strategies are available: POLICEwomen act like or outdo the men; policeWOMEN emphasize their femininity but fail effectively to exercise control on the street. A growing number of women have merged elements of these strategies by striking a balance in doing gender and police work, achieving recognition as "real policewomen" and providing a new model for women. Regardless of which strategy they use to "fit in," however, women officers encounter difficult choices not faced by men in deciding whether to have a family and in juggling both work and family responsibilities. This is not easy in a hostile environment in which unsupportive organizational policies and informal norms convey the message that women are inadequate as both police and mothers.

Endnotes

1. Jones (1986) found that police occupational culture had several grounds for resisting inclusion of women, which she labeled "ritual arguments" that guided men's daily interactions with women officers. These arguments about women's ability to perform included their emotional unsuitability, discipline problems such as their lack of command performance, physical unsuitability, and costliness to the department given their higher turnover rate.

2. For example, in 2003, three women officers won a $3.5 million sex harassment case against the Glendale, California, police department for creating a hostile environment and failing to prevent sexual harassment.

CHAPTER 5

Women Entering the Legal Profession

Change and Resistance

> *Nature has tempered women as little for the judicial conflicts of the courtroom as for the physical conflicts of the battlefield. . . . Our . . . profession has essentially . . . to do with all that is selfish and extortionate, knavish and criminal, coarse and brutal, repulsive and obscene in human life. It would be revolting to all female sense of innocence and the sanctity of their sex.*

> (Chief Justice C. J. Ryan of the Wisconsin Supreme Court
> opposing admitting Lavinia Goodell to the bar,
> 1895, cited in Epstein, 1993, p. 269)

Though the practice of the criminal law occasionally may be "coarse," this decision reflects the images and stereotypes that associate the law with masculinity. These images were used to justify the virtual exclusion of women from the prestigious and powerful legal profession in the United States until the 1970s. Despite Justice Ryan's vivid language, the reasons for men's resistance to women lawyers "likely has to do with the law's close relationship to power in our society" (Morello, 1986, p. x). The legal profession structures power relations between groups and classes by shaping the rules and laws that open or limit opportunities without resort to force, making it the quintessential male power role (Hagan, Zatz, Arnold, & Kay, 1991).

For many years, by controlling its own membership, the legal community was able to limit both the number of lawyers and the social diversity of those admitted to practice. It did this by exercising both formal control over admissions to law school and bar membership, and informal referral and social mechanisms. These processes enforced the understanding that outsiders such as women and racial minorities would be excluded from the legal community or would be kept on its fringes in low-visibility, low-prestige specialties, serving others like themselves (Epstein, 1993).

Since the 1960s, the legal world has undergone several major changes. The number of lawyers has more than doubled. The nature and organization of legal work have also changed. There are fewer lawyers in solo practice and more who work in large law firms and in salaried positions with corporations and government agencies. Law firms have greatly increased in size and become more bureaucratized and hierarchical. New areas, such as public interest law, have emerged, and the number of women lawyers has mushroomed. Thus, women's growing presence in the law beginning in the 1970s occurred as part of the changing legal context, while the growing representation of women stimulates further change in the organization and activities of lawyers.

Women now comprise more than a quarter of the legal profession and about half of all law students, but their numerical gains have not yielded equivalent increases in power and opportunities. As the report of the American Bar Association (ABA) Commission on Women in the Profession, *The Unfinished Agenda* (2001, p. 5), concluded,

> Despite substantial progress toward equal opportunity, the agenda [established by this group in 1987] remains unfinished. Women in the legal profession remain underrepresented in positions of greatest status, influence and economic reward. . . . The problems are compounded by the lack of consensus that there are in fact serious problems.

This chapter explores the history of women in the legal profession, the nature and organization of the work done by attorneys, the changes that have occurred across the legal landscape, and the ways that gendered legal culture and its images have severely disadvantaged women lawyers. Chapter 6 looks more closely at the organizational logic that prevails in key legal settings and the strategies adopted by women lawyer to address the barriers that inhibit legal careers. In these chapters, we present a general discussion of women's integration into the legal profession rather than focusing explicitly on criminal law because no such specialized data are available and because most of the barriers to women are encountered across legal settings.

Historical Overview: Barriers to Women in Law Before 1970

In 1638, Margaret Brent became executor of the estate of Lord Calvert, governor of the Maryland colony (Morello, 1986). Although it is known that she was the first woman to practice law in colonial America, little else is known about women practicing law until the mid-1800s. Women were barred from both law schools and state bar associations. It is possible that a few women appeared in court in their own behalf and others practiced law in the frontier areas (Bernat, 1992). However, few women pursued legal careers.

In 1869, Iowa became the first state to admit a woman, Arabella Mansfield, to the bar (Morello, 1986). Three years later, Charlotte E. Ray, daughter of leaders of New York's underground railroad, became the first African-American woman admitted to the bar (Siemsen, 2006). In other jurisdictions, however, women applicants were denied membership. For example, in 1872, Myra Bradwell, who was denied admittance by the Illinois State Supreme Court, appealed to the U.S. Supreme Court claiming that her rights under the Equal Protection Clause of the Fourteenth Amendment had been violated. The Court, denying her appeal, stated,

> The natural and proper timidity and delicacy which belongs to the female sex evidently unfits it for the practice of law. . . . [Additionally] a woman has no legal existence separate from her husband . . . [so that] . . . a married woman is incapable, without her husband's consent, of making contracts which shall be binding on her or him, whereas unmarried women are "exceptions to the general rule" of marriage. (Cited in Morello, 1986)

The Court's decision in *Bradwell* permitted states to exclude women from practicing law. Since admission to a state bar is the prerequisite for practicing law in that state, women had to challenge their exclusion state by state in order to gain the right to practice law. It was not until 1920, 51 years after women first became lawyers in the United States, that women were permitted to practice law before the courts in every state (Feinman, 1986). Women also were excluded from membership in the ABA until 1918 (Abel, 1989) and from the prestigious Association of the Bar of the City of New York until 1937 (Epstein, 1993). Consequently, they were kept from the networks through which lawyers gain contacts, referrals, and power.

Between 1870 and 1950, American lawyers as a professional group successfully controlled the market for their services. They developed local, state, and national bar associations; created codes of ethics; and established disciplinary procedures to control the quality of legal services. They also maintained tight entrance requirements into the profession through control over the standards and admission practices of the emerging law schools (Abel, 1986). Thus, the ABA and state bars limited the numbers and controlled the characteristics of new lawyers. As a result, despite the vast economic growth during the first half of the 20th century in the United States, the population-to-lawyer ratio was the same in 1950 as it was in 1900, and the legal profession consisted of white men mostly in solo practice.

By the end of the 19th century, the professionalization of legal practice had led to an increasing proportion of lawyers with formal legal education. Until 1900, the most common route to the bar was "reading the law" and serving as an apprentice or "clerk" to a working lawyer. As apprenticeship routes disappeared, even these limited opportunities for women to enter law were reduced by women's exclusion from the academic route. Although Washington University in St. Louis was the first law school to admit women in 1869 (Morello, 1986), access to legal education remained very limited. Many law schools, particularly the most elite, denied admittance to women altogether. Columbia only opened its doors to women in 1928, and Harvard did so in 1950.

Even when women were admitted, quotas and other restrictive barriers kept their numbers small (Epstein, 1993). With a sufficient supply of qualified men applicants and in the absence of antidiscrimination laws, the academic gatekeepers excluded or limited the numbers of men and women of color and white women. For many decades, law classes typically had a maximum of three women. Although academics protested that the low numbers were due to women's disinterest, statistics that appeared in the *Harvard Law Record* in 1965 suggest a pattern of discrimination. Despite increasing numbers of women applicants, women constituted about 3 percent in each class between 1951 and 1965 (cited in Epstein, 1993). Women remained less than 5 percent of the enrollment at ABA-approved law schools until the 1970s (Abel, 1989). Both faculty and men students made the educational environment inhospitable to women. While all students were subject to ridicule, particularly if they did not provide the right response when called on in class, women were rarely called on, and on such occasions, they were subjected to questions designed to embarrass them (e.g., being asked to explain the details of rape cases) or were humiliated by such comments as "better go back to the kitchen" if they stumbled in recitation. Additionally, women knew they would be expected to respond on "Ladies' Day," which for many professors and men students was a show put on at the women's expense. For example, one professor sat in the audience asking questions and told all the women in the class to stand at the podium "rather like performing bears" (Epstein, 1993, p. 66).[1]

In 1972, passage of Title IX of the Higher Education Act prohibited discrimination based on sex in the enrollment of students and hiring of faculty. Facing denial of federal financial assistance if they continued to discriminate, law schools finally began to admit more women and allow them to compete equally with men. Since that time, women's enrollments have grown dramatically; in 2004, they constituted about half (48 percent) of the students enrolled in law school and 51 percent of those awarded JDs (ABA, 2006).

The next hurdle for women lawyers was finding a job. Even women with training from elite schools faced employment discrimination that was openly practiced well into the 1970s. For example, a 1963 survey of 430 law firms found that "female status" was the characteristic that got the most negative rating in selecting new recruits (Epstein, 1993). Thus, it is not surprising that in 1965, fewer than 20 percent of the 104 firms responding to a *Harvard Law Record* questionnaire employed any women lawyers (cited in Epstein, 1993).

Women who were able to obtain legal work often were offered opportunities in low-status specialties deemed appropriate for women, such as domestic relations and probate law. They received lower pay and were denied partnerships and opportunities for leadership in bar associations. For example, when former Supreme Court Justice Sandra Day O'Connor graduated third in her class at Stanford Law School in 1953, the only job that she was offered was as a legal secretary (*Time*, July 20, 1981, p. 12, cited in Epstein, 1993, p. 84).

Women also were rarely found on the bench. The first woman justice of the peace was appointed in 1890, but it was not until 1979 that a woman had served at some level of the judicial system in all 50 states (Slotnick, 1984). Similarly, the first woman on the federal bench, Francis Allen, was appointed by President Roosevelt to the Circuit (Appellate) Court in 1934. The next was appointed to the U.S. District Court in 1949 by President Truman. By 1977, only eight women had ever served in the federal judiciary at the District or Circuit Court level (E. Martin, 2004).

Women were not the only group excluded from the practice of law. In fact, the club-like homogeneity of law firms that hired only white Anglo-Saxon Protestant men has only gradually, and often grudgingly, moved toward greater representativeness. The first step was made by Jewish and Catholic men during the 1950s and 1960s. White women broke through by the late 1970s. Informal barriers against persons of color remain high.[2]

The history of the struggle of women in the United States to enter the legal profession was similar to women's struggles in England, other Commonwealth nations, and Europe. In England, the Inns of Court controlled entry into the ranks of barristers (as well as the judiciary that is drawn from this group) and succeeded in excluding women who sued for admission through several judicial interpretations of the law until 1918. In that year, Parliament passed the Sex Disqualification (Removal) Act largely as a reward for women's performance during World War I. But as in the United States, admission did not end discrimination, and through the 1950s, the number of women admitted to the bar grew even more slowly than in the United States (Corcos, 1998). In Canada, Clara Brett Martin sought but was denied admission to the Ontario Bar in 1891. The provincial government, however, swiftly asked the Ontario legislature to permit the Law Society of Upper Canada to admit women, although it took several years and two separate acts of the legislature in 1897 before Ms. Martin was called to the bar. In Australia, the various territories admitted women to the legal profession separately but mostly before the mother country did. Women were admitted to the bar in Victoria in 1903, followed by Tasmania (1904), Queensland (1905), South Australia (1911), New South Wales (1918), and Western Australia (1923; Corcos, 1998). Nevertheless, Australian women as late as 1980 were underrepresented in the profession and were consigned to certain areas of practice (primarily family law).

In France, much of the argument over the admission of women to the legal profession took place after their admission to the bar in 1900. Although the government had little difficulty in overturning what it considered a grievous wrong in a court ruling in 1897 that denied a woman the right to admission, the majority of members of the legal profession were not happy about the government's policy. Questions about women's competence lingered, and few women sought legal careers for the next several decades after they were permitted to do so. Across these diverse nations, many of the arguments used to exclude or limit women were similar: the law was and continues to be "constructed as male" (i.e., presumed to be rational, logical, dispassionate, objective, professional, intimidating and demanding), while women are presumed to lack these qualities (Corcos, 1998).[3]

Changing Laws and Job Queues: Opening Legal Practice to Women

In the past four decades, there have been a number of major changes in the legal profession. These include an enormous increase in the number of law schools and lawyers; an opening of the profession to white women and people of color; a shift in the type and organization of legal employment, including increases in firm size and bureaucratization; increases in the number of hours worked and the salaries paid to lawyers (particularly those in private practice); and a diminution of the legal profession's control over lawyers' behavior. Each of these changes has affected and been affected by the expanded role of women in law.

Changing Labor Queues and Demographics in the Legal Profession

From 1960 to the present, there has been a phenomenal growth in the number of lawyers and in the ratio of lawyers to the general population. The number of lawyers in the United States grew from about 222,000 in 1950 to 355,000 in 1971, 542,000 in 1980, 806,000 in 1991, and 909,019 in 2000 (Carson, 2004, p. 28). The growth rate was about 25 percent during the 1950s and 1960s and rose to about 50 percent in the 1970s and 1980s, but slowed down in the 1990s. The ratio of lawyers to the population of the United States also increased markedly. Between 1950 and 1991, the number of lawyers almost quadrupled, but the size of the U.S. population did not even double. Thus, while there was one lawyer for every 679 people in 1950, by 1991 this ratio stood at one lawyer for every 313 people (Kornhauser & Revesz, 1995), and in 2000 that ratio was 264 to 1 (Carson, 2004, p. 27).

One consequence of this growth is the legal profession's gradual loss of control over its composition. Restrictions on the training of lawyers prior to 1960 led to a shortage of lawyers, expansion in the number of law schools in the 1960s, and willingness to turn to less expensive women lawyers by the 1970s. Greater demand also led to higher starting salaries that, in turn, made the law a more attractive career option. The civil rights, women's, consumers,' and environmental movements of the 1960s expanded new areas of the law and the demand for lawyers. As racial and sexual barriers to entry into law fell, the number of aspiring lawyers more than doubled, while the number of law schools rose by 25 percent. The number of new lawyers being trained in the mid-1980s was three times greater than that in the mid-1960s (Abel, 1986, p. 11); since then, the expansion of the profession has continued, but the rate of growth is slower.

There have been dramatic changes in the demographic composition of the legal profession over the past 30 years. These include a vast increase in the proportion of white women and a small increase in men and women of color. But this increasingly young and diverse profession remains dominated by elderly white men. Since men's enrollment in law schools has remained stable while women's has multiplied, most of the growth in the profession represents an increase in the number of women law students and lawyers. In 1960, women comprised only 3.5 percent of the enrollees at ABA-approved law schools; in 1970, they comprised 8.5 percent; in 1980, they comprised 33.6 percent; and in 1986, they comprised 40.2 percent (Abel, 1989, p. 285). As of 2005, women represented virtually half (48 percent) of all law students in the United States (ABA, 2006). Of the new entrants to the bar in 2003, 46 percent were women, 17 percent were nonwhite (compared to 5 percent in 1970), and 2.5 percent were openly gay or lesbian (*After the JD*, 2004, p. 19).

Similarly, the number of women lawyers in Canada and Australia in the past 25 years has mushroomed. In 2004, women comprised just under 50 percent of law students in Australia compared with only 20 percent in 1970 (Thornton, 2004). In Canada, in 2003 women represented 53 percent of the law school graduates (Women in Law in Canada, 2005).

Changes in the Type and Nature of Legal Employment

The organization of legal work also has changed enormously since 1960. Most lawyers still work in private settings and either serve large corporations or serve small businesses and individuals. However, an increasing proportion of attorneys now work in law firms rather than as solo practitioners, and their work is increasingly specialized. Not only are there more law firms, but they are much larger in size and are increasingly hierarchical and bureaucratic. For example, the proportion of lawyers in solo practice declined from 61 percent in 1960 to about 34 percent in 2000 (Carson, 2004). At the same time, the number of lawyers in firms with 50 or more lawyers grew from 7.3 percent in 1980 to 18.2 percent in 2000 (Carson, 2004, p. 29). Increases in size and bureaucratization have occurred not only in private law firms but in corporation counsel's offices and government legal departments. A study of lawyers in Chicago (Heinz, Nelson, Laumann, & Michelson, 1998) found that the average number of lawyers in the private law firm in 1975 was 27; by 1995, the average firm had 141 lawyers. Similarly, the average size of house counsel offices (lawyers working in corporations and other private organizations) grew from 17 in 1975 to 55 in 1995, and on average, government law offices grew from 64 to 399 between 1975 and 1995. A result of these changes is an increase in the proportion of lawyers who are salaried workers. More lawyers work for government and private industry now than 50 or 20 years ago. The nature of the work also shifted, as an increasing proportion of lawyers' activities involved work for corporate/business clients rather than individuals.

The ideal of professional practice represented in the law firm traditionally rested on service to clients, the production of knowledge, and adherence to an ethical code. Partnerships were granted to associates on the basis of craftsmanship, the individual's skills in business development, and personal qualities and "fit" within the "brotherhood" of the firm. The social structure of firms began to change in the late 1970s and 1980s and accelerated in the 1990s as law firms mushroomed in size, hired persons from diverse backgrounds, and began recruiting associates laterally from competing firms by offering more money and a swifter move to partnership. Within the firm, competition and stress replaced "fraternity" and collegiality. Clients, once property of the firm, became property of individual lawyers. To support their rising costs, firms put growing emphasis on the bottom line, and with it came a change in compensation systems from those based on seniority to those emphasizing productivity, particularly client development (i.e., "rainmaking"). This shift advantaged men and disadvantaged women since much of rainmaking activity occurs on the golf course and in extra-work hours activities at bar association meetings and social clubs among persons who give single-minded attention to the job and avoid outside obligations. Firms compete by adding specialty departments in areas of high demand and striving to enhance profitability by increasing the ratio of associates to partners, as well as creating several types of partnerships.

With the economic downturn in the early 1990s, law firms for the first time laid off lawyers and decreased the proportion of associates elevated to partner. Currently, both partners and younger associate lawyers face enormous pressures to win and hold client. In addition, the number of billable hours (i.e., those chargeable to a particular client or account) per year expected of and actually worked by lawyers has increased from 1,800 to as much as 2,300 hours annually to meet the costs of spiraling salaries and growing demands of clients. For example, a study of practicing lawyers in Calgary, Alberta, Canada, found that they average 50 hours per week in the office and that more than half (52 percent) take work home, and their evening and weekend work adds another 5.5 hours, resulting in a median of 53 hours a week of work (Wallace, 2002).

These changes in the size, composition, structure, and function of the legal profession have affected its self-governance by breaking down the control formerly exercised by the ABA and state bar associations and subjecting lawyers to more external regulation. The changes also have increased stratification of the legal profession according to practitioner background, clientele, function, and reward. As sociologist Richard Abel (1986) predicted, and as will be elaborated shortly, increasing heterogeneity within the profession has resulted in differential ranking within the legal profession and segregation associated with racial and gender differences. Changing job queues and expanded demand for women lawyers have enabled them to enter the field, but these changes have occurred at the same time as the legal profession has become more stratified, bureaucratized, competitive, and specialized. Consequently, as will be shown, the legal profession remains gendered despite dramatic changes in the past three decades. To understand why, it is necessary to examine other factors that also have affected both changes in the profession and women's place in it in the past 40 years.

The Changing Legal Environment

Civil rights laws have contributed to change in the legal profession by opening the doors to law schools and legal work for women and persons of color. Title VII of the Civil Rights Act of 1964, the 1972 Amendments to Title VII, and the 1972 Educational Amendments Act were of particular importance to aspiring women lawyers.

The 1972 Amendments to Title VII extended antidiscrimination provisions to all employers with 15 or more workers, including many law firms, as well as to state and local government agencies and educational institutions. It also allowed the

Justice Department to bring "pattern or practice" lawsuits. When this provision was applied to include the placement offices of law schools that served as employment agencies and made them targets for lawsuits, they radically altered their gatekeeping functions.

The 1972 Educational Amendments Act prohibited sex discrimination in all public institutions of higher learning receiving federal monies, including major university law schools. This not only opened enrollment to women students, but affected the distribution of scholarships and the hiring and promotion of women faculty members. It also made it illegal for law firms to openly refuse to interview or hire women.

Women Lawyers Using the New Laws

Opening employment opportunities in law to women required lawsuits against the legal establishment. These suits have gradually brought about changes in the legal profession's treatment of women in practice, teaching, and the job market. At first, women students at New York University and Columbia Law Schools, with the participation of Columbia Law School's Employment Rights Project, set out to end exclusionary practices in elite Wall Street firms. Pooling information about job interview experiences, they concluded that these firms were not taking their applications seriously. They complained to their school's placement office, and with help from the Employment Rights Project (and funding from the Equal Employment Opportunity Commission), several women filed complaints with the New York City Human Rights Commission against 10 firms on behalf of all women law students in New York. In 1976, seven years after initiation of their suit, all of the firms agreed to settlements similar to those reached following findings of employment discrimination in two test cases.

In the first case decided, *Kohn v. Royall, Koegel and Wells,* the court determined that the firm had systematically discriminated against women in hiring. The firm agreed to a complex formula, including a guarantee that it would offer at least 25 percent of its positions each year to women. In the other case, the court found that Diane Blank's interviewer from the firm of Sullivan and Cromwell had admitted that the firm was biased, discouraged her interest in the firm, failed to examine her resume, and asked about her lawyer-husband's career. Sullivan and Cromwell also agreed to a settlement that included the provision that in addition to hiring women, it would not hold social events in clubs that excluded women. The other eight firms cited in the initial complaint adopted similar guidelines (Epstein, 1993, pp. 184–189).

Despite antidiscrimination laws, women law students and faculty had to keep up pressure on law school placement offices through the 1970s to force law firms to recruit women seriously or face sanctions. In some instances, women students sued placement offices (e.g., University of Chicago Law School). By the end of the decade, law firm recruiting had changed; while old prejudices remain, most firms have eliminated blatant discrimination.

The next legal barrier was posed by the partnership decision. In *Hishon v. King & Spalding* (1984), the U.S. Supreme Court legally recognized that promotion to partnership is an area covered under Title VII. Earlier, the courts had treated partnerships as voluntary associations that must be congenial for all concerned, because partners are liable for the negligent acts of any copartner. In *Hishon*, the Court rejected the argument that the choice of partners was protected under the First Amendment right to freedom of association. It ruled that Title VII does not force partnerships to accept less qualified individuals. Nevertheless, consideration for partnership is a "term, condition, or privilege" of the original employment contract covered under Title VII, and, as such, a partnership decision must be made on a fair and equal basis without regard to the applicant's sex (Madek & O'Brien, 1990).

The next hurdle for women was addressing discrimination in the actual decision-making process. Since the decision to admit an individual to a partnership usually involves both objective and subjective factors and a collaborative decision, identifying the "real cause" of such decisions often is impossible. In a 1989 decision, *Price Waterhouse v. Hopkins* (which actually dealt with issues of partnership in an accounting firm, but the issues raised in this case apply more generally to partnerships), a fragmented Supreme Court failed to establish either clear grounds for determining when discrimination has occurred or the rules of the fight.

The facts of the case were clear. Ann Hopkins, a senior manager at the Price Waterhouse accounting firm, was denied a partnership in a "mixed motive" case (i.e., one in which there were multiple reasons for denying partnership, only some of which were related to her gender). Ms. Hopkins had generated more new business for the firm than any of the 85 men who also applied for partnership at the same time; she was also known to be a demanding and difficult supervisor. In the usual manner, Price Waterhouse solicited comments from partners about candidates who had applied for partnership. Among the 32 comments regarding Ms. Hopkins were 13 supporting admittance and 8 for rejection. The decision was put on hold, and when two of Hopkins' supporters withdrew their support, partnership was denied.

The lower courts ruled that once a plaintiff has established that an illegal motive played a significant part in the decision to deny partnership, the burden of proof shifts to the defendant to show that no discrimination actually occurred. In the *Price Waterhouse* case, the lower court suggested that Ms. Hopkins' management style was a legitimate reason for putting her partnership application on hold. Nevertheless, the firm still was liable because the partnership process gave unacceptably great weight to negative comments that reflected unconscious sexual stereotypes by male evaluators. Among the suspect comments were statements that Ms. Hopkins needed a "course at charm school" and, from her primary supporter, that she would improve her chances of becoming a partner if she would "wear make up, have her hair styled, and wear jewelry" (at 1116–1117).

The Supreme Court overruled the lower courts and raised the threshold for showing discriminatory intent. The Court was split, with Justice O'Connor in the middle as the swing vote on two issues: the amount of evidence needed to show a discriminatory motive that triggers a shift in the burden of proof from plaintiff to the defendant, and the degree to which discriminatory intent is the cause of the decision.

As Madek and O'Brien (1990) predicted, such a split decision led to legislation to resolve these issues. In 1991, Congress amended Title VII of the Civil Rights Act with the provision that stated,

An unlawful employment practice is established when the complaining party demonstrates that race, color, religion, sex or national origin was a motivating factor for any employment practice, even though other factors also motivated the practice. (Civil Rights Act of 1991, Pub.L. No. 102-166, 105 Stat.1071 [1991])

In a recent case interpreting the scope of the statute with respect to the amount of evidence, *Desert Palace v. Costa* (2003), the Supreme Court unanimously adopted a straightforward application of the statutory provision. It ruled that "a motivating factor" means that if race or gender plays any role, however minor, in an employer's decision, the plaintiff has established liability. In that instance, all the employer can do is limit the amount of award for the plaintiff's full remedies. Thus, the requirement for "direct" evidence of discriminatory intent called for in Justice O'Connor's decision in *Price Waterhouse* was eliminated (Zimmer, 2004).

Challenging Discriminatory Practices: Gender Bias Task Forces

Women lawyers soon encountered discriminatory practices and gendered interactions in the courthouse that threatened their livelihoods. Because these practices often were perpetrated or tolerated by judges, women lawyers could not safely challenge them individually. Instead, attorneys from the National Organization for Women's Legal Defense and Education Fund, in cooperation with the National Association of Women Judges, designed a program to call attention to "gender bias" in the law, decision making, and courtroom interaction in state judicial systems. To make this change strategy palatable to judges and other gatekeepers in the legal system, the program was focused on collecting state-specific information about "gender bias." Such bias was defined as existing when

people are denied rights or burdened with responsibilities solely on the basis of gender; . . . people are subjected to stereotypes about the proper behavior of men and women which ignore their situations; people are treated differently on the basis of gender in situations where gender should make no difference; [and] men or women as a group can be subjected to a legal rule, policy or practice which produces worse results for them than for the other group. (Maryland Special Joint Committee, 1989, p. iii)

Thus, gender bias includes both overt discrimination and more subtle practices.

The program was designed as part of the judiciary's continuing judicial education efforts and employed a new approach, creation of gender bias task forces, to document such bias in the courts (Schafran, 1987). The first such body, the New Jersey Supreme Court's Task Force on Women in the Courts, was established in November 1982 by that state's Chief Justice to investigate three issues: whether gender stereotypes affect the substantive law or impact on judicial decision making; whether a person's gender affects his or her treatment in the legal and judicial environment; and, if so, how to ensure equal treatment for women and men in court.

Its "First Year Report," published in June 1984, found substantial gender bias and led to creation of similar task forces, similar findings across jurisdictions, general acceptance of the findings, and the introduction of judicial education about gender bias in many states. During the 1990s, several Federal Circuit courts also created task forces to focus on gender bias. However, in response to the Washington, D.C. Circuit Court's report that revealed slights experienced by many women involved in the justice system similar in nature to those identified in other reports, several men judges, upset at the report's recommendations, got Congress to block funding for further gender bias studies that had been proposed in the judiciary budget (Wald, 1996). Nevertheless, the tide has clearly turned; as of 2001, 45 states and most Federal Circuits had created similar task forces on gender bias in the courts (Schafran, 2004). Their findings have been both consistent and troubling. As will be further detailed in Chapter 6, a substantial proportion of women lawyers (and a much smaller proportion of men) has experienced various forms of gender bias including sexual harassment and demeaning behavior in courtroom proceedings. These task forces also inspired creation of similar task forces on racial and ethnic bias in many states as well as reports by the ABA's Multicultural Women Attorneys Network (Schafran, 2004).

In addition to the bench, in 1987 the ABA created the Commission on Women in the Profession chaired by Hillary Rodham Clinton to address gender discrimination throughout the legal profession. Its 1988 report to the ABA House of Delegates called on that body to recognize the persistence of discrimination against women in the legal profession and to affirm its commitment to ending barriers that prevent "full integration and equal participation of women in all aspects of the legal profession" (ABA, 1988, p. 1). Since putting the legal establishment on record as opposing discrimination more than 20 years after the first surge of women into the profession, the ABA has also amended both its Model Code of Judicial Conduct and the Model Rules of Professional Conduct to include prohibitions on bias. Additionally, it has issued a number of reports that document continuing progress as well as continuing discrimination against women and men of color throughout the legal profession, and has recommend agendas for change (ABA, 1994, 1995, 2001a, 2001b).

Lawyers' Jobs, Specialties, and the Division of Legal Labor

Although women comprised 27 percent of the legal profession as of 2000 (Carson, 2004, p. 27), their numerical gains have not yielded equivalent increases in power, status, and income. Table 5.1 shows that male and female lawyers have different employment patterns. In brief, women are proportionally underrepresented in private practice and overrepresented in government, corporate/private industry, and legal aid and public defender (PD) work. Additionally, within each of these organizational hierarchies, women are concentrated in the bottom rungs of prestige and income; they are underrepresented in the ranks of partner, general counsel, and

Table 5.1   Employment Distribution of Men and Women Lawyers in 2000

Employment Setting	Male Lawyers		Female Lawyers		Females as Percentage of Category
	Number	Percent	Number	Percent	
Private practice	506,829	75.0	166,072	71.2	24.7
Federal judiciary	2,221	0.3	939	0.4	29.7
Federal government	18,572	2.7	10,049	4.3	35.1
State/local judiciary	16,231	2.4	4,548	1.9	21.9
State government	25,698	3.8	14,476	6.2	36.0
Private industry	54,972	8.1	14,476	6.2	36.0
Private association	3,285	0.5	20,973	9.0	27.6
Legal aid/public defender	5,060	0.7	2,443	1.0	42.7
Legal education	5,060	0.9	3,997	1.7	44.1
Retired or inactive	5,908	5.5	3,135	1.3	15.3
Total	675,729	100	233,290	100	

Source: From Carson (2004). © The American Bar Association. All rights reserved.

supervisors. This section looks at the organization and work of lawyers as well as their distribution across specialties and workplaces to set the stage for examination of the factors responsible for and the impact of these employment patterns.

The Organization and Work Activities of Lawyers

In complex societies, the critical rules of social life are codified in law, and their meanings are interpreted and enforced by a group of experts on their proper application and use. These specialists in legal rules are lawyers, whose occupational specialty often is traced back to ancient Rome. The work of lawyers is advocacy or action directly or indirectly in defense of a client's interests in the courts and other forms of dispute resolution. Law is a theoretical and abstract discipline, and lawyers' work represents the practical application of legal theory and knowledge to solve real problems or advance the interests of those who have retained them for legal services. This occurs through the court system, where the rules of the legal system are applied. Legal work revolves around the court setting, where the rules of the legal system interact with specific interests of clients or relationships between clients and the state.

The public image of lawyers' activities focuses on the drama of the adversarial process in highly publicized criminal trials pitting the prosecution against the defense, with the judge serving as a referee. However, not all proceedings in court are adversarial. Most laws actually relate to civil matters that involve facilitating, regulating, or channeling activities (e.g., transmission of property, divorce, interpreting tax laws) in a given society. In handling cases, the lawyer's role is to adjust the needs, requests, and rights of the client in response to another party's assertion of rights, the rights of the state, or requests of the state for certain behavior (e.g., the payment of taxes). The judge's role is to exercise the authority of the legal system to constrain the activities of lawyers in their role as advocates.

In the United States, the division of legal work may be examined along two major dimensions: the specific kind of legal work done and the particular setting of the practice. In each, there is stratification based on the nature of the client served. Criminal law generally deals with the poor, whereas much of civil law has to do with business matters. More prestige and rewards accrue to lawyers who work for the elite since they become identified with the kind of clientele they associate with. Similarly, types of work settings also involve stratification. Usually, lawyers in solo practice work with poor or middle-class individuals; Wall Street and other lawyers in large and established law firms have powerful corporate clients. In between are smaller group practices, governmental legal activities, and house counsel work. Siemsen (2006) asserts that given the "moral division of labor" among lawyers, the attorneys who do society's "dirty work" by handling criminal defendants and the social problems of the poor and downtrodden are contaminated by their work and given low status; those who litigate (do trial work) with other populations are higher ranked; and at the top of the hierarchy are those who handle civil matters.

Lawyers also are stratified by specialty. Most lawyers enter civil work, and the elite among these go into business-related legal specialties. The work of Wall Street lawyers often involves helping corporate clients manage the private sector of the world economy. However, most lawyers work in smaller firms on the cases involving middle-class individuals and families and deal with wills, accidents (torts), and divorces. In addition to practicing attorneys, a number of persons with law degrees pursue careers in business, politics, teaching, or government and often move from one practice setting to another over their career.

In the past quarter century, there has been an erosion of the independence and autonomy of lawyers, resulting in the "postprofessional world" (Kritzer, 1999). Three key forces have undermined professional control: increasing specialization, the loss of exclusivity, and the growth of technology to access information. As a result, services previously provided exclusively by lawyers now are being delivered by other occupational groups (e.g., accountants and public relations firms), and at the same time, individuals now access legal services and information on the Internet, without having to consult lawyers.

The practice of law rests on an institutional foundation, organizational constraints, and professional tasks. Although it is assumed that there are boundaries between a lawyer's work and private life, these are fluid because they are subject to open-ended demands from clients and from processes such as networking. At the task level, lawyers are expected to be endlessly available to pursue their careers in a single-minded manner. At the organizational level, they are assumed to be willing to work overtime without direct compensation as a sign of "commitment" (Epstein, Saute, Oglensky, & Gever, 1995; Sirianni & Welsh, 1991, p. 424). At an institutional level, professional autonomy rests on a system of private social support that is required to ensure release time from private (e.g., home and family) obligations. In addition to long work hours, professional success also requires some "leisure" time to pursue professional networking to make contacts and garner new clients (Seron & Ferris, 1995).

With respect to both work time and "leisure" time, professional men have an advantage over women because they can expand hours spontaneously, flexibly, and informally and thus can more easily meet the organizational expectation of professions that they put work first. The professional model thus rests on men's experience of release from domestic burdens; it gives men an implicit advantage that becomes visible by focusing on the ability to control professional time. This, in turn, rests on a "negotiated release from private time to have access to professional time" (Seron & Ferris, 1995, p. 27).

Private Law Practice

About three quarters of lawyers are in private practice, as shown in Table 5.1. However, there is wide variation in the kinds of practice, their positions within firms, the types of legal work they do, and their incomes. Women currently are only slightly less likely to enter private practice than their male counterparts; however, they leave private practice earlier and at a higher rate than their male counterparts in both the United States and Canada (Kay, 1997; Reichman & Sterling, 2004). The turnover rate is compounded for women who encounter discrimination (Kay, 1997) and women of color. A recent study found that from 1998 to 2003, nearly two thirds (64.4 percent) of minority females left private firms within 55 months of being hired (National Association for Law Placement Foundation, 2003).

Women are more likely than men to be in solo practice (53 percent versus 47 percent, respectively (Carson, 2004, p. 29). Among lawyers in firms, women are more likely than men to enter large firms that offer higher starting salaries, greater prestige, and more advancement potential than small or medium-sized firms. This apparent initial advantage was offset during the 1990s, however, by the reduction in the percentage of lawyers in private practice elevated to partnership, just as large numbers of women became eligible for elevation. In practice, this change has had a more pronounced effect on women's chances for partnerships than men's. As a result, a disproportionate number of women lawyers have remained at the associate level, and the rate at which women have moved from private practice to other employment sectors is higher than that of men. For example, in a recent survey of law graduates between 1970 and 1999 from five elite law schools (Columbia, Harvard, Boalt Hall, University of Michigan, and Yale), 51 percent of the men but only 40 percent of the women who entered private practice remained with a law firm in 2000, and 55 percent of the men but only 33 percent of the women remaining in firms had become partners (*Women in Law*, 2001). Additionally, women move up firm mobility ladders 37 percent more slowly than men and appear to be increasingly ghettoized within the legal profession (Kay, 1997).

In-House Counsel and Corporate Law

In 2000, about 8 percent of lawyers worked in corporations or for private industry (Table 5.1). Women constituted nearly a quarter of this group in the mid-1990s and more than a third in 2000 (Catalyst, 2002, note 22, cited in ABA, 2001b). However, they are not distributed evenly across in-house counsel departments of different sizes or types of business firms. They comprise 15 percent of the general counsels (i.e., top legal officers) in Fortune 500 organizations (ABA, 2006).

Despite similarities in their educational credentials, there are gender differences in the routes by which men and women found such jobs and in their current positions, salaries (Roach, 1990), and promotion opportunities (*Women in Law*, 2001). Men employed as in-house counsels disproportionately worked for corporations in the manufacturing sector and in large departments that offer substantial salaries and opportunities for advancement. In contrast, women holding in-house counsel positions were concentrated in the financial services sector and in medium-sized legal departments offering lower pay and fewer mobility opportunities. In the study of graduates from five elite law schools, the women and men in corporate legal departments differed regarding advancement. In 2000, more than half of the men but only one third of the women were general counsels; women were disproportionately represented at the assistant and associate general counsel ranks despite having two years more tenure than the men (*Women in Law*, 2001).

Women and Men in Government Work

A disproportionately large number of women attorneys are employed in government work, particularly at the state and local levels. In 1980, 17 percent of women lawyers but only 9 percent of men lawyers worked for a government. An additional 4.8 percent of women and 1.2 percent of men worked in legal aid or PD offices (Curran, 1986). In 2000, as shown in Table 5.1, the gender gap was reduced, as 10.5 percent of women and 6.5 percent of men lawyers worked for federal, state, or local governments, and 1.7 percent of women and 0.7 percent of men worked for legal aid or PD offices (Carson, 2004). As women have increased their representation in law, more have found work in private practice. Nevertheless, as column 5 in Table 5.1 indicates, more than a third of the lawyers in each of the government and PD settings are women. Women of color are especially likely to work in these settings (ABA, 2001b).

Several factors have contributed to the concentration of women in government and PD legal work. It may be attractive to women because it offers more regular and flexible hours, requires little "rainmaking" activity (i.e., bringing in clients), and is a less hostile work environment given the greater presence of other women. It also may be a "fallback" rather than the preferred option, particularly for African-American women. In a study of black women lawyers in New York, Simpson (1996) found that of the 44 percent who began their careers in government, only 21 percent stated that was their first choice of position they sought. Despite these advantages, women rated the government work environment lower than the environment in private legal settings in terms of opportunities for salary increases, professional development, and achieving career goals than did women in law firms (Rosenberg, Perlstadt, & Phillips, 1993).

Prosecutors constitute the small fraction of government lawyers involved directly in the criminal justice system. National data on the number and positions of women in these offices are not available. Nevertheless, several individual women have achieved high visibility as chiefs of important prosecutor's offices. The best know is Janet Reno, who was Attorney General of the United States during the Clinton administration (1992–2000).

The Judiciary

Because judges have great power and prestige and appointment to the bench usually occurs as a "reward" for a successful legal career, it is not surprising that women comprise a smaller proportion of the judiciary than the legal profession. There were very few women judges before 1970, but since that time, the number of female judges at both the state and federal levels has grown, particularly in the 1990s. Despite recent gains, women still are underrepresented on the bench.

At the start of 2001, women accounted for 22 percent of federal district and appellate judges (166 out of the 760 judges serving on the U.S. Court of Appeals and U.S. District Courts (ABA, 2001b). This is double the percentage in the early 1990s. At the state and local level, there has been similar growth: in 1970, there were only 200 women state court judges, when they comprised 1 percent of the state court judiciary (Feinman, 1986, p. 118). In 1991, 10 percent of the judges on courts of last resort and 10 percent of intermediate appellate court judges were women (ABA, 1988). By 2005, women comprised 22 percent of district court judges, 25.6 percent of circuit (appellate) court judges, and 28 percent of the justices on state courts of last resort (ABA, 2006).

The first breakthrough for women at the federal level came during President Carter's term (1976–1980), when 40 new women, including seven blacks and one Hispanic, were appointed to the bench. President Reagan appointed the first woman, Sandra Day O'Connor, to the U.S. Supreme Court in 1981. President Clinton appointed 100 women judges (29 percent of his judicial appointments), nearly triple the number appointed by Presidents George H. W. Bush and Reagan; he also appointed a second woman, Ruth Bader Ginsberg, to the Supreme Court in 1993. Additionally, 25 percent of Clinton's appointees were persons of color, compared with 15 percent of Reagan's and 12.4 percent of G. H. W. Bush's appointees (Pastore & Maguire, 2005, pp. 57–58).

Women have also slowly increased their representation on the bench in England, Wales, Canada, and Australia. In England and Wales, in 1998 women comprised 10.3 percent of the judiciary. By October 2004, they comprised 15.4 percent of court judges (and ethnic minority group members comprised 3.4 percent). Nevertheless, the representation of each group decreases the higher one goes in the judicial system. Thus, only 9 of the 107 High Court Judges and 1 of 12 Law Lords (the most senior judges) are women (Smith-Spark, 2004).

In Australia, the first woman judge, Dame Roma Mitchell, was appointed to the judiciary in 1965, but few women were appointed to the bench for another 30 years. A major catalyst for addressing "gender bias in the judiciary" occurred in 1993. A judge of the South Australian Supreme Court, during the course of a marital rape trial, stated that "rougher than usual handling" was acceptable on the part of a husband toward a wife unwilling to engage in conjugal relations. This led to a public outcry, government reviews of practices for making judicial appointments, and several commissions of inquiry. Although the number of women in the judiciary has grown, there currently are no women on Australia's High Court. In contrast, three of Canada's nine Supreme Court justices (including the Chief Justice) are women (Thornton, 2004).

Law School Teaching

Only 1 percent of lawyers go into full-time law school teaching, as shown in Table 5.1, yet they have a disproportionate effect on the law as role models, gatekeepers, and shapers of the next generation of practitioners. In addition, their legal writing affects lawyers' arguments and judicial decisions.

Initially, the barriers to women achieving faculty positions in law schools were even higher than those facing legal practitioners. In 1950, there were only 5 women law faculty members; they accounted for less than 0.5 percent of tenure-track faculty in law schools (Fossum, 1980). By 1977, the number of women had grown to 391 professors, who made up 8.6 percent of the tenure-track faculty, mostly at a few new and generally low-status law schools (Epstein, 1993). A decade later, Richard Chused's (1988) survey of law school faculty composition during the 1986–1987 academic year indicated that women comprised 20 percent of full-time faculty, including 45 percent of the professional skills teachers of legal writing and clinical law (who often are not considered regular faculty). His study also provided evidence that women were being denied tenure at high-prestige law schools at disproportionate rates. While about half of both the men and women law faculty candidates overall were given tenure, schools with a low proportion of women faculty, including a disproportionate share of prestigious schools, granted tenure to women at lower rates (41 percent) than men (51 percent). Additionally, he found that data on the representation of men and women of color on law school faculties suggested continuing discrimination in hiring (Chused, 1988, p. 539).

In the past two decades, women in legal education have made substantial progress, although they still are not fully represented in leadership positions and are clustered in the least prestigious academic specialties and positions. As of the 2004–2005 school year, women comprised 35 percent of law school faculty but only 25 percent of tenured faculty. They also were 19 percent of law school deans but 67 percent of the assistant deans who generally have staff positions that are not stepping-stones to deanships (ABA, 2006). Of the women faculty and deans, 11 percent were African-American women, 4 percent were Hispanic, and 3 percent were Asian-American (ABA, 2006).

Angel (2000) documented the continuation of the trend earlier noted in Chused's (1988) study that suggests that within legal education a new caste system is emerging. The majority of legal writing and clinical skills instructors, who usually are not on a tenure track, comprise the new lowest caste in that emerging system, and most of these instructors are women. In both clinical practice and legal writing fields, men are a minority, but they are overrepresented in tenured or tenure-track positions, while women disproportionately occupy the nontenure contract slots and receive lower pay. For example, women comprise 50 percent of clinical skills teachers. However, 55 percent of the men but only 37 percent of these women clinicians are tenured or in tenure-track positions. Similarly, women comprise 70 percent of the legal writing teachers, but men are twice as likely as women legal writing instructors to be tenured (13 percent versus 7 percent, respectively; Angel, 2000).

Angel's (2000) study also indicates a new trend in law schools and universities: a decrease in the percentage of faculty hired for tenure-track positions and the replacement of tenured faculty with contract faculty. Thus, just as women appear poised to make substantial gains in legal teaching and other academic specialties, they encounter new barriers that disproportionately limit their career opportunities.

During the 1990s, the gender balance in law faculty hiring changed to women's disadvantage. In 1992–1993, women made up 50 percent of the newly hired associate professors (i.e., those who were presumably on tenure track). In 1997–1998, they comprised only 39.6 percent of those hired. At the same time, they made up 60 percent of the new lecturers and instructors in 1992–1993 and 66 percent of those hired in 1997–1998 (presumably in contract rather than tenure-track positions), suggesting the growth of the "women's ghetto" in law school faculties (Angel, 2000, p. 10).

As these data suggest, women and men lawyers have different career paths. A study of Chicago lawyers who graduated after 1970 clearly illustrates the ways these paths increasingly diverge over time. At the start of their careers, women are underrepresented in solo practice and small firms and overrepresented in public sector jobs. These differences grow over the course of the career as women move out of both large and small firms and into non-firm settings in government, legal aid, and corporate work. Conversely, men are less likely to leave large firms and more likely to leave government employment as their careers develop (Hull & Nelson, 2000). These patterns suggest that women "choose" to leave firms due to inflexible work schedules that create tension between the competing demands of practice and family. But Hull and Nelson (2000, p. 253) also question whether this should be characterized as an exercise of "choice" or is, "in significant part, the product of the dynamics of gender inequality within legal employment" (labeled "gender constraints," which we will explore next. The issue of career patterns and "choices" also differs for white and black women. Simpson's (1996) study of black women lawyers in New York found that of the 42 percent who stated a desire to work in a law firm on completion of law school, only 27 percent found employment with a firm.

Gendered Legal Occupational Culture and Barriers to Women

In many ways, the legal culture is a quintessentially male world from which women have been excluded. Professional opportunities are defined by informal social networks, private (formerly all-men's) clubs, and bar associations that order status and power. Each serves as a barrier that reinforces the other. Thus, in circular fashion, the images of the law as "masculine" strengthen men's resistance to including women in informal socializing and bar association activities; their absence from informal networks and professional activities, in turn, supports the view that women do not "fit" in the profession, are not skilled at client development, and lack "commitment" to the practice of law.

Participation in the informal social world of lawyers occurs before or after long hours of legal work and means that a legal career is defined as total commitment to a "workaholic" schedule. Such work-related expectations were created when the prototypic lawyer had a wife taking care of the home and family. Most men regard the expectation of round-the-clock availability as an aspect of the legal culture that simply is one of the inevitable and necessary norms of the profession. While most women lawyers now share these professional norms, for many these work-related expectations generate difficult choices on a daily basis. When women opt not to or cannot create the impression of open-ended availability, their commitment is questioned, particularly that of women with families. Conversely, men with families are assumed to be committed out of financial necessity and are rewarded with higher salaries.

Because the prototype of the lawyer is a man, the characteristics generally associated with masculine dominance are used to explain men's successes; their failures are explained as "bad luck." Thus, men's success is regarded as a function of innate analytic and rhetorical abilities that presumably make them more suitable for practicing law. But women's success is attributed to luck, chance, or inappropriate use of their sexuality; their failures are explained as inability to "think like a lawyer" (D. Rhode, 1988). Such gender-based schemas affect promotion and salary decisions as well.

Women lawyers encounter a number of gender stereotypes and "second generation" gender bias that affect their careers. In contrast to "first generation" patterns of bias that resulted largely from deliberate intentional exclusion, "second generation" bias involves social practices and patterns of interaction among groups within the workplace that gradually exclude nondominant groups (Sturm, 2001, p. 259). Often, these behaviors rest on subtle cognitive processes including "homophily preferences" (i.e., tendencies for people to prefer to associate with others like themselves) and "status expectations" (i.e., beliefs about the superiority of some people over others in relation to some task; Roth, 2004). Together, these generate barriers for women since the men in the firm prefer to associate with others who are like themselves with whom they can communicate easily and share common interests. They also tend to expect superior performance from men compared with women and from whites compared to persons of color. Because men are valued as having higher status than women, women's competence is often evaluated more harshly than men's regardless of their numerical proportions in work groups, even when they exhibit equal performance. These disparities arise even in the absence of the evaluator's motivation to discriminate; rather, they rest on such stereotypic beliefs as the assumption that women lack aptitude for dealing with complex financial matters, are presumed not to be competent, lack commitment, and tend to overreact to criticism. Women have to work to overcome stereotypes by which they are evaluated by demonstrating superior performance (confirming women's assertion that they have to work harder to be seen as equally competent).

Bias also may take the form of excluding a woman from key social interactions, mentoring, assignment to "big" cases, or exposure to important clients. Such behaviors individually may appear gender neutral when considered in isolation since they also are experienced by men associates. However, they cumulatively produce a pattern of gender bias when connected to broader exclusionary patterns. For example, even if a woman is willing to work around the clock, often firms make decisions based on stereotypes and assume that she will not be available or believe that she should not be (Reichman & Sterling, 2002). Opportunities for such a woman are limited if the partner does not give her an assignment based on the assumption that she does not want to travel or because she is pregnant. These assumptions would not be made about an otherwise equally qualified male associate and cumulatively create a pattern of bias.

Scripts prescribe norms of professional interaction such as who can do what, with whom, and under what circumstances. They also reflect the broader cultural beliefs about gender dominance and deference. Men's positions of power and authority as partners and their general status superiority give them the right to control the structure and content of professional conversation. By controlling the professional context, men behave in ways that show that other men are taken seriously and accorded respect. Conversely, the way men talk about women and their appearance treats women as invisible, devalues them, and affects their ability to perform effectively.

For example, when a judge allows the opposing attorney to label a woman attorney's appearance a "distraction," it signals to others that it is acceptable to use a woman's looks as the basis for objecting against other women attorneys. Similarly, a judge may defer to a man attorney who monopolizes argument time or displays an aggressive style, but penalize a woman who displays the same behavior as "shrill" or too aggressive. Yet, if a woman adopts a less combative, more soft-spoken lawyering style, it is assumed to be because she is a woman, and she is regarded as "not tough enough" and treated as less effective. When a man displays a similarly non-combative style, it is viewed as simply a different style and may be regarded as "negotiating skill."

This dilemma was made clear by sociologist Jennifer Pierce (1995) in her study of litigation attorneys. In the adversarial system, where cases have winners and losers, these lawyers' emotional presentation of self is an element of their strategy and a means to dominate and control others. Litigators, who are mostly men, rely on intimidation and "strategic friendliness" to accomplish their professional goal. As Pierce notes, "Rambo litigators" do masculinized emotional labor since intimidation is associated with domination and control, and strategic friendliness is a form of emotional manipulation in competitive gamesmanship. Women litigators must contend with a situation in which the emotional labor associated with their work clearly conflicts with their gender identity and others' expectations. They face a double bind in doing litigation at the same time that they do gender in the courtroom. If they are aggressive and manipulative as zealous advocates, they risk being seen as pushy and unfeminine; if they adopt a less confrontational style, they risk being seen as too nice and ill-suited to the litigator role.

By not fitting the professional image, women lawyers are highly visible and face constant behavioral dilemmas. They must either model their professional behavior after a masculine image and suppress their femininity, or "act like women" and thus exhibit characteristics incongruent with the professional prototype, which leads to being discounted by men colleagues. Women lawyers who act "like men" are resented for being inflexible or too tough; those who act "like women" are, by definition, not acting in a "professional" (i.e., masculine) manner. Thus, women lawyers have to seek ways to be "demure but tough" (D. Rhode, 1988). Women are presumed not to be competent while their male counterparts receive the presumption of competence. In addition, feminist legal scholars encounter gendered expectations when they produce legal scholarship that gets labeled "feminist propaganda." Their critics assume that traditional legal canons are value-free, rather than representing a masculine perspective and interests.

Mentors are important teachers, advocates, and career launchers for junior associates. They help polish their mentees by giving them expanding responsibilities, opportunities to prove themselves, and exposure to clients. Many men do not want to mentor a woman because they are uncomfortable interacting with women as peers, are concerned about accusations of sexual intimacy, or do not want to invest time and energy in a woman whom they expect to leave legal work when she starts a family. The few senior women who might become mentors often lack power within the firm and have limited time for mentoring given their work and family obligations. With few mentors available, women have had difficulty learning the norms of informal behavior in the male-dominated community, "fitting in," and forming client and collegial relationships.

When women do find mentors, they tend to experience the mentoring process differently from men. Men's mentoring talk is full of ways that they are helped to belong. In contrast, Reichman and Sterling (2002) found that women describe mentoring as making them feel good about themselves, but the sense of friendship and personal bonding characteristic of the mentoring men experience is largely absent and sometimes based on a parent-child model where traditional gender roles spill over and affect the mentoring relationship.

The result of the lack of mentoring is that many female lawyers remain out of the loop of career development. For women who are denied challenging high-visibility assignments, excluded from social events that yield career opportunities, and unaided in efforts to develop marketing skills, the barriers to success often become self-perpetuating. Senior attorneys are reluctant to spend time mentoring women whom they perceive as likely to resign; women who are not aided are, in fact, more likely to leave, which "perpetuates the assumptions that perpetuate the problem," particularly for women of color (ABA, 2001, p. 6). Thus, what appears to be a choice to leave private practice "may be as much about a push away from work as it is about the pull of family" (Reichman & Sterling, 2002, p. 975).

Lawyers meet, socialize, secure clients and business contacts, plan policy, provide leadership opportunities, and set the rules of their profession through informal gatherings and formal meetings of the ABA and in the 1,700 state and local bar associations in the United States. Through the 1970s, women lawyers were denied memberships in many private clubs and positions of influence within local, state, and national bar associations. These exclusionary practices greatly hampered their legal careers.

Today, women are no longer denied membership in clubs, and some hold leadership roles in bar associations (i.e., in 2005 women comprised about one third of the membership, 27 percent of the ABA Board of Governors, and more than a quarter of its section/division chairs and committee chairs; ABA, 2006), but the continued importance of informal networks and mechanisms for securing clients and making informal social contacts with powerful bar members puts them at a disadvantage. Men and women very early in legal careers show different networking patterns. Men are more likely than women to have breakfast or lunch with partners where they strengthen informal bonds and foster "affiliating masculinities" (P. Y. Martin, 2001, p. 206), through "sucking up," doing self-promotion, and giving the partners a chance to get to know them personally and professionally so that they will be remembered when partners assign "big cases." The men join law firm governance committees; women are more likely than men to be asked to participate in less influential firm committees (e.g., recruitment) that provide service to the firm but do not translate into advancement (*After the JD*, 2004). In this way, their work "disappears" because it is seen as the so-called "softer" side of organizational practice and not as "real work."

In the courtroom, law office, and informal work-related activities, women lawyers encounter an occupational culture uncomfortable with their presence. Bringing business into the firm is an important criterion for success that generally occurs through participation in informal networks. Women now are permitted to participate in private clubs and bar association activities, but these organizations remain male dominated, and their structures, decision-making logic, and controlling images continue to pose problems for women lawyers. Participation requires that women extend their workday and "socialize" primarily with men who may be uncomfortable with their presence.

Even informal interactions such as making small talk with colleagues pose dilemmas (Epstein, 1993). A woman lawyer who is friendly is suspected of "coming on"; one who is too serious is rejected as unfriendly. Ignoring sexist jokes and comments signals tacit approval; failure to laugh leads to the label "humorless." Women get touched and interrupted more but cannot make "a thing" about this without being labeled "thin-skinned." They cannot simply behave "like lawyers"; they must negotiate their interpersonal power and find an acceptable style. Thus, gender serves as a "screen" for professional interactions so that a woman lawyer is evaluated, above all else, as a woman.

Women perceive that they are "at a disadvantage because they are operating in an alien culture" (ABA, 1988, p. 13) but have difficulty in conveying their perceptions convincingly to men. For example, between two thirds and three quarters of women lawyers report experiencing bias, but only a quarter to a third of men state they have observed it, and even fewer report experiencing it (ABA, 2001b). Worse yet, the men often trivialize women's complaints. Women's disadvantage becomes cumulative through the organizational logics and opportunity structures in the profession that calls for total career commitment, raising tensions between family and workplace issues. These and women's coping mechanisms are the focus of Chapter 6.

Summary

Before the 1970s, the number of women in law and their career opportunities were very limited. They were excluded from many law schools and denied job opportunities and bar association leadership roles. In the past three decades, large numbers of women have entered law and have made remarkable advances in the profession. At the same time, the legal profession has undergone several major changes. These include rapid expansion of the number of lawyers, changes in the nature of practice (e.g., a decline in solo practice and growth in large firms and in salaried work in public sector and corporate organizations), development of new areas of law (e.g., public interest law), and the opening of the profession to white women and to persons of color. Within private practice, changes include increased pressure for billable hours and "rainmaking," competition that has reduced collegiality within firms, and lower rates of partnership along with increasing firm size, specialization, and bureaucratization. Despite these changes, the law remains stratified by specialty and type of practice and, increasingly, by gender and race-ethnicity.

Men and women follow different legal career paths that increasingly diverge over the course of a career. To a large extent, these different trajectories are the result of the dynamics of gender inequality within the legal world. Women are more likely than men to begin in government employment and public interest work, and their representation in these sectors increases over time as they move out of private practice. Those in private practice are concentrated in less prestigious and remunerative specialties, are less likely to have mentors, and are less likely to become partners than their male counterparts. Nevertheless, it is important to recognize the enormous strides made by women lawyers. They have become partners as well as judges, law school deans, and general counsels for large corporations in increasing numbers despite the remaining obstacles posed by the legal culture.

A number of informal and sometimes invisible barriers posed by the legal culture limit women's career mobility. The prototype of the lawyer is a man with a continuous career trajectory and total availability day and night. Behavioral scripts and images of the successful recruit or partner are gendered. Referrals of clients and opportunities for leadership rest on opportunities provided by a mentor and participation in social networks and bar association activities. Women are excluded from these networks and often lack mentors. Tracked into lower status specialties, they lack visibility in the "right" specialties and do not appear to "fit in" or demonstrate "commitment" through total dedication to the law and unlimited availability. Thus, women are perceived as less competent, insufficiently committed, and too emotional to succeed in law. Less frequently given the opportunity to move onto the occupational fast track, women face subtle but often self-perpetuating cycles of gender bias that limit their career choices.

Endnotes

1. To help end "Ladies' Day" at Harvard, women of the class of 1968 on the designated day simultaneously dressed in black, wore glasses, and carried black briefcases. When the professor asked the question whose punch line was "underwear" and which was supposed to embarrass the women, the women opened their brief cases and threw fancy lingerie, instead humiliating the professor (Epstein, 1993).

2. In 1981, in the 50 largest U.S. law firms, only 20 of 4,251 partners were black (less than one half of 1 percent), and 151 of 6,408 associates (2.4 percent) were black (cited in Epstein, 1993, p. 183). According to the *National Law Journal* in 1995, there were 1,641 African-Americans working in the nation's 50 largest firms, including 351 who were partners (cited in Wilkins & Gulati, 1996, p. 7). While the numbers have increased, the proportions suggest otherwise. In 1995, African-Americans comprised the same proportion of lawyers in corporate firms as in 1981 and only 1 percent of partners. Unfortunately, these data, like many of the data provided by the ABA and National Association of Law Career Professionals broken down by gender and race ethnicity, do not present breakdowns by both demographic factors at the same time.

3. For further information on the history and status of women in law outside of the United States, see Hagan and Kay (1995) and Kay and Hagan (1998, 1999) for information on Canada; Thornton (1996) regarding Australia; Raday (1996) on Israel; and Corcos (1998) regarding women in law in the United Kingdom and other Commonwealth nations.

CHAPTER 6

The Organizational Logic of the Gendered Legal World and Women Lawyers' Response

A fair trial in a truly adversarial setting may be impossible when one of the attorneys is reduced to a laughingstock by a judge. In this way justice is defeated. Clients, confronted with such bias, are given a none-too-subtle message: get yourself a male lawyer or lose the case.

(Report of the Florida Supreme Court, 1990, p. 920)

Women pursuing legal careers encounter an alienating culture in the workplace that includes both gendered images and sexist treatment in the courtroom and other work-related settings. In addition, gendered organizational logics operating through formal policies and informal practices reinforce each other, creating "rules of the game" that are stacked against women. Together, these create dilemmas that require women lawyers to maneuver through diverse stressful "double bind" situations and to make life choices not required of most of their male counterparts.

Women have moved well beyond "token" representation and now comprise 30 percent of the legal profession. Nevertheless, they still encounter patterns of discrimination in law school classrooms and in key workplace outcomes, including financial rewards, promotions, and partnership decisions. They also face more subtle but insidious barriers, including stereotyped assumptions about their interests and skills, a lack of mentors, and consequent failure to be assigned "big" cases and introduced to the "right" clients, as discussed in Chapter 5. The long-term impact of these gender-related barriers limits women's opportunities for partnerships, judgeships, and other career options. Women lawyers also experience gender and sexual harassment and the dilemmas resulting from the continuing masculine image of a lawyer that hinder their ability to practice law.

This differential treatment, termed "gender bias," has been closely scrutinized by the legal community itself in the past two decades. Many reports have found that it pervades the organizational logic, legal culture, work-related interactions, and professional identities of lawyers (Resnik, 1996; Schafran, 2004). When such treatment occurs in the courtroom, it undercuts women lawyers' credibility and professionalism, creates double standards of performance, and affects the justice afforded litigants.

Organizational and occupational barriers confronting women in law vary across work sites and specialties. Nevertheless, across the legal landscape, the division of legal labor is gendered, as are the symbols and images of the profession (e.g., the language, dress, and ideology of law) and the interaction processes through which dominance and submission are displayed before both other lawyers and clients. These reinforce gender differences and result in gendered identities that, in turn, sustain organizational logic that supports and magnifies the growing difference in wealth and power among lawyers.

In addition to these barriers, women are disproportionately affected by inflexible workplace structures that make it difficult to mesh work and family life. Women, but not their men counterparts, often must choose between career and children and find ways to avoid long-term derailment from mobility opportunities if they take time out or seek a reduced schedule in order to have and raise children.

The "myth of meritocracy" also adversely affects women lawyers (D. L. Rhode, 1996). Despite substantial improvements for women in law in the past three decades, the "partial progress" creates barriers to further reform since "women's growing opportunities appear to be evidence that 'the woman problem' has been solved" (D. L. Rhode, 1996, p. 585). Yet three reports based on divergent approaches (American Bar Association [ABA], 2001b; Epstein, Saute, Oglensky, & Gever, 1995; Nossel & Westfall, 1997) indicate that problems remain for women in law. Progress has resulted in the dominant perception that women have moved up and that full equality is just over the horizon. Many presume that women lawyers already have achieved proportionate representation across professional contexts and that remaining disparities are due to women's own "different" choices and capabilities.

This chapter examines the organizational logics or mechanisms operating over a legal career and within various specialties that limit the career options of women; their consequences in terms of income differentials, career patterns, and occupational identities; and the manner in which women in law have sought to address and alter these limits on their careers.

Gender Bias in Law School and Its Impact on the Learning Environment

Gender bias against women seeking legal careers begins in the law school environment that emphasizes a white and middle-class masculinity. By the turn of the

21st century, women comprised half the students. Although a few studies suggest that differences in the experiences, performance, or satisfaction of law students have disappeared (e.g., Wrightman, 1996), others have found that the curriculum, pedagogy, and climate remain problematic for women. The ABA Commission on Women in the Profession (2001b) reported that women law students are more likely than men to experience sexual harassment and silencing in the classroom that are part of the lingering "hidden curriculum" of law school. In many schools, women are underrepresented in prestigious activities such as law review, moot court, and student government.

Several studies report that women are more dissatisfied than men with law school and alienated from what they regard as an inhospitable educational system that marginalizes women's issues and exposes them to "unconscious stereotypes." For example, one Yale torts professor wondered in class if there is such a thing as "the reasonable woman" (D. L. Rhode, 1997). Weiss and Melling (1988) identified four aspects of women's alienation from law school: alienation from themselves, from the law school community, from the classroom, and from the content of legal education. Alienation from the law school community, for example, includes discomfort with the competitive environment, sexist attitudes of men, and a masculine atmosphere that are part of the gendered legal culture. A follow-up study (Gaber, 1998) conducted at the same law school (i.e., Yale) also found feelings of estrangement and alienation among women students, lower classroom participation rates and lower grades than men, and diminished self-confidence during law school.

Research on students at Boalt Law School (in Berkeley, California), the University of Pennsylvania, and Harvard all indicate that women are much less likely than men to actively participate in class. The majority of women in the Boalt study, as well as most people of color, stated that they never asked questions or volunteered answers in class, in contrast to nearly two thirds of white men who stated they had done both with some frequency. Their reluctance to participate, which may have begun in the instinct for self-preservation, appears to reflect "a countercode of classroom ethics" and an active decision not to compromise the integrity of their beliefs by submitting them to the narrow legal analysis of the classroom (Homer & Schwartz, 1990). At Harvard, women volunteer to speak less often than do men, make up a significantly smaller proportion of frequent class participants, receive slightly lower grades than men (31 percent of the grades for men and 25 percent of women's grades were A– or better), and are half as likely as the men to assess themselves as being in the top 20 percent in their class in legal analysis (15 percent versus 33 percent; Working Group on Student Experiences, 2004).

A study conducted at the University of Pennsylvania Law School concluded, "the law school experience of women in the aggregate differs markedly from that of their male peers" (Guinier, Fine, Balin, Bartow, & Stachel, 1994, p. 2). Despite having identical entry-level credentials, graduating men have higher grades and more honors. Their more successful performance is established in the first year of law school and maintained over the next two years. In contrast, many women in the first year experience a "crisis of identity." When they enter law school, they are much more likely than their men classmates to be ready to fight for social justice; by the end of law school, they leave with corporate ambitions but less competitive academic credentials.

A number of factors affect women's academic performance. Many women, even those who do well academically, are alienated by the manner in which the Socratic method is used in classroom instruction.[1] They report being significantly less likely than men law students to ask questions or volunteer answers in class. They also report that men enjoy greater peer tolerance of their remarks, receive more attention from faculty during classes, get called on more often, and get more post-class "follow-up" than women. Men appear to be more comfortable speaking with faculty of either gender than women students.

Law rests on shared assumptions, but in discussions of race and gender, these assumptions are not shared, nor is it easy to talk about them. For example, when rape is discussed in criminal law class, women worry about being raped, white men fear being falsely accused by dates, and black men worry about all possible accusations. Discussion of the issues involving a rape prosecution should acknowledge that students are differently situated with respect to these issues, but often does not. Instead, discussion is abstract and impersonal to avoid polarizing the class and stirring up feelings that are difficult to control. However, as C. P. Wells (2000, pp. 524–525) asserts, "the suppression of real differences between groups inevitably marginalizes those who are not members of the dominant group."

Additionally, women's sexuality is used to keep them "in their place." When a woman expresses concerns with sexist language or assumptions or speaks too frequently, she is rumored to be a lesbian, labeled "feminazi" or "man-hater," or subject to male peers' laughter at her comments. As one of Guinier et al.'s (1994, p. 52) informants stated, "women don't speak partially because our sexuality becomes implicated as soon as we act 'too much like men' for their liking." This tends to silence those women who try to challenge the men, particularly when such incidents of bias are dismissed or ridiculed by faculty or students as "overemotional" or "ultra-feminist." This also undermines all women's sense of comfort and competence.

For many of the University of Pennsylvania's women law students, learning to think like a lawyer means learning to "become a gentleman," which exacts academic and personal costs. Rather than criticizing the intimidating learning environment, they come to regard themselves as "stupid." The combination of visible, competitive pedagogical strategies in large first-year classrooms, peer hazing, and "the emphasis on replacing 'emotions' with 'logic' and 'commitments' with 'neutrality'" socializes even those trying to resist to "stay in their place" (Guinier et al., 1994, p. 71).

For women of color, racism sometimes compounds sexism. As C. P. Wells (2000, p. 529) points out, individual incidents may seem trivial, but these "microaggressions" accumulate for women of color. For example, in a newsletter distributed to students titled "2nd Annual International Girls Night Out: Bodies in Lotion," meant to parody a student-sponsored symposium on women's rights, the students made up a panel called "The TOYS-R-US Lecture: Women as Property: How to Get the Most Work Out of Your Mail Order Chilean Bride: You Too Can Own Your Own in Fee Simple for a Simple Fee." Since sexual exploitation of third world women is a real problem and deeply resonates with the experience of many women students, many do not see this as humorous.

In addition, the curriculum often is remote from women's concerns. Mary Jo Frug (1992) identified several ways in which apparently "gender-neutral" law courses and casebooks on contract law are gendered. First, the parties in cases are predominantly men, and they represent many different occupations and roles; the few women in illustrative cases are found in stereotypically women's occupations and domestic roles. Language in both text and cases sometimes uses "he" to refer to persons of both genders. In addition, cases used to illustrate principles such as "mutuality of assent" are drawn from commercial settings in which men predominate, even though issues of concern to women, such as reproductive technology and cohabitation, also might illustrate contractual principles. Frug (1992, p. 71) adds,

> By confining issues that particularly concern women to domestic relations or sex discrimination courses, casebooks combine with standard law school curriculums to perpetuate the idea that women's interests are personal, concerning only themselves or their families. Men, in contrast, are concerned with the rest of life.

Even topics of obvious importance, such as rape in criminal law, are sometimes excluded "because the issues appear too politically or emotionally freighted for 'rational' discussion'" (D. L. Rhode, 1997, p. 220). Issues of particular concern to lesbians and women of color are also largely absent. And, when matters involving race or sexuality arise, affected students are questioned about their experiences, which then may be discounted by classmates as self-interested.

Gender Bias in the Firm, Office, and Agency

On the job, women lawyers' activities and rewards differ from those of men. These result in lower rates of partnership, lower income, and greater dissatisfaction with their compensation and other working conditions.

Partnership and Gender

By the mid-1980s, women should have had enough time in the profession to have attained their share of partnerships, yet they did not. For example, a study of the Harvard Law School class of 1974 found that by 1985, only 23 percent of the women had made partner, compared with 51 percent of their male classmates (Abrahamson & Franklin, 1986). A decade later, the New York City Bar's "Glass Ceiling" study of eight large firms found that women were three times less likely to become partners as men (Epstein et al., 1995). A survey of Chicago lawyers sponsored by the American Bar Foundation (Hull & Nelson, 2000, p. 14) reported that

> in spite of improvements over time, . . . only 60 percent as many female lawyers were partners in law firms . . . as would have been expected had women been fully represented among partners. Moreover, when representation is controlled for age, women are persistently under-represented in all age groups.

A 1990 survey of lawyers called to the bar from 1975 to 1990 in Ontario, Canada, indicated that by 1990, 45 percent of the men were partners compared with 25 percent of the women. Additionally, men were nearly 50 percent more likely than women to attain partnership after controlling for a variety of factors such as family background, law school grades, and hours worked (Kay & Hagan, 1998). A follow-up study of these lawyers conducted in 1996 found that the men were 110 percent more likely than women to become partners, and that even after controlling for such factors as specialization in a prestigious field and higher billable hours, women overall experienced lower chances for partnership than their male colleagues (Kay & Hagan, 1999).

In an additional analysis of their data, Kay and Hagan (1998) broke the sample into exceptional, average, and below-average men and women. They found that exceptional women did as well as exceptional men. Average and below–average men also were as likely to become partners as exceptional men. However, that was not the case for average and below-average women. Only women who endorse firm culture with exceptional intensity approach men's partnership success, while men become partners regardless of their disposition to firm culture. In explaining this finding, the authors observe that the partnership selection process seems to include a predisposition not to offer women partnerships. Rather, it requires them to demonstrate exceptional qualities that make it difficult for the firm to deny advancement. Women must show extraordinary work commitment by bringing in new clients, establishing a large network of corporate clients, returning quickly from maternity leave, continuing to docket high numbers of hours per week, and expressing a commitment to firm culture by endorsing practice-oriented career goals. Thus, they are required to embody standards that are an "exaggerated form of a partnership ideal and these standards are imposed uniquely on women" (Kay & Hagan, 1998, p. 741). In sum, to attain partnership, women must overcome the unstated assumption that they are less committed to their careers than men.

Gender Differences in Income

There are also consistent differences in the income of men and women lawyers that can only partially be accounted for by factors other than discrimination. Differences in the type and size of the firm in which they work, legal specialty, and partnership status each also contribute to these income differences. *After the JD* (2004), a national study of lawyers admitted to the bar in 2000, reveals a significant difference in the earnings of men and women at the earliest stage of their career. Women's median salary in their first job as a lawyer is $66,000, compared to $80,000 for men (i.e., women make 83 cents per each dollar made by a man). The difference is not attributable only to the practice setting. In law offices of 251 or more lawyers, there is a $15,000 difference in men's and women's salaries. Large gaps also are found in pay in corporate law departments.

Sociologists Nancy Reichman and Joyce Sterling (2004) used Colorado Bar Association survey and interview data collected in 1993 and in 1999 to investigate changes in the gender pay gap over the legal career. They report that the gender gap in pay decreased from 1993 to 1999 for lawyers with 1 to 3 years of experience (women earned 82 percent of men's income in 1993 and 92 percent in 1999) and for those with four to nine years of experience (women earned 86 percent of men's income in 1993 and 96 percent in 1999). However, the differential between earned income of men and women lawyers grew slightly for those in the group with less than one year of experience (women made 96 percent of men's income in 1993 and 92 percent of their income in 1999) and for those with 10 to 20 years of experience (women made 76 percent in 1993 and 74 percent of men's incomes in 1999; Reichman & Sterling, 2004, p. 10–11). Controlling for type of position provided mixed results. Women partners in 1999 narrowed the pay differential, but the gap grew for women associates, who had made 94 cents to the dollar earned by male counterparts in 1993 but only 65 cents to the dollar in 1999.

Huang's (1997) study of the gender wage gap compared 950 lawyers who graduated from four law schools in the classes of 1969–1971, 1980, and 1990. The study found evidence of occupational segregation by legal specialty and by sector; women disproportionately are found in low-status specialties and in the public sector and suffer a negative income effect for this, as do men, but to a lesser extent. However, differences in the earnings structure of the legal profession over time and across graduating groups explained most of the gender gap in wages. Within each sector, the men graduates in the first two groups surpassed the women graduates in those groups in terms of promotions and earnings increases. Those women who did become partners got smaller income premiums on their advancement than those received by men. In addition, men were rewarded financially for marrying and were not penalized for taking time out of the labor force; women were penalized both for marriage and for taking time out of the labor force or working part-time.

After controlling for these and other factors, Huang (1997) found the gap between men's and women's income increased from 5 years after law school to 10 years after law school. The proportion of unexplained gender wage gap was greater for lawyers working at private firms than for all lawyers. This suggests that there is a higher degree of wage discrimination in private law firms than elsewhere in law. Huang (1997, p. 298) concludes, "while it is difficult to separate choice from forced segregation . . . occupational segregation does exist within the profession of law and men and women follow different career patterns and experience different benefits and penalties."

Kay and Hagan (1998) studied the factors contributing to the large differences between the incomes of men and women lawyers in private practice in Toronto, Canada. They distinguished between the effects of discrimination and nondiscriminatory "composition" factors, which include differences attributable to specialty, experience, and practicing in a growing sector of the law. Among lawyers in private practice, men not only earn more than women after controlling for experience and specialty, but they also get a much larger financial return than women both from going to an elite school and from years of experience. Consequently, for each year of experience, the gender income gap grows larger.

Other Gender Differences in Practice

Another aspect of discrimination against women lawyers that results in dissatisfaction is their failure to get the challenging and visible assignments. A study of women lawyers in one Midwestern capital reported that substantial proportions of women working in private law firms (45 percent) and courts (46 percent) claimed they received less interesting and challenging assignments. This form of discrimination was the factor that most negatively affected women's view of the work environment and undermined their expectations of opportunities for professional growth, promotion, and commitment to law (Rosenberg, Perlstadt, & Phillips, 1993). Other studies (Epstein et al., 1995; Reichman & Sterling, 2004) also find that women report being assigned to less challenging cases. This pattern appears to result from the lack of a mentor to steer good assignments to them. Without such a sponsor, those making assignments do so on the basis of stereotypes and assumptions: women have feminine personalities and are perceived as not tough enough to handle business law and courtroom stresses or as simply lacking commitment to their careers. This puts women in a "no win" situation: accept the low-visibility and less challenging cases (reinforcing the stereotype of a lack of ambition), or complain and risk being perceived as a "whiner" or worse. "Tough" women face disapproval from both men and women colleagues for adopting a masculine model of behavior; women who conform to culturally emphasized feminine behavior are viewed as behaving in un-lawyerly ways. In addition, in many law firms, for associates without mentors, monitoring is loose and performance evaluations are subjective. These problems are compounded when evaluators/supervisors have little accountability and the persons evaluated are women of color or lesbians. Women of color often encounter higher performance demands and negative stereotypes that attribute their positions to affirmative action rather than professional qualifications (ABA, 2001b, p. 15).

The Impact of Gender Bias on Women Attorneys in Court and Beyond

Credibility is crucial for any attorney, especially for those who work in the courtroom. Yet in this setting, women attorneys often are subjected to treatment that undermines their ability to act as effective advocates for clients, biasing the rendering of justice.

The nature, extent, and impact of gender bias in the courtroom and other legal environments have been amply documented in the past two decades (ABA, 2001b; Epstein, 1993; Gellis, 1991; Hensler & Resnik, 2003; MacCorquodale & Jensen, 1993; Maryland Special Joint Committee, 1989; Report of the Florida Supreme Court, 1990; Resnik, 1996; Schafran, 1987, 2004). These studies found the legal world filled with sexist jokes, disparaging or patronizing treatment, inappropriate terms of address, remarks that call attention to the woman's gender, and other displays of a lack of respect. In addition, women lawyers encounter inappropriate touching and *quid pro quo* sexual harassment. These behaviors hamper women's work performance by undermining their self-image and credibility as lawyers.

Sexual Harassment

Many gender bias task force reports identified sexual harassment as a widespread problem for women in law. As illustrated in Table 6.1, these reports documented the

Table 6.1   Percent of Women Lawyers Reporting
Inappropriate Behaviors in State Gender Bias Reports

State	Inappropriate Names		Comments on Appearance	
	Attorneys	Judges	Attorneys	Judges
Indiana		64		59
Maryland	73	45	76	54
Minnesota	59	35	59	42
New Hampshire	67[a]	18	56[a]	11
New Jersey	85	61	68	54
Rhode Island	85		53	
North Carolina	57	32	35	18
Florida	75	53	74	47

Sources: Data from Gellis (1991) and Padavic and Orcutt (1997).

a. Outside courtroom; comparable figures for the same behavior in chambers or court are 40 percent and 23 percent.

frequent occurrence of two forms of harassment that make the work environment a hostile one: inappropriate terms of address and comments on appearance. In addition, they found that women lawyers often encounter disparaging remarks, sexist jokes, and *quid pro quo* harassment. For example, the Indiana gender bias report found that 11 percent of the women lawyers in that state had experienced physical sexual harassment, and 40 percent reported verbal harassment related to their work (Gellis, 1991). In Maryland, 47 percent of the women surveyed by the task force said women attorneys are subjected to verbal or physical sexual advances by other counsel (Maryland Special Joint Committee, 1989). A quarter of the women lawyers in a Midwestern capital reported unwanted sexual advances in a professional situation, and 85 percent of those reported their occurrence more than once in the prior year (Rosenberg et al., 1993).

Even as women have moved beyond token representation in law, they continue to have greater visibility with respect to their physical appearance than to their legal skill or reputation (see Table 6.1) and encounter patterns of offensive behavior that are directed most often at female participants in the legal system (Resnik, 1996). A survey of lawyers in Pima County, Arizona, testing the effects of tokenism found that women reported frequent compliments on their appearance but infrequent praise for handling a case or for their legal reputation; men reported complements on their legal activities but not on their appearance. Moreover, 38 percent of the women but only 6 percent of the men believed men counsel get more attention and credibility from judges than women counsel; no respondents believed women get more. This gives women a message that they are valued only for appearance (MacCorquodale & Jensen, 1993).

Sexist jokes contribute to a hostile work environment. In the Rhode Island gender bias study, 53 percent of the women reported hearing sexist jokes; in the Minnesota study, 63 percent of the women respondents had heard such jokes or demeaning remarks (Gellis, 1991); in the Pima County study, over 80 percent of the

women heard judges and attorneys make sexist jokes and remarks at least occasionally, more often at social events than at meetings, and rarely in court (MacCorquodale
& Jensen, 1993).

The frequency and type of sexual harassment vary across types of legal work
sites. Comparing three types of private sector work settings (solo practice, law firm,
and in-house counsel) and three categories of public sector settings (government
agencies, courts, and other settings) in one city, Rosenberg et al. (1993) found that
harassment was widespread, but it was more common in private than public sector
work. Nearly a quarter of the women overall and nearly half of those employed in
law firms experienced sexual advances.

Data from the Eighth (Federal) Circuit Gender Fairness Task Force indicate that
75 percent of women had experienced some type of incivility in the court in the
past five years in the context of federal litigation compared to half of the men. The
types of incivility differed by the gender of the target (Cortina, Lonsway, Magley,
Freeman, Collinsworth, Hunter, & Fitzgerald, 2002). About half of the women had
experienced gender-related incivility, and another 9 percent encountered unwanted
sexual attention, while only 13 percent experienced only general incivility. In comparison, 14 percent of the men experienced gender-related incivility, and only
1 percent were subjected to unwanted sexual attention, although 34 percent experienced only general incivility. Many women's descriptions of specific incidents
indicated the gendered nature of disrespectful behaviors. These included derogatory comments about an attorney's pregnancy, being excluded by male judges or
attorneys who engaged in discussions of mutual interests, professional discrediting,
and gender disparagement involving sexist or sex-role stereotypic jokes or comments. Less frequently, women reported sexually suggestive comments about their
physical appearance, being mistaken for nonlawyers, and physical or sexual touching. Male attorneys were the principal source of both gender-related incivilities and
the unwanted sexual attention.

Several illustrations suggest the nature and impact of such gender-related incidents. The Indiana Commission on Women in the Profession reported that one
county bar association invited its members to attend a dinner in which a featured
event was "to get drunk and come on to babes." In response to a letter of complaint
from a woman bar member, the association printed her letter on the place mats
used at the dinner (Gellis, 1991). Similarly, an attorney testified at hearings in
Florida that her sexual harassment complaint to a judicial ethics commission was
made public and, as a result, she was ostracized by the legal community.[2]

Sexist jokes and remarks heighten group boundaries by reinforcing tokens' feelings
of isolation, polarizing gender divisions, and testing women's loyalty (Kanter, 1977).
When a sexist joke is told, others wait to see if the woman will react "like a woman,"
with offense and anger, or will respond like "one of the boys" by laughing, even if it is
at the expense of women. Such jokes also reflect the status hierarchy, because they are
told about out-groups rather than those in the power structure. A woman telling a joke
about men's sexuality would be regarded as a display of "bad taste."

A recent report of the ABA observed that by the turn of the 21st century, there
has been "considerable progress" in the legal profession in addressing sexual harassment, at least at the formal level. The vast majority of law firms have adopted

sexual harassment policies that generally follow federal regulations prohibiting sexual advances and conduct that creates a hostile working environment. Yet, as that report continues, "the gap between formal prohibitions and actual practices remains substantial" since recent surveys indicate that "between half and two thirds of women lawyers report experiencing or observing sexual harassment" (ABA, 2001b, p. 19). In addition, an even higher percentage believe it remains a problem in their workplaces.

The individual costs and larger consequences of harassment are high. At the individual level, though few women make complaints, men express concerns about unjust accusations. This results in reported reluctance to mentor or socialize informally with younger women for fear of the appearance of sexual impropriety, thus depriving women of opportunities open to men. In addition, sexual harassment may serve to maintain the status quo of male dominance and female subordination by using hostility to women as a means of maintaining control. Thus, "seemingly trivial incivility can perpetuate the relegation of women to the margins of professional society" (Cortina et al., 2002, p. 256).

Undermining Women Lawyers' Credibility in the Courtroom

Women lawyers often face displays of disrespect in the courtroom from judges and other attorneys. Forms of disparagement that reinforce gendered cultural images include condescending treatment, allusion to a woman's gender characteristics or sexuality, and restatement of arguments. Women are addressed through infantilizing terms (e.g., "honey," "doll"; shown in Table 6.1), by their first name, or by another term that emphasizes social status ("woman attorney"), while men are addressed as "Mr." or by a term emphasizing professional status ("counselor"). Such behavior may undermine a client's confidence in his or her attorney's ability to handle a case and diminish credibility in the eyes of jurors and other court personnel. When it occurs in open court, a lawyer faces a bind: confront the issue and threaten the interest of the client or remain silent and accept a tarnished professional image. For a lawyer whose livelihood depends on attracting clients, often by having a "track record" of winning cases, the effects of such disrespectful behavior may be devastating. Thus, doing "femininity" and successful trial work are not compatible.

Byrna Bogoch (1999) used quantitative and qualitative analyses of actual observational data identifying judges', lawyers', and witnesses' terms of address, challenging comments, and use of directives in Israeli district courts. She found that women judges and lawyers were shown less deference than men judges and lawyers, and that their professional competence was challenged more frequently. These experiences threaten and engender the woman's professional identity. For example, in addressing men judges, about one third of the address forms used by lawyers were courtroom specific (i.e., "your honor," "the court"); for women judges, the comparable forms were used less than half as often (14 percent of the time). She also observed that in the courtroom, women lawyers were interrupted more often than men lawyers. Both men and women judges interrupted women prosecutors and defense attorneys (DAs) more than they did men prosecutors or DAs. Similarly, women prosecutors were interrupted more often by DAs and witnesses of both sexes than men prosecutors. If these interruptions reflect power differentials, they suggest that courtroom participants feel more powerful in relation to women lawyers than men lawyers.

Bogoch's (1999) analysis of comments made in the courtroom also suggests gender differences that undermine women lawyers. The adversarial relationship between lawyers was intensified when men and women attorneys were on opposite sides in a trial, as the conflict took on an element of a challenge to the woman attorney's professional performance. When judges called lawyers to task or challenged their role performance, women attorneys were criticized for mistakes and weak arguments, whereas men attorneys were challenged for being too aggressive (e.g., leading witnesses). When a woman attorney became angry, the judge tended to tell her not to be so emotional; when a man lawyer showed anger, the judge merely described him as angry. Thus, only the women were taken to task for emotionality, reinforcing Pierce's (1995) observation that men's use of intimidation is a taken-for-granted norm of their masculine adversarial tactics in the courtroom, while women face structural constraints on their use of masculine aggressive emotional labor in the courtroom. Bogoch (1999, p. 367) concludes that men's competence is taken for granted, while women lawyers are addressed and treated "in ways that undermined their professional status," hampered their ability to perform, and imply that women lawyers cannot be trusted to perform as ably as their male counterparts.

Men's Perceptions of Gender Bias

Men often claim to be unaware of the diverse forms of gender-biased behavior. Thus, while more than two thirds of the women in nearly every gender bias survey indicated they had experienced various forms of discriminatory treatment, less than a third of the men reported observing such behavior. For example, in Florida, 70 percent of the women attorneys and 58 percent of women judges but only 45 percent of men attorneys and 25 percent of men judges (who tend to be older, and age was also associated with lack of recognition) stated that men attorneys make demeaning remarks and jokes displaying disrespect for women colleagues (Padavic & Orcutt, 1997). Most men not only fail to perceive gender bias, they appear to regard complaints of discrimination as imaginary or as an overly sensitive reaction to their well-intentioned acts (P. Y. Martin, Reynolds, & Keith, 2002). These views persist despite the consistency of gender bias task force report findings. Other studies report high rates of bias based on race, sexual orientation, and disabilities as well as their invisibility to dominants (ABA, 2001b).

Organizational Logic and Limiting Opportunity Structures

In law, as in many occupations, there is an "opportunity structure," or set of positions that usually lead to obtaining the credentials and visibility needed to achieve a highly coveted position such as judge, law school dean, or police chief (Kanter, 1977). Women face a "glass ceiling," or limit on opportunities to climb beyond certain lower steps on the career ladder. Recently, some even have suggested that a "sticky floor" on which women are stuck is the more appropriate metaphor for the barriers that result in some women's failure to advance, their discouragement, and their dropout from legal work (Reichman & Sterling, 2002).

The processes through which gender differences arise across types of work settings, areas of specialization, income, and other employment outcomes rest, in part, on gendered organizational logic. Across the spectrum of legal practice, the rules and informal practices on which advancement decisions are based continue to rest on a linear, masculine "professional" model. In that model, work comes first, work-related social and professional organizational activities play a key part in cultivating contacts that contribute to the career, domestic and family responsibilities are limited, and the lawyer's career is uninterrupted. Since the time demands on which this model rests are open-ended and in part unpaid, professions require a system of "social capital," or private social support that allows the professional to give work tasks priority and ensure release time from private (e.g., family) obligations (Kay & Hagan, 1998, 1999; Seron & Ferris, 1995). Bias or discriminatory practices emerge from ongoing behavior that is shaped by the structure of daily decision making and workplace relationships. These include patterns of interaction, informal norms, networking, training, mentoring, and performance evaluation. First generation (i.e., overt) discrimination has been supplanted by "second generation employment discrimination" (Sturm, 2001), which affects women and minorities through discretionary decision making and the absence of systematic assessments of the fairness of these decisions in the aggregate. Advancement depends on informal decisions about case assignment, access to training, and exposure to important clients. Mentoring blurs the line between personal and professional interaction. Because many law firms do not do systematic tracking of work assignments and promotions, firm management is unaware of problems of bias that arise from ongoing patterns of interaction. These, in turn, are shaped by organizational culture and emerge from workplace conditions. Over time, they come to constitute the structure for inclusion or exclusion.

Women who do not play by these "professional" rules (e.g., they eat lunch at their desks, take advantage of flexible working hours or maternity leave, and do not attend bar association meetings) generally are disadvantaged in promotion decisions or are stigmatized as "double deviants" (as lawyers and women; Epstein, Seron, Oglensky, & Saute, 1999). From women's perspective, they are efficient and the men are wasting time by doing interpersonal rather than instrumental tasks. Men, however, do not consider that the women may be more efficiently using their time in the office. Instead, they criticize the women for failing to do gender as the men do (e.g., lingering after meetings and dropping by others' desks to chat and "do affiliative masculinity"; P. Y. Martin, 2001). How such gendered organizational logics operate at various career stages and sites is illustrated at three points in a legal career by our examination of selective job recruitment mechanisms, judicial selection practices, and the tenuring of law professors.

Organizational Logic, Gendered Job Recruitment, and the Hiring Process

As new lawyers, women encounter barriers in the recruitment, job interview, and selection processes. Although questions about their marital status, plans for pregnancy, and husband's occupation are prohibited, several gender bias task forces documented numerous instances of women still being asked just such questions through the 1980s (ABA, 1988; Gellis, 1991).

Sociologist Elizabeth Gorman (2005) examined law firms' structural mechanisms and recruitment practices that ostensibly are gender neutral but actually have differential impacts on men and women. She also explored the interactional mechanisms that influence decision makers evaluating job candidates. She found that gender-related mechanisms begin with employers' classification of candidates for jobs into sex categories. This triggers two important processes: the application of cultural schemas and stereotypes, and favoritism toward members of the decision maker's own sex. She observed that when selection criteria include more stereotypically masculine characteristics, women comprise a smaller proportion of new hires; conversely, when criteria include stereotypically more feminine traits, women represent a higher proportion of new hires. Additionally, women hiring partners fill more vacancies with women than do men in that position. Even when an open position is not sex-typed, there is a corresponding role-incumbent schema that may include stereotypical gendered abilities and traits, sometimes based on the characteristics of prior incumbents in the position.

The hiring of entry-level associates by large firms involves a three-step process. Initially, firms typically send one or more representatives to campuses to conduct interviews at law schools. Students only need to submit a resume and sign up for the interview without prior screening. The campus recruiters send their evaluations and the applicants' resumes and transcripts to the law office's hiring partner. That partner alone or with a committee selects candidates for "callback" visits to the office. Candidates are interviewed by several partners and associates, who send their impressions to the hiring partner. Based on this feedback, the hiring partner decides whether to extend an offer to a candidate.

Gorman (2005) found that 40 percent of new associate hires were women, whereas 43 percent of those initially interviewed at the law schools were women. Greater numbers of hiring criteria that were stereotypically masculine had a more negative effect on women's selection. One additional masculine attribute lowered the odds that a job would be filled by a woman by about 6 percent; conversely, the increase of one feminine criterion increased the odds of filling a vacancy with a woman by about 16 percent. In addition, when the hiring partner was female, women's likelihood of being hired increased by 13 percent. The proportion of current associates that were women also had a strong positive effect on the proportion of women hired. Gorman (2005) concluded that the gender-stereotypicality of ideas about the kind of people who are likely to perform well in a given job (as indicated by selection criteria) affects the gender composition of new hires; organizational decision makers view men and women candidates through the lens of gender stereotypes. In addition, the gender of the organizational decision maker matters; firms with female hiring partners fill a higher percentage of openings with women.

In a related vein, E. Chambliss and Uggen (2000) found minority partner representation itself also had a positive effect on the representation of women and minority associates. For women, African-American, Hispanic, and Asian-American lawyers, a large proportion of such partners increased their representation as associates in the firm. This may arise due to self-selection of the associates, active efforts by minority partners to promote the interests of minorities in their workplace, a change in the criteria by which minorities are evaluated, or all of these factors. These findings illustrate the operation of the preference for homophily (Roth, 2004) and may also, conversely, suggest some of the processes that disadvantage African-American lawyers in elite firms (Wilkins & Gulati, 1996).[3]

Merritt and Reskin (1997) examined tenure-track hiring for first-time law faculty at accredited law schools between 1986 and 1991. Focusing on the effects of race and sex and affirmative action, they found little evidence that law schools gave preference to women or persons of color over white men in the applicant pool. After controlling for academic credentials, work experience, and personal characteristics, there was a modest preference for white women and minority men over white men with similar credentials at the more prestigious schools. That advantage was small and was offset by other factors. Women of color got no affirmative action benefit. They fared no better than comparably qualified white men in getting jobs at prestigious institutions.

The study also found evidence of persistent sex bias in law faculty hiring. Men (both white and nonwhite) were more likely to begin teaching at a higher professorial rank (i.e., associate professor or professor) than white women and women of color who began at the assistant rank, even after controlling for credentials and publication records. The men also received higher starting salaries. Having a nonemployed partner greatly increased the likelihood of a high-ranking appointment (and the higher salary it conferred). While this factor would appear to be gender neutral on its face, far more men than women have non-employed partners, further disadvantaging women. Finally, men were more likely than women to teach constitutional law, a higher-status course, whereas women were more likely than men to teach trusts and estates or skills courses, although the men's and women's work experiences cut against the sex-based difference in teaching area. The authors conclude that given the stated commitment of law faculties to affirmative action during the time under examination, there is "surprisingly little evidence that sex or race preferences advantaged women or minorities" and clear evidence that women of color "face distinctive sex and race biases in the job market" (Merritt & Reskin, 1997, p. 275).

Gender Barriers to a Judgeship

Traditionally, a judgeship has been the final step and highest achievement in a long legal career. Not surprisingly, women are underrepresented on the bench because they are still underrepresented in the law, have less time in the profession, and have fewer of the experiences considered "prerequisites" for a judgeship. Nevertheless, they have made great progress in the past 25 years. Traditionally, the "fast track" to a federal judgeship has involved graduation with honors from an elite university and law school, a prestigious clerkship, partisan political experience, experience in the U.S. Department of Justice, and partnership in an elite law firm. Factors associated with state judgeships are similar but include greater emphasis on localism (i.e., being born and educated in state), experience as a prosecutor or legislator rather than federal government experience, and local political activism that creates ties to "the good old boys." Many of these factors continue to work against women's appointment to the bench.

Although women now are equally represented in elite law schools, their grades tend to be lower, which may contribute to their getting a lower proportion of the top clerkships with judges. For example, among the 385 Yale Law School graduates from the classes of 1988 through 1996 who clerked for the U.S. Court of Appeals, only 132 (34 percent) were women, and 12 of the 49 students who clerked at the Supreme Court (24 percent) were women. Clerkships at Federal District Courts and state court clerkships were more evenly split (*Yale Law School Faculty and Students Speak about Gender,* 2001–2002).

Women also are disadvantaged along the primary routes to the bench. In private practice, they are slower and less likely to make partner than their male counterparts. They also are underrepresented on elite law school faculties. The third route to prestigious judgeships, through service on local or municipal courts and in politics, may still be blocked by political party power brokers and other "gatekeepers," many of whom regard a candidate's male gender as an unwritten qualification for a judgeship.

In addition, the judicial selection process itself often rests in the hands of nominating bodies that apply different standards to men and women applicants. In Florida, for example, the Judicial Nominating Commission gave greater weight to certain areas of law perceived as traditionally masculine (e.g., commercial law) while disparaging areas of specialization (e.g., family law) perceived to be more "feminine." The Commission favored lawyers in private practice, while women disproportionately were employed in public sector work (Report of the Florida Supreme Court, 1990).

Despite these barriers, many women have attained judgeships across the spectrum of courts in the past two decades. By the turn of the 21st century, women represented 20 percent of the judiciary at the Federal District and Circuit Court levels (E. Martin, 2004) and 24 percent of justices of state supreme courts (E. Martin & Pyle, 2002). Political scientist Elaine Martin (2004) identified three primary ways by which the representation of women among judges can increase. First, the eligible pool of women lawyers available and qualified for judgeships can increase. As the ratio of women to men lawyers increases, so does the pool of women, although this process is very slow. Second, official gatekeepers (e.g., presidents, governors, or voters) may deliberately select women beyond their limited proportion within the eligible pool. As is shown in Table 6.2, Presidents Carter, Reagan, G. H. W. Bush, and Clinton all sought out and selected a higher percentage of women judges than was in the pool even if one defined the pool as broadly as all women lawyers (many of whom lack the legal experience required for a judgeship). The third way to increase the number of women judges is to redefine the eligible pool so as to include variables more characteristic of women's careers in law, thereby increasing the number and proportionality of women in the actual eligible pool. The three methods are

Table 6.2   Presidential Appointments of Women Judges and Eligible Pool Percentages: 1976–2000

Court Level	Clinton 1992–2000		Bush 1988–1992		Reagan 1980–1988		Carter 1976–1980	
	Percent	Number	Percent	Number	Percent	Number	Percent	Number
District court	28.9	88	19.6	29	8.3	24	14.4	29
Appeals court	32.8	20	18.9	7	5.1	4	19.6	11
Supreme court	50.0	1			25.0	1		
Women as Percentage of Eligible Pool								
	1993		1987		1980		1977	
State supreme	11.2		6.5		3.6		3.0	
State trial	8.5		7.3		2.4		2.5	
Lawyers	19.0		13.0		8.0		6.0	
New law degrees	45.0		40.0		30.0		12.0	

Source: Data from E. Martin (2004).

not mutually exclusive, and all operated in the last quarter of the 20th century, as each of the U.S. presidents from Jimmy Carter (1976–1980) through Bill Clinton (1992–2000) to varying degrees diversified the federal bench.

To increase the number of women judges, President Carter altered the traditional selection criteria and process. First, he modified appointment procedures to expand the number and types of people participating in the judicial selection process by establishing Circuit (appellate) Court nominating panels and encouraging use of merit selection panels to nominate judges to the District (lower) Courts. In addition, Carter expanded the eligible pool of potential women judges by seeking women with different career characteristics than the men in the eligible pool.

As a result of the change, Carter appointed 40 women to the federal bench out of his 258 judicial appointments (16 percent). Carter's women judges were younger (most were under 50; most of the men were over) and less likely to be partners in traditional law firms. They were also more likely to have worked in a prosecutor's office than the men he appointed (24 versus 48 percent, respectively) and were more likely than the men to have had judicial experience (58 versus 55 percent, respectively) or to come from a law school faculty (13 percent versus 6 percent). The women judges also were more likely than the men to have attended an elite college and law school and to have graduated with honors, but less likely to have been politically active. Men of color appointed by Carter also were drawn from the lower judiciary and were more likely than white men to have been public defenders prior to coming to the bench. Carter's white men candidates, in contrast, tended to follow the well-worn path to a federal judgeship: after long legal experience largely in successful private practices, having been active in partisan politics, their "merit" was rewarded by appointment to the bench.

Because white women and men and women of color followed different legal career paths, President Carter used alternative procedures and selection criteria to appoint them to the federal bench. Opposition to Carter's changes was muted by passage of the Omnibus Judgeship Act of 1978, which created 152 new federal court judgeships so that all groups could make gains.

President Reagan abolished Carter's nominating commission and relied instead on the recommendations of White House and Justice Department officials. A key element in their choice was the candidate's ideological "correctness." He appointed fewer women than Carter (28 women out of 368 or 7.6 percent of vacancies went to women). George H. W. Bush's approach continued Reagan's process and goals of selecting judges as a way to cultivate conservative elements in his political base. However, in the last year of his term, he sought to locate more women for appointment and named more than half of all his women judicial appointments in the year in which he ran unsuccessfully for reelection. The result was the appointment of 36 women to the 185 vacancies he filled (19 percent). President Clinton dramatically increased the number and proportion of women on the federal bench. During his first term, white males comprised less than half of his appointees to federal District Courts. Despite difficulties with the Senate in his second term, overall Clinton appointed 108 women out of 366 seats (30 percent; E. Martin, 2004).

Comparing the four presidents' federal District Court appointees, Carter and Clinton were most likely to select women already on the bench; Reagan and Bush were most likely to select women in private practice. Most of the women appointed by all four presidents had either judicial or prosecutorial experience. The women appointed by all four presidents were, on average, younger at the time of appointment than the men.

E. Martin (2004) concludes that the paths to the bench for women (at least those appointed by Democrats) have changed since 1976. Carter drew strongly from state court benches for his appointments, while Clinton relied both on sitting judges and on government attorneys. These changes seem to be associated with changes in women lawyers' career patterns. Overall, women continue to be less likely to come from private law firms and are still more likely than their male counterparts to have judicial and prosecutorial experience. These differences reflect the reality of the career differences between men and women lawyers.

E. Martin and Pyle (2002) conducted a similar study focusing on gender and racial diversification of state supreme courts, which historically have been overwhelmingly white and male. Here, too, the number of women judges has increased dramatically, from a handful nationwide in 1980 to as many as 20 percent of the bench in some states. At the beginning of 1999, the women comprised 16 percent of the 325 state supreme court justices. On average, all judges in 1999 were younger than their counterparts in 1980 largely because white women and nonwhite men and women judges were younger. Between 1980 and 1999, an increasing proportion of state supreme court justices had served as prosecutors and trial judges prior to their elevation to the bench. They also were less likely to have been born and educated in the state in which they serve. The differences from previous justices' backgrounds are most visible for women and African-American judges, who are more likely to have government legal experience as well as experience as a lower court judge than white men, who still come largely from private practice. This suggests that the eligible pool from which judges are selected also has broadened in many states. Since nearly half of the women and all of the African-American justices in states with elected judges gained their initial term through a gubernatorial appointment, E. Martin and Pyle (2002) also suggest that governors have had a key role in the continued diversification of state high courts, although women continue to be underrepresented.

Barriers to Law School Tenure

Gendered organizational logic also contributes to the difficulties women have in getting tenure at prestigious law schools. As previously discussed, there is gender bias in law school hiring of new faculty. Not surprisingly, the disadvantages with which women start out affect them in the tenuring process. Tenure decisions formally rest on such criteria as good teaching, research, and service, although the meaning of "good teaching" is not clear.[4] Both senior faculty members and students expect a teacher to adopt an adversarial, "Socratic" stance; they mistrust a teacher who is willing to explore different approaches and values. The research and writing of women faculty may be judged negatively because it often concerns "insubstantial" subjects such as family law and women's issues. Women's service contributions often are considerable but denigrated. For example, little weight is given to advising women law students or serving on university committees on the status of women, which take considerable time (Angel, 1988). In addition, the informal decision criteria often rest on "collegiality," which generally means how well one fits with the rest of the faculty and how well one is liked. As Angel (1988) notes, when "the rest" are men judging women, the latter often do not seem to fit.

By the early 1990s, women had made progress in the legal academy. Between 1986 and 1991, white women took 30 percent of tenure-track positions filled at law schools, while women of color gained 8 percent of those positions. Women with about 10 years of experience were as likely as men to have served as academic deans or program directors (Merritt & Reskin, 2003). Nevertheless, during this same period, women were far more likely than men to take nontenure-track positions at law schools, and men moved faster from nontenure to tenure-track slots than women. Two factors contributed to men's faster advancement. First, men on tenure track were assigned to teach the prestigious constitutional law classes, while women were assigned the less prestigious trusts and estates or skills courses. Second, women and persons of color abandoned teaching at much higher rates than white men, increasing opportunities for white men to move up the promotion ladder. This further skewed the race and sex distributions among tenured law faculties and perpetuated the difficulties encountered by junior women on law faculties (Merritt & Reskin, 2003).

McBrier (2003) focused on the factors that explain the slower advance of women than men within the law academic market from nontenure to tenure positions. She found that men and women began with similar credentials, constraints, and experiences but that women moved across the job sector boundary about 33 percent more slowly than their men colleagues, even after controlling for family obligations and geographic job search constraints. Several factors slowed women's rate of mobility. Geographic limits on the job search had a positive effect for men but a negative effect for women. Being married increased men's rate of mobility but decreased women's mobility rate. Women also got less payoff for nonacademic employment experience than men. Being a prosecutor helped men's movement to tenure track but had no effect on women's; government experience had no impact on men's mobility but slowed women's. Thus, women with characteristics, credentials, and constraints similar to those of men still gain unequal returns on these factors. While these factors appear to be gender neutral, in fact, career mobility in law academia appears to rest on cognitive biases against professional women. The women encounter differing expectations, which lead to negative sex-based stereotypes and biased outcomes. For example, having prosecutorial experience may accelerate men's movement into tenure-track law teaching jobs because it is perceived as conforming to the stereotype of the "Rambo litigator," while the same experience does not help women's movement into the tenure track because it contradicts expectations of "appropriate" behavior for women. Thus, law schools opt to reward men but not women for aggressive work styles while naturalizing women's presence in nontenure-track law teaching, which increasingly is labeled "women's work."

Women's Responses to Gender Bias: Adaptation and Innovation

Women lawyers have adopted a variety of coping strategies for dealing with gender bias. Like women in policing and corrections, they attempt to strike a balance between identities that will be regarded as "too tough" and "too feminine," seek sponsors or mentors, and try to avoid sexual harassers or deal with harassment informally. Other adaptive strategies include reducing stresses by choosing work settings and legal specialties deemed more appropriate for women and avoiding those where they are less welcome, delaying or avoiding marriage and children, changing jobs or seeking part-time work when they have a family, or leaving the legal profession.

At the same time, women lawyers' strategies differ somewhat from those of women in policing and corrections, due to the structure of the legal world and the nature of the work. First, they have organized far more effectively than women in other criminal justice system occupations. They have formed local women's bar associations and have stimulated gender bias task forces in more than 40 states and a number of federal courts whose findings have identified problems that have led to changes in policies and practices within the legal profession. Second, they have used their training to develop feminist jurisprudence that challenges the premises of legal reasoning and have applied it in lawsuits challenging discriminatory practices of their own employers—law schools and law firms as previously illustrated.

Despite these successes, other changes in the organization and practice of law identified in Chapter 5 have created greater stresses, time demands, and dissatisfaction across the legal profession that disproportionately disadvantage women lawyers. In addition, despite growing numbers of women lawyers and organizational efforts to eliminate discrimination and sexual harassment, these practices continue. Similarly, although the great majority of law firms and other legal work sites have adopted flexible work policies, their use is very limited. Thus, it is likely that time alone will not eliminate the pervasive gender inequalities in the legal profession. Structural changes are needed to address the "gendered constraints" (Hull & Nelson, 2000) that differentially affect women's and men's legal careers.

Women's Bar Associations and Gender Bias Task Forces

To foster their careers, women have established separate women's bar associations. The Women Lawyers' Club (which became the National Association of Women Lawyers) was formed in 1899; by 1951, its more than 1,000 members represented about 20 percent of women lawyers. Women's bar associations have helped women participate in professional life by serving as friendship groups and centers for mutual support, giving leadership opportunities, and providing visibility. However, these groups also have been criticized for diverting women from full integration into the profession (Epstein, 1993, p. 258).

As leadership opportunities in state bars and the ABA opened to women, many have resisted joining a separate organization, instead becoming active in the ABA. By 2005, women comprised 33 percent of the ABA members and 27 percent of the members of its Board of Governors; two women have been president (ABA, 2006).

The rationale and findings of gender bias task forces have made clear the nature and extent of discrimination in the law and have forced the legal profession to confront its own injustices. Nevertheless, their recommendations remain advisory. As the title of the most recent assessment of the status of women lawyers conducted by the ABA Commission on Women in the Profession states, despite progress, the agenda for change remains "unfinished" (ABA, 2001b). Women's opportunities are limited not only by conscious prejudice but by "unconscious stereotypes, inadequate access to support networks, inflexible workplace structures, sexual harassment and bias in the justice system" (ABA, 2001b, p. 5).

Feminist Jurisprudence and Legal Action

While doing their jobs as lawyers, women have written and presented arguments affecting employment opportunities for women in many occupations, including the legal profession. The efforts of feminist lawyers have not only reshaped the law regarding employment discrimination, but also increasingly have challenged the gender biases embedded in legal reasoning and the ways they affect such diverse areas of law as contracts, family relations (including treatment of domestic violence and child support law), and criminal sentences. Thus, feminist jurisprudence has questioned the law's entire perspective on and treatment of women.

Initially, feminist legal scholars challenged rules or laws that treated men and women differently, focusing on so-called "women's issues" such as rape and pregnancy. They also demanded to be admitted to law schools and allowed to practice on equal terms with men. But they discovered formal equality could be a double-edged sword and began exploring a variety of biases in the legal system. For example, they noted that ostensibly "objective" legal rules rest on the perspectives of "the reasonable man."

By the 1980s, feminist jurisprudential examination had expanded to explore what law and legal process would be like if it embodied a worldview that is more inclusive, less abstract, and more caring, and took the reality of women's lives into account. Although different approaches to feminist jurisprudence have developed, these share an analysis of law in the context of the reality of women's experiences and concerns and an effort to understand how the law works from women's perspectives so that law can be used to address actual problems in women's lives. Initially regarded as "radical," feminist jurisprudence now has penetrated the mainstream of legal thinking. As Resnik (1996) observed, the activities associated with task forces on gender bias in the courts have, within a decade, led to the exploration of the relationships among feminist theory, feminist practice, and one legal institution—the courts. The task force approach broke away from the paradigm of examining discrimination in a framework of a case-by-case approach and identified systemic discrimination and disparities in treatment. Consequently, judicial officials across the United States have implemented notable changes. Many jurisdictions have developed sexual harassment policies, rewritten the canons of ethics, and initiated programs to address the problems of victims of violence. In addition, Congress adopted the Violence Against Women Act in 1994 and renewed the law in 2000 and 2005. Clearly, this effort has led to increased sensitivity of bench, bar, and the public regarding gender bias.

Similarly, the issue now identified as "sexual harassment" illustrates the impact of feminist jurisprudence on the law. Until 1978, what is now called sexual harassment was an unnamed condition women had long endured. Feminist theorist Catharine MacKinnon labeled certain types of behavior "sexual harassment" and provided a legal theory that enabled women to identify certain behaviors as a form of actionable employment discrimination covered by Title VII (MacKinnon, 1978). As noted in Chapter 1, courts gradually have accepted MacKinnon's reasoning, and feminist jurisprudence has expanded to examine how domestic violence and pornography as well as sexual harassment subordinate women.

Another group of feminist scholars has challenged the "gender essentialism" of the mainly white middle-class feminists. Pioneers, including Kimberle Crenshaw and Mari Matsueda, developed critical race feminism centered on the experiences of black women and women of color more broadly. Their work theorizes the intersectionality of race, class, and gender as crucial in understanding their disadvantage in terms of simultaneous gender- and race-based oppression.

The Time Crunch: Meshing Work and Family Life

Because the legal profession demands an open-ended commitment of practitioners' time and energy, women lawyers face a particularly acute "time crunch." Moreover, the work pressures and conflicts faced by lawyers have increased over the past two decades due to changes in the organization and practices of law firms. As previously noted, the average number of hours billed annually by lawyers working in firms (which does not fully reflect the time devoted to their profession) has risen from about 1,700 in the 1960s to between 2,000 and 2,400 today. This translates into 60-hour workweeks for persons who expect to make partner and a median of 53 hours per week (Wallace, 2002). A 40-hour workweek is considered part-time (ABA, 2001a).

Meshing work and family is the last and greatest hurdle for women in law. Women carry most of the family responsibilities, particularly those related to child care, and balance the perceived demands of home and work differently than their men colleagues (ABA, 2001a; Chambers, 1989; Epstein et al., 1999). These "choices," in turn, have affected women's career opportunities. Several studies have found that women opt to leave private practice for work environments that are more "family friendly" (Hull & Nelson, 2000; Reichman & Sterling, 2004). Others encounter workplace constraints in private practice that lead to "phasing out" women who have children. When they return from maternity leave, these women are given mundane work assignments and find that relations with colleagues become unsatisfactory (Kay, 1997). Ironically, the *Women in Law* study (2001) found that although two thirds of the women selected their jobs in corporate counsel's offices based on anticipated work/life balance, technological changes and downsizing have altered the work so that in-house counsel now face time and performance pressures similar to those experienced in law firms. Thus, 66 percent of women in corporate legal departments find balancing work and private life difficult due to excessive workloads and fast turnarounds. Fewer of these women (9 percent) than those in law firms (22 percent) believe they can use part-time or flexible work schedules and still advance in their careers.

Joan Williams (1990, p. 351) observed that women lawyers internalize both an ideology of work success and a belief that successful motherhood is essential to adult life. Meeting expectations of the "ideal worker," however, prevents women in law from meeting their children's daily needs for care and affection. This leaves three options: avoid having children; spend very little time with them; or become part-time lawyers, reducing career activities and opportunities for advancement.

Each option reflects a system of gender privilege rather than a "free choice" and demonstrates that, in fact, men and women are not similarly situated with respect to legal work. Men but not women generally have access to the domestic labor of their spouses. The work schedule of elite American lawyers both reflects and reinforces this system of gender privilege. It ensures that a disproportionate number of women will be effectively barred from elite jobs by choosing to marry and have a family since they still carry a greater share of household and child care responsibilities than their husbands/partners (ABA, 2001a; Wallace, 2002; J. Williams, 2000).

Marriage and Children

To reduce career-limiting domestic demands, women may remain single or hire a housekeeper. In the past, women attorneys were forced to choose between career and marriage. Men attorneys not only were expected to be married, but their wives sometimes were interviewed informally to assure that they understood the firm's demands on their husband's time and that they "fit" into the social life of the firm. According to U.S. Census data on the marital status of lawyers and judges by sex, in

1960, 46 percent of the women and 87 percent of the men lawyers and judges were married (cited in Epstein, 1993, p. 330). More recent figures indicate that these figures have not changed much: just over half of women lawyers currently are married compared with 85 percent of men, and fewer women than men have partners who are primary caretakers (ABA, 2001a).

The parental role is even more demanding and likely to conflict with professional life, particularly for women who have primary responsibility for child care. Consequently, many women lawyers opt to remain childless. Among lawyers who have children, a higher proportion of women than men report delaying starting a family because of their careers, taking parental leave when they had children and remaining on leave longer than their male counterparts (Epstein et al., 1999; Wallace, 2002).

The availability and length of maternity leave as well as its impact on women's careers vary among employers. The ABA Commission on Women in the Profession's report, *Balanced Lives* (2001a), states that 95 percent of law firms permit part-time work and half have parental leave policies (prompted by the Family and Medical Leave Act of 1993). Yet there is a vast gap between policy and actual practice: only 3 to 4 percent of lawyers take advantage of the part-time and other flexible work policies. This is because most lawyers (correctly) believe that their employers do not really support flexibility or alternative schedules and find that colleagues also resent the added burden a part-timer creates for them (ABA, 2001a; Epstein et al., 1999; Reichman & Sterling, 2004; *Women in Law*, 2001).

Child care responsibilities, even more than pregnancy and childbirth, create demands for more flexible hours and part-time work. Many younger professionals, seeking more balanced lives, are challenging the legitimacy of the time demands of law firms. Thus far they are fighting a losing battle. Organizations that appear to grant more flexible and shorter hours also define those who take them as "time deviants." As Epstein et al.'s (1999, p. 29) study of "the part-time paradox" concludes, "part-time lawyers are stigmatized." They face coworker verbal and nonverbal disapproval, clients' objections, symbolic treatment that highlights different status (e.g., exclusion from the company's organization chart), and pension inequalities. Since most part-timers are women, they also are stigmatized as inadequate parents and uncommitted lawyers.

Working part-time, even for a short time, results in career derailment because the most interesting work goes to those willing to be available at all times. Left with more mundane tasks, part-timers lose the opportunity to be visible or assume leadership. Mentors are less willing to sustain relationships since they expect that a part-timer will not become a partner. To avoid the penalties for working part-time, some women select firms that do not have quick turnaround pressures, develop a legal specialty in particularly high demand, or prove themselves to be exceptional in order to justify the accommodation to their reduced hours (Epstein et al., 1999).

The absence of part-time opportunities and inflexibility of law firms and, increasingly, of corporate employers regarding accommodations for pregnancies and family life exacerbate the frustration of women in law. These issues also highlight the gendered nature of legal organizations. Family responsibilities are not viewed as an acceptable reason to ask for professional scheduling adjustments; lawyers who ask for extended leave are said to display "reduced professional commitment" or demand "special treatment." In contrast, when a man who was a member of a law firm decided to run for the presidency of the state bar, he too limited his activities in the firm for a defined period of time. Nevertheless, his commitment to the firm or the law was not questioned (Report of the Florida Supreme Court, 1990).

Even accommodations like provision of an on-site child care facility have proven to be a double-edged sword. They have enabled firms to increase expectations of young lawyers, pressuring them to work later and come in on weekends, bringing the children if necessary.

Reshaping the Profession: Work-Family Balance and Quality of Life

The increasing number of women in law has led some scholars to speculate on women's impact on the law and legal practice and its effect on them. Studies find that women and men lawyers generally are equally satisfied with their careers (Chambers, 1989; Reichman & Sterling, 2004; Wallace, 2002). For example, Chambers (1989) found that five years after graduation from the University of Michigan law school, women members of the classes of 1976–1979 were as satisfied with their careers as men. However, the marital and family status of the respondents were related to their level of work satisfaction. Single persons of both sexes were less satisfied than those with spouses or partners, and among women lawyers, those with children were significantly more satisfied than those who were childless. For women but not for men, having children was significantly related to career satisfaction (Chambers, 1989). Chambers suggests this probably is because they achieved a healthier balance between career and the rest of life by accepting and resolving the work-family tension and adjusting personal standards accordingly. Nevertheless, these women paid a price not exacted of men in work-related stress and/or derailment of their career from the "fast track."

More recent studies (Reichman & Sterling, 2004; Wallace, 2002; Women in Law in Canada, 2005) have found that both men and women report similar high levels of overall job satisfaction but differ in their specific sources of dissatisfaction. For example, Reichman and Sterling (2004) observed that their women respondents tended to be less satisfied than the men with their compensation and job opportunities as well as with relationships at work. In interviews, both men and women spoke about tension between work and personal life, but responded to the push/pull of career versus family differently. Women moved away from traditional private practice and took jobs that reduced their compensation. Men facing work/life dilemmas tended to remain in the practice of law but to expand or reshape their professional networks. These responses reinforce gendered expectations about commitment and competence (Reichman & Sterling, 2004).

Beyond a Reasonable Doubt (2005), Catalyst's study of attorneys in Canadian law firms, found significant differences by both gender and position in lawyers' difficulty managing the demands of work and personal/family life. While 61 percent of men partners were satisfied with their ability to balance work/family responsibilities, only 41 percent of women partners, 37 percent of men associates, and 27 percent of women associates were satisfied with their ability to manage work and personal/family responsibilities. Women associates (75 percent), men associates (64 percent), and women partners (59 percent) were significantly more likely than men partners (46 percent) to agree that advancement in their firm depends on putting career before personal/family life. Most women partners and associates and men associates stated they would consider working in another firm if the environment were more supportive of family and personal commitments.

As the first report of the ABA Commission on Women in the Profession (1988, pp. 16–17) noted, the pressures on lawyers to produce more billable hours has resulted in "dehumanized" lawyers who are "24-hour a day workaholics." Women have taken the lead in challenging these pressures and forcing the legal profession to examine the direction in which it is moving, although they are not alone in their dissatisfaction. In a recent survey, about two thirds of both male and female lawyers expressed discontent and frustration with work/life tensions (ABA, 2001b). While the report states that there is an ongoing dialogue occurring within the profession, solutions are elusive, and the outcome is still evolving. Moreover, it is unlikely that these work/life tensions will be addressed satisfactorily until they are seen as the problems of the profession and symptomatic of larger social structural issues rather than as "women's problems" (J. Williams, 2000). In the interim, however, women's challenges to the profession still accentuate the ways in which women are "outsiders."

More than 15 years ago, Joan Williams (1990) asserted that in order to resolve the work/family dilemma, what is needed is to "restructure the entire society's work around the time commitments of responsible parenting" by allowing people to slow down during parenting years. This solution, however, would require a whole cultural shift regarding work-family relations so that employers who demand 12-hour days and parents who work them are regarded as irresponsible.

Summary

This chapter has examined gender bias in diverse legal settings and how it is related to organizational logic and the legal culture. For many women, legal education is an alienating experience that presses them to "become gentlemen." Across diverse legal work sites, women are paid less and advance more slowly than men with similar education and experience, and these differences are magnified over time. Additionally, women are more likely than men to be denied partnerships in firms and tenure at elite law schools. Part of these career path differences are due to "composition" factors like women's specialties. However, even after controlling for confounding factors, women lawyers still pay a price simply for being women, and the price is compounded for women of color.

In various work settings, women encounter deprecating and harassing behaviors that affect their morale, satisfaction, commitment, and professional advancement opportunities. Sexist jokes and demeaning comments also undermine women's credibility as lawyers and their ability to effectively represent clients.

Organizational logics limit women's opportunities for advancement. The path to partnership, the bench, or tenure on a law faculty favors those who "fit," and such persons are men. This is the result of several factors. Fewer women than men are able or willing to pursue the workaholic life of lawyers, particularly those on the "fast track." Achieving a judgeship, for example, traditionally has required a prestigious clerkship and partnership in a commercial law practice as well as political involvement and the support of gatekeepers with gendered images of judges. Men continue to follow this traditional path to the bench. Women's representation on the bench, in contrast, has been greatly expanded by deliberate efforts by American presidents and state governors to widen the pool of persons considered eligible for a judgeship by including judicial and prosecutorial experience more characteristic of women's career paths. Some attribute gender differences in career patterns to the fact that women bear children and continue to shoulder responsibility for their rearing. Yet, both those women who choose to forgo families and those who work part-time or take a leave of absence face a number of interrelated barriers. These constraints push them to make fundamentally different "choices" than men with respect to the directions of their careers and their personal lives. Many women opt for work in less high-pressure environments than law firms or in specialties that are less prestigious and financially rewarding than commercial law. Those who are wives and mothers also must find a balance between extraordinary work demands and family responsibilities without institutionalized assistance. Whether the women who are challenging the pattern of success based on continuous and total commitment will succeed in altering the legal profession rather than reshaping themselves to fit the mold remains to be determined.

Endnotes

1. The Socratic or case-study method teaches law through the study of case decisions. Typically, the class session is spent with the professor questioning students about details of the court's decision to get them to extrapolate the legal principles embedded in the opinion. This method is designed to aid the student in developing legal reasoning and critical thinking skills. However, the questioning can get quite intimidating and can be used to humiliate students who are unprepared or question the logic of the decision from an unconventional perspective.

2. Nearly 40 percent of respondents to the survey of the Florida Supreme Court Gender Bias Study Commission reported that they wanted to file a complaint but did not do so because of the fear of ostracism, other reprisals, and the failure of the commission to take action (Report of the Florida Supreme Court, 1990).

3. While there has been significant growth in the absolute numbers of black lawyers in corporate firms, the percentages remain "microscopically small." According to Wilkins and Gulati (1996), a 1996 *National Law Journal* survey reported that blacks constituted only 2.4 percent of the lawyers in corporate firms and just over 1 percent of partners. These percentages are similar to those reported in 1980 and lag behind figures achieved by other legal employers. For example, minority lawyers occupied 19.5 percent of the supervisory positions in government legal offices as compared to 1.6 percent of the partnerships in large Chicago firms, and 2.5 percent of executive or managerial positions in private sector industries, twice the number of partners in elite corporate law firms.

4. Angel (1988, p. 830) describes the bind women face regarding student evaluations:

If the student evaluations and "they" (the tenured faculty) like the faculty member being evaluated, the student evaluations are valid. If the student evaluations are good and "they" don't like the faculty member, the evaluations show that students are being spoon-fed and are not being intellectually stimulated. If the student evaluations are bad and "they" like the faculty member, the evaluations reflect that the teacher is being "tough on the little bastards." . . . If the student evaluations are bad and "they" don't like the faculty member, the evaluations just prove how awful the faculty member is.

CHAPTER 7

Women in Corrections

Advancement and Resistance

For more than a century, the women working in corrections were volunteers or specialists assigned to supervise women inmates and juvenile offenders. The 1970s witnessed significant expansion in the number and types of jobs women held in U.S. corrections. Similar expansions occurred in Canada, Australia, the United Kingdom, and continental European countries in the 1970s and 1980s. These increases have included growing numbers of women working in formerly all-men's jobs (King, 2000; Morton, 1991b; Szockyj, 1989). As discussed in Chapter 1, these increases were precipitated, on the one hand, by legal and social movement pressures for women's work opportunities and, on the other hand, by the growing numbers of jobs available in arresting, processing, and imprisoning individuals for street crimes. Political rhetoric and public panics about crime and immigration, and the enactment of myriad get-tough policies have swelled prison populations worldwide, with the United States leading the trend (Christie, 2000). The shortage of available men for correctional positions greatly facilitated the movement of women into formerly all-men's work areas of this field.

As women's employment in men-dominated jobs increased, and as they have proven themselves in these jobs, some of the overt opposition to their presence has subsided. However, women remain a minority in these fields, and with the erosion of old forms of gender subordination, ironically, new and sometimes invidious forms have emerged. Prisons are highly gendered and sexualized organizations in ways that are disadvantageous to the growing populations of women inmates and correctional officers alike (Britton, 2003; Cowburn, 1998). Women working in corrections continue to confront embedded and often subtly gendered organizational practices that hinder their job performance and advancement in the field. Along with women prison and jail inmates, women officers experience devaluing and subordination to masculine norms of prison behavior. Despite women's advancement over the past two decades, the close association of prison work with a correctional discourse conflates worker competence with cultural ideals about working-class masculinity and supports work cultures that oppose women. At the same time, women officer successes are actively challenging these cultural norms.

This chapter examines the history of women's work in corrections, especially their entry into the men-dominated occupation of correctional security work in men's prisons. To be consistent with American Correctional Association (ACA) terminology and wishes expressed by men and women working in the field, we use the terms "corrections" and "correctional officer" (CO) to describe work in prisons and jails. However, as noted in Chapter 1, the accuracy of the labels corrections and COs is contested.

History of Women in Corrections: 1860s to 1960s

In 1793, Mary Weed became the first known woman correctional administrator. As the principal keeper of the Walnut Street Jail in Philadelphia, she was known for her humane administration over men and women inmates (Morton, 1992). In 1822, the first woman was hired as a jail matron; the term "matron" was to apply to a virtuous, dutiful woman who would mother and nurture women prisoners. The first women were hired as prison "guards" in 1832, but until 1861, women correctional workers were still extremely rare (Freedman, 1981).

Between 1860 and 1900, small groups of U.S. women took up women prisoners as their special cause. They followed Elizabeth Fry in England, who organized volunteer programs to visit and aid women inmates (Rafter, 1990). Women were then housed in the same facilities as men but were usually segregated into crowded, isolated areas. Reformers guided by religious beliefs visited prisons and questioned prevailing images of women inmates as depraved (Freedman, 1981; Rafter, 1990).

Gradually, women prisoner aid societies joined with prison boards and other social welfare groups to advocate changes in the treatment of women inmates. Reformers were predominantly elite and middle-class women with the desire and free time for social activism. Prison reform was one of several movements aimed at underprivileged and disenfranchised groups. Women reformers had been active in other causes, such as the abolition of slavery, temperance, and aid to the needy (Rafter, 1990). They hoped to transform societal images of women inmates by portraying them as victims of economic disadvantage and sexual exploitation by men. Women reformers argued that women were different from and morally superior to men (Freedman, 1981) and that all women, rich and poor, shared a common bond of innate, womanly spirit. Their vision of appropriate "womanly" behavior was a middle-class construction of femininity that disapproved of the behavior of lower-class women and girls.

At a prison conference in 1870, women and other reformers demanded separate prisons for women. They envisioned women's institutions as homelike atmospheres of rehabilitation that would be controlled and run by women. Reformers also worked to establish the modern juvenile justice system to serve as a "protective parent" for wayward youth, especially lower- and working-class girls. Their design of the juvenile system actually inspired some of the reforms recommended for women's institutions (Rafter, 1990). Women gained authority over public institutions that housed women and, by the end of the century, were employed in the growing fields of charities and corrections. They became administrators and jail matrons in women's prisons and juvenile detention centers (Freedman, 1981). The reform movement for women's prisons was also important for men's prison reformers. A man who was an administrator of a women's institution, Zebulon Brockway, also headed the first U.S. men's prison reformatory, the Elmira reformatory. It opened in 1876 and reflected many of the ideas that emerged from the 1870 reform conference (Clear, Cole, & Reisig, 2006).

Women were able to enter correctional work in the late 19th and early 20th centuries by emphasizing womanly qualities (Heidensohn, 1992; Rafter, 1990). Middle-class women held the professional jobs of reforming women and girls of the lower, more "dangerous" classes (Rafter, 1990). They claimed that their inherently emotional and sympathetic natures prepared them for work as professional role models for "fallen women" (Freedman, 1981; Rafter, 1990). According to Jennifer Brown and Frances Heidensohn (2000) and others (e.g., King, 2000; Schulz, 1995), this activism spanned numerous countries and included advocacy for women to work in policing as well as in corrections and other helping professions. It also made professional work both an acceptable component of middle-class femininity and an avenue for imposing middle-class constructions of femininity on women and girls in the lower classes.

By 1900, separate women's prisons were a reality in many U.S. states and in England, but as the prison reform movement waned, the success of women's institutions was partially due to their increasing resemblance to men's prisons and their reliance on programs that conformed to middle-class gender stereotypes. Women's prisons took on more of the institutional and warehouse-like character of men's prisons, and more were headed by men. From 1900 to 1920, progressive women reformers tried unsuccessfully to drop sexual distinctions and to diversify training. Although reformers did carve out new categories of work for women in corrections, their specialist strategies reinforced culturally emphasized images of femininity and ultimately limited women's work opportunities (Dobash, Dobash, & Gutteridge, 1986; Freedman, 1981).

From the 1930s to the 1970s, women worked as administrators, security officers, and counselors in juvenile and women's detention facilities, and as probation and parole officers for women and juvenile offenders. Women also worked as volunteers and as administrative and clerical staff but were rarely allowed to supervise men inmates (Feinman, 1986). Women inmates and prison matrons became second-class citizens in a correctional system planned around the demands of men's prisons (Rafter, 1990). During this period, correctional work, especially in women's and juvenile facilities, was characterized by long hours and low pay. The director of the New Jersey Reformatory for Women reported in 1940: "Our cottage staff work practically 24 hours a day and receive $50 to $70 a month, plus maintenance. Men guards in reformatories for men work eight hours and receive a minimum of $150 per month" (Hawkes, 1991, quoted in Morton, 1992, p. 84).

Despite these barriers, a few women were recognized as outstanding in the field. In 1863, Edna Mahan, superintendent of the New Jersey State Reformatory for Women, was the first woman to receive the ACA's achievement award; she revived the Women's Correctional Association. Grace Oliver Peck chaired Oregon's Institutions Committee and worked to modernize its entire correctional system (Morton, 1992).

The gender ratios of men and women correctional workers remained steady throughout the 1950s. In the 1960s and 1970s, the Civil Rights and second-wave feminist movements began to sow the seeds of change for women correctional workers.

Social Change and Changing Queues for Women COs in the 1970s

Over the past three decades, women have begun to participate fully in all areas of corrections. The occupational realm that has been the most resistant to the inclusion of women has been security work in men's prisons as well as leadership positions in men's prison administration. Since most prisons are for men, and most resources are devoted to men's programs, women have a large stake in obtaining employment in men's facilities. Women began working as COs in U.S. men's prisons in the late 1970s. This expansion of women's roles was prompted by a confluence of factors both external and internal to correctional organizations.

Socio-Legal Changes and Women COs

Civil rights and women's movements of the 1960s and 1970s launched ideological and political attacks on the principle of "separate but equal" in all realms of social life. With regard to women prisoners, critics exposed the inequality of their vocational training and longer indeterminate sentences. Some radical feminists have advocated closing women's prisons (A. Y. Davis, 2003; Feinman, 1986). Feminists worldwide have stressed the need to extend equal work opportunities in corrections and to revitalize rehabilitative values with a feminist grounding in humane treatment for inmates (Carlen, 2001; Feinman, 1986). Legal pressure is frequently cited as the major impetus for expanding women's roles in corrections (Feinman, 1986; Zimmer, 1986). The equal employment opportunity legislation and regulations discussed in Chapter 1 were crucial to their expansion.

However, legal support for women COs working in men's prisons was uneven. Some courts denied employment opportunity to women in men's prisons. In 1977, the Supreme Court allowed Alabama to exclude women from CO positions in men's facilities because they represented a threat to security (*Dothard v. Rawlinson*, 1977). The suit was filed by Diane Rawlinson, who was denied a job as a CO because her weight was below minimum requirements. As noted in Chapter 1, her class action suit challenged these requirements, as well as a regulation that prevented women COs from "continual close proximity" to inmates in maximum security prisons for men—the "no-contact rule."

The Supreme Court held that height and weight requirements were not legitimate (i.e., bona fide) occupational qualifications because they disproportionately disqualified women. However, the Court affirmed the no-contact rule, citing the danger of attack on women by "predatory sex offenders" and arguing that their vulnerability would weaken security and endanger others. There was little evidence for either assertion, but the majority opinion was strongly influenced by the extremely dangerous (and unconstitutional) conditions that characterized Alabama prisons. The reference to the "jungle atmosphere of the penitentiary" in the court ruling also illustrates the implicitly racialized images that inform many opinions about prisons in the United States (*Dothard v. Rawlinson*, 1976, cited in Maschke, 1996; Hawkins & Alpert, 1989). The direction of court opinion later shifted in favor of women's rights to equal employment opportunities, but these early suits served as a rationale for many facilities to continue restricting women COs' work assignments. Although legal and social movement pressures for equal employment opportunity were crucial for women's efforts to expand their roles in corrections, seemingly gender-neutral challenges to prison conditions indirectly supported the introduction of women to traditional men's jobs.

By the 1930s, a rehabilitation ethos had been adopted by U.S. states; even so, programs and services were often poor to nonexistent. Reports that rehabilitation programs did not work (e.g., Martinson, 1974) were circulated throughout the media and fueled a political and public backlash against rehabilitation mandates (Cavender, 2004). Further criticism grew out of reports that promises of rehabilitation were used as justification for long prison sentences and covered harsh and abusive treatment of inmates. The general instability within prisons became more apparent during the 1960s and 1970s and included several high-profile inmate riots. These riots and associated investigations drew public attention to squalid living conditions and abusive treatment in prisons (Clear et al., 2006).

By the late 1970s, most U.S. states had withdrawn mandates for prison rehabilitation. Despite the heightened emphasis on inmate incapacitation and security functions, prisons were mandated by court rulings in inmate suits to reform their treatment of inmates and, accordingly, to fulfill roles as human service providers. The source of many of these court orders came from inmate rights movements both inside and outside the prison. These movements combined with the highly publicized prison riots to produce increased inmate access to courts. This court intervention eventually produced significant changes in corrections, changes which encouraged the diversification of correctional staffs (Jurik & Martin, 2001).

Inmate Suits and Pressures for Prison Reform

Prior to the 1960s, most courts refrained from involvement in prison affairs (i.e., a "hands-off policy"), and only a few states recognized rights for prisoners. After that time, however, prisoners began to argue successfully that some aspects of their incarceration violated their constitutional rights. The greatest departure from the hands-off policies of the past came when the Supreme Court ruled that inmates had the right to sue state officials in federal court over such issues as brutal treatment by staff, inadequate nutrition and medical care, theft of personal property, and denial of basic rights (*Cooper v. Pate*, 1964). Initial rulings in favor of inmates focused on issues of brutality and inhumane living conditions; later rulings focused on issues of inmates' right to communication with the outside world and with each other, mail censorship, access to religious services, unreasonable strip searches, right to counsel at disciplinary hearings, and access to law libraries (Clear et al., 2006, pp. 105–115).

By the late 1980s, the Supreme Court became less supportive of expanding inmates' rights, and Congress passed legislation in 1996 that limited the authority of federal judges to intervene in the operations of correctional institutions. Nevertheless, the prisoner rights movements of the 1960s through the 1980s were the impetus for many correctional reforms. Federal and state courts mandated due process requirements for inmate discipline, releases for inmates in overcrowded facilities, improvements in prison living conditions, access to law libraries, and the introduction of job skill and "resocialization" programs (J. B. Jacobs, 1983, p. 33–60). Many suits were settled by consent decrees or mutual agreement between the litigants that changes would be made in the prison facility. The implementation of these agreements were then monitored by the court, and in some cases, receivers were named to manage state prisons. As a result of these changes, national accreditation standards were developed and prisons were increasingly centralized and bureaucratized in the hope that they would become more rational organizations (J. B. Jacobs, 1983). Reformers wanted to replace traditional, informal, and arbitrary prison management with formal and universal rules and regulations; they wanted to professionalize prison staff (Useem & Goldstone, 2002). The continuing reform and professionalization discourses supported hiring women in a wider range of correctional jobs, including security work in men's prisons.

Prison Reform Ethos and Changing Labor and Job Queues for Women COs

With the intention of ensuring that line COs exercised their responsibilities in a manner consistent with these reforms, new administrators concentrated on upgrading job qualifications (Task Force on Corrections, 1973). Policy makers and administrators believed that the professionalization of prison custodial staff would produce more humane, treatment-oriented practices (R. Johnson, 1987; Owen, 1988).

Prior to the 1970s, white men predominated as COs in U.S. men's prisons. Embarrassing publicity, which revealed that all of the COs at Attica Prison during the 1971 riot were white, and federal mandates for equal employment opportunity pressured prisons to hire more men of color as COs (Hawkins & Alpert, 1989). COs of color were expected to be more sympathetic to the needs of inmates of color. Correctional agencies began recruiting blacks and other men of color in the early 1970s. For example, in Illinois, "recruitment trailers and sound trucks were sent to the inner city to interview and hire guards from African American communities" (J. B. Jacobs, 1977, p. 126).

Changes in penal philosophy that favored human service delivery functions, the humane treatment of inmates, and equal employment practices encouraged the assignment of women to security jobs in men's prisons. Consistent with the discourse of 19th-century women prison reformers, 1970s policy makers believed that the addition of women to prison staff would promote humane treatment of inmates. Women COs were expected to bring to the prison culturally emphasized feminine qualities, including a greater sensitivity to inmates, communication skills, and conflict-diffusion abilities (Kissel & Katsampes, 1980; Owen, 1988).

Shortages of men workers also stimulated the growth of women's employment in corrections. Prisons, especially in isolated rural areas, were unable to find enough men for CO positions. For example, when Louisiana's Angola prison could not find enough local men to service its inmate population, administrators took men off the guard towers and replaced them with women (Crouch & Alpert, 1982).

In the late 1970s, the "push" of economic recession, the high unemployment in non–criminal justice system jobs, and growing numbers of single mother–headed households increased the numbers of women seeking jobs in corrections. At the same time, affirmative action policies and the increasing social acceptance of women working in nontraditional jobs converged with relatively low entrance requirements and improvements in pay level to "pull" women into CO ranks (Belknap, 1991; L. E. Zimmer, 1986).

Since the 1970s, the numbers of women in traditionally men's correctional jobs have risen—at first quickly, and then more slowly in recent years. In large part, this progress was the result of challenges by prison reformers, equal rights proponents, and women workers themselves, but huge increases in prison populations were also very important. These increases prompted significant prison employment growth. Also, since the 1980s, the private sector has dramatically increased its role in operating jails and prisons and thus has further expanded correctional employment opportunities (Hallett, 2002).

By mandating improvement in prison administration and inmate treatment and programs, courts indirectly fostered the extension of correctional employment opportunities to a more diverse workforce that would include men of color and women. However, court intervention also spawned inmate activism that challenged women working in men's prisons.

Inmate Rights to Privacy and Equal Work Opportunities

A series of suits by inmates challenged policies of cross-gender supervision, claiming that their constitutional right to privacy was violated. Women officers also filed suits against some departments of correction that restricted their work assignments due to inmate privacy claims. Women officers and some corrections departments challenged inmate claims by arguing that refusing to assign officers to cross-gender supervision jobs violated equal employment opportunity mandates (Maschke, 1996, p. 42). Early court decisions prohibited women's presence in some areas of men's prisons. In *Reynolds v. Wise* (1974), a Texas district court ruled that excluding women from working in men's prison dorms reasonably accommodated inmate privacy interests and did not unduly discriminate against women (W. Collins, 1991). However, most later decisions preserved employment opportunities for women by demanding that prisons accommodate women's employment and men inmates' privacy. In *Hardin v. Stynchcomb* (1982), the court ordered officials to erect privacy screens and juggle work schedules to increase the number of positions available to women in men's prisons. Courts have held that the limited observation of men in the nude by women COs does not violate inmate rights, nor does it require officials to modify the institution or to juggle work schedules (*Grummett v. Rushen*, 1985; W. Collins, 1991). Although cross-gender strip searches have been viewed as justifiable in emergency situations, searches by same-sex officers are still preferred.

Women inmates filed suits with regard to cross-sex supervision by men officers, and some decisions have ruled in inmates' favor. In *Forts v. Ward* (1978, 1980), the circuit court ruled that women should wear night clothes that completely covered their bodies if they were concerned about being seen by men officers. In a later case, *Torres v. Wisconsin* (1988a, 1988b), prison officials argued that preventing men officers from working in the women's prison was necessary for inmate rehabilitation and privacy. Officials justified this policy by noting that, nationwide, a high percentage of women inmates had been physically and sexually abused by men, and that 60 percent of the women in their institution had been victims of such abuse prior to incarceration. The Court of Appeals issued two separate rulings: one that denied women inmates' claims, and a second binding ruling that prison officials were justified in prohibiting men COs from working in the women's prison (Maschke, 1996). Another case (*Jordan v. Gardner*, 1993) held that the use of men officers to perform body searches of women inmates constituted cruel and unusual punishment for women suffering from prior sexual victimization (cited in Belknap, 2001, p. 385).

These court cases demonstrate the complex conditions that affect prison operations. These include, for example, inmate right to privacy. Against this argument is the argument that inmates have much less of a right to privacy than other citizens. In addition, invasions of privacy may be experienced differentially by women inmates and men inmates, and defining equal rights to privacy as the same for men and women is problematic. In particular, women inmates who have been sexually abused by men experience strip searches by men COs as a traumatic invasion of privacy (A. Y. Davis, 2003; V. Young & Reviere, 2006). Inmate privacy rights can also conflict with the employment rights of correctional workers. Again, equality is not sameness because women COs are more likely than men COs to be employed in cross-gender supervision jobs. Accordingly, to limit women COs because of men inmates' privacy rights would greatly curtail if not end their careers. Promotional and other career opportunities are most strongly associated with working in men's prisons. And of course, all of these issues should not distract from the context of soaring prison populations. Indeed, some scholars (e.g., Chesney-Lind & Pasko, 2004) argue that these debates about privacy and employment rights distract from the shortcomings of policies that are swelling our prison populations.

Although the specter of inmate suits continues to be used as a justification for restricted women's assignments in men's prisons, the reform/service ethos that resulted from inmate rights movements was indirectly very supportive of women's expanded roles in corrections. Also, the unfortunate and explosive growth in inmate populations has spawned continued increases in demands for correctional workers.

Women's Movement Into CO Jobs
in Men's Prisons: 1970s to Present

Women's employment in both line staff and administrative positions in the field of corrections at federal, state, and local levels has steadily increased over the past three decades. Women are well represented among the workers in privately operated prisons, which have assumed an increasing role in corrections since the 1980s. Women have also established a stronger presence in correctional leadership positions since the 1970s. Although this section focuses on women's expanded presence as correctional security staff and administrators, it is important to keep in mind that many women in corrections work in professional and technical jobs and in administrative/clerical support positions. In support jobs, women perform daily, taken-for-granted operating tasks, and often contribute extra hours and talent to expanded roles without the accompanying pay and title (Morton, 1992, p. 77).

A 1988 study of U.S. prisons reported that although women comprised 65 percent of the CO force in women's prisons, they made up only 13 percent of the CO force in men's prisons. However, this 13 percent figure represented a doubling of 1978 estimates (Morton, 1991b). In 1988, The U.S. Federal Bureau of Prisons reported that approximately 8 percent of its COs were women (Morton, 1991b). At the same time, 21.5 percent of the total CO force in 107 of the largest U.S. jail facilities were women, although some counties reported that women constituted over 40 percent of their jail guard force. However, jail figures are misleading because jails are mixed sex institutions, and women employees may supervise the areas for women inmates. As more non-prison jobs opened up for white women during the 1970s and 1980s, and as the numbers of jobs in prisons expanded, black and Hispanic women also began to assume more jobs in the correctional sphere (Jurik & Martin, 2001).

Overall, the staff at U.S. state and federal prisons increased by 24 percent from 1995 to 2000. In 2000, women constituted 33 percent of all staff in U.S. state, federal, and privately operated prisons, a 4 percent increase over 1995 estimates (up from 29 percent). Women constituted 23 percent of the correctional security staff in U.S. state prisons. Comparisons of the gender of COs assigned to men's state prisons over time reveal that women COs increased their proportionate representation in men's prisons by 5 percent during the five-year period from 1995 to 2000 (from 16 percent to 21 percent; Bureau of Justice Statistics, 2003).

Table 7.1 summarizes the percentages of COs by gender in U.S. jails and prisons for 1999 and 2000, respectively. These figures reveal that women comprise 23 percent of COs in state prisons, 14 percent in federal prisons, and 28 percent in publicly run jails. These data show the improvements in women's representation over the 1980s data cited earlier. Even the much lower 14 percent figure for women's representation among federal prison CO staff represents an increase over the 7 percent figure reported for 1988 (Morton, 1991a). As would be expected, women comprise a much higher percentage of the CO workforce (56 percent) in women's state prisons, but it is important to note that 79 percent of all women COs work in men's prison facilities.

Table 7.1   Gender of Correctional Officers in Adult Jails and Prisons: 1999–2001

	Total Number of COs	Men COs (%)	Women COs (%)	Total Number of Administrative	Men Admin. (%)	Women Admin. (%)
Federal prisons[a]	14,746	86	14	—	—	—
State prisons						
All	241,783	77	23	8,896	68	32
Men's prisons	212,614	79	21	7,532	71	29
Men's maximum	95,995	77	23	2,661	74	26
Women's prisons	12,955	43	56	513	40	60
Private prisons						
All	14,352	62	38	1,443	58	42
Men's prisons	10,615	65	35	1,054	65	35
Women's prisons	668	35	64	118	37	63
Public jails	141,663	71	28	13,722	80	20
Private jails	2,617	59	41	413	62	38

Sources: Prison data are drawn from Bureau of Justice Statistics (2003), and data on jails are drawn from Bureau of Justice Statistics (2001).

a. Due to rounding, not all percentages total 100%.

Jails and prisons also report data on the race of COs and other staff. These breakdowns are similar across facility types. The breakdowns for federal facilities are shown in Table 7.2. Approximately 60 percent of federal COs are white, 25 percent are black, 12 percent are Hispanic, and 3 percent comprise "other" racial-ethnic groups. Although not shown in the table, breakdowns for state and private facilities differ in that whites comprise a greater percentage (65 percent) of the CO workforce in state and private prisons, and blacks and Hispanics comprise lower percentages (25 and 12 percent, respectively) of COs in state and private than in federal prisons.

The Federal Bureau of Prisons also reports simultaneous breakdowns for its CO work force by race and gender. These data are also shown in Table 7.2. They reveal that African-American women outnumber white women in the federal CO workforce. The 908 black women comprise 6 percent, and the 847 white women comprise 5.7 percent of the total federal CO workforce. When considering racial composition of the general U.S. population, it is clear that these data reaffirm prior findings that African-American women are actively assuming CO work roles in prisons of the 21st century (Belknap, 2001; Maghan & McLeish-Blackwell, 1991). Hispanic women comprise 1 percent of the federal CO workforce, although their representation in southwestern U.S. regions is significantly greater. Unfortunately, state and private prison data do not provide breakdowns of CO gender and race simultaneously.

When women began working in men's prisons in the 1970s, researchers anticipated that the greatest resistance to women COs would occur in maximum security prisons. However, actual differences across security levels reported by the late 1980s were slight: women comprised 12.7 percent of COs in men's maximum, 13.4 percent

Table 7.2   Gender and Race of Correctional Officers in Federal Prisons

	Total[a]		White		Black		Hispanic		Other[b]	
	Number	%	Number	%	Number	%	Number	%	Number	%
Total	14,746	100	8,878	60	3,622	25	1,821	12	425	3
Gender										
Men COs	12,737	86	8,031	91	2,714	75	1,609	88	383	90
Women COs	2,009	14	847	10	908	25	212	12	42	10

Source: Federal Bureau of Prisons (2002).

a. Due to rounding, not all percentages total 100%.

b. The "other" category includes Asian, Native American, and non-Hispanic employees in Puerto Rico.

in men's medium, and 15 percent in men's minimum security prisons (Morton, 1991b). Table 7.1 shows that the proportion of COs who were women in men's maximum security prisons did not differ from the percentages for all security levels combined. However, in a separate analysis of the 2000 staff data for new super-maximum security prisons (not shown in the table), women comprised only 18 percent of COs in these facilities (Bureau of Justice Statistics, 2003). These data suggest that the trend toward building more and more supermax prisons may not create as many new positions for women officers as might be expected.

The growth of privately-run detention facilities is also evident in the data presented in Table 7.1. Private companies now contract with governments to manage jails and prisons for profit. In 2000, women comprised significantly higher percentages of the CO staff in privately run prisons (38 percent) and jails (41 percent) than in state or federal facilities. Unfortunately, the lower pay and benefit packages and inferior training opportunities associated with security work in private prisons and jails means that women's greater presence there is mixed news (American Friends Service Committee, 2003; Blakely & Bumphus, 2004; Raher, 2002).

Despite their increases in CO ranks, women continue to comprise a small minority of top-level administrators in corrections. However, their proportions have improved significantly over past years. Data from the early 1990s suggest that women constituted less than 10 percent of the wardens and supervisors in U.S. adult correctional institutions, including women's prisons (Hunter, 1992). Women comprised 39.5 percent of the staff in juvenile correctional facilities but only 23 percent of the wardens and supervisors in these facilities (M. H. Young, 1992). The Bureau of Justice Statistics data reported in Table 7.1 suggest that women have improved their representation in administrative ranks. They comprise 32 percent of administrative employees in state prisons generally and 29 percent in men's state prisons. Their representation in public jails is lower at 20 percent, but in private jails and prison, they comprise 35 to 42 percent of administrative staff. As a caveat, the administrative category in the survey that provided the source for these data included, "Wardens, superintendents, administrators, and others in administrative positions" (Bureau of Justice Statistics, 2003, p. 5). Thus, this administrative category may include individuals in many traditionally women's jobs such as those of administrative assistant and office manager. Information from the ACA suggests that the estimates in Table 7.1 overestimate women's rise in traditionally male and upper-echelon administrative positions. ACA officials report that women comprise 23 percent of the wardens and superintendents in adult corrections and 32 percent of comparable administrators in juvenile facilities (Gondles, 2005). Women are also now the directors or commissioners of corrections in nine states (Waters, 2005). Although significantly less than the percentages listed in Table 7.1, these figures still indicate that women have advanced into higher-echelon correctional positions (also see Green, 2005; McCauley, 2005).

The same conditions that produced changes in women's roles in prisons generated opportunities for women in community corrections. In probation and parole, women initially were restricted to supervision of women clients, but a 1974 survey revealed that cross-gender supervision had become common practice in all U.S. state probation and parole agencies (Schoonmaker & Brooks, 1975). More recent data indicate that women comprise 49.1 percent of U.S. probation employees and 50.6 percent of the workforce in U.S. parole agencies (Hunter, 1992; T. Wells, Colbert, & Slate, 2006). Similar trends have been described for probation officers in the United Kingdom (Cowburn, 1998).

The numbers of women working in all aspects of corrections, including men's and women's prisons and jails, juvenile facilities, and probation and parole, continued to grow worldwide into the 21st century (Christie, 2000; A. Y. Davis, 2003). For example, since 1988, the U.K. Prison Service officially adopted an equal opportunities approach to staff postings that enabled women officers to work in men's prisons (Carlen & Worrall, 2004). However, the rate of assignment of women to U.K. men's prisons appears to lag behind figures reported for the United States. Only 17 percent of officers in U.K. prisons are women, and the proportion of women officers ranges dramatically across facilities (e.g., 3 percent in one men's prison and 90 percent in one women's prison). However, 35 percent of new officer recruits were women in 1999–2000, compared with 27 percent women in 1996–1997 and 20 percent three years earlier. As in the United States, most British women officers are assigned to jobs in women's prisons. Women comprise about 14 percent of the "governor" (administrative) grades in British corrections (Liebling & Price, 2001).

As women have moved forward, research has described their experiences and achievements as well as the continuing barriers they face. Reports from women correctional pioneers (e.g., Byrd, 2005; Green, 2005; McCauley, 2005) chronicle the myriad successes of women in the field but warn of a persistent masculine culture that is problematic both for women and for corrections in general. We consider these issues in the following sections.

Characteristics of Women COs in Men's Prisons

Although there are no comprehensive national studies of women and men COs, numerous case studies provide information on women COs including their demographics, educational attainment, reasons for taking the CO job, and attitudes and work orientations. Women COs in state prisons tend to be more highly educated, are more likely to come from professional urban families, and are less likely to be married than men COs (Farkas, 1999b). In her New York and Rhode Island samples, Lynne Zimmer (1986) found that women and men COs had similar education levels. Before assuming CO positions, women were either unemployed or had worked in low-paying, traditionally women's jobs. Several studies find that men COs have more law enforcement or military experience than do their women counterparts (e.g., Britton, 2003; Carlson, Anson, & Thomas, 2003).

As noted earlier, a large proportion of women COs are women of color. The limited data on gender-by-race composition suggest that men and women COs of color comprise anywhere from 20 to 80 percent of the CO force in prisons across the country (Owen, 1988; Van Voorhis, Cullen, Link, & Wolfe, 1991). Jess Maghan and Leasa McLeish-Blackwell (1991) reported that 24.7 percent of New York City Department of Corrections COs were women. Of these, 84 percent of the women COs were black, 10 percent were Latina, 0.2 percent were Asian-American, and 6 percent were white. Joanne Belknap (1991) reports that 43 percent of the women COs in her jail sample from a Midwestern city were black; 57 percent were white. Latina and American Indian representation varies considerably depending on the demographics of the region.

Women may enter correctional occupations for different reasons than men. In some U.S. samples, women were more likely to report intrinsic reasons, such as an "interest in human service work" or in "inmate rehabilitation," as primary reasons for taking the job (e.g., Farkas, 1999b; Jurik & Halemba, 1984; Walters, 1992). The human service dimensions of correctional work have been associated with increases in women applicants for CO positions in Australia and Canada as well (King, 2000; Walters & Lagace, 1999). One U.S. study, however, found that men and women jail officers valued service over security goals to about the same extent (Stohr, Lovrich, & Wood, 1996). Men more often ranked "salary," "job security," and "having no other job" as primary reasons for becoming COs (Britton, 2003; Jurik & Halemba, 1984). L. E. Zimmer's (1986) women respondents ranked salary and a lack of alternative employment options as most important. Belknap (1991) found that women COs working in a county jail chose the job for the salary, benefits, and experience but hoped to eventually get jobs as police officers. The black women in her study were more interested in a career in corrections and less interested in moving into police work than were their white counterparts. Relative to white women COs, women COs of color are more likely to be single heads of households. Maghan and McLeish-Blackwell (1991) found that 46 percent of black women COs in their survey were single. They were attracted to corrections by salary, benefits, and potential job security.

Researchers have also examined women COs' attitudes on gender issues. L. E. Zimmer's (1986, pp. 43–44) sample appeared to be conservative. Only 17 percent supported the Equal Rights Amendment; 56 percent disapproved of a woman working during her children's formative years. In Belknap's (1991) sample, the women COs held more liberal attitudes with respect to parity between men and women in the workplace. Although the women in a more recent study by Stojkovic, Pogrebin, and Poole (2000) supported equality with men in the workplace, they were not as liberal about gender equality in the home.

CO Jobs as a Resource for Doing Gender

Despite improved opportunities, surviving and advancing in corrections has been difficult for women in the United States, the United Kingdom, and Canada (Britton, 1997; Cowburn, 1998; King, 2000; Szockyj, 1989). In the United States, women entered CO positions approximately five years after most men's prisons began hiring men of color. Like men of color, women of all races and ethnicities confronted overt and covert hostilities and exclusion from coworkers and supervisors. Although they shared some common problems with men of color, women COs faced unique problems, including paternalistic protectionism, sexual harassment, and the refusal of their right to work in men's prisons. By the early 1970s, racial discrimination, which was legally prohibited, remained strong in the informal culture of corrections, but the denial of work opportunities to women in men's prisons remained part of official policy in many departments (P. Johnson, 1991; L. E. Zimmer, 1986).

Research suggests that although the attitudes and behavior toward them are more positive than was the case two decades ago, women continue to face resistance from coworkers, supervisors, and inmates, as well as from friends and family members outside of corrections. Yet, such attitudes and behavior cannot be understood apart from the larger occupational and cultural context of CO work.

Correctional literature stresses that the culture of the prison, not personality variables, is primary in shaping COs' responses to the job (G. M. Sykes, 1958). Craig Haney, Curtis Banks, and Philip Zimbardo (1973) conducted an experiment to test for evidence of the "guard mentality," a syndrome of traits that officers allegedly bring to the job. These traits reflected popular stereotypes of "prison guards." They randomly assigned men volunteers to "guard" and "prisoner" groups. Prior to assignment, the researchers ran personality tests on each group to ensure that they had not disproportionately assigned individuals with authoritarian personalities to either group. The experimental prison environment turned normal college students into a group of prison guards who derived pleasure from threatening and dehumanizing their peers (Haney et al., 1973, p. 84). A normative culture among "guards" emerged that defined strength and weakness according to power. As Haney et al. (1973, p. 90) noted,

> Not to be tough and arrogant was seen as a sign of weakness. . . . Even good guards who did not get drawn into the power syndrome . . . respected the implicit norm of never . . . interfering with the actions of a more hostile guard on their shift.

The Zimbardo experiment was many years ago, but research suggests that its conclusions remain relevant. Sarah Tracy and Clifton Scott (2006) argue that a discourse of masculine toughness and emotional control pervades the CO culture (also see Britton, 2003; Tracy, 2005). In the next sections, we examine the links among occupational cultures, the CO job, and interpersonal resistance to women COs.

The Nature of Work in Corrections

The CO job involves a variety of ambiguous and conflicting tasks centered around controlling unwilling inmates (G. M. Sykes, 1958). Although prisons assume some responsibility for rehabilitating, educating, and training inmates, "custody and control are the nucleus" of the job (Clear et al., 2006). COs' primary duties are the supervision of residents and maintenance of security, order, and discipline.

Like police departments, prisons are hierarchical, paramilitary organizations, but COs have less discretion than police. CO salary and prestige are low, turnover is high, and work hours include nights, weekends, and holidays (Clear et al., 2006). Inmate control is fostered by physical barriers, regimented schedules, and the regulation of all inmate movements. Several times a day, prisoners must return to their cell or dormitories for the "count." If an inmate is missing, all other activity stops until the counting error is corrected, the missing inmate is found, or an escape is detected. Outsiders coming into the prison are closely monitored to prevent the introduction of contraband, especially weapons and drugs. COs also are responsible for monitoring physical objects such as the packages, prison equipment, or supplies that might be used as weapons. Beyond the preventive control functions, COs are responsible for policing inmate violations of rules, ranging from illegal acts such as assault to infractions peculiar to prison such as violations of grooming standards.

The CO job involves considerable "body work," which ranges from performing body cavity and strip searches, to shower supervision, to the enforcement of organization rules regarding inmate sexual behavior and physical conflicts, and to some degree, the management of inmate health care and illness issues (Britton, 2003). In doing these tasks, COs often confront unsanitary and unpleasant prison conditions. These aspects of the CO job lead some analysts to describe it as part of a category of societal "dirty work," positions that are physically, socially, or morally tainted and challenge the worker's self-esteem (Tracy & Scott, 2006). Related to these often undesirable duties, the CO job involves the management of intense and stressful emotions on the part of both inmates and staff (Tracy, 2005).

COs face danger. Even more than police, they work with a clientele who resent the restrictions imposed by imprisonment. COs can "act tough" and punish all violations, or they may tolerate some minor infractions in an attempt to build working relationships with inmates. Most research concludes that COs must rely on some inmate cooperation to maintain order. Such cooperation arises through tacit agreements between officials and inmates regarding which rules will be strictly enforced. Since COs are outnumbered by inmates, they learn to enlist cooperative inmates and give them special privileges for keeping other inmates "in line" (Hawkins & Alpert, 1989, p. 344). They hope that earning some inmate respect may increase compliance, reduce conflict, and reduce the danger of being taken hostage, assaulted, or killed. Either this "corruption of authority" or excessive rule-minded "toughness" can have negative consequences and lead to harm of or disciplinary actions against COs (Stojkovic & Farkas, 2003; G. M. Sykes, 1958; L. E. Zimmer, 1986, p. 22).

Despite this potential for excitement and danger, most CO work is repetitive and uneventful. Prisons are bureaucratic organizations, and so COs spend considerable time writing reports and managing activity records. As noted earlier, 1970s and

1980s court decisions and consent decrees afforded new rights to U.S. prisoners, and resulting procedures require increased documentation and justification for formerly routine decisions (Stojkovic & Farkas, 2003). These changes have increased officer paperwork. Such mundane tasks often challenge officer perceptions of themselves as aggressive law enforcement officers who fend off prison violence.

Prisons in a variety of other countries (e.g., Australia, Canada, Germany, Korea, United Kingdom) have incorporated a human service ethos into their expectations for COs (Carlen & Worrall, 2004; Dunkel, 1995; King, 2000; Micucci & Monster, 2004; Moon & Maxwell, 2004). Thus, in addition to their security roles, contemporary COs have been asked to view themselves as basic human service providers. For some officers, the service orientation has made their jobs more attractive, but for others, it has undermined their ideal CO image (Jurik & Martin, 2001; Tracy & Scott, 2006). Nevertheless, the emphasis on offender services and programs has introduced new job tasks for which many COs are ill-prepared, and the training and resources to implement these programs have been lacking. The implementation of a service orientation have been complicated by a number of factors that increased the danger and tedium of prison work (Kommer, 1993). We will discuss these challenges to corrections in Chapter 8.

CO Work Cultures and Masculinities

The nature of CO work and prison organization give rise to distinctive work cultures. Many COs feel underappreciated because their occupation is not highly regarded by the public (Tracy & Scott, 2006). This is especially the case as many citizens renew attacks on the dangerous and abusive conditions in prisons across the globe (A. Y. Davis, 2003; McMahon, 1999). Danger makes COs dependent on one another for backup, and the unusual hours and isolated locations of prisons encourage them to socialize after work. As in police departments, correctional administrators have developed rules that COs cannot follow "to the letter" and still perform their jobs. Nevertheless, rule violation leaves COs constantly vulnerable to arbitrary punishment. These conditions increase the informal sanctions against COs who "snitch" on other COs for rule violations.

Occupational cultures are not gender neutral. The social control and danger dimensions of the work, and past identification of the job as a working-class occupation, encourage an association of CO competence with dominant notions of working-class masculinities. Because overt displays of fear can undermine authority, CO occupational cultures have stressed physical and verbal aggressiveness as essential qualities for controlling inmates (Cowburn, 1998; Tracy & Scott, 2006). Women COs threaten the association between the CO job and working-class masculinities (Jurik & Martin, 2001).

Several factors also foster conflict among COs. Limited promotion opportunities generate considerable competition (Britton, 2003; Hawkins & Alpert, 1989, pp. 338–339). Some COs resent advances in inmate rights, and attempt to sabotage related regulations. Other COs are generally supportive of inmate rights and associated policies (Carlen, 2001; Farkas, 1999a).

Despite their differing views, most COs believe that they are treated unfairly and denied the due process rights granted to inmates (Hawkins & Alpert, 1989, pp. 352–353). Many COs are alienated and isolated (Morgan, Van Haveren, & Pearson, 2002; Poole & Regoli, 1981). They often feel caught in the middle, having to enforce rules developed by courts or prison administrators into which they have little input (Stojkovic & Farkas, 2003; Tracy, 2004b). Yet, if problems arise from enforcing the rules, COs are accountable for the consequences. In response to these problems, COs have organized in unions. However, in the past, unionization efforts have divided COs along race and gender lines when unions defended individuals charged with racial and sexual harassment (J. B. Jacobs, 1977). Some COs have sought other avenues of prison reform, including support for inmate rights movements (Carlen, 2001; R. Johnson, 1987).

Despite the unified image presented in much classic prison literature (e.g., Haney et al., 1973; G. M. Sykes, 1958), COs are not a monolithic group (Stojkovic & Farkas, 2003). Racial and gender integration and the reform-professionalization ethic have undermined solidarity based on social similarity, and fragmented the "old-guard subculture" (Britton, 1997; Marquart & Crouch, 1985). However, even before the entry of women and COs of color, researchers identified diverse CO "work styles." For example, Lucian Lombardo (1981) distinguished COs according to whether they regard their authority as emanating from their own personal legitimacy or from their formal position. Michael Gilbert (1989) identified four CO occupational styles: the professional, who seeks compliance through communication; the reciprocator, who just tries to get along; the enforcer, who rigidly enforces the rules; and the avoider, who minimizes contact with inmates.

Other researchers have argued that it is doubtful if a single "guard subculture" ever existed (R. Johnson, 1987; Klofas & Toch, 1982; Lombardo, 1981). In any case, corrections work today involves multiple occupational cultures, each with its own images and work styles. Moreover, work styles and strategies vary across and within race and gender groups (Britton, 1997; Owen, 1988; L. E. Zimmer, 1986). Despite growing diversity, work cultures continue to be influential in shaping CO behavior (Tracy & Scott, 2006). Diverse occupational groups can provoke struggles in daily interactions over the job and definitions of CO competence.

Sites of Struggle: Gendered Interactions, Gendered Identities

The nature of CO work and gendered occupational cultures frame the routine social interactions of women COs with men inmates, coworkers, supervisors, and those outside the work environment. Cultural images of correctional work converge with popular images of femininities and masculinities to make daily work in prisons a resource for doing gender.

Prisons are gendered organizations in that they are structured in ways consistent with culturally dominant images of gender. Dana Britton (2003) documents how gender, race, class, and sexuality are dynamic and interactive features of prisons, and we will elaborate this analysis in Chapter 8. It will suffice to say here, however, that the effects of gender can be found in all aspects of the prison from the development of the institutions to the direct day-to-day experiences of both workers and inmates. Beliefs about poor and working-class manhood and the masculinities of men of color are pervasive in media imagery and policy maker ideas about prison life. Prisons are presumed to be violent places and masculinity is conflated with that image, and interactional mechanisms often reinforce the "naturalness" of gender distinctions (Tracy, 2005).

Drawing attention to "feminine" characteristics of women COs becomes a mechanism for highlighting the "masculinity" of men COs. For some women COs, "doing masculinity" is conflated with demonstrating competence. Images of feminine incompetence portray women as "little sisters" who accept men's protection, or as "seductresses" who accept men's sexual advances (Kanter, 1977). Accordingly, for many men COs and inmates, projecting a masculine identity means demonstrating superiority to that which is feminine (Tracy & Scott, 2006). Some inmates, men coworkers, and supervisors support women COs who challenge these images of feminine incompetence and construct opposing images of feminine competence in corrections. However, women who refuse men's protection and sexual advances and seek to demonstrate competence risk being labeled as too mannish, or as "man-haters" and "lesbians." Moreover, regardless of the image of femininity that is emphasized, categorizing women COs' sexuality is a constant source of interest for men coworkers, and images of competence as masculine permeate social interactions in the prison (Britton, 2003).

The many changes in corrections that we described earlier in this chapter have heightened the struggles between competing notions of worker competence and concurrent constructions of femininities/masculinities. CO work cultures continue to associate competence with notions of masculinity as manifested in physical strength and emotional toughness (Tracy & Scott, 2006). Such notions of masculinity are integrally associated with poor, white, working-class, or even rural cultures (Messerschmidt, 1993). In contrast, reform-oriented visions of prisons tend to view such versions of competence as authoritarian and as cultivating a sadistic, violent culture among COs (Farkas, 1999a; Stojkovic et al., 2000). Reform visions call for more educated (read: middle-class) COs who are rational and rule-oriented (Stojkovic & Farkas, 2003). They must oversee inmates using conflict management and communication techniques. If they conform to this discourse of bureaucratic professionalism, educated white women and men and women of color can be competent COs. This version of professionalism appears to be gender neutral and more supportive of women, but it still draws on many male-centered standards of body image and conduct to form the image of ideal officers. For example, professional ideals in our society typically assume a cool, emotionless demeanor; male-like business attire and camaraderie; and an organizational loyalty and availability devoid of childbearing, child care, and other family-related obligations that tend to be owned more by women than by men (Jurik & Martin, 2001; I. M. Young, 1990).

Men Inmates and Women COs

Most studies (e.g., Lawrence & Mahan, 1998; L. E. Zimmer, 1986) suggest that men inmates respect women COs. Many inmates indicate that the presence of women COs exerts a calming and normalizing effect on life in men's prisons (Holeman & Kreps-Hess, 1983; Kissel & Katsampes, 1980). However, it is important to keep in mind that these constructions of masculinity are neither uniform over time nor universal to all inmates. For example, one study argues that inmate views of women COs vary by security level (Cheeseman, Mullings, & Marquart, 2001). Given some men inmates' concerns that women COs violate their right to privacy, pat searches and situations in which women COs see inmates nude may challenge masculinity, and increase tension and resentment (L. E. Zimmer, 1986).

Men inmates typically haze new COs, and the hazing is gendered. Inmates may whistle, flirt, openly stare, or otherwise declare their own masculinity and the femininity of women COs. Women COs report that hazing usually subsides once they have demonstrated competence, or "established their authority." Some inmates may try to engage women COs in conduct that violates regulations regarding staff-inmate boundaries (e.g., bring in contraband, form a sexual or emotional bond) and then brag about their "conquest" later (Marquart, Barnhill, & Balshaw-Biddle, 2001; Worley, Marquart, & Mullings, 2002).

Women COs have to "prove themselves to be fair and emotionally strong with inmates" (Farkas, 1999b). Some inmates may then assist women COs by providing important information necessary to perform the job, especially if men COs have refused to supply such information (Britton, 2003; Owen, 1988; L. E. Zimmer, 1986).

The relationships between women COs and inmates are organized along race as well as gender lines (Britton, 2003). Men and women COs of color feel some tension about their authority over inmates of their own race, perhaps from their own neighborhood, who, like themselves, have been victims of racial discrimination and economic disadvantages (Maghan & McLeish-Blackwell, 1991). One writer argues that persons of color should not seek employment in the "racist" criminal justice system (T. Jones, 1978). Charges of racism in the criminal justice system have proliferated with heightened public awareness of the highly disproportionate rates of incarceration for men and women of color. In fact, the history of prisons is laden with racist incarceration practices (Britton, 2003, Chapter 2; A. Y. Davis, 2003). Moreover, black COs in the both the United States and the United Kingdom have levied charges of racist treatment that included both institutional racist practices and blatant episodes of racist language (Global News, 2006).

Some black inmates may exhibit resentment toward black women COs because they regard them as violating racial unity and participating in a racialized system of incarceration. Maghan and McLeish-Blackwell (1991, p. 93) argue that black women COs with incarcerated family or friends experience the "concomitant stress and emotional pain . . . [of] this situation in their lives on and off the job." Alternatively, other men inmates of color are highly supportive of women COs, especially women of their own race or ethnicity.

There have been cases in which women COs have been sexually assaulted by men inmates (Villa, 2004), but systematic studies report lower rates of assaults against women COs when compared to rates for men COs (Holeman & Kreps-Hess, 1983; Rowan, 1996; Shawver & Dickover, 1986). In fact, Rowan (1996) concludes that the introduction of more women COs might actually reduce prison violence overall. Although a lawsuit cited the harassment of women COs by men inmates, plaintiffs claimed that inmates' behavior promoted a hostile environment primarily because it was tolerated and encouraged by men coworkers and supervisors (*Antonius v. King County*, 2004; *Holloway v. King County*, 2000). The attitudes and behavior of men line staff and supervisors have been more problematic for women than the actions of inmates.

Men Coworker, Supervisor, and Subordinate Resistance

As noted earlier, women threaten the close association between the CO job and the production of masculinity. If women can do the job as well as men, the job is no longer a viable resource for constructing masculinity. Some men are supportive: CO attitude surveys indicate that men COs are less hostile toward women COs than in days past (Carlson, Thomas, & Anson, 2004; Hemmens, Stohr, Schoeler, & Miller, 2002). However, the details of attitudinal studies indicate differing degrees of acceptance of women COs by men. For example, younger, more educated, and less experienced men officers are more accepting of women COs, while older, less educated, and more experienced men officers with military backgrounds are more negative (Carlson et al., 2004; Hemmens et al., 2002; Lawrence & Mahan, 1998). Generally, women still identify men supervisors and coworkers as their major opposition in men's prisons (Britton, 2003; L. E. Zimmer, 1986), and research documents hostilities from men that are still pervasive (Pogrebin & Poole, 1997). In addition, women of color continue to face both racialized and gendered resistance (Britton, 2003).

Men individually tend to do gender in ways that underline their difference from women. They may mobilize masculinities intentionally or unconsciously in ways that bond men but separate or devalue women (P. Y. Martin, 2001). Some men supervisors and coworkers contrast "masculine" and "feminine" behavior arguing that women are too weak, physically and emotionally, to work CO jobs in men's prisons. They argue that due to "natural" physical weaknesses, women cannot perform adequately in violent encounters and will be injured. Emotional weakness means that women will be too fearful or depressed to do the job, or will be "taken in" by inmates. Some men COs report that they "step in to protect women" in conflict situations with inmates and are injured while protecting women, or when women fail to "back them up" (Jurik, 1985).

Many men supervisors and coworkers are fearful that women COs will become too "friendly" with inmates. They scrutinize and sexualize women's interactions with men inmates, watching for situations in which women get "too close." Women COs complain that men COs' interactions with inmates are rarely monitored so closely (Farkas, 1999b; Pogrebin & Poole, 1997; Stojkovic et al., 2000; L. E. Zimmer, 1986). Such scrutiny disadvantages women since interaction with inmates is a necessary part of the job and some boundary violations are inevitable in prison work. Negotiation with inmates lies at the heart of the social order of the prison (Britton, 2003; Owen, 1988; G. M. Sykes, 1958). This problem is magnified for women COs of color who may even know inmates as neighbors or relatives. They are sometimes transferred to less desirable work sites. Officers of color are also fearful about reporting the abuse of inmates of color by other staff. In such cases, women and men COs have experienced retaliation including abusive language, investigation, and disciplinary infractions (Equal Opportunities Commission, 2006; Maghan & McLeish-Blackwell, 1991).

Sexual Harassment and Women COs

Unwanted sexual attention or sexual harassment is another mechanism for constructing masculine dominance over women (Gruber & Morgan, 2005). Harassment ranges from outright statements of opposition and propositions by men COs and supervisors to more subtle forms such as joking, teasing, and name-calling (L. E. Zimmer, 1986, p. 90–105). Sexual rumor mills undermine women through frequent allegations of sexual liaisons between women officers and either staff or inmates (Britton, 2003; Sweet, 1995). The proportionately fewer men who work with women inmates also express much concern about false allegations of sexual misconduct with inmates, but they are generally supported by their women colleagues (Britton, 2003). Women COs who refuse men's protection or attention are ridiculed as lesbians, and women's perceived or real deviation from heterosexual norms constitutes a serious threat to "masculinist" work cultures (L. E. Zimmer, 1986).

Research reveals the pervasiveness and seriousness of sexual harassment in corrections and its negative impact on women COs' work experiences (Pogrebin & Poole, 1997; Savicki, Cooley, & Gjesvold, 2003). Thirty-one percent of the women COs in Belknap's (1991) jail survey said that sexual harassment had been a problem. L. E. Zimmer's (1986) intensive interviews revealed that all of the women respondents reported at least one incident of sexual harassment. Women probation officers in the United Kingdom and women COs in Canada also report flagrant sexual harassment, a men's "canteen culture," and in one case, the gang rape of women officers by men peers (Cowburn, 1998; McMahon, 1999).

Belknap's (1991) respondents distinguished between "nonsexual" but gendered "put-downs" (gender harassment) and offensive sexual comments or behaviors (sexual harassment). The first type of harassment claims that women are less capable or intelligent than men. Overtly sexual behavior includes whistling, pressuring women for sex, or comments on their bodies (Belknap, 1991, pp. 103–104). A pattern of either type of harassment may correspond to the legal concept of hostile environment sexual harassment (Gregory, 2003).

In-depth studies of sexual harassment in prisons are rare, but information gained from discrimination lawsuits provides some further details of sexual harassment in some extreme situations. For example, in one suit, women COs charged that sexual innuendo and harassment ran rampant in the prison where they worked. Complaints were met with neglect and, if they persisted, with retaliation. In the same case, women COs claimed that they were pressured to perform sexual acts in exchange for favorable work shifts (Word, 2003). In another suit, a woman supervisor in a men's prison claimed that she was subjected to rumor and disrespect from subordinates who went so far as to have their wives call child protective services to falsely accuse her of child neglect (Sweet, 1995). In a Canadian case, men COs were charged with the gang rape of two women staff in a departmental training academy (McMahon, 1999).

Perception and reporting of harassment vary among women along age and racial lines. Younger women appear more likely than older women to report sexual harassment. White women are more likely than black women to report it (45 and 13 percent, respectively), and white women also are more likely to report that men as a group "put women down" (Belknap, 1991). Racial variations in perceptions of sexual harassment may be due to the blurring of gender and racial harassment for women of color. Some women may define harassment as racial; some may perceive it as sexual. In reality, the two types of discrimination are not as easily separable as sexual harassment laws imply (Crenshaw, 1990). Comments about a black woman's sexuality may be linked to racist images of black women as sexually promiscuous (P. H. Collins, 2000). Owen (1988) reported that white women COs who were married to or dating men COs of color experienced harassment from white men coworkers.

If they are harassed by men COs of their own race, women of color face additional dilemmas. Although women COs of color generally describe men COs of their race as "very supportive" (L. E. Zimmer, 1986), when men of color harass them, women of color feel betrayed by the very group that should understand discrimination. This harassment reinforces the "outsider" status of these women. However, they may avoid reporting it because they fear that such reports will further emasculate men of their own race. Some may believe that their claims of harassment are taken less seriously than those of white women COs (Maghan & McLeish-Blackwell, 1991).

Evidence demonstrates that supervisor and coworker harassment is a source of mistrust, resentment, and job-related stress for women COs (Cullen, Link, Wolfe, & Frank, 1985; Savicki et al., 2003). Harassment reinforces the definition of women as outsiders and subordinates in the organization, and punishes them for entering men-only domains. We discuss organizational policies for dealing with harassment issues in the next chapter.

Resistance From Women Coworkers, Family, and Friends

No matter how frequent or severe, work-related stress can be reduced by social supports at home and in the workplace (Cullen, Lemming, Link, & Wozniak, 1985). For women COs, stress that accrues from the resistance of inmates and staff can be mediated by the support of women colleagues in the same predicament, or from family and friends outside of work. Unfortunately, these spheres are not always supportive of women COs.

Women COs are not a homogeneous group; some women colleagues are hostile toward other women (L. E. Zimmer, 1986). At least one study reports that men COs rated their women colleagues as a group more highly than women COs rated themselves as a group (Carlson et al., 2004). Some women COs resent being supervised by other women (Belknap, 1991). Women who have different styles of doing their job sometimes oppose one another (Jurik, 1988; L. E. Zimmer, 1986). Women COs of color may encounter racial prejudice from white women coworkers (Britton, 2003; Owen, 1988). Although women COs have tried to establish networks for coping with the barriers to women, men supervisors who fear such alliances have tried to block them (Jurik, 1985).

For most of us, family and friends can provide support and respite from workday pressures. However, this dimension of the woman CO's life is not always trouble free.

Some women COs encounter resentment of their nontraditional jobs from husbands, dates, friends, or other family. Some husbands define their wives' careers as challenges to their masculinity. They are insecure if their wives have higher job status and resent wives' long hours and rotating shifts. L. E. Zimmer (1986) found that COs' husbands were more supportive if their wives accepted the protection of men colleagues at work. Black and white women COs identify problems with marginally employed or unemployed mates (Maghan & McLeish-Blackwell, 1991). Other COs report that their mates see their job as "unfeminine." Some black women COs say that their spouses have a difficult time "seeing me in uniform" (Maghan & McLeish-Blackwell, 1991).

Children and parents may fear for women COs' safety. The woman CO may respond by hiding fears and refusing to discuss work-related problems with fearful or hostile family members. This containment of emotions can heighten work-related stress. Several studies find that regardless of gender, COs experience family-work conflict (Hogan, Lambert, Jenkins, & Wambold, 2006; Lambert, Hogan, & Barton, 2004), but another study reports that women COs experience more of such conflict than do men COs (Triplett, Mullings, & Scarborough, 1999).

Although women colleagues and outside friends and family often offer support to women COs, this pattern is inconsistent. For women COs, social supports can be hard to find (Sweet, 1995).

Proponents of Women COs: Alternative Gendered Identities

Despite the diversity that now characterizes prison work culture, gender is one of its fundamental organizing features. The exclusionary and hostile interactions surrounding women COs, as well as the negative images of women that justify such exclusion, are part of larger occupational, cultural, and societal dynamics that devalue women (Acker, 1992).

Although other men and some women coworkers and supervisors continue to oppose affirmative action and rationalization principles, pro-reform, professional cultures have presented formidable challenges to anti-reform "old-guard" cultures that devalue women. To the "old-guard" culture, bureaucratic paperwork, limitations on CO discretion, and emphasis on dispute management and communication skills represent attempts to feminize the job (Hunt, 1990; Tracy & Scott, 2006).

Working against the "old-guard" culture, Robert Johnson (1987) emphasized the emergence of new human service–oriented COs who support correctional reform, professionalization, and women COs. In more recent studies, scholars in several countries report similar trends (Carlen, 2001; King, 2000; Moon & Maxwell, 2004; Szockyj, 1989; Walters & Lagace, 1999). In the United States, these human service–oriented COs include some white men COs, staff, and supervisors, as well as white women and men and women of color at all ranks (Denborough, 2001; Farkas, 1999a; Stohr, Lovrich, & Mays, 1997; Walters, 1993). Such work cultures advance a different vision of CO competence from that of "old-guard" cultures. They emphasize the custodial and service/counseling aspects of the job, and gender-neutral models of professional competence (Farkas, 1999b; Jurik, 1988).

Some supporters of women, including COs, supervisors, women's rights advocates, and prison reformers, have constructed alternative images of competence that emphasize women's unique capacities and their positive contribution to work in men's prisons. Like 19th-century women reformers and modern cultural feminists, they view women COs as different from men COs in ways that can actually improve CO-inmate relations and the prison environment. This image of women COs contrasts with opponents' arguments that women's differences are harmful to prison order and discipline. Proponents suggest that different gender role socialization patterns give women better communication skills, which enable them to diffuse conflict more effectively than men can (L. E. Zimmer, 1986). Prison literature refers to this phenomenon as the "calming effect" of women COs on men inmates. Men inmates have reported that women COs help normalize the prison environment (King, 2000; Kissel & Katsampes, 1980).

At the same time, the construction of "women as different" carries potential dangers. First, these unified images of femininity ignore the diversity of behavior among women COs. Second, readily accepting the existence of preemployment "feminine" differences from men can reinforce the existence of other, more negative and limiting images of feminine capacities (e.g., Marquart et al., 2001; Worley et al., 2002). Moreover, as prison overcrowding has undermined reform agendas, "old-guard" definitions of masculine competence may undermine the importance of "feminine" virtues (Britton, 2003; Jurik & Martin, 2001).

Difference arguments also overemphasize the power of individuals or small groups to effect change in large organizations (Anleu, 1992). If women do not exhibit the predicted differences in job performance, some may question the necessity of hiring and promoting women. At a more general level, emphasis on "feminine styles" continues to focus on assessing women COs as a homogenous group by comparing them to men as a homogenous group.

The emphasis in the literature on women in corrections clearly exemplifies the preoccupation with men as a standard for evaluating women COs. Studies that compare women CO demographics, attitudes, and behavior to those of men COs continue to proliferate. Such studies fluctuate between arguments that women do the job the same and just as well as men and claims that women do the job differently and better than men. In either case, men's behavior serves as the norm against which women COs are assessed. This research will be discussed in the next chapter.

Summary

Women have played prominent roles in corrections since the late 1800s, but it was not until the 1970s that women supervised men inmates. Changes in women's correctional jobs were precipitated by a variety of societal and organization-level changes: social activism, economic recession, equal employment opportunity laws, prison reform efforts, and explosions in prison inmate populations.

Despite their increasing numbers, women continue to face barriers in nontraditional correctional jobs. Their presence limits the CO job as a resource for constructing masculinity. Although more positive than in initial stages of women's expanded roles in corrections, men opponents continue to construct images of feminine physical and emotional vulnerability. Racism and diverse occupational styles still divide women COs into sometimes hostile camps. Women's behaviors are still sexualized.

The roots of imagery about women's inappropriateness in men's corrections are best understood within the context of the job and its surrounding work cultures. Some work cultures, built on a shared sense of masculinity and dominated by white, rural, working-class definitions of masculinity, have been shaken by the entrance of new types of workers that include white women, men and women of color, and also college-educated, urban, reform-oriented and bureaucratically oriented administrators and staff. Prison organizations continue to base structure and practice on culturally dominant images of masculinity. Men's behavior is still the norm by which women COs and inmates are judged.

Drawing on discourses of reform and affirmative action, prison experts and supportive staff have constructed opposing images of competence arguing that "feminine talents" are an asset in modern prisons. Women may exert a "calming effect" through superior communication and conflict-diffusion skills, or because of men inmates' reluctance to be disrespectful to them. However, these images, as well as those of opponents, perpetuate images of women and men COs as largely undifferentiated and opposing groups.

Missing in research on women COs are more in-depth analyses of the experiences of women working in corrections, especially examinations of the experiences of women of color, lesbians, and women of different ages and at different stages of their careers. Also given the increasing presence of privately operated prisons, more studies are needed about women's work experiences in such facilities.

These gendered interactions, identities, and work cultures are located within larger organizational contexts. Chapter 8 focuses on the gendered and racialized organizational logic of modern correctional agencies and its impact on the career progression of women COs. It discusses women COs' individual and collective responses to barriers, and the significance of their actions for the social control world of corrections.

Gendered Organizational Logic and Women CO Response

I n the last chapter, we examined women's expanding roles in the correctional system, specifically focusing on women working as correctional officers (COs) in men's prisons. We argued that discourses of equal employment opportunity and prison reform were supportive of women's entry into traditionally all-men's correctional spheres in the late 1970s and 1980s. Although one research study (e.g., Marquart, Barnhill, & Balshaw-Biddle, 2001) and the anecdotal impressions of men coworkers and supervisors (Britton, 2003; L. E. Zimmer, 1986) suggest that women COs are more vulnerable to physical attack and seductions by inmates, most research suggests that women do the job as effectively as men (Holeman & Krepps-Hess, 1982). However, justifications for women's presence grounded in reform discourses argue further that women officers actually promote a more orderly and humane prison environment (Kissell & Katsampes, 1980).

Of course, for women to have a significant impact on the prison environment, most agree that it is necessary for them to reach a critical mass. Gender-neutral organizational theory (Kanter, 1977) suggests that until a minority social type (e.g., gender, racial group) comprises at least 15 percent of the work group, members of the minority group will experience performance pressure, ostracism, and negative stereotyping by those in the majority. Since women now comprise more than 15 percent of the security force in many men's prisons, it is reasonable to ask (1) whether the barriers to women COs have vanished or greatly lessened over time as their numbers have increased and (2) whether women have made prisons more humane through a uniquely feminine approach.

Although these queries follow logically from a number of popular arguments about women's experiences in and impact on traditionally male fields, we will see in this chapter that such questions do not have simple answers. On the one hand, women's proportions in traditionally men's prison jobs are increasing, and research indicates that men COs are more positive about them (e.g., Carlson, Thomas, & Anson, 2004). On the other hand, men's support for women COs varies considerably, and women still report a variety of barriers that stem from the masculinist culture of corrections (Britton, 1997; Lawrence & Mahan, 1998).

With regard to women's impact on the field of corrections, some research suggests that women COs do effect reductions in violent incidents within men's prisons and that they are more positive about the rehabilitative or human service dimensions of their jobs (Lariviere & Robinson, 1996; Rowan, 1996). Yet, most research on COs indicates that women hold more values in common with than differences from men coworkers (Stohr, Lovrich, & Mays, 1997). Reports of the inmate abuses by women as well as by men officers in the U.S.-run Abu Ghraib prison indicate graphically that women are not exempt from the inhumanities associated with war and prison life (Wikipedia, 2006). In addition, today's prisons seem to be as dangerous, and reports of inhumanities in them seem to be as widespread as ever (A. Y. Davis, 2003; V. Young & Reviere, 2006). Even prison systems that have a history of humane treatment for inmates (e.g., the Netherlands, West Germany) are becoming less rehabilitative and more punitive than in previous times (Christie, 2000; Kommer, 1993). Officers do exhibit differences in attitudes and deeds, but these variations occur as much within gender groups as across them, and again, the similarity of officer viewpoints across gender, age, race, and tenure is always daunting for those of us who want to argue that a few individuals can change the world (Britton, 1997; Stohr, Lovrich, & Wood, 1996).

The key to understanding the continued barriers to women officers and the limited impacts that women have made on the field lies in understanding the power of the prison as an organization. The experiences and behavior of prison staff and inmates as individuals cannot be understood without reference to the nature of prison organizations and the larger societal context in which they are located. Social forces such as cultural images and divisions of labor and power simultaneously shape organizations like prisons and the behavior of those in them. Cultural ideas about gender, race, and sexuality structure the prison organization and frame the routine interactions there. However, it is also important to stress that social forces and prison organizations do not fully determine behavior. Human identities are emergent features of prison interactions that can reproduce but also challenge existing organizational practices and even the social arrangements outside prison walls. In this chapter, we outline how prison organizations are gendered, racialized, and sexualized in ways that are intended or unintended, and conscious or unconscious. We focus especially on the ways that organizational arrangements shape women COs' work experiences and struggles to do good jobs and perhaps even make a difference in today's prisons.

Gendered, Racialized, Sexualized, and Embodied Prison Organizations

Despite popular ideology, prisons are not neutral with regard to issues of gender, race, and sexuality. Gendered, racialized, and sexualized practices are deeply embedded within the history and contemporary reality of prison operation (Sabo, Kupers, & London, 2001). Many of these practices serve to devalue inmates and staff alike, but especially women inmates and officers. Class issues also frame popular images and functions of prisons. Most prison and jail inmates are poor, have less than a high school education, and have been charged with or convicted of street crimes. Critics of incarceration practices charge that prisons function as warehouses for the poor and unemployed in capitalist societies (Parenti, 1999). The management of bodily functions and behavior are also a key component of life and work in prisons, and women's bodies are especially problematic in these settings.

Angela Y. Davis (2003), Dana Britton (2003), and Don Sabo and colleagues (2001) provide in-depth descriptions of the ways that gendered and racialized images and practices formed U.S. prisons. The prototypical inmate is a poor man of color; he is expected to exhibit a tough, emotionless demeanor and physically aggressive behavior. He may exhibit violence and uncontrollable sexual urges (Aiken, 1983–1984) but can be managed through emotionless, tough, and consistent masculine discipline (Britton, 2003; Tracy, 2005).

Racialized Prisons

A. Y. Davis (2003), Britton (2003), and other scholars (e.g., V. Young & Reviere, 2006) trace the racialized history of prisons that included special offense codes designed to incarcerate African-Americans and use them as prison farm labor long after slavery was abolished. Modern-day legislation provides stiff penalties for drugs more typically used by persons of color and less severe penalties for drugs typically used by middle-class whites. The revival of chain gangs in today's prisons and jails also conjures up images of past all-black slave and later prison farm chained work crews (A. Y. Davis, 2003). COs must often deal with tensions among diverse racial and ethnic groups in prisons, and these tensions may characterize relationships among officers themselves. Inmate membership in gangs organized along racial, ethnic, and neighborhood lines fuel these conflicts, although they are sometimes encouraged by corrupt prison staff.

COs of color feel tension if they complain about abusive treatment of inmates of their own race. They also feel pressured to avoid the appearance of being too close with inmates of their own race (Owen, 1988). This expectation of social distance is more than a little ironic given that an important argument for hiring more officers of color was that they might better relate to the disproportionate numbers of inmates who are persons of color.

Racial and ethnic tensions in jails and prisons have been further heightened by anti-immigrant rhetoric and imprisonment policies, and the angers and fears concerning terrorist acts against the United States and other Western nations (Summerill, 2005). U.S.-run prisons in Afghanistan and Iraq have been the sites of acts of physical cruelty and culturally loaded abuse of inmates by U.S. detention staff (Wikipedia, 2006). Since some of the abused victims had not been charged with any crimes, the acts appear all the more heinous. These incidents, especially in the context of official orders about the treatment of "military detainees," again raise the specter that inhumane treatment of prison inmates is acceptable.

Prisons as Gendered

Prisons and programs for inmates were also developed in ways that reflect the gender stereotypes that men are violent and dangerous while women are in need of guidance and direction. Facilities for men were oriented toward containment and surveillance. The buildings were often designed in a panoptic style, which permits anonymous and sweeping views of inmates. Women's facilities were designed more like cottages and emphasized a more homelike atmosphere and the resocialization of inmates so that they would become "proper" women. Even today, disciplinary orders in prisons reflect these distinctions, with men's prisons being more rigidly rule bound and women's prisons entailing more flexible regimes. Historically, women of color were often exempt from this kinder, gentler treatment and sometimes imprisoned in men's facilities long after practices of separate incarceration became widespread (Britton, 2003; A. Y. Davis, 2003; Rafter, 1990).

Both men and women COs express preferences for working with men inmates. They view the design and disciplinary structure of men's facilities as "the way real prisons should be." They believe that the architectural design and disciplinary structure of women's facilities fosters a chaotic and unpredictable atmosphere where they too easily become ensnared in women's emotional problems and disputes (Britton, 1999). In part, the greater flexibility in women's prisons represents the relatively less severe criminal histories that characterize women as a group, but it is also consistent with cultural stereotypes that construct women as emotional and passive. Apart from any gender stereotyping of inmates, it is the case that advancement in corrections has been greater for those working in men's prisons. This difference is certainly in part due to the greater size of men's facilities and consequent number of advancement slots, but is also due to the construction of women's facilities as deviations from the generic (men's) prison (Britton, 1999).

Regardless of the historical differences between prisons, women's facilities are increasingly subjected to an "equality with a vengeance"; that is, their design and disciplinary practices are becoming more akin to the strict and harsh treatment of men's prisons (Chesney-Lind & Pasko, 2004). Thus, even with notions of equality, men's standards are the benchmark for women. Despite this purported equality with regard to level of punitiveness, vocational programs are still less prevalent in women's than in men's facilities, and where they exist, they continue to reflect gender-stereotypic job training and therapeutic regimens (Micucci & Monster, 2004).

Prisons as Sexualized

Although prisons ostensibly prohibit sexual liaisons on their premises, behaviors of both inmates and officers are highly sexualized (Sabo et al., 2001). Officers are privy to exposure of inmate bodies in showers, cells, and elsewhere. Even when officers make strong efforts to behave professionally, these interactions may take on sexualized meanings that violate both inmate and officer sense of dignity and privacy (Carlen & Worrall, 2004). Sometimes, these interactions are also used by officers or inmates to embarrass or demean one another (*Holloway v. King County*, 1999).

Another prevalent form of sexuality in prison includes sexual relationships between same-sex inmates; some are consensual and others are the result of peer pressure, intense fear, or sheer physical force. Prison rape is an under-researched topic, but extant research and human rights commission investigations suggest that it is a widespread problem all over the world (Amnesty International, 1999; Sabo et al., 2001). Although inmates who are known as gay are often segregated in men's facilities and viewed as less than real men, most sex among inmates is typically regarded by staff as a consensual and temporary adaptation to prison life. It may at times be the subject of humor, but often it is ignored. Staff view men's liaisons as the result of pure physical need, but women's more family-like relationships are seen as emotional yet trivialized attachments (Britton, 2003). Staff responses to sexual relationships among inmates in specific situations are framed by these images.

Sexual relations between staff and inmates are strictly prohibited, and officially result in disciplinary procedures for inmates and termination for staff. The rape of women inmates by men staff has been the subject of inmate lawsuits and citation of prisons worldwide for human rights abuses, but even routine strip searches of women inmates by men officers are also highly contested issues in prisons today (A. Y. Davis, 2003). These searches are particularly traumatic for the many women inmates who have a past history of sexual abuse (V. Young & Reviere, 2006). Feminist and human rights activists dispute definitions of any officer-inmate sexual relationship as consensual (A. Y. Davis, 2003). Regardless of their status as "chosen" or forced, sex between officers and inmates is viewed as a danger to prison security and inmate welfare.

Although there have been cases in which women COs have been taken hostage and raped by men inmates (P. Johnson, 1991; Liebling & Price, 2001; Villa, 2004), these incidents have not been systematically analyzed. Extant research indicates that women are less likely to be injured by inmates than are men COs (Rowan, 1996; Shawver & Dickover, 1986). Sexual relationships between women officers and men inmates are more typically constructed as either "consensual" or the outcome of women's seduction by men inmates (Britton, 2003). Even "consensual" sexual relationships between COs and inmates are viewed as serious disciplinary infractions (Marquart et al., 2001). Opponents often try to discredit women COs by claiming that such seductions are a common occurrence. However, qualitative evidence suggests that women COs are monitored far more closely than men COs and that reports of woman CO–man inmate liaisons take on mythic proportions. The details of an alleged seduction were recounted repeatedly throughout several facilities, and each storyteller claimed the seduction had occurred in his prison (Jurik, 1985; also see Britton, 2003). Women officers complain that even routine interactions with inmates often lead to false charges of disciplinary infractions to the point that they have difficulty doing their jobs properly (Britton, 2003; L.E. Zimmer, 1986). It is difficult to assess even official reports of women COs' boundary violations with men COs because of the surveillance faced by women working in men's prisons (Farkas, 1999b). Inappropriate liaisons between staff and inmates of the same sex are rarely a topic of discussion or official records (Marquart et al., 2001).

Relationships between women and men staff in prison settings are highly sexualized. Evidence presented in a number of lawsuits and research studies suggests that the sexual harassment of women COs by men peers and supervisors is still extensive. Sexual harassment policies are important organizational features that can further limit women's careers in corrections.

Sexual Harassment Policies and the Gendered Organization

In Chapter 7, we discussed the problem of sexual harassment. Strong and well-implemented sexual harassment policies are an organizational method for prohibiting and punishing some of the most egregious offenses in this realm. Since the late 1980s, most correctional agencies have adopted sexual harassment policies, and women COs report that many of the most overt forms of hostilities toward women have subsided (Britton, 2003). Yet, women correctional staff continue to experience more harassment than do men COs, and their reports include both gender and sexual types of harassment (Altendorf, 2003; Savicki, Cooley, & Gjesvold, 2003). Sexual harassment policies in some agencies remain vague, and organizations lack adequate training and administrative follow-through for sanctions against harassing behaviors (Pogrebin & Poole, 1997; Sweet, 1995; Word, 2003). Women COs also still fear reprisals for reporting sexual harassment (Britton, 2003). Even women prison wardens experience sexual harassment from colleagues and subordinates that they do not report (Altendorf, 2003). Consequently, the vast majority of problems with sexual harassment are ignored or handled on an informal and individual basis with mixed success. Both racial and sexual harassment contribute to job burnout, stress, and turnover for men of color and women working in corrections (Savicki et al., 2003; Stojkovic & Farkas, 2003).

Sexual and racial harassment is most problematic for COs when they work in an organizational context that promotes and/or tolerates such conduct. Although most formal sexual harassment complaints involve abuses by men coworkers or supervisors (Morton, 1991a), even harassment by inmates becomes problematic if COs are not given the organizational support to manage it. For example, women COs working in Seattle's King County jails claimed that they were routinely subjected to the sexually offensive, oppressive, and threatening behaviors of inmates. They argued that efforts to report and discipline inmates for such behavior were undermined by men officers and supervisors. Plaintiffs also complained that administrators and supervisors routinely disciplined inmates for threats made toward men officers and for less severe behavioral problems. Men COs also brought in pornographic materials for inmates to view. Women COs were told that inmate threats and offensive sexual behaviors were part of the conditions of work in the jail facilities. Women COs who continued to complain about these conditions were subjected to less desirable work assignments and disciplinary actions. This suit was resolved with a consent decree that mandated a number of organizational changes to address problems that the plaintiffs had identified. These will be discussed in the final section of this chapter (*Antonius v. King County*, 2004; *Holloway v. King County*, 1999, 2000).

Maeve McMahon (1999) details a scandal case in the Canadian Correctional Services (CCS) in which two female staff were sexually assaulted by men colleagues at a training school run by the ministry. Further investigation revealed a long-term pattern of gender-based discrimination and sexual harassment in facilities within the CCS. McMahon concludes that this pattern was reinforced by lack of administrative follow-through in the implementation of affirmative action and sexual harassment policies, and also by a backlash against the additional opportunities extended to women in the CCS. Although women had been hired to work in the CCS, very little was done to address the masculine culture of the organization that prevailed long after women's entry into the department.

In many organizations, the handling of harassment complaints is sometimes insensitive to the concrete experiences of workers who are being harassed. One-size-fits-all policies also equate different forms of harassment (e.g., rape versus harassing talk or touching) and the different experiences of men and women across racial and ethnic groups (McMahon, 1999). For example, sexual harassment policies rarely are sensitive to the work experiences of women COs of color. Their harassment is often linked to their race as well as their gender, and they may fear reporting even more than do white women (Maghan & McLeish-Blackwell, 1991). Additional research is needed to develop adequate policies to confront such problems. There also has been insufficient research on the harassment experiences of openly gay and lesbian correctional staff although research suggests that harassment due to actual and suspected homosexual workers is frequent and severe in the workforce in general, and in the criminal justice workforce in particular (Miller, Forest, & Jurik, 2003; Schneider, 1982, 1991).

Like other work organizations, correctional agencies have made significant progress in developing, disseminating, and enforcing sexual harassment policies. However, in order to promote an environment that welcomes rather than devalues women's contribution, existing practices need improvement. Since departments tend to handle sexual harassment complaints internally, this permits information leaks and corruption of investigations by informal friendships (McMahon, 1999; Sweet, 1995). Although unions have adopted more explicit prohibitions against discrimination and harassment than in preceding years, they are often in the position of defending men officers who are the subjects of repeated sexual harassment complaints by women officers who are also union members (AFSCME Union, 2006; L. E. Zimmer, 1986).

Some researchers suggest that increasing percentages of women in corrections will lessen sexual harassment and other hostilities (Stohr et al., 1997). However, others suggest that gender is still so closely associated with work in corrections that the more women enter and perform well within the field, the more resentful men colleagues will become (Pogrebin & Poole, 1997). Without strong administrative support and follow-through that include training, periodic reviews, and systematic sanctions reflecting the gravity of the offenses, informal hostilities persist (L. E. Zimmer, 1989). Sexual harassment policies must also be informed by understandings of the ways in which the gendered, racially, and sexually charged atmospheres of prisons give rise to diverse forms of harassing behaviors.

Corrections as Embodied Work and Women as Embodied Workers

The work of COs entails tending to many aspects of inmate bodies. COs chaperone inmates to bathrooms, conduct bodily searches, and sometimes clean up inmate bodily messes (Tracy & Scott, 2006). Prison policies regulating bodies assume that the typical inmate and typical CO are men.

Women inmate and women CO bodies constitute deviations that pose problems in prison life. Women inmates experience difficulties because medical services are based upon male models of care that are often inadequate for women's bodily needs. Examples of such needs are gynecological problems and issues related to pregnancy and childbirth (A. Y. Davis, 2003). Staff in prisons often view women's bodies as messy and entailing unpleasant extra work. For prison administrators, women inmates' bodily needs are organizationally problematic (Britton, 1999). Women COs face similar problems. Work in corrections, including the physical requirements to qualify for the position, uniforms for the job, scheduling priorities, and associated health care and sick leave policies are also based upon men's bodies. The shape, functions, and problems associated with women's bodies do not comport well with such employment policies.

Women COs working in men's prisons experience a range of other issues related to bodies. Women must routinely cope with exposure to inmate bodies, including displays designed to humiliate, threaten, or otherwise undermine women (*Holloway v. King County*, 1999; L. E. Zimmer, 1986). Women COs are also confronted with the need to manage their own bodies in a traditionally all-male environment. Women who pioneered these jobs report issues of managing the discomfort associated with wearing uniforms designed for men's bodies (L. E. Zimmer, 1986). In one facility, women were forced to use restroom facilities not only designed for but occupied by men colleagues (Jurik, 1985). A woman CO, who was one of the first two women assigned to work in an Arizona men's prison, was ordered to strip search two busloads of men inmates while her men coworkers stood around watching (Sweet, 1995).

Women COs must also deal with the rigors of work in corrections and handle the bodily issues surrounding pregnancy and childbirth with limited time for maternity leaves. Despite widespread publicity surrounding the "growing gender equality" in the 1970s and 1980s, women continue to provide a primary and disproportionate share of home care, child care, and extended family care (J. A. Jacobs & Gerson, 2004). Predominant models of paid work (e.g., rigid work schedules, absence of paid family leave) presume that employees lack responsibilities for the day-to-day care of children and other family members. Corrections is no exception. The CO's job is inflexible: absence or tardiness may jeopardize an entire unit; there is a constant demand for shift coverage. Continuing societal patterns whereby women bear the primary responsibility for household and family matters produce conflicts between work and home obligations for women COs, especially working mothers (Triplett, Mullings, & Scarborough, 1999).

When women's roles in corrections first began to expand, many agencies lacked any consistent pregnancy leave policy, and in many cases, pregnant women were forced to take unpaid leaves of absence or simply quit. Forced leaves caused financial hardship and disadvantaged women for future promotions (Morton, 1991a). By the late 1980s, many agencies had established policies. An American Correctional Association survey revealed that most responding state correctional agencies have instituted pregnancy and maternity leave policies (Morton, 1991a). Paternity leave was allowed by 39 percent of the departments surveyed, but the policies varied greatly across states. Only 14 states provided for the reinstatement of employees on sick leave to their former or equal-status jobs. Adherence to these maternity policies was also problematic. New research is needed to determine the current nature and extent of pregnancy and family leave policies in corrections agencies today and to evaluate the degree to which they are being properly implemented.

Without strong and adequately implemented family leave policies, women must choose between or compromise both their jobs and their families. Some women COs defer advancement opportunities in order to have a family and continue working. Balancing family responsibilities with paid work is a dilemma for women and leads to increased work-family stress among women COs (Triplett et al., 1999).

Promoting Equality in Prison Organizations: A Case Example

The purpose and cultural significance of prisons remains hotly contested ground, and gender and racial subordination remain embedded in prison organizational practices. However, in some cases, administrators have been able to successfully challenge past organizational practices and cultures and promote institutional reforms that include racial and gender equality (Chivers, 2001; Janofsky, 1998).

Director Perry Johnson of the Michigan Department of Corrections describes his efforts to change the correctional work culture and improve conditions of inmate confinement in his agency (P. Johnson, 1991). When Johnson assumed command during the 1970s, like many departments, Michigan corrections was under orders to improve prison operations and conditions. Its workforce was predominantly composed of white men. Johnson decided to diversify his staff to promote reform in prison operations and avail his department of the increasing numbers of qualified men of color and women in the workforce at the time. His efforts and those of his successors led to significant changes in department demographics over the past 30 years. In 1975, the department's personnel office set a goal that at least 15 percent of hires for entry-level positions would be persons of color, women, or ex-offenders. The percentage of women COs at that time constituted about 12 percent of the department workforce. By 1984, that figure had risen to 29 percent. As of 2004, women constituted 38 percent of the department workforce. In addition, 44 percent of wardens and 38 percent of top management staff were women (Withrow & Burke, 2005).

It is important to stress that Johnson not only increased the numbers of women in the department, he also analyzed prison culture and operations looking for unnecessary barriers to the successful job performance of new entrants, especially women and persons of color. For example, he scrutinized training to determine if it was sufficient to meet the needs of new entrants who might not have law enforcement backgrounds. Central academy training was followed by a program of on-the-job support to prevent initial training from being undermined by old-guard–oriented officers. Johnson sent new administrators to intensive leadership training sessions to bolster their confidence. Facilities installed screens for inmate showers to provide privacy for them while women COs monitored their living quarters. Johnson noticed that the guns used in guard towers had so much recoil that many women had difficulty handling them. He replaced these guns with newer and better weapons that had less recoil. The department also provided a sexual harassment hotline to circumvent problems with having to report harassment up the chain of command. The hotline was supplemented with a network of experienced women staff who could assist a complainant in assessing options (P. Johnson, 1991, p. 11). Johnson (1991) argues that, typical of the many changes he made to accommodate a diversifying workforce, these adjustments improved prison life for inmates, operational efficiencies, and the work environment for all staff. The department used a variety of other techniques to recruit and successfully integrate men of color and women into its ranks. These included (1) enlisting assistance from community colleges and universities for applicant referral, (2) providing financial assistance to pay moving expenses for job relocation, (3) employing former inmates, (4) downgrading jobs for training purposes to "open doors" for newer staff, (5) reviews of examinations to determine if they contained unnecessary gender and cultural barriers, and (6) reexamination of positions formerly held only by men to see if women could qualify (Withrow & Burke, 2005).

Women officers and administrators employed during Johnson's term provide testimonies about his organizational successes and support of women staff (Withrow & Burke, 2005). These women also added training, mentoring, and networking groups for new recruits. The first black director of the department, Bob Brown, was appointed in the 1980s, and he continued affirmative hiring practices. For example, he appointed Denise Quarles, who was the first woman deputy director in the department. The diversification of staff paralleled improved ratings for organizational performance and conditions of prisoner confinement in the Michigan system. They also facilitated the department's release from a federal consent decree (Withrow & Burke, 2005). The Michigan case exemplifies the success that can be derived from serious commitments and administrative follow-through in changing correctional organization cultures. It also demonstrates the presumed link that we described in Chapter 7 between efforts to reform prison conditions and diversification of the correctional workforce.

Despite nationwide efforts in the United States aimed at humanizing inmate treatment and reducing both overt and institutionalized gender and racial discrimination, some groups both within and outside of prisons opposed the demise of traditional prison cultures. Even more problematic for achieving prison reform goals has been the expansion of inmate populations worldwide wrought by get-tough crime control strategies during the 1980s and 1990s. Although crime control and increased incarceration strategies were ostensibly gender neutral, they nevertheless promoted negatively gendered, racialized, and dangerous prison organizations. They reinforced images in the minds of men and women officers, supervisors, policy makers, and the general public that generic inmates are poor men of color and that the COs who guard them must be strong, aggressive men. Women inmates and women officers are devalued deviations from these norms.

Social Context and the Shifting
Organizational Logic of Corrections

During the last third of the 20th century, a variety of social pressures converged to impede both prison reform and efforts to challenge masculinist prison cultures. There have been large-scale changes in corrections, especially in jails and prisons. Most concretely, public anger and fears about crime have been stimulated by media and political rhetoric about rising crime rates in the 1970s, drug crimes in the 1980s, and terrorism in the aftermath of the 2001 destruction of the World Trade Center (W. J. Chambliss, 1995; Clear, Cole, & Reisig, 2006). Citizens have supported politicians who advocate get-tough-on-crime measures, and these include longer and harsher punishments and the demise of inmate rehabilitation policies. Crime policy has become even more racialized through the so-called "Southern Strategy" wherein racism masqueraded as anticrime sentiments (e.g., differential penalties for crack and powder cocaine and the 1988 presidential campaign ad featuring Willie Horton, a "dangerous" black criminal who was "too easily" released from prison; Beckett & Sasson, 2000).

As we discussed in Chapter 1, these policies were not isolated but were part of a larger social, political, and economic context. From the 1980s on, there has been a conservative political trend fueled by economic insecurity, exaggerated claims of reverse discrimination, and anticrime rhetoric (Davey, 1995). This mood has supported reduced government spending for social investments (e.g., welfare, education, medical care), challenges to affirmative action programs, the individualization of social responsibility, and a faith in the market as the best means for solving social problems. Media and political campaigns often contain vilifications of criminals, women on welfare, beneficiaries of affirmative action, immigrants, and "profit-hungry" disaster victims that inspire public awareness of the dangers inherent in too easily extending a helping hand to unworthy persons, especially those who are poor people of color.

These trends have converged to produce record incarceration levels in the United States. By the end of 2004, U.S. prisons and jails incarcerated over 2.1 million persons. These figures are produced by rates of incarceration of 123 women inmates per 100,000 women and 1,348 men inmates per 100,000 men. These general rates hide the racial differences in rates of incarceration: 3,218 black men, 1,220 Hispanic men, and 463 white men are incarcerated per each 100,000 population of the total number of men in their racial group, respectively (Bureau of Justice Statistics, 2005). African-American women are imprisoned at a rate eight times that of white women, and Hispanic women are imprisoned at a rate four times that of white women (V. Young & Reviere, 2006). Although violent crime rates have fallen over the past several years, incarceration rates are still rising. Today's inmate populations constitute a record proportion of individuals incarcerated in the United States. The number of those incarcerated continued to increase as we entered the 21st century. Jails and prisons continue to operate significantly above capacity (i.e., at 16 percent above capacity for prisons and 94 percent above capacity for jails), and inmates continue to be sentenced for longer durations (Bureau of Justice Statistics,

2005). The rate of incarceration in the United States significantly surpasses rates for other nations, with Russia being the country that comes the closest to U.S. rates (Christie, 2000; A. Y. Davis, 2003). The differential between African-American and white inmates is so dramatic that several analysts have described the U.S. prison system as the American Gulag, thus likening the U.S. system to that of Russia at the height of its repressive Stalinist regime (Christie, 2000). However, the rates of incarceration in other nations are increasing, and prison overcrowding is a global problem that threatens inmate programs and services as well as the safety of staff and inmates alike (Christie, 2000; MacDonald, 2003).

At the same time that more inmates are serving longer prison terms, there are fewer resources for prison services and programs, especially those that might be rehabilitative. Some human service sentiments remain and are increasingly shared by many COs (Farkas, 1999a; Stohr et al., 1997), but the security concerns associated with extreme prison and jail overcrowding continually challenge and often trump human service discourses. In addition, the deterioration of mental health care that has accompanied cuts in social services means that poor people with mental problems wind up in the criminal justice system as a treatment of last resort (T. White, 2005). Anti-immigration laws and terrorist fears have led to the detention and incarceration of growing numbers of legal and undocumented immigrants, many of whom have committed no criminal offense (Summerill, 2005). The care of these groups constitutes a mandate for corrections that is largely unfunded. Drug-addicted, mentally ill, and immigrant detainees and offenders may also need special treatment and health care programs. Without them, jails and prisons become more violent and serve as breeding grounds for both future crimes and infectious diseases (e.g., AIDS, hepatitis, tuberculosis). The size of the prison population and the range of problems associated with these new inmates make incarceration increasingly more costly and prison work more difficult.

Although many prisons and jails have long relied on private vendors to provide food, medical, and other services for inmates, the 1980s chronicle the development and expansion of privately operated prisons in the United States, Canada, England, Europe, and Australia (James, Bottomley, Liebling, & Clare, 1997). Public officials sought to reduce the exploding costs associated with operating jails and prisons, and the private sector was hailed as a quick solution. By 2000, there were 264 private prisons for adults in the United States and Puerto Rico with a capacity of over 91,000 inmates. They now house about 7 percent of U.S. inmates (Bureau of Justice Statistics, 2003). Private prisons and jails constitute well over a billion-dollar business (Hallett, 2002) and are a source of expanding employment for correctional workers, especially for women working in line staff and administrative categories (as reported in Table 7.1). However, the training, benefits, and pay associated with these jobs are typically inferior to those of positions in publicly operated facilities (Blakely & Bumphus, 2004; Raher, 2002). Private prisons are also associated with problems of quality and accountability of services and, in some cases, outright abuse of inmates (Sclar, 2000; Useem & Goldstone, 2002). Private prison corporations have also been criticized for the use of racialized imagery in selling their "product" to the general public at the same time as they help to transform inmate bodies into commodities that they are paid to keep (Hallett, 2002). Although CO unions have been very vocal opponents of prison privatization, there is also a more general movement to demand increased monitoring of and accountability for inmate and staff treatment in these facilities (American Friends Service Committee, 2003; Hallett & Lee, 2000; Raher, 2002).

Despite the widely publicized need to improve the services in private prisons, their purported "cost-effectiveness" has spawned a wide-ranging effort to emulate businesslike operations in publicly operated facilities (Jurik, 2004; Sclar, 2000). Such new managerial discourses justify further reductions in the programs and services available for inmates in public prisons, and increase the pressures on staff in all facilities to "do more with less."

Conflicting Correctional Organizational Directives

Prison and jail overcrowding stifles the implementation of inmate services and programs and promotes a more dangerous milieu for both inmates and staff (Useem & Goldstone, 2002). This climate also bolsters fears about women COs in men's prisons (Jurik & Martin, 2001). When conflicts arise, security concerns and the continued conflation of competence with masculinity prevail (Tracy & Scott, 2006; Walters, 1993, p. 57).

Conflicts between security and service directives are heightened by another correctional dilemma, which concerns just how punitive prison life should be. The U.S. Supreme Court has addressed this issue, for example, when it considered whether inmates could be subjected to corporal punishment or other physical mistreatment (Murton & Hyams, 1969). Although the issue of physical mistreatment has ostensibly been resolved (*South Carolina v. Edwards*, 1963), public sentiment in some sectors remains high that in addition to the punishment associated with incarceration alone, prisons should inflict further pain (Cavender, 2004). The popularity of elected officials like Sheriff Joe Arpaio in Arizona, who gained fame for his get-tough policies toward inmates, illustrates the popular support for deteriorating rather than improving jail and prison living conditions. Arpaio's policies include reviving jail chain-gang work crews, ongoing Web broadcasts of jails and inmates to the general public, serving green baloney to inmates, and a variety of other high-profile and symbolic get-tough measures. Also, contemporary debates surrounding the abuses of prisoners in U.S.-operated detention facilities at Guantanamo Bay and prisons like Abu Ghraib in Iraq, as well as the abuse and torture associated with the U.S. policy on rendition of terrorist suspects to foreign nations, all indicate the continuing public ambivalence about torture and mistreatment even in cases where individuals have not been charged with, much less convicted of, any crimes (N. Bernstein, 2006; Golden, 2006).

Inadequate Implementation of Human Service and Affirmative Action Reforms

Given the conditions just described, it is not surprising that prison reform agendas of the 1980s were never fully implemented. Despite court mandates to extend equal work opportunities, reform inmate treatment, and improve prison services, few agencies ever adequately planned or devoted sufficient resources for the diffusion of these innovations, even before the explosion of jail and inmate populations. In fact, corrections agencies have seldom devoted adequate resources to monitor the implementation of new organizational practices (Clear et al., 2006; Useem & Goldstone, 2002).

In the face of mixed support from state and local legislative bodies, some correctional administrators only halfheartedly supported the extension of inmate rights, human service regimes, and the introduction of women into formerly all-men's jobs, and demonstrated little commitment to follow-through during implementation stages (Jurik & Martin, 2001; Useem & Goldstone, 2002).

Even when administrators supported reform and equal employment opportunity programs, the hierarchical, paramilitary structure of corrections agencies did not foster the training of veteran staff or encourage their understanding of, input into, and support for new policies (Kommer, 1993; Marquart & Crouch, 1985). Many opponents resented the "interference" in hiring, evaluation, and promotional decisions:

> Nobody asked us how we felt. . . . We don't even know why things are changed. . . . Sometimes we know a policy won't work. Those making the policy may never have even worked with inmates. (Man CO supervisor quoted in Jurik, 1985, p. 382)

Although many officers have supported the addition of human service responsibilities to their duties, they have been frustrated by a lack of the resources and autonomy that they needed to accomplish their jobs (Hepburn & Knepper, 1993; Kommer, 1993; Stojkovic & Farkas, 2003).

As a result of these correctional trends, jobs in corrections have become more plentiful for men of color and women. However, such positions may be far less desirable. Moreover, the amount of funds allocated to building and operating prisons has reduced the budgets for employment in other important areas of society (e.g., education, social services, parks and recreation). Sadly, the expansion of corrections has reduced alternative and socially meaningful work opportunities.

The neglect of implementation processes, and in some cases, the near abandonment of reform/affirmative action agendas, greatly empowered masculinist work cultures in corrections (Jurik & Martin, 2001). Women's prisons and women COs continue to be viewed as less than desirable deviations from the generic men's prison and the "need" for men security officers to manage it. To succeed, many women must prove they do can do the job like a man.

Prison Organizational Logic and Women's Careers

With the establishment of affirmative hiring and promotional policies and more and better sexual harassment and maternity leave policies, women have made significant advancements in the field of corrections. Despite these successes, disadvantages to women COs remain embedded in organizational practices at various points along correctional career paths. Women officers must prove themselves to be "exceptional," and this means pressure to emulate men COs' behavior. Because they still constitute a minority within most correctional organizations, women who successfully prove themselves may experience a heightened positive visibility that might help them advance up the promotional ladder. However, child care and other family responsibilities may still hinder women's advancement to higher levels and cause them to settle for lower-ranking and more flexible positions. Gendered correctional organizations negatively affect the careers of women COs at several crucial points: training, work assignments, and performance evaluations. At each stage, women face consequences for their "differentness" (Britton, 2003; Morton, 1991a).

Preemployment Experience and Training

Because women tend to enter correctional employment with less law enforcement or related experience, on-the-job training is important for providing them with the requisite skills to do their job. However, staff shortages and prison overcrowding restrict training. Jurik & Musheno (1986) reported that 33 percent of COs surveyed were offered no entry-level training before their first day of work. Both Britton (2003) and L. E. Zimmer (1986) found that, in the absence of adequate formal training and in the face of hostile men coworkers, inmates trained women COs. Owen (1988) and Maghan and McLeish-Blackwell (1991) report that many black women COs received training from black men inmates. This surprising feature of learning the job is common to COs in general (Clear et al., 2006).

Training should disseminate information about routine procedures, self-defense, and service policies supportive of women COs. Training programs should include information about such issues as communication skills, nonviolent techniques for resolving disputes, and handling mentally disturbed inmates, but conflicts between security and rehabilitative functions produce inconsistent programs. COs in one department reported conflicts in the philosophy of different training classes within the same prison (Jurik, 1985), and recent surveys reveal that COs desire more training in communication and human service–related tasks (Stohr et al., 1996, 1997). Moreover, training that is provided outside prison work units often seems irrelevant to the day-to-day work of COs (Britton, 2003) and fails to even confront, much less resolve, competing correctional directives (Tracy, 2004b).

Without training in communication and crisis intervention skills, COs are inept at using alternative tactics rather than intimidation to control inmates. The "old-guard" discourse of masculinity—stressing physical strength and mental aggressiveness—endures, and women COs are devalued. Along these lines, Britton (2003) argues that prison training exaggerates the potential violence of the job and of the work environment. Officers in her study noted that trainers took particular delight in telling "war stories" about prison violence and showing films that chronicled events of prison riots while many routine functions of officers were neglected. Although both men and women recruits received this training, women were reportedly more discouraged by this training emphasis—an emphasis that underrates the fact that 91 percent of U.S. state and federal prisons reported no riots, and 96 percent reported no deaths of officers during the time of the study (Britton, 2003, p. 97). This type of training emphasized the handling of violent, typically maximum security men inmates. Routines for handling inmates at lower security levels and inmates in women's facilities received short shrift. It made such inmates appear to recruits as exceptions to work in "real" prisons. New training packages for COs that emphasize the handling of communication, inmate discipline, and diversity in prisons are now more widely available from the American Correctional Association, but staff training continues to be inadequate and insufficiently relevant to the work and problems faced by COs (Tracy, 2004a, 2004b).

Work Assignments

The assignments of COs affect their integration and career advancement. Although most COs hold the same rank, their activities vary greatly. Assignments affect COs' attitudes toward their work, departments, chances for advancement, and themselves. Women are assigned to a wider range of custody and duties than was previously the case. Morton (1991b) reported that the number of agencies restricting women CO work assignments significantly decreased from 1978 to 1988, but considerable inconsistencies across agencies remained. Issues surrounding inmate privacy rights and concerns about women COs' physical strength have continued to promote ambiguity and inconsistency among administrators regarding women's work assignments (Britton, 2003; Morton, 1991b, p. 37; L. E. Zimmer, 1989).

Administrators' failure to monitor gender allocation patterns leads to inconsistencies even within the same institutions. Assignments reflect supervisor discretion and views of women COs' "proper place" in the prison (Britton, 2003; Jurik, 1985; L. E. Zimmer, 1989). Although inmate privacy rights may require some restrictions on women COs' work assignments, actual practices suggest gross inconsistencies and the use of privacy rationales as excuses for limiting women's deployment. For example, in one state department of corrections, the official policy was to assign women to all areas of men's prisons unless it violated inmate rights to privacy, that is, strip searches and viewing inmates nude. In reality, the interpretation of the policy varied from prison to prison, among supervisors, and across time (Jurik, 1988; Morton, 1991b, p. 37).

Britton (2003) found that supervisor discretion in assignments was greater in state than in federal prisons, where assignment patterns were more bureaucratized. Women COs' deployment in state prisons was greatly influenced by the association of masculinity with physical prowess. Women COs were less likely to be assigned to positions that were viewed as "unsafe," that is, positions that involved a lot of contact with inmates who were viewed as more violent. Women officers were assigned to control rooms, visitation areas, and duties that might entail typing. Many women COs resent such restrictions as unwarranted, but some women accept protection even though they later pay for their adaptation with weaker evaluations and more limited opportunities for promotion (Britton, 2003).

In women's prisons, Britton found that men were restricted from work in women inmate cells but were given far more desirable roving work assignments and brought in as "enforcers" when women inmates became violent. Ironically, the restrictions on women COs in men's prisons led to a devaluing of women's contribution there, but the restrictions on men COs' assignments in women's facilities led to a valorization of men's role in those prisons (Britton, 2003).

Without experience in a wide range of assignments that includes inmate contact, women COs' promotion opportunities are limited. This pattern has led to the informal identification of "women's slots" in areas of the prison that are viewed as safe for women. Women COs must either try to prove they can do the job like a man or compete for these few valued "women's" assignments (Jurik, 1985, p. 385). Ironically, restricted work assignments fuel the resentment of men coworkers over "reverse discrimination" or the "special treatment" given to women (Britton, 2003; Owen, 1988). Absence of the opportunity to demonstrate competence in all aspects of the job reaffirms images of feminine incompetence.

Performance Evaluations and Promotions

Performance evaluations become part of the CO's permanent work record and are scrutinized when COs apply for promotions. Correctional reforms have emphasized "universalistic" and objective criteria based on formal organizational rules instead of "particularistic" and subjective judgments based on friendship or partisanship. Despite these bureaucratic reforms, supervisor discretion and subjectivity surround the evaluation process, and often seemingly gender- and race-neutral criteria for evaluations and promotions can disadvantage men of color and women.

The difference between performances labeled "successful" and "outstanding" can mean loss of merit pay or promotional prospects. Subjective judgments about performance quality can be unconsciously swayed by issues of demeanor, appearance, and tone of voice that do not reduce CO effectiveness but constitute gender and cultural differences from those of the supervisor doing the assessments (I. M. Young, 1990). Zimmer (1987) has found that women COs who use unique work strategies receive less favorable evaluations because their performance differs from men's. Jurik's (1985, p. 386) content analysis of CO performance evaluation forms in one agency suggested that security was emphasized and service responsibilities were ignored: of the 18 categories, only one dealt with any service function, administering first aid. Communication skills, conflict diffusion, and other service functions were not addressed. Communication and conflict diffusion are skills that may be more often associated with women (also see L. E. Zimmer, 1987).

The evaluation process can formalize informal suspicions that surround women COs through employment records. As noted earlier, supervisors scrutinize and record women COs' interactions with men inmates more carefully than encounters between men COs and men inmates (Belknap, 1991; Pogrebin & Poole, 1997). This may also be true for men of color who are suspected of being overly sympathetic or lenient toward inmates of their race (Owen, 1988).

Like evaluations, promotional decisions can be gendered and racialized in subtle ways. The continued emphasis on paramilitary custodial and security functions supports status quo images of CO work that conflate masculinity with competence (Britton, 2003). Get-tough discourses may discourage many women from seeking promotions in today's prison if they do not identify with this ethos (Hayes, 1989). Even for women who do not "opt out," the amount of supervisor discretion in promotion decisions may exclude women who do not appear to be "tough enough" for some prison climates.

Given prison overcrowding and threats of prison privatization, new management philosophies aimed at enhancing cost-effectiveness heighten the pressure on supervisory and administrative staff to be available for longer and less flexible work hours than ever. Because relative to men, women typically have greater family responsibilities, these schedules may also lead more women to opt out of promotional tracks.

Like evaluations, promotion decisions are characterized by considerable discretion. Both men and women staff believe that promotions are associated with informal ties to supervisors (Britton, 2003; Jurik, 1988). Research suggests that men of color and women often either are excluded by others or choose to exclude themselves from informal after-hours socializing. Women often avoid it because of family responsibilities and fears of sexual harassment (L. E. Zimmer, 1986). Men and women of color may be excluded from or feel uncomfortable in informal associations with predominantly white staff. An absence of informal networking can cause individuals to lose both peer and supervisory support for their advancement.

The discretion and ambiguity surrounding promotion also increase women COs' vulnerability to sexual harassment. Women COs fear retaliation from supervisors if they resist or complain about sexual harassment (Britton, 2003). Ironically, when white women and men and women of color receive favorable evaluations, the ambiguities in the process prompt white men's claims of "reverse discrimination," or, for women, insinuations that the promotion was due to sexual favors (Maghan & McLeish-Blackwell, 1991; Owen, 1988). Without clear and equality-promoting standards for evaluations, COs must rely on the goodwill of individual supervisors, who are still most often white men.

In spite of these barriers, more men of color and women are being promoted within corrections. Although their numbers are still small, improvements have been made in training, mentoring, and networking opportunities that are more supportive of organizational diversity in corrections. These will be discussed later in this chapter.

Women's Performance: Adaptation and Innovation

Systematic research on CO performance relies on indirect measures that range from the examination of official prison records, field observations, and interviews, to staff and inmate surveys. The vast majority of studies have focused on men staff and inmate attitudes toward women COs, and comparisons of men and women CO attitudes. These studies report differences between men and women but also many striking similarities. Recent research identifies some significant differences in work-related attitudes within gender groups, including variations along the lines of race and ethnicity, as well as age, educational level, rank, and time on the job. Most research concludes that organizational climate and institutional characteristics are more important in shaping worker orientations than are the attributes of individuals. Given these findings, it is disappointing that there is so little recent research on the organizational and institutional conditions within corrections today, especially investigations that are mindful of gendered, racialized, and sexualized organization dynamics. In this section, we examine the extant research on women's work-related attitudes and job performance focusing on the ways in which women COs both adapt and seek to change organizational conditions.

Work-Related Attitudes

Survey research indicates that men and women COs agree on a variety of work-related issues, including opportunities for advancement, learning, variety, influence in policy making, and job satisfaction. Notable exceptions are the differential assessment made by men and women about the level of discretion on the job: men COs want more discretion; women COs prefer more structure. Both men and women COs rated administrators and supervisors as the groups that caused them the most problems, but women COs rated coworkers as the next major source of problems in their jobs. Men COs were more likely to list inmates second and coworkers last (Belknap, 1991; Jurik & Halemba, 1984).

Most survey and qualitative studies (e.g., Farkas, 1999b; Kissell & Katsampes, 1980; Stohr, Hemmens, Kofer, & Schoeler, 2000; Walters & Lagace, 1999; L. E. Zimmer, 1986) report that women COs hold greater regard for inmate rehabilitation and service functions than do men COs, although one study indicated that both men and women COs valued service over security functions (Stohr et al., 1997). Women wardens were more supportive of services for inmates than were their male counterparts (Kim, DeValve, DeValve, & Johnson, 2003). Perhaps consistent with this service orientation, stress studies suggest that relative to men, women COs have similar levels of stress and burnout, but women are less likely than men to let stress cause them to respond negatively and impersonally to inmates (Hurst & Hurst, 1997; Morgan, Van Haveren, & Pearson, 2002). Surveys do suggest that men and women officers desire similar amounts of social distance between themselves and inmates (Freeman, 2003), but one study reports that women COs score higher on tests of correctional ethics than do men COs (Stohr et al., 2000).

Sexual harassment bothers women COs to a greater extent than it bothers men (Pogrebin & Poole, 1997; Savicki et al., 2003), and women experience more conflict stemming from the spillover of work into home life (Triplett et al., 1999). Despite concerns about harassment and work-home conflict, women still report greater senses of job-related personal achievement and accomplishment than do men COs (Carlson, Anson, & Thomas, 2003), and most findings suggest that women's levels of job satisfaction are about equal to men's (Griffin, 2001; Jurik, Halemba, Musheno, & Boyle, 1987; Wright & Saylor, 1991). In contrast to survey estimates, qualitative research finds women to be highly frustrated with working conditions, especially with the lack of supervisory support and hostilities from coworkers (Owen, 1988; L. E. Zimmer, 1986). Perhaps disgruntled women COs are more likely to consent to interviews in qualitative studies, or workers may simply inflate their satisfaction assessments when asked to respond in written form. Either way, this is a common discrepancy in qualitative and quantitative studies of job satisfaction and work orientations (Britton, 1997).

Vignette studies suggest that women are as disposed as, or even more disposed than, men toward using aggressive tactics to control inmates in hypothetical scenarios (Farkas, 1999b; Jenne & Kersting, 1996). Race and gender were not correlated with the methods that COs selected to handle rule violations (Freeman, 2003), but qualitative interviews with women COs suggested that they felt pressured to prove themselves as aggressive and tough with inmates (Farkas, 1999). To some extent, women COs must adapt to the masculinist organizational culture. According to a woman CO,

> It's a macho environment, and I have to act aggressively to succeed. I work here all day, talk loud, act tough. I go home at night and find myself talking in a deep, loud voice to my kids. (Woman CO quoted in Jurik, 1988, p. 303)

Despite the important gender differences that research suggests, it is essential not to forget the many similarities between women and men officers as groups. Moreover, studies of CO orientations produce as many variations within as across gender groups. For example, Britton (1997) finds important variations in COs' work-related assessments along gender and race lines. Black and Hispanic men COs feel more effective in working with inmates than do white men officers. Efficacy in work relations with inmates is also strongly associated with positive assessments of work environment and lower stress levels for black and Hispanic men COs. However, although COs who are men of color report lower levels of stress, they are more dissatisfied with their jobs than are white men officers. In contrast, supervision is most important to white women: white women COs who evaluate supervision more positively report higher levels of satisfaction with their work than do white men. Black women COs do not report the same sense of efficacy with inmates identified by black men COs, and they also register lower levels of job satisfaction than do white men COs. Even in this study where individual characteristics predict differences in worker attitudes, the characteristics of the prisons in which officers worked were still important. Those who worked in prisons with a high proportion of inmates of color and a high proportion of white men custody staff viewed their work environment more negatively. This finding may reflect the organizational tensions that the corrections literature has often attributed to the control of inmates of color by white male staff (Britton, 1997; J. B. Jacobs, 1977). In addition to race and gender, dimensions of identities such as age, length of service, military history, and level of education influence CO work-related attitudes. Higher levels of education are associated with more positive attitudes toward both women COs and the provision of inmate services, but education is negatively associated with CO job satisfaction (Jurik & Halemba, 1984; Jurik et al., 1987; Walters, 1993). Further research is needed to assess the ways in which these different features of human identities converge within actual correctional settings.

Job Performance

The few systematic evaluations of the job performance of women and men COs again reveal as many cross-gender similarities as differences. Comparisons of 168 matched pairs of women and men COs found no significant difference between gender groups in performance appraisal ratings, number of commendations or reprimands, or use of sick leave (Holeman & Krepps-Hess, 1982). Most studies that evaluated women COs' performance in men's prisons have been quite positive. Still, there are significant differences across and within gender groups when COs evaluate themselves and coworkers. In most studies, women rate their job performance more positively than they do men's (Kissel & Katsampes, 1980), but women COs who accept men's protection on the job tend to rate men higher than women (L. E. Zimmer, 1986).

We have noted the myriad concerns for women's vulnerability and safety in men's prisons. One study (i.e., Marquart et al., 2001) reported a greater number of officially recorded boundary violations by women COs with men inmates. However, the validity of these findings must be questioned given the relatively higher scrutiny accorded to women's than to men COs' behavior in men's prisons. Although men COs working in women's prisons may also be heavily scrutinized, there are far fewer COs assigned to women's prisons. The vast majority of COs work in men's facilities.

With regard to safety issues, one study revealed that women COs had a greater fear of victimization than did men, but as a group, women still tended to feel safer at work than did men COs (Griffin, 2001). Continued informal restrictions on women CO work assignments make it difficult to assess their actual safety in men's prisons compared to that of men COs. However, available evidence suggests that women COs suffer significantly fewer assaults than men COs; when women COs are assaulted, they are no more likely to be injured than are men (Shawver & Dickover, 1986). It is also important to note that increases in the number of women COs in a prison do not increase the number of assaults against men COs (Shawver & Dickover, 1986). Another, more recent study of physical assaults on men and women COs in a sample of U.S. maximum security prisons in all 50 states reports that men officers were assaulted almost 4 times more often than women officers (Rowan, 1996).

Work Styles: Adaptation and Innovations

The similarities between men and women COs suggest the importance of the prison organization in molding its workers (Kanter, 1977). So often, women COs feel that they must emulate hegemonic forms of masculinity to be accepted on the job. Research simulations (e.g., Haney, Banks, & Zimbardo, 1973) and real-world events demonstrate the problematic and abusive behavior that prison organizations can generate.

In 2003, numerous widely publicized cases of detainee abuse at the U.S.-run Abu Ghraib prison and other U.S. detention facilities associated with the "war on terror" highlight the power of organizations to shape the behavior of those in them. Some women guards participated in these atrocities. Perhaps most prominent among these was reservist Spc. Lynndie England, who was featured in a series of photographs depicting inmate abuses at Abu Ghraib. For example, in one photograph, she was shown leading a nude detainee on a leash (Wikipedia, 2006). Spc. Sabrina Harman also testified that she put wires on the hand of a hooded detainee who was standing on a platform and told him that "if he fell off he would get electrocuted" (Benjamin, 2006). The detention staff in these cases argued that they were given orders from superiors directing them to humiliate and intimidate detainees so that they would cooperate with interrogators. U.S. officials countered that these abuses constituted a few isolated cases in which individuals behaved inappropriately or criminally. Regardless of which of these explanations one accepts, the involvement of women in such incidents suggests the flaw in arguments that women are uniformly more ethical or humane than men. There are tremendous variations among workers regardless of gender. These abuse cases illustrate how a particular organizational setting can shape individual behavior in ways that go beyond gender, race, or other dimensions of social identities. However, these incidents still illustrate the sexualized, gendered, and racialized dimensions to prison security work. Much of Spc. England's behavior was linked to her association and alleged sexual affair with a Spc. Charles Graner, who was identified as an instigator of abuse at Abu Ghraib; in some coverage she appeared to be little more than his sexual pawn. Moreover, the abusive actions in these cases were informed by and infused with cultural meanings for both detainees and keepers (e.g., the humiliation of Muslim men by photographing them nude with U.S. women looking on).

Despite the sometimes striking similarities in men and women COs' attitudes and behavior, research suggests that some women COs develop innovative CO work styles that they believe are compatible with competence and femininity as well as more humane inmate treatment (Belknap, 1991; Britton, 2003; L. E. Zimmer, 1986, 1987). Studies describe a "woman's style" in terms of a "calming effect" on men inmates. Zimmer (1987, pp. 422–423) argues that

> most . . . women who work as guards in men's prisons have neither the desire nor the capacity to perform the job as it has been traditionally performed by men. . . . [They] are . . . more likely to have a social worker's orientation toward the job and to spend . . . time listening to inmate problems. . . . Women rely on . . . skills of communication and persuasion.

However, women do not do the job or do gender in uniform ways. Styles and strategies vary with differences in race, age, educational level, sexual orientation, length of service, and other dimensions of identities. L. E. Zimmer (1986) has argued that women COs adopt one of three "roles." In the "institutional role," women adhere closely to prison rules and try to maintain a "professional" stance. Although they try to enforce all rules fairly and consistently, inmates and other staff view them as rigid and inflexible. Corrections researchers claim that it is impossible to enforce all rules and still maintain order in institutions (G. M. Sykes, 1958). The "modified role" is a compromise for women who do not think that they can perform the job as well as men. They rely on men COs to "protect them" from men inmates. Finally, women in "innovative roles" rely on inmate guidance to do their jobs.

Arguing for a more dynamic conception of job performance, Jurik (1988) has suggested that women COs use a variety of strategies, not set role types, to challenge organizational policies and informal staff resistance. Women COs use these strategies to "strike a balance," or do gender in ways that avoid negative gender images, and combine notions of femininity and competence (Jurik, 1988, pp. 291–292; also see Kanter, 1977).

First, women COs adopt a "professional demeanor," which they perceive to be a gender-neutral performance strategy. This strategy requires adherence to institutional rules but, in contrast to Zimmer's institutional role, does not require the enforcement of all rules at all times. This discourse of professionalism emphasizes consistency and fairness, but also flexibility in dealing with inmates and staff. Conflict management techniques replace "old-guard" approaches to inmate confrontations. Sexuality is explicitly excluded from the professional demeanor; sexual comments and overtures are considered unprofessional in workplace interactions.

"Emphasizing unique skills" allows women COs to identify the contributions that they make to the men's prison. Some define these contributions in terms of their feminine nature or socialization, such as women's "superior" feminine abilities to communicate with and calm inmates. By using this strategy, women COs increase the value of so-called "feminine" talents and devalue talents that are viewed as the domain of men (e.g., physical aggressiveness or macho demeanor). At other times, women may simply identify talents that are unique to themselves as individuals. By distinguishing unique individual skills (e.g., writing, counseling, public speaking), women COs may reduce their competition with men COs and minimize performance pressures that stereotype them either as failures or as "rate busters." Regardless of their alleged source, it is important that the organization value these "unique" talents in promotion and retention decisions. Moreover, there is always a danger that emphasizing any difference may reinforce gender stereotypes that cause a woman's work to be devalued relative to men's.

Highlighting organizational policies that require "teamwork" is another strategy used by women COs. This policy requires that in a potential confrontation situation, COs must call for backup. Enforcement of such rules helps counter criticisms based on women's "inherent physical inferiority to men."

Women COs use "humor" to distance men COs who harass them, while simultaneously avoiding the negative images that plague women who formally report harassment. However, the humor strategy can backfire in the event that a woman later reports harassment; supervisors may then claim that the record indicates that she enjoyed the harassment. Additionally, if the humor strategy involves the use of offensive language, women COs can be sanctioned for violating rules that prohibit such conduct (Gregory, 2003).

Finally, "sponsorship" is a method that women COs use to advance in prison organizations. Supportive sponsors give women COs visibility and information essential to promotion in an organization with a strong informal opportunity structure. Men COs also seek sponsors. However, since powerful sponsors are typically men, women COs face potential rumors about sexual liaisons with their sponsor.

> When I . . . got promoted, they said I was sexually involved with the captain. . . . I tried to maintain a good relationship with him, but also . . . to use the attention I was getting to demonstrate my abilities, to show that I was an independent thinker. It was a good thing because, he got . . . transferred and demoted. (Woman CO quoted in Jurik, 1988, p. 302)

The presence of more women in supervisory and administrative ranks is important for improving the mentoring prospects for new women COs (Green, 2005).

The use and effectiveness of these strategies vary over time, across situations, and from one women CO to the next (Jurik, 1988). The strategies used vary for women of different ages, marital statuses, levels of seniority, and racial-ethnic groups (Belknap, 1991; Britton, 2003). Differences sometimes lead to resentment and conflict, not only between men and women, but among women, and conflicts between individuals distract from a collective awareness of organizational problems.

Regardless of whether women as a group exert a "calming effect," or whether there are distinctive women's styles, some women openly challenge "old-guard" cultural images and try to develop innovative strategies for doing their job and doing gender in it. Stojkovic, Pogrebin, and Poole (2000) describe the ways in which women officers construct and justify unique and "womanly" styles of work in county jails. In interviews, women deputy sheriffs referenced many of the strategies described previously, and contrasted their "styles" of work with those of men officers, whom they described as more confrontational and less communicative. Women officers drew on discourses of humane treatment and inmate service provision to justify work styles that deviated from standards based on the past practices of men deputies. Future research might examine the success of women's arguments and strategies in jails that are operating at above capacity since such conditions may challenge service discourses such as those referenced by the women in these studies (Stojkovic et al., 2000).

Literature on "grassroots" corrections and critical analyses of masculinities in prison demonstrate the mistake of dichotomizing the behavior of men and women COs (R. Johnson, 1987; Sabo et al., 2001). In some prisons, progressive, human service–oriented COs who are men have also adopted innovative work strategies, including conflict mediation and other techniques for avoiding oppressive, physically aggressive displays of masculinity with inmates (Gilbert, 1990; R. Johnson, 1987; Sabo et al., 2001). There are men line staff and administrators as well as inmates who actively support the presence of women COs and progressive and innovative models of working in prisons (Burton-Rose, 2001; Denborough, 2001; P. Johnson, 1991). Changes in prison facilities and policies made to accommodate women COs (e.g., partitions for inmate privacy in showers, additional diversity training for correctional environments) may actually improve the benevolence and efficiency of the organization. More extensive studies of the ways in which contemporary organizational contexts encourage or inhibit progressive innovation in corrections are desperately needed. Systematic and direct observations would undoubtedly shed much light on the variations in work strategies both across and within gender groups.

The Costs: Stress and Turnover

Even for women COs who "strike a balance" and avoid negative feminine stereotypes, there are costs to working in nontraditional fields like corrections (Jurik, 1988). The ethic of professional reform is more compatible with women COs' presence, but professional visions of unfailing worker dedication and emotionless objectivity are still gender-laden (Connell, 1993). Culturally emphasized femininity in society at large and in modern professional corrections still associates women with emotionalism and lack of objectivity. Women's sexuality is viewed as disruptive in the professional work environment, and, when sexual problems arise in the prison, women are the usual suspects (Britton, 2003; Marquart et al., 2001).

Correctional administrators may not exhibit open hostility to affirmative action programs but may underfund them (Jurik & Martin, 2001). The few mentoring programs that corrections organizations sponsor for women place the burden of change on women workers rather than on the organization. Women bear the burden of their "differentness" with regard to behavior and physical appearance (e.g., ill-fitting uniforms). Women COs of color face additional cultural biases regarding dress and appearance (Britton, 2003; Maghan & McLeish-Blackwell, 1991).

Professionalism continues to mean that the job comes before family commitments and that work negatively affects home life (Triplett et al., 1999). These conflicts may be greatest for women of color, who are disproportionately single mothers (Maghan & McLeish-Blackwell, 1991).

Some studies of CO work-related stress in men's prisons suggest that women's stress levels are higher than those of men (e.g., Cullen, Link, Wolfe, & Frank, 1985). In contrast, other studies report that men's and women's stress levels are similar, but the factors that influence stress and responses to it are different for men and women COs (Hurst & Hurst, 1997; Morgan, Van Haveren, & Pearson, 2002; Savicki et al., 2003). Variation may also occur within gender groups according to race, age, and years of experience on the job. Sexual harassment is a source of work- and non–work-related stress for women COs (Savicki et al., 2003). Some researchers have argued that, due to sexual harassment, women's turnover rates in nontraditional fields are higher than those of men (Gutek & Nakamura, 1982).

Research on gender and turnover is equivocal but increasingly suggests that women's rates are higher. The New York City Department of Corrections reports that men COs resign from jails at higher rates than do women COs (Steier, 1989). Jurik and Winn (1987) found that COs of color are significantly more likely than white COs to resign or to be dismissed, but discovered no significant differences between men and women COs' turnover rates. In this study, a small sample size prevented the computation of turnover rates for women of different racial groups. In a larger and more recent study, Scott Camp (1994) found that women's turnover was higher than men's in the Federal Bureau of Prisons.

Organizational Movements for Change

Thus far, discussion of responses and strategies has focused on the individual. Although the evidence is largely anecdotal, there are indications that some agencies have made organizational changes to create a better environment for women. Many have established sexual harassment and family leave policies. To varying degrees, agencies have developed training programs for correctional staff and administrators that address the contributions of women workers (P. Johnson, 1991). Agencies now report more extensive organizational changes to accommodate women COs. Innovations include implementation of cross-gender officer supervision teams. These teams comprise COs with different levels of physical strength, communication, and counseling skills as needed to work troubled areas within the prison (Waters, 2005).

Women's correctional associations are also playing larger roles in promoting networking and organizational change efforts (Gondles, 2005). Although some supervisors and administrators discouraged the formation of support groups by women COs in the past, national women's professional association movements have stimulated the development of women's task forces in local and state agencies (Morton, 1992). In 1973, the American Correctional Association formed women's caucuses to compile research and advocate policies supportive of women workers (Morton, 1992). In 1985, the first National Conference for Women Working in Corrections and Juvenile Justice was held and attracted over 350 participants. The conference is now held every other year and has approximately 1,000 participants. The Association of Women Executives in Corrections has also been organized to offer leadership training and support for women correctional administrators. In some local departments, women have formed training workshops and mentoring groups to facilitate women's survival and promotion to supervisory and administrative levels (Byrd, 2005; McCauley, 2005).

Women COs have also filed class action lawsuits against their departments. A suit in the District of Columbia alleged that sexual harassment—demands for sex and threats of retaliation for refusal—is "standard operating procedure" at all levels in the D.C. Department of Corrections (Harriston, 1994). Some suits have led to consent decrees. As part of a consent decree in the state of Washington, women officers developed an outline for organizational changes that included better education for staff and inmates with regard to sexual harassment, improved procedures for making sexual harassment complaints, and improved procedures for handling inmate disciplinary infractions (*Holloway v. King County*, 2000).

Despite these many advancements, collective action by women COs is still extremely limited. Collective avenues of resistance and change and a recognition of the shared problems confronted by officers and inmates alike clearly are necessary for women to bring about significant and organizational-level changes in corrections.

Summary

This chapter has examined the gendered, racialized, and sexualized dimensions of prisons as organizations. We also considered the ways in which changes in the broader society influenced the internal operations of today's prisons. Changing social and organizational contexts shape the everyday interactions and construction of identities within prison facilities. Accordingly, gender, race, and sexuality are fundamental organizing features and outcomes of correctional work, and more organizational studies of these prison dynamics are needed.

Just as some societal and organizational changes expanded women's work in corrections, others have reinforced formal and informal barriers to women. Although their proportions in all spheres of corrections have grown, women still experience the increased visibility and scrutiny that accrue to numerical minorities in work organizations. Get-tough-on-crime discourses reinforce cultural ideologies that assume prisons to be men's domains. Within this context, women are scrutinized—especially women who try to do "men's jobs"—and women's increased visibility is typically detrimental.

Pressures to conform to "old-guard" images of masculine competence weigh heavily on women COs. They may at times emulate or exceed the worst of stereotypic masculine aggressiveness and punitiveness. Women COs often join men in devaluing women inmates and each other without recognizing that in so doing they are contributing to the negative stereotyping and devaluing of themselves. However, researchers and advocates also find that many women COs bring distinctive communication and conflict management styles to men's prisons. Yet, women's performance is not monolithic and neither is men's. Officer performance may vary in ways that simultaneously reflect gender, race, ethnicity, sexual orientation, age, class, education, and other dimensions of identities. Women rely on diverse styles: some accept the protection of men, some rely on sympathetic inmates, some try to emulate aggressive forms of masculinity, some utilize innovative and grassroots reform strategies to challenge the organizational status quo. As they have advanced through the correctional ranks, women have begun to form informal and formal organizations to support other women and also men of color. Despite the power of correctional organizations, women officers sometimes as individuals and sometimes as groups are managing to "strike a balance" among competing negative stereotypes and do gender in ways that promote success and fairness on the job.

CHAPTER 9

Doing Justice, Doing Gender Today and Tomorrow

Occupations, Organizations, and Change

I n the preceding chapters, we have explored the social reproduction of a gendered workforce in the justice system. Women began work in the criminal justice system (CJS) as specialists supervising women and children. The few women lawyers before 1970 were limited to specialties that focused on family issues. Over the past three decades, women's work opportunities in the justice system have greatly expanded. We have focused on the formerly all-men's criminal justice (CJ) fields of police patrol and correctional security in men's prisons, and more broadly on legal practice. In each field, growing numbers of women have entered positions formerly closed to them and gained a degree of acceptance on the job. These shifts have been facilitated by social and legal change movements as well as other seemingly gender-neutral shifts in the nature of policing, corrections, and legal work organizations. Consequently, women encounter less overt hostility in their daily work lives. Nevertheless, they continue to confront more subtle barriers that are deeply embedded in daily interactions, occupational cultures, and the logic of work organizations. As a result, the gendered division of labor in these occupations continues to be contested terrain.

In this chapter, we begin with a brief review of our theoretical approach. We next compare the opportunities and barriers that women confront in these occupations and assess the justice system's effects on women workers and women's impact on justice fields. In particular, we consider the social control implications of women's inclusion in justice occupations. The chapter concludes with a discussion of the contribution of our analysis toward a theory of workplace gender segregation and toward policies that promote gender equality.

Our Theoretical Approach: A Recap

We began this volume by identifying workplace gender differentiation as part of a general cultural tendency to divide our world and people in it into opposing categories, with one category dominating the other. People tend to value the traits of the dominant group as good and devalue the other as different (I. M. Young, 1990). The dominant group becomes the standard by which other groups are judged. Socially constructed relations of dominance and subordination differentiate according to race, ethnicity, class, and sexual orientation, as well as according to gender. Hierarchies of social relations are constructed in routine interactions and located within a larger structural context of divisions of labor, power, and culture. These structured actions reinforce beliefs that dominant and subordinate groups differ in essential ways and that such differences are "natural" (West & Zimmerman, 1987).

Our analysis of the social construction of a gendered labor force in justice occupations identifies four institutional sites of struggle over gendered divisions of labor, power, and culture. These sites are the family, state, labor market, and work organization. Within work organizations, interactions reference and shape organizational cultures, rules, and procedures, as well as other social institutions (Acker, 1992). Through these structured actions, workers do their jobs and "do gender" (West & Zimmerman, 1987). They are simultaneously constructing race, ethnicity, sexual orientation, and class as well as other features of social identities (e.g., age, ability, disability; West & Fenstermaker, 1995). The ways in which individuals experience their bodies also figure prominently in these interactions, and interactions, in turn, shape the ways that people perceive their bodies.

Comparison of Opportunities, Barriers, and Women's Responses

Similarities in Women's Opportunities and Barriers

In the past three decades, sociopolitical and legal changes have challenged traditional constructions of femininity, especially those related to women's work. These changes also challenged the close association between worker competence and masculinity in justice fields (Jurik & Martin, 2001). The adoption of equal educational and employment opportunity laws facilitated women's paid labor force participation. The social upheaval and reform movements of the 1960s and 1970s altered CJ organizations and increased the employment opportunities for women. Economic recession and demographic shortages of white men workers, together with occupational growth and explicit equal employment opportunity mandates to hire women and "minorities," not only increased the number of women in CJS fields, but also expanded their work assignments to police patrol and supervision of men prison inmates. Similarly, expansion of the demand for lawyers led to the opening of new law schools, which, combined with antidiscrimination legislation, provided new opportunities for women attorneys.

Although professionalization and reform movements expanded justice work opportunities for women and men of color, they have not removed all barriers to women in these fields. Professionalization, reforms, and unionization have not given line police and correctional officers (COs) a greater voice in formulating major policy. Instead, justice professionals face increasing workloads that include growing numbers of clientele with unique and intensive sets of service needs. At the same time, there are increased demands for both accountability and cost-effectiveness without substantial increases in power, despite the rhetoric of new managerialism and programs like community policing that promise greater line staff discretion.

The CJS has continued to expand dramatically over the past three decades. Police, courts, and prisons are frequently overwhelmed by the exponential growth in the number of cases and individuals that they must handle. These populations of "criminal offenders" include growing numbers of individuals who are mentally ill, drug addicts, undocumented immigrants, and "terrorist" suspects, many of whom are poor, learning disabled, and victims of sexual and physical abuse and economic exploitation (e.g., work in sweatshops or sex industries). Because of the length of criminal sentences, the U.S. prison population is aging and will increasingly be composed of senior citizens. Many of the offender populations just described have needs that have not traditionally been accommodated by the CJS (e.g., drug treatment, domestic violence counseling, mental health counseling, English language skills, disability resources). Despite these enormous program needs, the money allocated to the CJS has been consumed by the sheer volume of cases now within its purview; we have more prisons instead of prison programs.

Get-tough discourses converge with backlash against affirmative action to reinforce the continued definition of competence in terms of hegemonic masculinity. Although there are competing discourses to the contrary, in many agencies and situations, women must continue to prove that they can do the job like a man.

Within legal practice, changes in the organization of work have diminished the autonomy of individual lawyers and lawyers' control over the legal profession itself. Elite law firms face competition among themselves to gain and keep clients, turf challenges with other occupations (e.g., accountants), and growing demands for accountability and cost containment from clients. Higher salaries and new technologies have resulted in pressures on lawyers for more billable hours, longer work days, and availability to clients round the clock. The proportion of solo practitioners and lawyers in small firms has declined; more lawyers now work in large, bureaucratic law firms, corporations, and government agencies (Abel, 1989; Hull & Nelson, 2000; Kritzer, 1999).

Lawyers' practices also have shifted. An increasing proportion of work, particularly at the elite large law firms, is in the area of commercial law for large corporations. Economic pressures have led to a decrease in pro bono work, while public funding for legal services has decreased the access to legal services available to poor and middle-class individuals. A disproportionate number of women and men of color are employed as government attorneys, including prosecutors, who typically have lower status and lower salaries than those working in private practice. Those men of color and women who begin as associates working in private practice are more likely than white men to resign prior to being considered and to fail to gain partner status (Carson, 2004; Kay, 1997; Wilkins & Gulati, 1996).

As women enter changing justice fields, they encounter considerable resistance to their presence. The opposition to women workers is associated not only with men's fears that women will compete with them for jobs and promotions, but also with concerns that women will change the nature and organization of the work itself. Justice occupations focus on exercising formal social control through making, interpreting, and enforcing society's rules. Men's resistance to women in justice occupations is related to their reluctance to share control over the definitions of "illegal" behavior and imposition of social order, in particular, the exercise of authority over men's wrongdoings. The issue of "equal access to control of social control" reflects a "deeper concern about who has a right to manage law and order" (Heidensohn, 1992, p. 215). Furthermore, policing, corrections, and law traditionally have been so closely associated with men that the jobs have offered a resource for doing masculinity. Women's presence in these fields threatens this close association between work and manhood.

Men's resistance, framed by gendered work cultures and gendered organizational logics, produces forms of gender bias common to all three justice occupations. The resulting gendered dynamics undermine women's efforts to gain acceptance, training, experience, favorable evaluations, and promotions. Women often receive differential treatment during the training process, including a lack of mentors and informal help in "learning the ropes." Women face discriminatory treatment including sexual harassment and other effects of being represented in token numbers, such as heightened visibility, performance pressure, and subordinating feminine images. There often are double standards of evaluation, resulting in both greater and lower expectations for women than for men. Women of color face discrimination based upon race and gender. They sometimes feel as ostracized by white women as they do by white men. Men of color may support them or view them as out of place in a man's world. Lesbian workers sometimes believe they are more accepted than their gay men counterparts, but it is also the case that they may be rejected by men and women colleagues alike. Organizational mandates for the extension of equal work opportunities regardless of sexual orientation have been an important source of support to gay and lesbian police officers (Miller, Forest, & Jurik, 2003). Such interventions illustrate the importance of organizational policies in framing even if not determining the experience of social difference in the workplace.

Although men have resisted women's presence as coworkers, they are not abandoning justice occupations as they have in the case of several other feminizing occupational fields (Padavic & Reskin, 2002). None of the three fields show signs of resegregating as "women's work," nor do such trends seem likely because the work centers on exercising responsibility for making society's rules, enforcing its laws, and controlling men violators. Instead, there is a growing concentration of women in the less prestigious assignments and specialties within each occupation. Even within specialties such as community policing, the work women do is feminized (seen as "natural" for women to do), while men's work is hailed as demonstrating strong technical, communication, and leadership skills.

Finally, the constraints of the contemporary workplace converge with institutional patterns of family life and state policy to produce conflicts between women's family and work commitments. Workers in any field are supposed to prioritize their work above other time commitments, including household and family responsibilities. The structure of workdays in all three justice occupations is problematic for women with families. Full-time working women experience a double workday as they perform paid work for eight or more hours each day, and unpaid household and child care labor "after work." Problems loom large with the expectation of workweeks of 80 hours or more for lawyers and the frequent special details, shift changes, and unpredictable overtime demands for police and COs. The pressure for unending organizational commitment has grown with increased competition among law firms and with the growth of new managerialism in policing and corrections. In all three spheres, idealized businesslike operations promote demands for increased efficiency, total dedication, and unbroken career patterns among workers who have expanding work responsibilities (Jurik, 2004). Because women can have babies and need flexibility to care for them, they are suspected of lacking proper commitment to their occupation.

Differences in Opportunities, Barriers, and Responses

Despite common patterns, there are important differences in justice occupations that affect women's work opportunities. The job and labor queues of these occupations vary because of differences in hiring requirements, the nature of the work, working conditions, and job rewards. Historically, all three fields have been closely associated with masculinity, but the exact nature of this link varies across occupations. Differences are greatest between law and the two CJ occupations, but police and corrections also differ from each other in several ways.

Because the work of both police and corrections involves the physical control of "dangerous" lower-class men, officers traditionally were selected for brawn rather than for interpersonal or intellectual skills. Because neither occupation required extensive training or offered high salaries, policing and corrections were white working-class men's fields (e.g., Schulz, 1995).

Competence among police and COs has typically been equated with dominant cultural images of traditional, white working-class masculinity. Highly valued traits included physical aggressiveness, emotional reserve, and trustworthiness (Hunt, 1990). Accordingly, men's resistance to women colleagues was justified by claims that women were too physically or emotionally weak to withstand the demands and danger of the work. Women were viewed as unreliable partners, and their job performances were devalued as indicative of "natural," feminine incompetence or "unnatural," unwomanly conduct.

Both policing and corrections adopted military-style, hierarchical organizational structures to prevent corruption and control line staff behavior. Despite such controls, police and COs continued to hold considerable degrees of discretion, and were divided by numerous divisions and cliques (Hunt, 1990, p. 8). The discretion and danger of work in these fields gave opponents ample opportunities to expose women to dangers not typically experienced by men staff. Women's vulnerability was then attributed to their "natural physical weaknesses." However, any additional danger that women faced was less likely to be the manifestation of physical differences from men than to arise from systematic discriminatory practices that denied women adequate training and backup support and placed them in situations designed to frighten, humiliate, and endanger them (S. E. Martin, 1980).

The workplace is sexualized in myriad ways, as we have outlined in the preceding chapters. This includes "locker-room" language and stories of sexual conquest, as well as sexual relationships with and among staff and offenders. Presumptions of heterosexual and masculine sexual dominance facilitate solidarity among men in police and corrections work. When women enter the occupation, such language may be heightened, and women are treated as sex objects. At the same time that they are sexually harassed, women are socially isolated and resegregated into newly defined "women's job assignments." Although much of the overt sexual and gender harassment that pioneering women faced in the 1970s and 1980s has diminished, complaints of "reverse discrimination" often accompany the entry and advancement of women with the same effects. Many men of color and women themselves feel compelled to speak against affirmative action to gain the respect of those around them. Although men and women of all races believe that informal influence is an essential key to promotion such that advancement is as much the result of who you know as what you know, they fail to recognize that such informal relationships and influence patterns are part of the rationale behind affirmative action policies (Britton, 2003; I. M. Young, 1990). The consequences of environmental pressures include unique stressors and, in some cases, higher turnover rates, as women enter and depart from these occupations. These practices also lead some women to defer applying for advancement and to accept the "women's assignments" where there is less resistance to them (Reichman & Sterling, 2002; Silvestri, 2003).

Increasing efforts to rationalize and otherwise reform policing and corrections have challenged the discourse of white working-class masculinity and sought to replace it with a middle-class version of masculinity as rational, professional, and rule-oriented. Professionalization, reform, and affirmative action programs threatened "old-line" occupational cultures in these fields. By rationalizing hiring and promotion standards, these changes challenged the often arbitrary practices of pre-reform eras and facilitated the entry and advancement of women and men of color. By mandating equal employment opportunity, due process rights of clients, and a human service approach, reforms encouraged pockets of men staff, supervisors, and administrators to support new definitions of competence on the job and women colleagues' place in it (P. Johnson, 1991). But these organizational changes also brought resentment and active resistance in police and corrections agencies. New entrants represented outsiders, who, like many reform agency policies and administrators, were viewed as oppositional to the "real work" of line staff. To many line staff, resulting regulations and paperwork symbolize a loss of control over offenders, job satisfaction, and advancement opportunities.

Jennifer Hunt (1990, p. 10) has argued that women symbolize outsiders in the worldview of many men police officers because "sex, violence, and corruption are seen as masculine, and therefore, as opposed to service work, non-violence, and non-corrupt behavior that are feminine." Community policing programs are seen as more feminine and service oriented, while crime control programs accentuate the more masculine aspects of the job (S. L. Miller, 1999). Similarly, in corrections, "old guard" COs associate women with unwanted reforms and human service (read: feminine) dimensions of the work (Jurik, 1985).

In many agencies, such symbolic associations have crystallized into differential work assignment patterns that delegate the "feminine" aspects of the jobs to women. Women police are often assigned to station, dispatcher, or juvenile assignments, and women COs are assigned to supply room, inmate grievance procedure, or communication room duties. Men are then left to the "real" work of crime fighting in the streets or control of inmates in the cell blocks.

Although reforms have challenged these old-line views, CJS resources for implementing and enforcing them have been grossly inadequate, and the explosion of prison population, post-9/11 tensions, and the general decline in support for affirmative action goals among governmental authorities have attenuated the implementation of reform and have led to the demise of affirmative action programs in many agencies. These problems have reinvigorated old-line discourses that emphasize force, and weave together physical strength, masculinity, and competence (Jurik & Martin, 2001).

Because it emphasized communication and mediation over forceful coercion, the professionalization-reform ethic has been embraced by many women justice workers and their supporters as a discourse that is supportive of women, or that is at least gender neutral (Stojkovic, Pogrebin, & Poole, 2000). However, professionalism and bureaucratic rationality are not gender neutral, but are closely associated with culturally dominant views of elite white masculinity as the apex of rationality, objectivity, and emotionless affect. This association is well-demonstrated in the field of law.

In contrast to the working-class occupations of police and corrections, lawyers historically have exemplified a culture of elite white masculinity; law has been an occupation reserved for the sons of the aristocracy. Lawyers have been responsible for making the rules of society through rational debate and the assertion of universalistic principles, while simultaneously working to preserve the power of those in authority.

The limitations of professionalism discourses become most apparent when examining resistance to women lawyers. The legal profession seldom poses the physical perils of police and corrections work, so objections to women in law could not center on their physical weaknesses. Instead, the legal fraternity has focused on women's ostensible lack of mental agility and "toughness" in the face of "coarse" public life. Because of their emotional natures and "lower" level of moral reasoning, women are not thought to be sufficiently rational and objective for legal work. Resistance tactics in the legal profession have focused on withholding sponsorship and important cases, tracking into less prestigious specialties, excluding women from key referral networks, and verbal and nonverbal displays of disrespect that discourage potential clients and threaten the livelihood of women attorneys. The professional ethic of law is gendered, and legal work is a resource for doing masculinity.

Do Women Make a Difference?

In the introduction to this book, we asked if the addition of women to new fields within justice-related occupations prompts any significant changes in those occupations, the organizations in which they work, or the quality of services delivered to clients. Assessment of women's effects on an occupation is closely linked to the debates within the feminist movement regarding whether women are essentially different from or essentially similar to men.

Early advocates of policewomen on patrol suggested that women would diffuse violence, be less threatening, and thereby reassure citizens and improve police-community relations (e.g., Milton, 1972). Supporters of women COs have suggested that they have calming and normalizing effects in men's prisons (Rowan, 1996).

Scholars have also debated whether women might behave differently enough from men to change the legal profession. Feminist legal scholar Carrie Menkel-Meadow (1986) argued that women's experiences and values differ from those of men, and that their presence in sufficient numbers could transform the organization and practice of law. Although her argument focused on law, it is relevant to the three justice occupations covered here. She suggested that with greater numbers and more power, women may increase an emphasis on "feminine values" that include less litigation, more mediation, greater empathy for subordinate groups, and more concern about how law can promote the general good. In all three occupations, women might inspire work structures that are less hierarchical, more consensual, and more accommodating to the family.

In contrast to difference feminists like Menkel-Meadow, others suggest that organizational norms, expectations, and job constraints severely restrict individuals' ability to change work organizations (Haney, Banks, & Zimbardo, 1973; G. M. Sykes, 1958). Kanter (1977) argued that it is more likely that jobs make workers than that workers make jobs. She suggested that given similar organizational conditions, women and men workers would behave similarly. Without assuming that women and men would behave exactly the same, others have argued that the difference approach credits women with too much ability to change legal practice; they agree that work organizations restrict options (Anleu, 1992).

The difference model views femininity as a more or less fixed aspect of individual identity. Historically, assigning certain attributes to women, particularly caring and nurturing, has resulted in disadvantage, regardless of whether these attributes are viewed as biological or social (MacKinnon, 1989). So-called "feminine traits" are "deceptive distinctions" that rest on a paradigm specifying a set of essential differences between men and women. This paradigm diverts attention from the similarities between men and women and the differences among women. For example, assertions that women lawyers are more interested in conflict resolution than in adversarial courtroom combat magnify small gender differences and create double binds for women who prefer the adversarial approach (Epstein, 1988).

For some "radical" feminist scholars, "feminine" attributes are neither natural nor constitutive of a "woman's voice"; they are the by-products of masculine dominance (MacKinnon, 1989). Masculine dominance structures and controls behavior and produces different access to resources and power in social institutions. This dominance perspective suggests that law and the CJS are so imbued with masculine values of objectivity and abstract equality that there is little room for women to make a difference.

The social construction of gender approach that we have employed suggests that none of these competing approaches offers an accurate description of the effect of women workers on the justice system. These dichotomies reify the behavior of a few women and men into opposing images of a fixed, unified masculinity and its opposite, femininity. Patricia Hill Collins (2000) seeks to avoid dichotomous thinking by adopting a both/and approach. Women may be both similar to and different from men, and they may be both similar to and different from each other. At all times, the actions of men and women shape and are framed by larger social divisions of labor, power, and culture.

Women's Responses to Barriers

Women actively respond to barriers through a variety of strategies that vary over time and across occupations, individuals, and situations. Several response patterns characterize women in justice occupations. Although some have adhered to one pattern almost entirely, most women alternate among patterns, depending on the circumstances and other emergent features of social identities such as race, sexual orientation, age, and class.

Sometimes, women have accepted constructions of femininity that required men's protection. Such paternalistic constructions of femininity usually have not been available to women of color or to lesbians in the justice workplace. Cultural images of women of color as "mules of the white man" or as sexually promiscuous, and images of lesbians as "tough" and sexually deviant rarely elicit masculine protectionism.

In other cases, women have adapted to the standards of the gendered organization and demonstrated competence by doing masculinity on the job, that is, by emulating styles of reasoning, speech, and demeanor thought to characterize men. Use of this adaptive strategy in all three occupations illustrates the extensive power of the organization to mold its workers. Even women who have avoided this adaptation have felt pressured to act like men.

Women in policing and corrections also have developed conscious strategies for constructing femininity in ways that make it more compatible with images of competent job performance. They have presented themselves as "professionals." Nonetheless, even seemingly gender-neutral professional images accentuate characteristics historically associated with elite white masculinity, namely rationality, objective impartiality, and organizational loyalty; they leave little room for emotions and concerns with personal relationships or social locations. The failure of work organizations to make significant changes to the definitions of "real work" and the structure of the workday result in second-generation discrimination. Within this context, men still are treated as disembodied workers totally loyal to the organization, and women are regarded as embodied workers with family lives that diminish their organizational worth.

Some women have challenged the work structures in justice occupations. Women lawyers in private firms have been more successful in carving out career paths that are sensitive to childbearing and child rearing responsibilities than women in the other occupations. In England and Australia, police agencies also provide for part-time work and job sharing. However, "flexible" career paths continue to impose costs in terms of lower incomes and decreased advancement opportunities (Epstein, Seron, Oglensky, & Saute, 1999).

Adaptation and resistance are always framed by situational and organizational contingencies. Moreover, these contingencies are inextricably bound with race, ethnicity, age, sexual orientation, seniority, and other dimensions of social relations.

Gender, Job Perspectives, and Performance in Justice Occupations

Evidence comparing the work attitudes and behavior of men and women in our three occupations refutes any notion of strict gender dichotomies of performance quality or style. It reveals both similarities and differences in men's and women's job perspectives and performance, and also significant differences in viewpoints and performance within gender categories.

Two studies suggest that men and women police officers have similar attitudes toward their departments, citizens, and their work (Worden, 1993) and that their primary sources of stress are comparable (Morash & Haarr, 1995). Both studies found some gendered patterns, but there were also significant race and ethnic differences that crosscut sex categories.

Early evaluations of gender differences in police officers' job-related behavior found that relative to men, women on patrol made slightly fewer arrests and received fewer citizen complaints and disciplinary reprimands. Few other significant differences were found (see Chapter 5 for details). Anecdotal evidence reported by men and women officers suggests that women tend to handle situations differently from men: they are more likely to reason and less inclined to use force or threat (Belknap & Shelley, 1992; Heidensohn, 1992; Hunt, 1984; S. E. Martin, 1980). Newer studies based on observational data indicate that the situation rather than officer gender shapes the likelihood that the officer will provide comfort and use coercion in dealing with citizens (DeJong, 2004; Paoline & Terrill, 2004).

Women COs do not hold any more positive or lenient attitudes toward inmates than do men COs, but they may be more supportive of inmate rehabilitation and CO service responsibilities than are men. Men and women also tend to have similar amounts of organizational stress, although the sources of that stress and the way they respond to it differ. With increasing seniority, many of women's and men's work attitudes and behavior converge, but some women in leadership positions still attempt to change correctional training and practice. There is also support for prison reform, rehabilitation, and gender equality among some men in corrections (Hemmens, Stohr, Schoeler, & Miller, 2002). In men's prisons, reports indicate that women COs help to diffuse tensions and mediate conflict among men inmates and between men COs and inmates. Men inmates perceive that women's presence normalizes and humanizes the prison environment (Kissell & Katsampes, 1980).

Women wardens are more supportive of providing humane services to inmates than are men wardens (Kim, DeValve, DeValve, & Johnson, 2003). Some correctional workers are also critical of prison conditions for inmates and understand that both they and inmates are sometimes treated as human waste (Denborough, 2001). Thus, get-tough discourses are not without opposition, and women have provided some leadership for change. Nevertheless, research reveals the power of police and corrections work organizations to shape employees regardless of gender, and women feel pressured to behave aggressively (Britton, 2003; Farkas, 1999b).

Observers of the legal profession disagree about women's ability to change the profession. One line of research has focused on women judges. It examines whether they sentence criminal defendants differently from men judges, are more sympathetic in deciding cases affecting women, particularly sex discrimination, and use different criteria or legal reasoning in their decision making. Studies of trial judge behavior in criminal cases suggest that the effects of judges' gender on sentencing outcomes are "small or negligible," but where differences exist, women judges are harsher (Steffensmeier & Herbert, 1998, p. 1166). In sex-discrimination cases that have been decided at the Appellate or Supreme Court levels, women judges consistently are stronger supporters of women' rights claims than their men colleagues. Additionally, the literature suggests that having even one woman on the bench is a strong predictor of decisions favoring women's sex-discrimination claims, which suggests that the integration of women into the American judiciary has fostered positive changes in the outcomes of sex discrimination cases (Palmer, 2001). There is no consensus in the literature examining the question whether women judges speak in a "different voice" or use different legal reasoning.

The numerous state and federal gender bias task force reports suggest that women judges and attorneys are more sensitive to gender-biased behavior than are men judges and attorneys. In the courtroom, women judges are less likely to undermine women lawyers with sexist and demeaning remarks and less likely to tolerate men's harassment (Bogoch, 1999). The reports and their recommendations clearly have had a major impact on the legal community and standards of behavior in and around the courts. However, the effects of women attorneys on clients or case outcomes have not yet been studied using actual cases.

Our analysis reveals the multiplicity of differences in work-related attitudes and job performance among women. Just as there are wide variations among men in their job performances and, therefore, no "men's style" of policing, litigating a case, or guarding inmates, there is diversity among the women's experiences, attitudes, and performance. Both men's and women's work strategies vary considerably by race, ethnicity, sexual orientation, class, and length of service. In some cases, women of color are less likely than are white women to perceive and report men's behavior as sexually harassing (Belknap, 1991). They tend to experience harassment as both sexually and racially motivated. Women of color often perceive men of their race as more supportive of them than are their white women coworkers. Lesbian and gay police officers sometimes feel ostracized by men and women coworkers, but also believe that their social marginalization makes them more empathetic and effective police officers (Miller, Forest, & Jurik, 2004).

In all three occupations, women and men experience many common problems. Men and women both are likely to join large law firms but are unlikely to find mentors or to become partners. As associates both experience a lack of autonomy and feel pressures from the firm to increase the number of hours billed and from clients who want immediate responses, growing numbers of both women and men are unwilling to make the extreme personal and family life sacrifices required to attain a partnership (Epstein et al., 1999).

In corrections and policing, both men and women officers are concerned about declining resources, bureaucratization, heavier workloads, increased client rights, and their inability to affect organizational policy. Both police and COs have increasingly joined unions for support, but unions have not always promoted unity among officers. Some women have opted out of promotional tracks as "conscientious objectors" to the new managerialism and get-tough policies (Hayes, 1989).

Although women in law have substantially higher average incomes than women in policing and corrections, the income differences between men and women in law also are much greater than are the gender income gaps in corrections and policing. Thus, women lawyers are relatively advantaged and disadvantaged, depending on the group with which they are compared. Their legal skill, social status, and income—as well as the nature of the work (which can be done out of the office) and the greater flexibility of the private organization in which most work—provide them with more options and opportunities to demand organizational accommodations for childbearing and child rearing (e.g., part-time tracks). They can more easily obtain and afford part-time, temporary, or other flexible work arrangements than women police and COs, but such individualistic solutions are harmful to women as a group in the long run.

Women's Collective Responses

In addition to individual-level responses, women lawyers and, to a lesser extent, women in policing and corrections have organized and initiated legal actions to challenge discriminatory environments. The success of women workers and their collective organization provide powerful challenges to perceived "natural" links between these occupations and masculinity. However, many forces undermine women's collective action in justice fields.

In all three occupations, women have formed professional associations for women in their fields. For women in policing and corrections, these efforts have typically been more successful at the national level than at local levels. Many department-based organizations have floundered because of disinterest, fear of reprisals from men, or tensions among women from different race and ethnic groups. Statewide organizations are gaining presence. National organizations of women in policing and corrections primarily serve those in, or aspiring to, administrative positions. For example, the National Conference for Women Working in Corrections has tried to expand its network to a wider array of women beyond just administrative ranks. But class disadvantages for lower ranks in corrections make it impossible for most women to travel to meetings even if family permitted, so local and regional associations are a key ingredient of networking and support across agencies (Goldhart & Macedonia, 1992).

The International Association of Women Police (IAWP) has a 50-year history in the United States but limited visibility among rank-and-file women officers. It has financial support only from dues and a few small donations. Its annual meeting and publications attract primarily women supervisors. The National Center for Women & Policing is a division of the Feminist Majority Foundation (which is its primary source of funding). Since its founding about a decade ago, it has served as a center for research and advocacy for increasing the number of women officers and their career opportunities in policing.

Outside of the United States, in addition to national organizations of women officers (e.g., the British Association for Women in Policing), the European Network of Policewomen (ENP), created in 1989, has fostered cooperation across countries. Unlike the IAWP, the ENP since its inception has received a subsidy from the Dutch Ministry of the Interior and now receives financial support from a number of police forces and training academies in Western Europe. It is more research oriented than the IAWP and publishes an annual report and materials on women in policing. It has representative women from 25 countries either as board members or as contact persons (Schulz, 1998). Although these organizations differ, they each are addressing common challenges to women police around the world, including entry standards, affirmative action, harassment, integration into specialized units, and promotion to leadership positions in the male chains of command.

The growing numbers of women of color in policing and corrections fields is also an area that is ripe for organization as well as for research on their experiences in CJS occupations. As pressures in the occupations mount and as corrections in particular increasingly is perceived as part of society's dirty work (Tracy & Scott, 2006), one might hypothesize that entry positions in these fields will increasingly be relegated to men and women of color. The racism that permeates the CJS affects not only victims, detainees, offenders, and inmates, but the workers within it (Britton, 2003). It may also be necessary for men and women of color to organize further to demand better treatment within that system.

The advancement of gay and lesbian officers in some areas has been supported by organizational changes that prohibit discrimination based on sexual orientation. In addition, some "out" gay and lesbian police officers have begun to form associations, primarily in urban areas. However, like officers of color, they sometimes face hostility from their straight colleagues and those within the gay and lesbian communities for becoming a part of law enforcement agencies that have so often mistreated their community (M. Bernstein & Kostelac, 2002; Miller et al., 2003). The rising public discourse against gay marriage and adoption may pose additional barriers to the increased mobilization of gays and lesbians and supportive organizational climates for them within the CJS; it is hoped that the momentum for greater acceptance of lesbian, gay, bisexual, and transgender staff in the CJS will continue.

Class-based differences among men in justice-related occupations are also found among women. As noted earlier, women in law (like men) tend to come from more middle-class and elite backgrounds than do correctional and police officers. By virtue of their status and profession, many women lawyers have assumed leadership positions in the women's movement. They have been active in shaping the legal challenges to gender discrimination throughout society, and in questioning the premises and processes of law. Their activities have extended beyond the concerns of women clients to question the bases of social relationships and the allocation of power in society.

Local women's bar associations have provided more support and contacts than has the National Association of Women Lawyers, which has very limited membership and visibility. In the past decade, women have slowly gained positions of responsibility in state bar associations and the American Bar Association, and have used such positions to bolster women's power in the profession (e.g., through the American Bar Association's Commission on Women in the Profession), as well as challenge continuing patterns of gender discrimination.

Women law professors have formed legal associations and centers within their law schools to address the gendered nature of law. The feminist legal studies movement has led efforts to reform laws and promote gender justice in areas that include inequalities in employment, divorce and family law, as well as in laws related to violence against women (including rape, prostitution, sexual trafficking, pornography, sexual harassment, domestic violence), and the treatment of women who kill battering husbands. This group was central in developing theories of feminist jurisprudence to understand the deeply embedded nature of gender inequality in law. While Catharine MacKinnon's (1989) work has pioneered the examination of sex/violence systems of gender power, others (e.g., A. D. Davis, 2001; J. Williams, 2000) are seeking to "unbend gender" in exploring work-family conflict and the gendered bases and assumptions of workplace discrimination against family caretakers. Feminist jurisprudence has also merged with schools of critical race theory to challenge many other traditional perspectives on legal subjects. Critical race legal scholars have developed research that analyzes the convergence of gender and racial inequality in law. Critical Race Feminists and Latino/Latina Critical (i.e., Lat/Crit) scholarship has dealt with the gender and race dimensions of harassment, hate speech, immigration, terrorism, and welfare reform (Wing, 2003).

Women's Contribution and the Future

We have argued that gender is a fundamental organizing feature of life in justice work organizations. Gender makes a difference in virtually every social context. Even when women prefer that they not be treated as women, their actions continue to be held accountable by others and by themselves as appropriately feminine or not. The sameness approach treats men and women as essentially the same; the difference approach treats all women as uniformly different from men but similar to each other (e.g., nurturing to clients); the dominance perspective views women as passive victims of masculine dominance. Sameness, difference, and dominance arguments all provide one-dimensional views of women: they ignore class, race, ethnic, cultural, and situational differences among women (as well as personality variations among individuals). None of these perspectives grasps how social structure and institutional arrangements simultaneously limit and permit variation, resistance, or innovation at work (Anleu, 1992).

Legal scholar Kenji Yoshino (2006) has argued that discrimination now targets people within marginalized groups who refuse or resist assimilation. Thus, individuals are pressured to hide or minimize their "difference," such as women who must camouflage their lives as mothers and gays in the military who must not "tell." Yoshino sees potential in legal models that require organizations to offer reasonable accommodation to the physically disabled and religious "minorities" within their ranks. However, defining what is "reasonable" in organizational accommodation and determining from whose perspective these definitions will be derived are still matters of controversy. Even so, accommodation models at least offer precedent for requiring organization changes to accommodate new and "minority" social types. Many feminists now argue that women themselves must determine when difference is relevant so that they can be both the same and different across situations and individuals (P. H. Collins, 2000). The goal must not be "equality but equivalence, not sameness for individual men and women, but parity for women as a sex or for groups of women in their specificity" (Cockburn, 1991, p. 10). The goal is neither simple assimilation nor moral superiority, but to transform the nature and operation of work organizations and the political-economic system.

Our analysis of justice system changes that have increased work opportunities for women demonstrates the difficulty of isolating women's impact on the system or its clients. Increases in the range of jobs available to women are inextricably linked to societal changes (e.g., the state of the economy and availability of jobs, the women's movement, equal opportunity struggles, increase in numbers of women workers, changing family roles) and justice system-level changes (e.g., CJS reform efforts, increasing numbers of CJS clients, the shifting organization of legal work). Thus, assessing the effect of women's expanded presence on the justice system, its services, or clients is indeed a complicated matter.

Arguments that women's presence will facilitate the implementation of a human service ethic in justice fields may overstate the benefits of such orientations to client groups (e.g., Stohr, Hemmens, Kifer, & Schoeler, 2000). Bureaucratization, professionalization, reform policies, and women's entry may have shaped client treatment, but in ways that may mean more effective, not simply more humane, social control. The French social thinker Michel Foucault (1979) noted that penal reforms in the 18th century—a shift from heavy reliance on capital punishment to prisons—were not designed to punish less, but to punish better. Foucault's characterization may be apt for the changes that we have described in the justice system. From the 1960s through today, new personnel and new regimes in the CJS may increase and intensify the state control of more individuals; management and human service techniques may further legitimate expanded and unjust forms of social control (Cohen, 1985). Although some women staff may relate more humanely to clients on an individual basis, women's presence in these justice system jobs is not indicative of an overall feminist ethic, nor does it guarantee that all clients will receive improved treatment.

If anything, the prevailing mean spirit that pervades public discourse about crime and social services makes one question whether women or anyone should want jobs in the CJS. In some ways, it is reminiscent of arguments advocating women and gay men's "rights" to go to war. However, our analysis in this book illustrates that progressive change is a struggle that requires advocates on both the inside and the outside of the target institutions.

In a similar vein, we have noted that progressive reforms have been more overtly supportive of women working in the system, but these are neither pro-feminist nor gender neutral. Much research affirms that gender distinctions (like so many other dichotomies) and the preoccupation with similarity versus difference are indeed vestiges of a faulty cultural belief system. However, these cultural beliefs have real material consequences (bodily, economic, and social).

Building Feminist Theory and Policy

Our analysis has implications both for developing theory and altering policy. The implications of women's work as controllers in new and changing systems of social control continue to be an important avenue for feminist inquiry. When women act as social-control agents, the social roles of victim and perpetrator no longer can be dichotomized along gender lines (Heidensohn, 1992). Instead, women's presence as controllers suggests that, in some way, they are "part of the problem" and share, however meagerly, in the system of oppression, hovering at the periphery of the power structure of gender (Connell, 2002).

Our analysis illustrates the usefulness of a dynamic social construction approach to the study of occupational segregation. Popular media analyses continue to treat women's lower incomes and lesser occupational achievement as the result of differential socialization or women's failure to sufficiently invest in "human capital." Work organizations in general and justice work organizations in particular are still portrayed as gender neutral.

We have traced the social construction of a gendered workforce through struggle over gender ratios at interactional, organizational, and societal levels. Our analysis has described the mechanisms whereby gendered divisions of labor are socially constructed but appear to be the natural outcome of individual characteristics (learned or innate). Our approach shows how gender, race, ethnic, sexual orientation, and class distinctions are constructed simultaneously through categorization and differentiation in the family, state, labor market, and work organization and at various levels of social action. We also show these constructions of difference to be embodied social practices: bodily experiences both frame and are shaped by life in justice organizations.

Our conceptualization of the dynamic and emergent construction of workplace identities makes it easier to understand the panoply of women's and men's experiences and behaviors. It also causes us to emphasize the need for more in-depth ethnographic studies of legal and CJ workplaces, especially research sensitive to the variety of worker experiences across race, sexual orientation, seniority, and other dimensions of difference. Further research that simply compares the attitudes and behavior of men and women without an adequate understanding of the variations within gender groups and the dynamics that give rise to those variations will not sufficiently advance our understanding of the justice workplace.

Our analysis has numerous implications for social policy. The historical review of women's changing roles in the justice system reveals that federal requirements to promote affirmative action hiring policies can effectively increase the hiring of women. These pressures are probably most effective when attached to funding criteria rather than being court ordered. The recent attempts to end affirmative action are already having negative consequences on the gender ratio in some work organizations. Within the context of attacks on affirmative action, it is all the more important to analyze work organizations for embedded practices that unnecessarily disadvantage workers who are women, persons of color, gay or lesbian, or disabled or who come from a disadvantaged class background. Research associated with activism in the realm of informal hiring and promotional systems can attack unfair disadvantages to a wide array of workers. It is also time to attack the resurgence of family-unfriendly work policies and practices such as the new managerialism and traditional definitions of workplace commitment. These place greater burdens on women, but also negatively affect men who want to be active fathers or provide care to their elderly parents. Along these lines, rather than simply working to preserve existing affirmative action programs, activism might focus more on extending the legal principles of accommodation models to women as well as to gay and lesbian workers (e.g., improved family leave policies; gay and lesbian rights to work without a hostile environment), and improving these models.

We have discussed how and why men isolate, harass, and otherwise pose visible, daily resistance to women. In the face of such opposition (despite official policies of assimilation), an important survival strategy is for subordinated social group members to identify themselves as an interest group and as potential agents of organizational change.

However, collective organization is made more difficult by differences within gender groups. It is important that women's organizations recognize and appreciate the variations in situations, needs, and desires among women. Alliances across boundaries are needed, but they must be formed with sensitivity and must aim to promote work climates that will accept and appreciate difference (I. M. Young, 1990, pp. 226–260).

In addition, much can be gained from emphasizing the common problems that women and men staff, offenders, and clients share in the work environment. Some CJS unions are beginning to recognize that many problems experienced by women (e.g., maternity leave issues) stem from larger organizational flaws that also pose problems for men workers (e.g., inflexible workdays and leave policies). All staff can benefit from safer work environments, more satisfied clients, and increased input into organizational policies and procedures. Women can begin by forming fluid alliances with each other and with supportive men. Then they must consider how they might make their case to hostile factions by identifying workers' common needs. In all efforts to form alliances, negotiations that recognize both difference and sameness will be key.

References

Abel, R. L. (1986). The transformation of the American legal profession. *Law & Society Review, 20,* 7–17.

Abel, R. L. (1989). *American lawyers.* New York: Oxford.

Abrahamson, J., & Franklin, B. (1986). *Where they are now: The story of the women of Harvard Law 1974.* Garden City, NY: Doubleday.

Acker, J. (1990). Hierarchies, jobs and bodies: A theory of gendered organizations. *Gender & Society, 4,* 139–158.

Acker, J. (1992). Gendered institutions: From sex roles to gendered institutions. *Contemporary Sociology, 21,* 565–569.

AFSCME Union. (2006). *Preventing sexual harassment.* Retrieved February 11, 2006, from http://www.afscme.org/about/wom.htm

After the JD: First results of a national study of legal careers. (2004). Overland, KS: NALP Foundation for Law Career Research & Education and the American Bar Foundation. Retrieved December 12, 2005, from http://www.nalpfoundation.org

Aiken, J. H. (1983–1984). Differentiating sex from sex: The male irresistible impulse. *New York University Review of Law and Social Change, 12,* 357–377.

Almanac of Policy Issues. (2006). The Americans with disabilities act: Statutory language and recent issues. Retrieved March 12, 2006, from http://www.policyalmanac.org/social_welfare/archives/crs_ada.shtml

Altendorf, K. (2003). *Success strategies of female prison wardens: Managing gender identity in a nontraditional occupation.* Unpublished doctoral dissertation, Oklahoma State University, Stillwater.

American Bar Association. (1994). *The burdens of both, the privileges of neither: Report of the multicultural women attorneys network.* Washington, DC: Author.

American Bar Association, Commission on Women in the Profession. (1988). *Report to the House of Delegates* [Mimeograph]. Washington, DC: Author.

American Bar Association, Commission on Women in the Profession. (1995). *Unfinished business.* Washington, DC: Author.

American Bar Association, Commission on Women in the Profession (2001a). *Balanced lives: Changing the culture of legal practice.* Washington, DC: Author. Retrieved January 23, 2006, from http://www.abanet.org/women/reports.html

American Bar Association, Commission on Women in the Profession. (2001b). *The unfinished agenda: Women and the legal profession.* Washington, DC: Author. Retrieved September 6, 2005, from http://www.abanet.org/women/reports.html

American Bar Association, Commission on Women in the Profession. (2006). *A current glance at women in the law 2005*. Washington, DC: Author. Retrieved March 12, 2006, from http://www.abanet.org/women/ataglance.pdf

American Friends Service Committee. (2003). *Overview of privatization in Arizona*. Retrieved February 1, 2006, from http://www.afsc.org/az/azprispriv.htm

Amnesty International. (1999, March). *"Not part of my sentence": Violations of the human rights of women in custody*. Amnesty International AI Index AMR51/01/99.

Amott, T., & Matthaei, J. (1996). *Race, gender, and work: A multi-cultural economic history of women in the United States* (2nd ed.). Boston: South End Press.

Andersen, M. L. (2005). Thinking about women: A quarter century's view. *Gender & Society, 19*(4), 437–455.

Angel, M. (1988). Women in legal education: What it's like to be part of a perpetual first wave or the case of the disappearing women. *Temple Law Review, 61*, 799–846.

Angel, M. (2000). The glass ceiling for women in legal education: Contract positions and the death of tenure. *Journal of Legal Education, 50*, 1–15.

Anleu, S. R. (1992). Women in law: Theory, research and practice. *Australian and New Zealand Journal of Sociology, 28*, 391–410.

Appier, J. (1998). *Policing women: The sexual politics of law enforcement and the LAPD*. Philadelphia: Temple University Press.

Bagilhole, B. (2002). *Women in non-traditional occupations challenging men*. New York: Palgrave.

Bartell Associates. (1978). *The study of police women competency in the performance of sector police work in the city of Philadelphia*. State College, PA: Author.

Bartlett, H. W., & Rosenblum, A. (1977). *Policewoman effectiveness*. Denver, CO: Civil Service Commission and Denver Police Department.

Bauer, L., & Owens, S. D. (2004). *Justice expenditure and employment in the United States, 2001* (NCJ 202792). Washington, DC: Bureau of Justice Statistics, U.S. Department of Justice.

Bayley, D. H., & Shearing, C. D. (2004). The future of policing. In Q. C. Thurman & J. Zhao (Eds.), *Contemporary policing: Controversies, challenges, and solutions. An anthology*. Los Angeles: Roxbury.

Beckett, K., & Sasson, T. (2000). *The politics of injustice: Crime and punishment in America*. Thousand Oaks, CA: Pine Forge.

Beemyn, B., & Eliason, M. (1996). *Queer studies: A lesbian, gay, bisexual, and transgender anthology*. New York: New York University Press.

Belknap, J. (1991). Women in conflict: An analysis of women correctional officers. *Women & Criminal Justice, 2*, 89–116.

Belknap, J. (2001). *The invisible woman: Gender, crime and justice* (2nd ed.). Belmont, CA: Wadsworth.

Belknap, J., & Shelley, J. K. (1992). The new lone ranger: Policewomen on patrol. *American Journal of Police, 12*, 47–75.

Bell, D. J. (1982). Policewomen: Myths and reality. *Journal of Police Science and Administration, 10*, 112–120.

Beneria, L., & Roldan, M. (1986). *The crossroads of class and gender: Industrial homework, sub-contracting, and household dynamics in Mexico City*. Chicago: University of Chicago Press.

Benjamin, M. (2006). *Salon exclusive: The Abu Ghraib files*. Retrieved February 25, 2006, from http://www.salon.com/news/feature/2006/02/16/abu_ghraib

Bernat, F. P. (1992). Women in the legal profession. In I. Moyer (Ed.), *The changing roles of women in the criminal justice system: Offenders, victims and professionals* (2nd ed., pp. 307–322). Prospect Heights, IL: Waveland Press.

Bernstein, M., & Kostelac, C. (2002). Lavender & blue: Attitudes about homosexuality and behavior toward lesbians and gay men among police officers. *Journal of Contemporary Criminal Justice, 18,* 302–328.

Bernstein, M., & Reiman, R. (2001). *Queer families, queer politics: Challenging culture and the state.* New York: Columbia University Press.

Bernstein, N. (2006, February 28). U.S. is settling detainee's suit in 9/11 sweep: Egyptian cited abuse at center in Brooklyn. *New York Times,* pp. A-1, A-21.

Beyond a reasonable doubt: Building the business case for flexibility. (2005). Retrieved July 19, 2006, from http://www.catalystwomen.org/files/full/canadalaw3%2014%2005%20 FINAL.pdf

Bianchi, S. M., Milkie, M. A., Sayer, L. C., & Robinson, J. P. (2002). Is anyone doing the housework? Trends in the gender division of household labor. In P. J. Dubeck & D. Dunn (Eds.), *Workplace/women's place: An anthology* (2nd ed., pp. 174–187). Los Angeles: Roxbury.

Bielby, W. T., & Baron, J. N. (1986). Men and women at work: Sex segregation and statistical discrimination. *American Journal of Sociology, 91,* 759–799.

Bird, C., & Briller, S. W. (1969). *Born female: The high cost of keeping women down.* New York: Basic Books.

Bittner, E. (1970). *The functions of police in modern society.* Chevy Chase, MD: National Institute of Mental Health.

Blakely, C. R., & Bumphus, V. W. (2004). Private and public sector prisons: A comparison of select characteristics. *Federal Probation, 68,* 27–31.

Bloch, P., & Anderson, D. (1974). *Policewomen on patrol: Final report.* Washington, DC: Urban Institute.

Bogoch, B. (1999). Courtroom discourse and the gendered construction of professional identity. *Law and Social Inquiry, 24*(2), 329–376.

Boni, N. (1998). *Deployment of women in policing.* Payneham, South Australia: National Police Research Unit.

Braverman, H. (1974). *Labor and monopoly capital.* New York: Monthly Review Press.

Britton, D. M. (1997). Perceptions of the work environment among correctional officers: Do race and sex matter? *Criminology, 35,* 85–105.

Britton, D. M. (1999). Cat fights and gang fights: Preference for work in a male-dominated organization. *The Sociological Quarterly, 40*(3), 455–474.

Britton, D. M. (2003). *At work in the iron cage: The prison as gendered organization.* New York: New York University Press.

Britton, D. M., & Williams, C. L. (2000). Response to Baxter and Wright. *Gender & Society, 14,* 804–809.

Brown, J. M. (1997). Women in policing: A comparative research perspective. *International Journal of the Sociology of Law, 25,* 1–19.

Brown, J. M. (1998). Aspects of discriminatory treatment of women police officers serving in forces in England and Wales. *British Journal of Criminology, 38*(2), 265–282.

Brown, J. M. (2002, October). *"You can't have it both ways": Being an officer and a lady (woman) in a male dominated occupation.* Paper presented at the Third Australasian Women and Policing Conference: Women and Policing Globally, Canberra, Australia. Retrieved November 28, 2005, from http://www.aic.gov.au/conferences/policwomen3/brown.html

Brown, J. M., & Grover, J. (1997). Stress and the woman sergeant. *The Police Journal, LXXI,* 47–54.

Brown, J. M., & Heidensohn, F. (1996). Exclusion orders. *Policing Today,* September, 20–24.

Brown, J. M., & Heidensohn, F. (2000). *Gender and policing: Comparative perspectives.* New York: St. Martin's Press.

Brown, M. K. (1981). *Working the street: Police discretion and the dilemmas of reform.* New York: Russell Sage Foundation.

Brush, C. (1992). Research on women business owners: Past trends, a new perspective, and future directions. *Entrepreneurship Theory and Practice,* Summer, 5–30.

Bureau of Justice Statistics. (2001). *Census of jails, 1999.* Retrieved February 7, 2006, from http://www.ojp.usdoj.gov/bjs/pub/pdf/cj99.pdf

Bureau of Justice Statistics. (2003). *Census of state and federal correctional facilities, 2000.* Retrieved February 6, 2006, from http://www.ojp.usdoj.gov/bjs/pub/pdf/csfcf00.pdf

Bureau of Justice Statistics. (2005). *Nation's prison and jail population grew by 932 inmates per week.* Retrieved May 25, 2005, from http://www.ojp.usdoj.gov/bjs/pub/press/pjim04pr.htm

Burgess-Proctor, A. (2006). Intersections of race, class, gender and crime: Future directions for feminist criminology. *Feminist Criminology, 1*(1), 27–47.

Burrell, G., & Hearn, J. (1989). The sexuality of organization. In J. Hearn, D. Sheppard, P. Tancred-Sheriff, & Burrell, G. (Eds.), *The sexuality of organization* (pp. 1–28). Newbury Park, CA: Sage.

Burton-Rose, D. (2001). The anti-exploits of men against sexism, 1977–78. In D. Sabo, T. A. Kupers, & W. London (Eds.), *Prison masculinities* (pp. 224–229). Philadelphia: Temple University Press.

Butler, E. K., Winfree, L. T., & Newbold, G. (2003). Policing and gender: Male and female perspectives among members of the New Zealand police. *Police Quarterly, 6*(3), 298–329.

Butler, J. (1990). *Gender trouble: Feminism and the subversion of identity.* New York: Routledge.

Byrd, M. V. L. (2005). Leadership & legacy. *Corrections Today,* October, 82–91.

California Highway Patrol. (1976). *Women traffic officer report: Final report.* Sacramento: Department of California Highway Patrol.

Camp, S. D. (1994). Assessing the effects of organizational commitment and job satisfaction on turnover: An event history approach. *The Prison Journal, 74,* 279–305.

Carlen, P. (2001). Death and the triumph of governance? Lessons from the Scottish women's prison. *Punishment and Society, 3*(4), 459–472.

Carlen, P., & Worrall, A. (2004). *Analysing women's imprisonment.* Cullompton, Devon, UK: Willan.

Carlson, J. R., Anson, R. H., & Thomas, G. (2003). Correctional officer burnout and stress: Does gender matter? *Prison Journal, 83*(3), 277–288.

Carlson, J. R., Thomas, G., & Anson, R. H. (2004). Cross-gender perceptions of corrections officers in gender-segregated prisons. *Journal of Offender Rehabilitation, 39*(1), 83–103.

Carson, C. N. (2004). *The lawyer statistical report: The U.S. legal profession in 2000.* Chicago: American Bar Foundation.

Cavender, G. (2004). Media and crime policy: A reconsideration of David Garland's *The culture of control. Punishment & Society, 6,* 335–348.

Cavender, G., & Jurik, N. C. (2004). Policing race and gender: An analysis of *Prime Suspect. Women's Studies Quarterly, 32,* 211–230.

Chambers, D. L. (1989). Accommodation and satisfaction: Women and men lawyers and the balance of work and family. *Law and Social Inquiry, 14,* 251–287.

Chambliss, E., & Uggen, C. (2000). Men and women of elite law firms: Reevaluating Kanter's legacy. *Law and Social Inquiry, 25,* 41–68.

Chambliss, W. J. (1995). Control of ethnic minorities: Legitimizing racial oppression by creating moral panics. In D. Hawkins (Ed.), *Ethnicity, race, and crime: Perspectives across time and place.* Albany: State University of New York Press.

Charles, M., & Grusky, D. B. (2004). *Occupational ghettos: The worldwide segregation of women and men.* Stanford, CA: Stanford University Press.

Charles, M. T., & Copay, A. G. (2001). Marksmanship skills of female police recruits: Impact of basic firearms training. *International Journal of Police Science and Management, 3*(4), 303–308.

Cheeseman, K. A., Mullings, J. L., & Marquart, J. W. (2001). Inmate perceptions of security staff across various custody levels. *Corrections Management, 5,* 41–48.

Chesney-Lind, M., & Pasko, L. (2004). *The female offender: Girls, women and crime* (2nd ed.). London: Sage.

Chivers, C. J. (2001, April 4). From court order to reality: A diverse Boston police force. *New York Times,* Final ed., Section 1, p. A-1.

Chodorow, N. (1978). *The reproduction of mothering: Psychoanalysis and the sociology of gender.* Berkeley: University of California Press.

Christie, N. (2000). *Crime control as industry: Toward gulags, western style* (3rd ed.). London: Routledge.

Chused, R. H. (1988). The hiring and retention of minorities and women on American law school faculties. *University of Pennsylvania Law Review, 193,* 527–569.

Cixous, H. (1971). Sorties. In E. Marks & I. Courtivron (Eds.), *New French feminisms* (pp. 90–98). New York: Schocken.

Clear, T. R., Cole, G. F., & Reisig, M. D. (2006). *American corrections.* Belmont, CA: Thomson.

Cockburn, C. (1991). *In the way of women: Men's resistance to sex equality in organizations.* Ithaca, NY: ILR Press.

Cohen, S. (1985). *Visions of social control.* Cambridge, MA: Polity Press.

Collins, P. H. (2000). *Black feminist thought: Knowledge, consciousness, and the politics of empowerment* (2nd ed). New York: Routledge.

Collins, S. C., & Vaughn, M. S. (2004). Liability for sexual harassment in criminal justice agencies. *Journal of Criminal Justice, 32,* 531–545.

Collins, W. (1991). Legal issues and the employment of women. In J. B. Morton (Ed.), *Change, challenge, and choices: Women's role in modern corrections* (pp. 13–18). Laurel, MD: American Correctional Association.

Connell, R. W. (1987). *Gender and power: Society, the person and sexual politics.* Stanford, CA: Stanford University Press.

Connell, R. W. (1993). The big picture: Masculinities in recent world history. *Theory and Society, 22,* 597–623.

Connell, R. W. (2002). *Gender.* Cambridge, UK: Polity Press.

Connell, R. W., & Messerschmidt, J. (2005). Hegemonic masculinity: Rethinking the concept. *Gender & Society, 19,* 829–859.

Cooper, C., & Ingram, S. (2004). *Retention of police officers: A study of resignations and transfers in 10 forces* (RDS Occasional Paper). London: Home Office. Retrieved January 13, 2006, from http://www.homeoffice.gov.uk/rds/pdfs04/occ86.pdf

Cooper, C. J. (1992, January 5). Women cops taking on harassment fight. *San Francisco Examiner,* pp. A1, 10.

Cooper Institute for Aerobics Research. (2004). *Common questions regarding physical fitness tests, standards and programs for public safety.* Retrieved June 2, 2006, from www.cooperinst.org/lawenf.asp

Cortina, L. M., Lonsway, K. A., Magley, V. J., Freeman, L. V., Collinsworth, L. L., Hunter, M., & Fitzgerald, L. F. (2002). What's gender go to do with it? Incivility in the federal courts. *Law and Social Inquiry, 27*(2), 235–270.

Corcos, C. A. (1998). Portia goes to parliament: Women and their admission to membership in the English legal system. *Denver University Law Review, 75,* 307–379.

Cowburn, M. (1998). A man's world: Gender issues in working with male sex offenders in prison. *The Howard Journal, 37,* 234–251.

Crenshaw, K. (1990). Demarginalizing the intersection of race and sex: A black feminist critique of antidiscrimination doctrine. In K. Bartlett & R. Kennedy (Eds.), *Feminist legal theory: Readings in law and gender* (pp. 51–80). Boulder, CO: Westview.

Crouch, B. M., & Alpert, G. P. (1982). Sex and occupational socialization among prison guards. *Criminal Justice and Behavior, 9*, 159–176.

Cullen, F. T., Lemming, T., Link, B. G., & Wozniak, J. F. (1985). The impact of social supports on police stress. *Criminology, 23*, 503–522.

Cullen, F. T., Link, B. G., Wolfe, N. T., & Frank, J. (1985). The social dimensions of correctional officer stress. *Justice Quarterly, 2*, 505–533.

Curran, B. A. (1986). American lawyers in the 1980s: A profession in transition. *Law & Society Review, 20*, 19–52.

Dalton, S., & Fenstermaker, S. (2002). "Doing gender" differently: Institutional change in second-parent adoptions. In S. Fenstermaker & C. West (Eds.), *Doing gender, doing difference: Inequality, power, and institutional change* (pp. 169–188). New York: Routledge.

Daly, M. (1984). *Pure lust: Elemental feminist philosophy.* Boston: Beacon Press.

Dantico, M., & Jurik, N. C. (1986). Where have all the good jobs gone? The effect of government service privatization on women workers. *Contemporary Crises, 10*, 421–439.

Davey, J. D. (1995). *The new social contract: America's journey from welfare state to police state.* Westport, CT: Praeger.

Davis, A. D. (2001). Straightening it out: Joan Williams on unbending gender. *American University Law Review, 49*, 823–849.

Davis, A. Y. (1981). *Women, race and class.* New York: Random House.

Davis, A. Y. (2003). *Are prisons obsolete?* New York: Seven Stories Press.

Davis, K. (1997). *Embodied practices.* Newbury Park, CA: Sage.

de Beauvoir, S. (1974). *The second sex* (H. M. Parshley, Trans.). *New York Modern Library.* New York: Vintage Books.

DeJong, C. (2004). Gender differences in officer attitude and behavior: Providing comfort to citizens. *Women & Criminal Justice, 15*(3/4), 1–32.

Denborough, D. (2001). Grappling with issues of privilege: A male prison worker's perspective. In D. Sabo, T. A. Kupers & W. London (Eds.), *Prison masculinities* (pp. 73–77). Philadelphia: Temple University Press.

Dick, P., & Jankowicz, A. D. (2001). A social constructionist account of police culture and its influence on the representation and progression of female officers: A Repertory grid analysis in the UK police force. *Policing: An International Journal of Police Strategies and Management, 24*(2), 181–199.

Dobash, R. E., Dobash, R. P., & Gutteridge, S. (1986). *The imprisonment of women.* Oxford, UK: Blackwell.

Dunkel, F. (1995). Imprisonment in transition: The situation in the new states of the federal Republic of Germany. *British Journal of Criminology, 35*(1), 95–113.

Echols, A. (1989). *Daring to be bad: Radical feminism in America 1967–1975.* Minneapolis: University of Minnesota Press.

Ehrenreich, B., & Hochschild, A. R. (Eds.). (2003). *Global woman: Nannies, maids, and sex workers in the new economy.* New York: Metropolitan Books.

Eldredge, M. (2005). The quest for a lactating male: Biology, gender and discrimination. *Chicago-Kent Law Review, 80*(2), 875–901.

Else-Mitchell, R. E., & Flutter, N. (Eds.). (1998). *Talking up: Young women's take on feminism.* North Melbourne, Victoria, Australia: Spinifex Press.

Embser-Herbert, M. S. (2005). A missing link: Institutional homophobia and sexual harassment in the U.S. military. In J. E. Gruber & P. Morgan (Eds.), *In the company of men:*

Male dominance and sexual harassment (pp. 215–242). Boston: Northeastern University Press.

Engel, R. S., & Worden, R. E. (2003). Police officers' attitudes, behavior and supervisory influences: An analysis of problem solving. *Criminology, 41*, 131–166.

Epstein, C. F. (1988). *Deceptive distinctions: Sex, gender and the social order.* New York: Yale University Press and Russell Sage Foundation.

Epstein, C. F. (1993). *Women in law* (2nd ed.). Urbana and Chicago: University of Illinois Press.

Epstein, C. F., Saute, R., Oglensky, B., & Gever, M. (1995). Glass ceilings and open doors: Women's advancement in the legal profession. *Fordham Law Review, 64*, 291–448.

Epstein, C. F., Seron, C., Oglensky, B., & Saute, R. (1999). *The part-time paradox.* New York and London: Routledge.

Equal Opportunities Commission. (2006). *Armitage, Marsden & HM Prison Service v. Johnson* [1997]. Retrieved February 6, 2006, from http://www.eoc-law.org.uk

Evans, G. (2000). *Play like a man, win like a woman: What men know about success that women need to learn.* New York: Broadway Books.

Faludi, S. (1991). *Backlash: The undeclared war against American women.* New York: Crown.

Farkas, M. A. (1999a). Correctional officer attitudes toward inmates and working with inmates in a "get tough" era. *Journal of Criminal Justice, 27*, 495–506.

Farkas, M. A. (1999b). Inmate supervisory style: Does gender make a difference? *Women & Criminal Justice, 10*, 25–45.

Fausto-Sterling, A. (2000). *Sexing the body: Gender politics and the construction of sexuality.* New York: Basic Books.

Federal Bureau of Prisons. (2002). *Characteristics of Federal Bureau of Prison correctional officers.* Retrieved March 20, 2005, from http://www.albany.edu/sourcebook/pdf/section1.pdf

Feinman, C. (1986). *Women in the criminal justice system* (2nd ed.). New York: Praeger.

Fenstermaker, S., & West, C. (2002). *Doing gender, doing difference: Inequality, power, and institutional change.* New York: Routledge.

Ferree, M. M., & Purkayastha, B. (2000). Equality and cumulative disadvantage: Response to Baxter and Wright. *Gender & Society, 14*, 809–813.

Fielding, N. (1994). Cop canteen culture. In T. Newburn & B. Stanko (Eds.), *Just boys doing the business? Men, masculinities and crime* (pp. 46–63). London: Routledge.

Fitzgerald, L. F. (2003). Sexual harassment and social justice: Reflections on the distance yet to go. *American Psychologist, 58*(11), 915–924.

Forst, B. (2000). The privatization and civilianization of policing. In *Boundary changes in criminal justice organizations: Criminal justice 2000 series, Vol. 2.* Washington, DC: National Institute of Justice.

Fossum, D. (1980). Women law professors. *American Bar Foundation Research Journal, 4*, 903–914.

Foucault, M. (1979). *Discipline and punish: The birth of the prison.* New York: Vintage.

Frankel, L. P. (2004). *Nice girls don't get the corner office.* New York: Warner Business Books.

Frankenberg, R. (1993). *White women, race matters: The social construction of whiteness.* Minneapolis: University of Minnesota Press.

Freedman, E. B. (1981). *Their sisters' keepers: Women's prison reform in America 1830–1930.* Ann Arbor: University of Michigan Press.

Freedman, E. B. (2002). *No turning back: The history of feminism and the future of women.* New York: Ballantine Books.

Freeman, J. (1989). Feminist organization and activities from suffrage to women's liberation. In J. Freeman (Ed.), *Women: A feminist perspective* (pp. 541–555). Mountain View, CA: Mayfield.

Freeman, R. M. (2003). Social distance and discretionary rule enforcement in a women's prison. *Prison Journal, 83,* 191–205.

Friedan, B. (1963). *The feminine mystique.* New York: Norton.

Frug, M. J. (1992). *Postmodern legal feminism.* New York: Routledge.

Fry, L. (1983). A preliminary examination of the factors related to turnover of women in law enforcement. *Journal of Police Science and Administration, 11,* 149–155.

Fyfe, J. (1987). *Police personnel practices, 1986* (Baseline Data Report Vol. 18, No. 6). Washington, DC: International City Management Association.

Gaber, P. (1998). "Just trying to be human in this place": The legal education of twenty women. *Yale Journal of Law and Feminism, 10,* 165–203.

Garfinkel, H. (1967). *Studies in ethnomethodology.* Englewood Cliffs, NJ: Prentice Hall.

Garner, J. H., & Maxwell, C. D. (2002). *Understanding the use of force by and against the police in six jurisdictions: Final report.* Washington, DC: National Institute of Justice.

Gellis, A. J. (1991). Great expectations: Women in the legal profession, A commentary on state studies. *Indiana Law Journal, 66,* 941–976.

Giddens, A. (1976). *New rules of sociological method.* New Haven, CT: Yale University Press.

Gilbert, M. J. (1990). *Working the unit: An inquiry into the discretionary behavior of correctional officers.* Ph.D. dissertation, Arizona State University, Tempe.

Gilligan, C. (1982). *In a different voice: Psychological theory and women's development.* Cambridge, MA: Harvard University Press.

Glenn, E. N. (1992). From servitude to service work: Historical continuities in the racial division of paid reproductive labor. *Signs, 18,* 1–43.

Global News. (2006). *CRE starts inquiry into prisons.* Retrieved February 6, 2006, from www.irseclipse.co.uk

Goffman, E. (1961). *Encounters.* Indianapolis, IN: Bobbs-Merrill.

Goffman, E. (1976). Gender displays. *Studies in the Anthropology of Visual Communication, 3,* 69–77.

Golden, T. (2006, February 26). A growing Afghan prison rivals bleak Guantanamo. *New York Times,* pp. A1, A4.

Goldhart, J. D. & Macedonia, A.T. (1992). Organizing in Ohio: Community corrections workers form alliance to promote women's professional development. *Corrections Today,* August, 96–100.

Goldstone, J. A., & Useem, B. (1999). Prison riots as microrevolutions: An extension of state-centered theories of revolution. *American Journal of Sociology, 104,* 985–1029.

Gondles, J. A. (2005). A salute to women working in corrections. *Corrections Today,* October, 6.

Gorman, E. H. (2005). Gender stereotypes, same-gender preferences and organizational variation in the hiring of women: Evidence from law firms. *American Sociological Review, 70,* 702–728.

Gossett, J. L., & Williams, J. E. (1998). Perceived discrimination among women law enforcement. *Women & Criminal Justice, 10*(1), 53–75.

Goward, P. (2002, October 20). *Both sides of the thin blue line.* Speech delivered at the Third Australasian Women and Policing Conference, Canberra, Australia. Retrieved June 2, 2006, from http://www.hreoc.gov.au/speeches/sex_discrim/thin_blue_line.html

Grant, D. R. (2000). Perceived gender differences in policing: The impact of gendered perceptions of officer-situation "fit." *Women & Criminal Justice, 12*(1), 53–74.

Gray, T. (1975). Selecting for a police subculture. In J. Skolnick & T. Gray (Eds.), *Police in America* (pp. 46–56). Boston: Little, Brown.

Green, B. A. (2005). A tribute to all "little women." *Corrections Today,* October, 78–81.

Greene, J. R. (2000). Community policing in America: Challenging the nature, structure and function of the police. In J. Homey (Ed.), *Policies, processes and decisions in the criminal justice system: Crime and justice* (Vol. 3). Washington, DC: U.S. Department of Justice.

Gregory, R. F. (2003). *Women and workplace discrimination: Overcoming barriers to gender equality.* New Brunswick, NJ: Rutgers University Press.

Griffin, M. L. (2001). Job satisfaction among detention officers: Assessing the relative contribution of organizational climate variables. *Journal of Criminal Justice, 29,* 219–232.

Gruber, J. E., & Morgan, P. (Eds.). (2005). *In the company of men: Male dominance and sexual harassment.* Boston: Northeastern University Press.

Guinier, L., Fine, M., Balin, J., Bartow, A., & Stachel, D. L. (1994). "Becoming gentlemen": Women's experiences at one Ivy League law school. *University of Pennsylvania Law Review, 143*(1), 1–110.

Gutek, B. A., & Nakamura, C. (1982). Gender roles and sexuality in the world of work. In E. Allgeier & N. McCormick (Eds.), *Gender roles and sexual behavior: Changing boundaries* (pp. 182–201). Palo Alto, CA: Mayfield.

Haarr, R. N. (2001). The making of a community policing officer: The impact of basic training and occupational socialization on police recruits. *Police Quarterly, 4*(4), 402–433.

Haarr, R. N. (2005). Factors affecting the decision of police recruits to "drop out" of police work. *Police Quarterly, 8*(4), 431–453.

Haarr, R. N., & Morash, M. (2005). Police workplace problems, coping strategies and stress: Changes from 1990 to 2003 for women and racial minorities. *Law Enforcement Executive FORUM, 4*(3), 165–185.

Hagan, J., & Kay, F. (1995). *Gender in practice.* New York: Oxford University Press.

Hagan, J., Zatz, M., Arnold, B., & Kay, F. (1991). Cultural capital, gender, and the structural transformation of legal practice. *Law & Society Review, 25,* 239–262.

Hale, D. C., & Menniti, D. J. (1993). Discrimination and harassment: Litigation by women in policing. In R. Muraskin & T. Alleman (Eds.), *It's a crime: Women and justice* (pp. 177–189). Englewood Cliffs, NJ: Regents/Prentice Hall.

Hall, E. J. (1993). Smiling, deferring and flirting: Doing gender by giving "good service." *Work and Occupations, 20,* 452–471.

Hall, R. H. (1994). *Sociology of work: Perspectives, analyses, and issues.* Thousand Oaks, CA: Pine Forge.

Hallett, M. A. (2002). Race, crime and for-profit imprisonment: Social disorganization as market opportunity. *Punishment & Society, 4,* 369–393.

Hallett, M. A., & Lee, J. F. (2000). Public money, private interests: The grass roots battle against CCA in Tennessee. In D. Shichor & M. J. Gilbert (Eds.), *Privatization in criminal justice: Past, present and future* (pp. 227–244). Cincinnati, OH: Anderson.

Haney, C., Banks, C., & Zimbardo, P. (1973). Interpersonal dynamics in a simulated prison. *International Journal of Criminology and Penology, 1,* 69–97.

Harriston, K. A. (1994, January 7). D.C. agency accused of harassment. *Washington Post,* p. A-1.

Hartmann, H. (1979). Capitalism, patriarchy, and job segregation by sex. In Z. Eisenstein (Ed.), *Capitalist patriarchy and the case for socialist feminism* (pp. 206–247). New York: Monthly Review Press.

Hawkes, M. G. (1991). Women's changing roles in corrections. In J. B. Morton (Ed.), *Change, challenge and choices: Women's role in modern corrections* (pp. 100–110). Laurel, MD: American Correctional Association.

Hawkins, R., & Alpert, G. P. (1989). *American prison systems: Punishment and justice.* Englewood Cliffs, NJ: Prentice Hall.

Hayes, M. (1989). Promotion and management: What choice for women? *Probation Journal, 36,* 12–17.

He, N., Zhao, J., & Archbold, C. A. (2002). Gender and police stress: The convergent and divergent impact of work environment, work-family conflict, and stress coping mechanisms of female and male police officers. *Policing: An International Journal of Police Strategies & Management, 25*(4), 687–708.

He, N., Zhao, J., & Ren, L. (2005). Do race and gender matter in police stress? A preliminary assessment of the interactive effects. *Journal of Criminal Justice, 33*(6), 535–547.

Heidensohn, F. (1992). *Women in control? The role of women in law enforcement.* New York: Oxford.

Heinz, J. P., Nelson, R. L., Laumann, E. O., & Michelson, E. (1998). The changing character of lawyers' work: Chicago in 1975 and 1995. *Law & Society Review, 32*(4), 751–775.

Hemmens, C., Stohr, M. K., Schoeler, M., & Miller, B. (2002). One step up, two steps back: The progression of perceptions of women's work in prisons and jails. *Journal of Criminal Justice, 30,* 473–489.

Hensler, D. H., & Resnik, J. (2003). Contested identities: Task forces on gender, race and ethnic bias and the obligations of the legal profession. In D. Rhode (Ed.), *Ethics in practice: Lawyers' roles, responsibilities and regulation.* New York: Oxford University Press.

Hepburn, J., & Knepper, P. (1993). Correctional officers as human service workers: The effect on job satisfaction. *Justice Quarterly, 10,* 315–335.

Hickman, M. J., & Reaves, B. A. (2001). *Community policing in local police departments, 1997 and 1999* (BJS Special Report NCJ 184794). Washington, DC: US Department of Justice.

Hickman, M. J., & Reaves, B. A. (2003a). *Local police departments, 2000* (BJS Special Report NCJ-196002). Washington, DC: U.S. Department of Justice.

Hickman, M. J., & Reaves, B. A. (2003b). *Sheriffs' offices, 2000* (BJS Special Report NCJ-196534). Washington, DC: U.S. Department of Justice.

Hochschild, A. R. (1989). *The second shift: Working parents and the revolution at home.* New York: Viking.

Hogan, N. L., Lambert, E. G., Jenkins, M., & Wambold, S. (2006). The impact of occupational stressors on correctional staff organizational commitment. *Journal of Contemporary Criminal Justice, 22,* 33–62.

Holdaway, S., & Parker, S. (1998). Policing women police: Uniform, patrol, promotion and representation in the CID. *British Journal of Criminology, 38,* 40–60.

Holeman, H., & Krepps-Hess, B. J. (1982). *Women correctional officer study final report.* Sacramento: California Department of Corrections.

Homer, S., & Schwartz, L. (1990). Admitted but not accepted: Outsiders take an inside look at law school. *Berkeley Women's Law Journal Annual, 5,* 1–74.

Hondagneu-Sotelo, P. (2001). *Domestica: Immigrant workers cleaning and caring in the shadows of affluence.* Berkeley: University of California Press.

Hossfeld, K. (1990). Their own logic against them: Contradictions in sex, race and class in Silicon Valley. In K. Ward (Ed.), *Women workers and global restructuring* (pp. 149–178). Ithaca, NY: ILR Cornell University Press.

Huang, W. R. (1997). Gender differences in the earnings of lawyers. *Columbia Journal of Law & Social Problems, 30,* 267–325.

Huffman, M. G., & Torres, L. (2002). It's not only "who you know" that matters: Gender, personal contacts, and job lead quality. *Gender & Society, 16,* 793–813.

Hull, K. E., & Nelson, V. (2000). Assimilation, choice or constraint: Testing theories of gender differences in the careers of lawyers. *Social Forces, 79*(1), 229–264.

Hunt, J. (1984). The development of rapport through negotiation of gender in field work among police. *Human Organization, 43,* 283–296.

Hunt, J. (1990). The logic of sexism among police. *Women & Criminal Justice, 1*, 3–30.

Hunter, S. M. (1992). Women in corrections: A look at the road ahead. *Corrections Today*, August, 8–9.

Hurst, T. E., & Hurst, M. M. (1997). Gender differences in mediation of severe occupational stress among correctional officers. *American Journal of Criminal Justice, 22*, 121–137.

Hurtado, A. (1989). Relating to privilege: Seduction and rejection in the subordination of white women and women of color. *Signs, 14*, 833–855.

Hutzel, E. (1933). *The policewoman's handbook.* New York: Columbia University Press.

Jacobs, J. A. (1989). *Revolving doors: Sex segregation and women's careers.* Stanford, CA: Stanford University Press.

Jacobs, J. A., & Gerson, K. (2004). *The time divide: Work, family, and gender inequality.* Cambridge, MA: Harvard University Press.

Jacobs, J. B. (1977). *Stateville: The penitentiary in mass society.* Chicago: University of Chicago Press.

Jacobs, J. B. (1983). *New perspectives on prisons and imprisonment.* Ithaca, NY: Cornell University Press.

James, A. L., Bottomley, K., Liebling, A., & Clare, E. (1997). *Privatizing prisons: Rhetoric and reality.* London: Sage.

Janofsky, M. (1998, June 21). Pittsburgh is showcase for women in policing. *New York Times*, Section 1, p. 14.

Jenne, D. L., & Kersting, R. C. (1996). Aggression and women correctional officers in male prisons. *Prison Journal, 76*, 442–460.

Johnson, P. (1991). Why employ women? In J. B. Morton (Ed.). *Change, challenge and choices: Women's role in modern corrections* (pp. 6–12). Laurel, MD: American Correctional Association.

Johnson, R. (1987). *Hardtime: Understanding and reforming the prison.* Pacific Grove, CA: Brooks/Cole.

Jones, S. (1986). *Policewomen and equality.* London: Macmillan.

Jones, T. (1978). Blacks in the American criminal justice system: A study of sanctioned deviance. *Journal of Sociology and Social Welfare, 5*, 356–73.

Jurik, N. C. (1985). An officer and a lady: Organizational barriers to women working as correctional officers in men's prisons. *Social Problems, 32*, 375–388.

Jurik, N. C. (1988). Striking a balance: Female correctional officers, gender role stereotypes, and male prisons. *Sociological Inquiry, 58*, 291–305.

Jurik, N. C. (1999). Socialist feminism, criminology and social justice. In B. Arrigo (Ed.), *Social justice/criminal justice* (pp. 30–50). Belmont, CA: Wadsworth.

Jurik, N. C. (2004). Imagining justice: Challenging the privatization of public life. *Social Problems, 51*, 1–15.

Jurik, N. C. (2005). *Bootstrap dreams: U.S. microenterprise development in an era of welfare reform.* Ithaca, NY: Cornell University Press.

Jurik, N. C., & Halemba, G. J. (1984). Gender, working conditions and the job satisfaction of women in a nontraditional occupation: Female correctional officers in men's prisons. *The Sociological Quarterly, 25*, 551–566.

Jurik, N. C., Halemba, G. J., Musheno, M. C., & Boyle, B. V. (1987). Educational attainment, job satisfaction, and the professionalization of correctional officers. *Work and Occupations, 14*, 106–125.

Jurik, N. C., & Martin, S. E. (2001). Femininities, masculinities and organizational conflict: Women in criminal justice occupations. In C. M. Renzetti & L. Goodstein, (Eds.), *Women, crime and criminal justice* (pp. 264–281). Los Angeles: Roxbury.

Jurik, N. C., & Musheno, M. C. (1986). The internal crisis of corrections: Professionalization and the work environment. *Justice Quarterly, 3*, 457–480.

Jurik, N. C., & Winn, R. (1987). Describing correctional security dropouts and rejects: An individual or organizational profile? *Criminal Justice and Behavior, 14,* 5–25.

Kanter, R. M. (1977). *Men and women of the corporation.* New York: Basic.

Kappeler, V. E., Sluder, R. D., & Alpert, G. P. (1998). *Forces of deviance: The dark side of policing.* Prospect Heights, IL: Waveland.

Kay, F. M. (1997). Flight from law: A competing risks model of departures from law firms. *Law & Society Review, 31*(2), 301–335.

Kay, F. M., & Hagan, J. (1998). Raising the bar: The gender stratification of law-firm capital. *American Sociological Review, 63,* 728–743.

Kay, F. M., & Hagan, J. (1999). Cultivating clients in the competition for partnerships: Gender and the organizational restructuring of law firms in the 1990s. *Law & Society Review, 33*(3), 517–555.

Kelly, R. M. (1991). *The gendered economy.* Newbury Park, CA: Sage.

Kessler, S. J., & McKenna, W. (1978). *Gender: An ethnomethodological approach.* New York: J. Wiley and Sons.

Kiczkova, Z., & Farkasova, E. (1993). The emancipation of women: A concept that failed. In N. Funk & M. Mueller (Eds.), *Gender and post-communism* (pp. 135–156). New York: Routledge.

Kim, A. S., DeValve, M., DeValve, E. Q., & Johnson, W. W. (2003). Female wardens: Results from a national survey of state correctional executives. *The Prison Journal, 83,* 406–425.

King, S. (2000, October/November). *Women and the changing work of prison officers.* Women in Corrections: Staff and Clients Conference. Australian Institute of Criminology, Adelaide.

Kissel, P., & Katsampes, P. (1980). The impact of women corrections officers on the functioning of institutions housing male inmates. *Journal of Offender Counseling Services and Rehabilitation, 4,* 213–231.

Kizziah, C., & Morris, M. (1977). *Evaluation of women in policing program: Newton, Massachusetts.* Oakland, CA: Approach Associates.

Klofas, J., & Toch, H. (1982). Guard subculture myth. *Journal of Research on Crime and Delinquency, 19,* 238–254.

Koehorst, P., & Koppers, A. (1995). *Report on a visit to prisons in the Ukraine.* Amsterdam: Prison Project Second World Center.

Kommer, M. M. (1993). A Dutch prison officer's work: Balancing between prison policy, organizational structure, and professional autonomy. *The Netherlands Journal of Social Science, 29,* 130–146.

Kornhauser, L. A., & Revesz, R. L. (1995). Legal education and entry into the legal profession: The role of race, gender and educational debut. *New York University Law Review, 70,* 829–964.

Kostelac, C. (2004). *Civilianization in policing: Trends and consequences.* Unpublished paper, Arizona State University, Tempe.

Kritzer, H. M. (1999). The professions are dead, long live the professions: Legal practice in a postprofessional world. *Law & Society Review, 33*(3), 713–759.

Labaton, V., & Martin, D. L. (2004). *The fire this time: Young activists and the new feminism.* New York: Anchor Books.

Lambert, E. G., Hogan, N. L., & Barton, S. M. (2004). The nature of work-family conflict among correctional staff. *Criminal Justice Review, 29,* 145–172.

Lariviere, M., & Robinson, D. (1996). *Attitudes of federal correctional officers towards offenders.* Ottawa: Research Division, Correctional Service Canada.

Lawrence, R., & Mahan, S. (1998). Women corrections officers in men's prisons: Acceptance and perceived job performance. *Women & Criminal Justice, 9,* 63–86.

Leinwand, D. (2004, April 26). Lawsuits of '70s shape police leadership now. *USA Today*, pp. A13–A14.

Liebling, A., & Price, D. (2001). *The prison officer.* London: The Prison Service Journal Press.

Lombardo, L. X. (1981). *Guards imprisoned: Correctional officers at work.* New York: Elsevier.

Lorber, J. (2001). *Gender inequality: Feminist theories and politics* (2nd ed.). Los Angeles: Roxbury Press.

Lorber, J., & Farrell, S. A. (1991). Preface. In J. Lorber & S. A. Farrell (Eds.), *The social construction of gender* (pp. 1–5). London: Sage.

MacCorquodale, P., & Jensen, G. (1993). Women in the law: Partners or tokens? *Gender & Society, 7,* 582–594.

MacDonald, M. (2003). *A comparative report of health care provisions in prisons in Poland, Hungary, and the Czech Republic.* Helsinki, Finland: The European Initiative for Crime Prevention and Control, affiliated with the United Nations.

MacKinnon, C. (1978). *Sexual harassment of working women.* New Haven, CT: Yale University Press.

MacKinnon, C. (1989). *Toward a feminist theory of state.* Cambridge, MA: Harvard University Press.

Madek, G. A., & O'Brien, C. N. (1990). Women denied partnerships: From Hishon to Price Waterhouse v. Hopkins. *Hofstra Labor Law Journal, 7,* 257–302.

Maghan, J., & McLeish-Blackwell, L. (1991). Black women in correctional employment. In J. B. Morton (Ed.), *Change, challenge and choices: Women's role in modern corrections* (pp. 82–99). Laurel, MD: American Correctional Association.

Maniloff, M. (1998). Policewomen in France. *European Network of Policewomen Newsletter,* June, 2–5.

Manning, P. K. (1997). *Police work: The social organization of policing* (2nd ed.). Prospect Heights, IL: Waveland Press.

Marquart, J. W., Barnhill, M. B., & Balshaw-Biddle, K. (2001). Fatal attraction: An analysis of employee boundary violations in a southern prison system 1995–1998. *Justice Quarterly, 18,* 877–910.

Marquart, J. W., & Crouch, B. M. (1985). Judicial reform and prisoner control: The impact of Ruiz v. Estelle on the Texas penitentiary. *Law & Society Review, 19,* 557–586.

Martin, E. (2004). Gender and presidential judicial selection. *Women & Politics, 26*(4), 109–129.

Martin, E., & Pyle, B. (2002). Gender and racial diversification of state supreme courts. *Women & Politics, 24*(4), 35–52.

Martin, P. Y. (1991). Gender, interaction and inequality in organizations. In C. Ridgeway (Ed.), *Gender, interaction and inequality* (pp. 208–231). New York: Springer-Verlag.

Martin, P. Y. (2001). Mobilizing masculinities: Women's experiences of men at work. *Organization, 8,* 587–618.

Martin, P. Y. (2003). "Said and done" versus "saying and doing": Gendering practices, practicing gender at work. *Gender & Society, 17,* 342–366.

Martin, P. Y., Reynolds, J. R., & Keith, S. (2002). Gender bias and feminist consciousness among judges and attorneys: A standpoint theory analysis. *Signs, 27*(3), 665–701.

Martin, S. E. (1978). Sexual politics in the workplace: The interactional world of policewomen. *Symbolic Interaction, 1,* 44–60.

Martin, S. E. (1980). *"Breaking and entering": Policewomen on patrol.* Berkeley: University of California Press.

Martin, S. E. (1990). *On the move: The status of women in policing.* Washington, DC: Police Foundation.

Martin, S. E. (1991). The effectiveness of affirmative action: The case of women in policing. *Justice Quarterly, 8,* 489–504.

Martin, S. E. (1994). "Outsider within" the stationhouse: The impact of race and gender on black women police. *Social Problems, 41*, 383–400.

Martin, S. E. (1999). Police force or police service? Gender and emotional labor in police work. *Annals of the American Academy of Political and Social Science, 561*, 111–126.

Martinson, R. (1974). What works? Questions and answers about prison reform. *Public Interest, 35*, 22–54.

Maryland Special Joint Committee. (1989). *Gender bias in the courts.* Annapolis, MD: Author.

Maschke, K. J. (1996). Gender in the prison setting: The privacy-equal employment dilemma. *Women & Criminal Justice, 7*, 23–42.

McBrier, D. B. (2003). Gender and career dynamics within a segmented professional labor market: The case of law academia. *Social Forces, 81*(4), 1201–1266.

McCauley, M. (2005). Reflections from a female pioneer. *Corrections Today*, October, 102–103.

McElhinny, B. S. (1993). *We all wear the blue: Language, gender and police work.* Unpublished Ph.D. dissertation. Palo Alto, CA: Stanford University.

McMahon, M. (1999). *Women on guard: Discrimination and harassment in corrections.* Toronto, Ontario, Canada: University of Toronto Press.

Menkel-Meadow, C. (1986). The comparative sociology of women lawyers: The "feminization" of the legal profession. *Osgood Hall Law Journal, 24*, 897–918.

Merritt, D. J., & Reskin, B. F. (1997). Sex, race and credentials: The truth about affirmative action in law faculty hiring. *Columbia Law Review, 97*(2), 199–311.

Merritt, D. J., & Reskin, B. F. (2003). New directions for women in the legal academy. *Journal of Legal Education, 53*(4), 489–495.

Messerschmidt, J. (1993). *Masculinities and crime.* Lanham, MD: Rowman & Littlefield.

Messerschmidt, J. (2004). *Flesh and blood: Adolescent gender diversity and violence.* Lanham, MD.: Rowman & Littlefield.

Messner, M. (2000). Barbie girl versus sea monsters: Children constructing gender. *Gender & Society, 14*, 765–784.

Meuser, M. (2003). Modernized masculinities? Continuities and changes in men's lives. In S. Ervo & T. Johansson (Eds.), *Among men: Moulding masculinities* (pp. 127–148). Aldershot, UK: Ashgate.

Micucci, A., & Monster, M. (2004). It's about time to hear their stories: Impediments to rehabilitation at a Canadian provincial correctional facility for women. *Journal of Criminal Justice, 32*, 515–530.

Mies, M. (1998). *Patriarchy and accumulation on a world scale: Women in the international division of labor* (2nd ed.). London: Zed Books.

Milkman, R. (1976). Women's work and economic crisis: Some lessons of the Great Depression. *Review of Radical Political Economics, 8*, 73–97.

Miller, J. (2002). The strengths and limits of "doing gender" for understanding street crime. *Theoretical Criminology, 6*, 433–460.

Miller, S. L. (1999). *Gender and community policing: Walking the talk.* Boston: Northeastern University Press.

Miller, S. L., Forest, K. B., & Jurik, N. C. (2003). Diversity in blue: Lesbian and gay police officers in a masculine occupation. *Men and Masculinities, 5*, 255–385.

Miller, S. L., Forest, K. B., & Jurik, N. C. (2004). Lesbians in policing: Perceptions and work experiences within the macho cop culture. In B. R. Price & N. J. Sokoloff (Eds.), *The criminal justice system and women* (pp. 511–526). New York: McGraw-Hill.

Miller, S. L., & Hodge, J. (2004). Rethinking gender and community policing: Cultural obstacles and policy issues. *Law Enforcement Executive Forum, 44*, 39–49.

Milton, C. (1972). *Women in policing.* Washington, DC: Police Foundation.

Mincer, J., & Polachek, S. (1974). Family investments in human capital: Earnings of women. *Journal of Political Economy, 82,* s76–s108.

Minow, M. (1988). Feminist reason: Getting it and losing it. In K. T. Bartlett & R. Kennedy (Eds.), *Feminist legal theory: Readings in law and gender* (pp. 357–369). Boulder, CO: Westview Press.

Mohanty, C. T. (2003). *Feminism without borders: Decolonizing theory, practicing solidarity.* Durham, NC: Duke University Press.

Moon, B., & Maxwell, S. R. (2004). The sources and consequences of corrections officers' stress: A South Korean example. *Journal of Criminal Justice, 32,* 359–370.

Moraga, C., & Anzaldua, G. (Eds.). (1983). *This bridge called my back: Writings by radical women of color.* New York: Kitchen Table, Women of Color Press.

Morash, M., & Greene, J. (1986). Evaluating women on patrol: A critique of contemporary wisdom. *Evaluation Review, 10,* 230–255.

Morash, M., & Haarr, R. (1995). Gender, workplace problems, and stress in policing. *Justice Quarterly, 12,* 113–140.

Morello, K. B. (1986). *The invisible bar: The woman lawyer in America, 1938 to the present.* New York: Random House.

Morgan, R. D., Van Haveren, R. A., & Pearson, C. A. (2002). Correctional officer burnout. *Criminal Justice and Behavior, 29,* 144–160.

Morton, J. B. (1991a). Pregnancy and correctional employment. In J. B. Morton (Ed.), *Change, challenge, and choices: Women's role in modern corrections* (pp. 40–50). Laurel, MD: American Correctional Association.

Morton, J. B. (1991b). Women correctional officers: A ten year update. In J. B. Morton (Ed.), *Change, challenge, and choices: Women's role in modern corrections* (pp. 19–39). Laurel, MD: American Correctional Association.

Morton, J. B. (1992). Women in corrections: Looking back on 200 years of valuable contributions. *Corrections Today,* August, 76–77.

Murton, T. O., & Hyams, J. (1969). *Accomplices to the crime.* New York: Grove Press.

Myers, K. A., Forest, K. B., & Miller, S. L. (2004). "Officer Friendly" and the tough cop: Gays and lesbians navigate homophobia and policing. *Journal of Homosexuality, 47*(1), 17–37.

Naples, N. A., & Desai, M. (2002). *Women's activism and globalization.* New York: Routledge.

Natarajan, M. (2001). Women police in a traditional society: Test of a Western model of integration. *International Journal of Comparative Sociology, XLII*(1–2), 211–233.

Natarajan, M. (2003). Women police in India: A tale of two cohorts. *International Journal of Comparative Criminology, 2*(2), 201–224.

National Association for Law Placement. (2005). *Women and attorneys of color at law firms, 2004.* Retrieved January 22, 2005, from http://www.nalp.org/press/details.php?id=53

National Association for Law Placement Foundation. (2003). *Keeping the keepers-2: Mobility and management of associates.* Overland Park, KS: Author.

National Center for Women & Policing. (2002a). *Equality denied. The status of women in policing: 2001.* Los Angeles: Author. Retrieved September 8, 2005, from http://www.women andpolicing.org/PDF/2002_Status_Report.pdf

National Center for Women & Policing. (2002b). *Men, women and police excessive force: A tale of two genders.* Los Angeles: Author. Retrieved February 14, 2006, from http://www .womenandpolicing.org/PDF/2002_Excessive_Force.pdf

National Center for Women & Policing. (2003). *Tearing down the wall: Problems with consistency, validity and adverse impact of physical agility testing on police selection.* Los Angeles:

Author. Retrieved February 14, 2006, from http://www.womenandpolicing.org/pdf/PhysicalAgilityStudy.pdf

National Crime Prevention Council. (2002). *Building the homeland security network: What will it take? The Wirthlin Report.* Washington, DC: Author.

National Research Council. (2004). *Fairness and effectiveness in policing: The evidence.* Washington, DC: National Academies Press.

Ness, C., & Gordon, R. (1995, August 13). Beating the rap. *San Francisco Examiner,* p. A11.

Nieva, V., & Gutek, B. (1981). *Women and work: A psychological perspective.* New York: Praeger.

Nossel, E., & Westfall, E. (1997). *Presumed equal: What America's top women lawyers really think about their firms.* New York: Career PR.

Omi, M., & Winant, H. (1994). *Racial formation in the United States.* London: Routledge.

Owen, B. A. (1988). *The reproduction of social control: A study of prison workers at San Quentin.* New York: Praeger.

Padavic, I., & Orcutt, J. D. (1997). Perceptions of sexual harassment in the Florida legal system: A comparison of dominance and spillover explanations. *Gender & Society, 11*(3), 682–699.

Padavic, I., & Reskin, B. (2002). *Women and men at work* (2nd ed.). Thousand Oaks, CA: Pine Forge.

Palmer, B. (2001). Women in the American judiciary: Their influence and impact. *Women & Politics, 23*(3), 89–99.

Paoline, E. A., III, & Terrill, W. (2004). Women police officers and the use of coercion. *Women & Criminal Justice, 15*(3/4), 97–119.

Parenti, C. (1999). *Lockdown America: Police and prisons in the age of crisis.* London: Verso.

Parsons, T., & Bales, R. (1955). *Family, socialization and interaction process.* Glencoe, IL: Free Press.

Pastore, A. L., & Maguire, K. (Eds.). (2005). *Sourcebook of criminal justice statistics* [Online]. Retrieved June 9, 2006, from http://www.albany.edu/sourcebook//pdf/t182.pdf

Pelfrey, W. V., Jr. (2004). The inchoate nature of community policing: Differences between community policing and traditional police officers. *Justice Quarterly, 21*(3), 579–601.

Pennsylvania State Police. (1974). *Pennsylvania State Police Female Trooper Study.* Harrisburg: Pennsylvania State Police Headquarters.

Perrucci, R., & Wysong, E. (1999). *The new class society.* Lanham, MD: Rowman & Littlefield.

Pierce, J. L. (1995). *Gender trials: Emotional lives in contemporary law firms.* Berkeley: University of California Press.

Pike, D. L. (1992). Women in police academy training: Some aspects of organizational response. In I. Moyer, *Changing roles of women in the criminal justice system: Offenders, victims and professionals* (2nd ed., pp. 261–280). Prospect Heights, IL: Waveland Press.

Pogrebin, M. R., & Poole, E. D. (1995). Emotion management: A study of police responses to tragic events. *Social perspectives on emotion* (Vol. 3). Greenwich, CT: JAI.

Pogrebin, M. R., & Poole, E. D. (1997). The sexualized work environment: A look at women jail officers. *Prison Journal, 77,* 41–57.

Polowek, K. (1996). *Retention of British Columbia's municipal police officers: An examination of reasons for leaving.* Vancouver, British Columbia, Canada: Ministry of Attorney General.

Poole, E., & Regoli, R. (1981). Alienation in prison: An examination of the work relations of prison guards. *Criminology, 19,* 251–270.

Poster, W., & Salime, Z. (2002). The limits of microcredit: Transnational feminism and USAID activities in the United States and Morocco. In N. A. Naples & M. Desai (Eds.), *Women's activism and globalization* (pp. 189–219). New York: Routledge.

Potts, L. W. (1983). Equal employment opportunity and female employment in police agencies. *Journal of Criminal Justice, 11*, 505–523.

Prenzler, T. (1994). Women in Australian policing: An overview. *Journal of Australian Studies, 42*, 78–88.

Prenzler, T. (1996, July 29–31). *Rebuilding the walls? The impact of police pre-entry physical ability tests on female applicants.* Paper presented at the First Australasian Women Police Conference, Sydney, Australia.

Prenzler, T. (1998). Gender integration in Australian policing: The evolution of management responsibility. *International Journal of Police Science and Management, 1*, 1241–1259.

Prenzler, T., & Hayes, H. (2000). Measuring progress in gender equity in Australian policing. *Current Issues in Criminal Justice, 12*(1), 66–91.

Prenzler, T., & Wimshurst, K. (1997). Blue tunics and batons: Women and politics in the Queensland Police 1970-1987. *Journal of Australian Studies, 52*, 88–101.

Price, B. R., Sokoloff, N. J., & Kuleshnyka, I. (1992). A study of black and white police in an urban police department. *The Justice Professional, 6*, 68–85.

Price, J. (1996, August). *Doing gender: Men and emotion.* Paper presented at the annual meeting of the American Sociological Association.

Prokos, A., & Padavic, I. (2002). "There oughtta be a law against bitches": Masculinity lessons in police academy training. *Gender, Work and Organization, 9*(4), 439–459.

Raday, F. (1996). Women in law in Israel: A study of the relationship between professional integration and feminism. *Georgia State University Law Review, 12*, 525–552.

Rafter, N. H. (1990). *Partial Justice, women in state prisons, 1800–1935* (2nd ed.). New Brunswick, NJ: Transaction Press.

Raher, S. (2002). *Private prisons and public money: Hidden costs borne by Colorado's taxpayers.* Colorado Springs: Colorado Criminal Justice Reform Coalition. Retrieved February 1, 2006, from http://www.ccjrc.org/pdf/CostDataReport2002.pdf

Reaves, B. A. (1997). *Federal law enforcement officers, 1996* (BJS Special Report NCJ-164617). Washington, DC: U.S. Department of Justice.

Reaves, B. A., & Bauer, L. M. (2003). *Federal law enforcement officers, 2002* (BJS Special Report NCJ-111115). Washington, DC: U.S. Department of Justice.

Reaves, B. A., & Hickman, M. J. (2002). *Census of state and local law enforcement agencies, 2000* (BJS Special Report NCJ 194066). Washington, DC: U.S. Department of Justice.

Reichman, N., & Sterling, J. (2002). Recasting the brass ring: Deconstructing and reconstructing workplace opportunities for women lawyers. *Capital University Law Review, 2*, 923–977.

Reichman, N., & Sterling, J. (2004). *Gender penalties revisited.* Retrieved December 13, 2005, from: http://www.cwba.org/pdf/GenderPenaltiesRevisitedfullreport.pdf

Report of the Florida Supreme Court Gender Bias Study Commission. (1990). *Florida Law Review, 42*, 803–981.

Reskin, B. F. (1988). Bringing the men back in: Sex differentiation and the devaluation of women's work. *Gender & Society, 2*, 58–81.

Reskin, B. F. (2002). Rethinking employment discrimination and its remedies. In M. Guillen, R. Collins, P. England, & M. Meyer (Eds.), *The new economic sociology* (218–244). New York: Russell Sage.

Reskin, B. F., & Roos, P. A. (1990). *Job queues and gender queues: Explaining women's inroads into male occupations.* Philadelphia: Temple University Press.

Resnik, J. (1996). Asking about gender in the courts. *Signs, 21*, pp. 952–960.

Reuss-Ianni, E. B. (1983). *The two cultures of policing: Street cops and management cops.* New Brunswick, NJ: Transaction Books.

Rhode, D. (1988). Perspectives on professional women. *Stanford Law Review, 40,* 1164–1207.

Rhode, D. L. (1996). The myth of meritocracy. *Fordham Law Review, 65,* 585–594.

Rhode, D. L. (1997). Whistling Vivaldi: Legal education and the politics of progress. *New York University Review of Law and Social Change, 23,* 217–224.

Rich, A. (1980). Compulsory heterosexuality and lesbian existence. *Signs, 5,* 631–660.

Riley, K. J., & Hoffman, B. (1995). *Domestic terrorism: A national assessment of state and local preparedness.* Santa Monica, CA: RAND.

Roach, S. L. (1990). Men and women lawyers in in-house legal departments: Recruitment and career patterns. *Gender & Society, 4,* 207–219.

Romero, M. (2002). *Maid in the U.S.A.* New York: Routledge.

Rosenberg, J., Perlstadt, H., & Phillips, W. R. F. (1993). Now that we are here: Discrimination, disparagement, and harassment at work and the experience of women lawyers. *Gender & Society, 7,* 415–433.

Roth, L. M. (2004). The social psychology of tokenism: Status and homophily processes on Wall Street. *Sociological Perspectives, 74*(2), 189–214.

Rowan, J. R. (1996). Who is safer in male maximum security prisons? *Corrections Today, 58,* 186–189.

Sabo, D., Kupers, T. A., & London, W. (2001). Gender and the politics of punishment. In D. Sabo, T. A. Kupers, & W. London (Eds.), *Prison masculinities* (pp. 3–18). Philadelphia: Temple University Press.

Sassen, S. (1998). *Globalization and its discontents.* New York: New Press.

Savicki, V., Cooley, E., & Gjesvold, J. (2003). Harassment as a predictor of job burnout in correctional officers. *Criminal Justice and Behavior, 30,* 602–619.

Schafran, L. H. (1987). Documenting gender bias in the courts: The task force approach. *Judicature, 70,* 280–290.

Schafran, L. H. (2004). Overwhelming evidence: Gender and race bias in the courts. In B. R. Price & N. J. Sokoloff (Eds.), *The criminal justice system and women: Offenders, prisoners, victims & workers* (3rd ed., pp. 457–472). New York: McGraw-Hill.

Schneider, B. (1982). Consciousness about sexual harassment among heterosexual and lesbian women workers. *Journal of Social Issues, 38,* 75–97.

Schneider, B. (1991). Put up and shut up: Workplace sexual assaults. *Gender & Society, 5,* 533–548.

Schoonmaker, M., & Brooks, J. S. (1975). Women in probation and parole, 1974. *Crime and Delinquency, 21,* 109–115.

Schultz, V. (1991). Telling stories about women and work: Judicial interpretation of sex segregation in the workplace in Title VII cases raising the lack of interest argument. In K. T. Bartlett & R. Kennedy (Eds.), *Feminist legal theory: Readings in law and gender* (pp. 124–155). Boulder, CO: Westview Press.

Schulz, D. M. (1995). *From social worker to crimefighter: Women in United States municipal policing.* Westport, CT: Prager.

Schulz, D. M. (1998). Bridging boundaries: United States policewomen's efforts to form an international network. *International Journal of Police Science and Management, 1*(1), 70–80.

Schulz, D. M. (2004). Invisible no more: A social history of women in U.S. policing. In B. R. Price & N. Sokoloff (Eds.), *The criminal justice system and women: Offenders, prisoners, victims, & workers* (3rd ed., pp. 483–493). New York: McGraw-Hill.

Sclar, E. D. (2000). *You don't always get what you pay for: The economics of privatization.* Ithaca, NY: Cornell University Press.

Scott, J. W. (1990). Deconstructing equality-versus-difference: Or, the uses of poststructuralist theory for feminism. In M. Hirsch & E. Fox (Eds.), *Conflicts in feminism* (pp. 134–148). New York: Routledge.

Seagram, B. C., & Stark-Adamec, C. (1992). Women in Canadian urban policing: Why are they leaving? *Police Chief, 59*, 120–128.

Seccombe, W. (1986). Patriarchy stabilized: The construction of the male breadwinner norm in nineteenth-century Britain. *Social History, 11*, 53–75.

Sedgwick, E. K. (1993). *Epistemology of the closet.* Berkeley: University of California Press.

Seron, C., & Ferris, K. (1995). Negotiating professionalism: The gendered social capital of flexible time. *Work and Occupations, 22*, 23–47.

Shawver, L., & Dickover, R. (1986). Research perspectives: Exploding a myth. *Corrections Today,* August, 30–34.

Sherman, L. J. (1975). Evaluation of policewomen on patrol in a suburban police department. *Journal of Police Science and Administration, 3*, 434–438.

Sichel, J. L., Friedman, L. N., Quint, J. C., & Smith, M. E. (1977). *Women on patrol: A pilot study of police performance in New York City.* Washington, DC: National Institute of Law Enforcement and Criminal Justice.

Siemsen, C. (2006). Women criminal lawyers. In C. M. Renzetti, L. Goodstein & S. L. Miller (Eds.), *Rethinking gender, crime and justice* (pp. 228–239). Los Angeles: Roxbury.

Siklova, J. (1993). Feminism and the roots of apathy in the Czech Republic. *Social Research, 64*, 258–277.

Silvestri, M. (2003). *Women in charge: Policing, gender and leadership.* Cullompton, Devon, UK: Willan.

Simpson, G. (1996). The plexiglass ceiling: The careers of black women lawyers. *The Career Development Quarterly, 45*, 173–188.

Sirianni, C., & Welsh, A. (1991). Through the prism of time: Temporal structures in postmodern America. In A. Wolfe (Ed.), *America at century's end* (pp. 421–439). Berkeley: University of California Press.

Skolnick, J. (1994). *Justice without trial: Law enforcement in a democratic society* (3rd ed.). New York: Macmillan.

Skolnick, J., & Bayley, D. (1986). *The new blue line: Police innovation in six American cities.* New York: Free Press.

Slotnick, E. E. (1984). Gender, affirmative action and recruitment to the federal bench. *Golden Gate University Law Review, 14*, 519–571.

Smith-Spark, L. (2004, October 25). Where are all the women judges? BBC News Online. Retrieved February 9, 2006, from http://news.bbc.co.uk/2/hi/uk_news/3739562.stm

Steier, R. (1989). Women flourishing in corrections departments. *American Justice Association Newsletter,* Winter, 1.

Stohr, M. K., Hemmens, C., Kifer, M., & Schoeler, M. (2000). We know it, we just have to do it: Perceptions of ethical work in prisons and jails. *The Prison Journal, 80*, 126–150.

Stohr, M. K., Lovrich, N., & Mays, G. L. (1997). Service v. security focus in training assessments: Testing gender differences among women's jail correctional officers. *Women & Criminal Justice, 9*, 65–85.

Stohr, M. K., Lovrich, N. P., & Wood, M. J. (1996). Service v. security concerns in contemporary jails: Testing general differences in training topic assessments. *Journal of Criminal Justice, 24*, 437–448.

Stojkovic, S., & Farkas, M. A. (2003). *Correctional leadership: A cultural perspective.* Belmont, CA: Wadsworth.

Stojkovic, S., Pogrebin, M. R., & Poole, E. D. (2000). Accounts of jail work: Women deputies' portrayals of their work worlds. *Perspectives on Social Problems, 12*, 217–231.

Sturm, S. (2001). Second generation employment discrimination: A structural approach. *Columbia Law Review, 101*(3), 458–568.

Sugden, N. (2005). *Disruptive bodies: Women performing policing.* Dissertation submitted for doctoral degree, Charles Stuart University, Queensland, Australia.

Sulton, C., & Townsey, R. (1981). *A progress report on women in policing.* Washington, DC: Police Foundation.

Summerill, J. (2005). Securing confidence in immigration reform. *Corrections Today,* October, 14, 16.

Sutton, J. (1996, July). *Keeping the faith: Women in policing, a New South Wales perspective.* Paper presented at the First Australasian Women Police Conference, Sydney, Australia. Retrieved June 2, 2006, from http://www.aic.gov.au/conferences/policewomen/sutton.pdf

Sweet, C. (1995). Flirting with disaster. *Phoenix Magazine,* January, 53–58.

Swerdlow, M. (1989). Men's accommodations to women entering a nontraditional occupation: A case of rapid transit operatives. *Gender & Society, 3,* 373–387.

Sykes, G. (1985). The functional nature of police reform: The "myth" of controlling the police. *Justice Quarterly, 2,* 52–65.

Sykes, G. M. (1958). *The society of captives.* Princeton, NJ: Princeton University Press.

Szockyj, J. E. (1989). Working in a man's world: Women correctional officers in an institution for men. *Canadian Journal of Criminology,* July, 319–328.

Task Force on Corrections, The President's Commission on Law Enforcement and Administration of Justice. (1973). *Task force report: Corrections.* Washington, DC: U.S. Government Printing Office.

Texeira, M. T. (2002). "Who protects and serves me?" A case study of sexual harassment of African American women in one U.S. law enforcement agency. *Gender & Society, 16*(4), 524–545.

Thornton, M. (1996). *Dissonance and distrust: Women in the legal profession.* Oxford, UK: Oxford University Press.

Thornton, M. (2004). *Gender, legality and authority.* Address to Australian Lawyers and Social Change Conference. Retrieved February 2, 2006, from http://law.anu.edu.au/alsc/ThorntonDiversity.pdf

Tracy, S. J. (2004a). The construction of correctional officers: Layers of emotionality behind bars. *Qualitative Inquiry, 10,* 509–533.

Tracy, S. J. (2004b). Dialectic, contradiction, or double bind? Analyzing and theorizing employee reactions to organizational tension. *Journal of Applied Communication Research, 32,* 119–146.

Tracy, S. J. (2005). Locking up emotion: Moving beyond dissonance for understanding emotion labor discomfort. *Communication Monographs, 72,* 261–283.

Tracy, S. J., & Scott, C. (2006, forthcoming). Sexuality, masculinity and taint management among firefighters and correctional officers. *Management Communication Quarterly, 20.*

Trice, H. M. (1993). *Occupational subcultures in the workplace.* Ithaca, NY: ILR Press.

Triplett, R., Mullings, J. L., & Scarborough, K. E. (1999). Examining the effect of work-home conflict on work-related stress among correctional officers. *Journal of Criminal Justice, 27,* 371–385.

United Nations. (2000). *The world's women 2000: Trends and statistics.* New York: Author.

U.S. Department of Justice, Bureau of Justice Statistics. (1992). *State and local police departments, 1990* (Bulletin NIC-133284). Washington, DC: Author.

U.S. Department of Justice, Federal Bureau of Investigation. (1981). *Uniform crime reports 1980*. Washington, DC: US Government Printing Office.

U.S. Department of Justice, Federal Bureau of Investigation. (1991). *Uniform crime reports 1990*. Washington, DC: US Government Printing Office.

U.S. Department of Justice, Federal Bureau of Investigation. (2001). *Uniform crime reports, 2000*. Washington, DC: US Government Printing Office.

U.S. Department of Justice, Federal Bureau of Investigation. (2005). *Uniform crime reports, 2004*. Washington, DC: US Government Printing Office.

U.S. Department of Labor. (2006). *Compliance assistance—Family and medical leave act*. Retrieved March 5, 2006, from http://www.dol.gov/esa/whd/fmla/

Useem, B., & Goldstone, J. A. (2002). Forging social order and its breakdown: Riot and reform in U.S. prisons. *American Sociological Review, 67*, 499–525.

Valocchi, S. (2005). Not yet queer enough: The lessons of queer theory for the sociology of gender and sexuality. *Gender & Society, 19*, 750–770.

Van Voorhis, P., Cullen, F. T., Link, B. G., & Wolfe, N. T. (1991). The impact of race and gender on correctional officers' orientation to the integrated environment. *Journal of Research in Crime and Delinquency, 28*, 472–500.

Villa, J. (2004, February 19). Lewis officer hurt in attack by inmate. *Arizona Republic*, pp. B1, 2.

Wald, P. (1996). Glass ceilings and open doors: A reaction. *Fordham Law Review, 65*, 603–618.

Walker, S. (1985). Racial minority and female employment in policing: Implications of "glacial" change. *Crime and Delinquency, 31*, 555–572.

Walker, S., & Katz, C. M. (2005). *Police in America: An introduction* (5th ed.). New York: McGraw-Hill.

Wallace, J. E. (2002). *Juggling it all: Exploring lawyers' work, home and family demands and coping strategies* (Law School Admission Council Research Report RR-00-02). Retrieved November 19, 2005, from www.lsacnet.org/Research/TOC-research-reports2.htm

Walters, S. (1992). Attitudinal and demographic differences between male and female corrections officers: A study in three midwestern prisons. *Journal of Offender Rehabilitation, 18*, 173–189.

Walters, S. (1993). Changing the guard: Male correctional officers' attitudes toward women as co-workers. *Journal of Offender Rehabilitation, 20*, 47–60.

Walters, S., & Lagace, D. (1999). Gender differences in occupational characteristics of Canadian correctional officers. *International Journal of Comparative and Applied Criminal Justice, 23*, 45–53.

Waters, K. L. (2005). Not all leaders look alike. *Corrections Today*, October, 92–94.

Weiss, C., & Melling, L. (1988). The legal education of twenty women. *Stanford Law Review, 40*, 1297–1344.

Wells, A. S. (1932). Twenty-two years a police woman. *The Western Woman, 7*, 15–16.

Wells, C. P. (2000). The perils of race and gender in a world of legal abstraction. *University of San Francisco Law Review, 34*, 523–535.

Wells, T., Colbert, S., & Slate, R. N. (2006). Gender matters: Differences in state probation officer stress. *Journal of Contemporary Criminal Justice, 22*, 63–79.

West, C., & Fenstermaker, S. (1995). Doing difference. *Gender & Society, 9*, 8–37.

West, C., & Zimmerman, D. H. (1987). Doing gender. *Gender & Society, 1*, 125–151.

Westley, W. (1970). *Violence and the police*. Cambridge: MIT Press.

Wexler, J. G., & Logan, D. D. (1983). Sources of stress among women police officers. *Journal of Police Science and Administration, 13*, 98–105.

White, S. E., & Marino, K. (1983). Job attitudes and police stress: An exploratory study of causation. *Journal of Police Science and Administration, 11*, 264–274.

White, T. (2005). Mental health programs: Addressing the unfunded mandate. *Corrections Today,* October, 108–115.

Wikipedia. (2006). *Lynndie England.* Retrieved February 8, 2006, from http://en.wikipedia .org/wiki/Lynndie_England

Wilkins, D. B., & Gulati, G. M. (1996). Why are there so few black lawyers in corporate law firms? An institutional analysis. *California Law Review, 84,* 493–625.

Williams, C. L. (1989). *Gender differences at work: Women and men in nontraditional occupations.* Berkeley: University of California Press.

Williams, C. L. (1995). *Still a man's world: Men who do women's work.* Berkeley: University of California Press.

Williams, J. (1990). Sameness feminism and the work-family conflict: Faulty framework: Consequences of the difference model for women in the law. *New York Law School Law Review, 35,* 347–360.

Williams, J. (2000). *Unbending gender: Why family and work conflict and what to do about it.* New York: Oxford University Press.

Wilson, N. K., & Moyer, I. L. (2004). Affirmative action, multiculturalism and criminology. In B. R. Price & N. Sokoloff (Eds.), *The criminal justice system and women: Offenders, prisoners, victims, & workers* (3rd ed., pp. 564–577). New York: McGraw-Hill.

Wimshurst, K. (1995). Anticipating the future: The early experiences and career expectations of women police recruits in post Fitzgerald Queensland. *Australian and New Zealand Journal of Criminology, 28,* 278–297.

Wing, A. (2003). *Critical race feminism: A reader* (2nd ed.). New York: New York University Press.

Withrow, P., & Burke, L. (2005). Introducing women into Michigan's correctional system: A conversation about changing culture. *Corrections Today,* October, 88–90.

Women in Law in Canada. (2005). *Catalyst Information Center: Quick takes.* Retrieved February 10, 2006, from http://www.catalystwomen.org/files/quicktakes/Quick%20 Takes%20-%20Women%20in%20Law%20in%20Canada.pdf

Women in law: Making the case. (2001). New York: Catalyst. Retrieved June 6, 2006, from http://www.catalyst.org/files/full/Women%20in%20Law%20-%20Making%20the% 20Case.pdf

Word, R. (2003, September 27). *Two female prison guards sue state alleging sexual harassment.* Associated Press Wire Service. Retrieved February 22, 2006, from http://www.angelfire .com/f14/fci/lawteylawsuit.html

Worden, A. P. (1993). The attitudes of women and men in policing: Testing conventional and contemporary wisdom. *Criminology, 31,* 203–242.

Working Group on Student Experiences. (2004, February). *Study on women's experiences at Harvard Law School.* Cambridge, MA: Author. Retrieved May 7, 2006, from http://www.law.harvard.edu/students/experiences/FullReport.pdf

Worley, R., Marquart, J. W., & Mullings, J. L. (2002). Prison guard predators: An analysis of inmates who established inappropriate relationships with prison staff, 1995–1998. *Deviant Behavior, 24,* 175–194.

Wright, K. N., & Saylor, W. G. (1991). Male and female employees' perceptions of prison work: Is there a difference? *Justice Quarterly, 8,* 505–524.

Wrightman, L. F. (1996). *Women in legal education: A comparison of law school performance and law school experiences of women and men.* Law School Admission Council Research Report Series. Newtown, PA: Law School Admission Council.

Yale Law School faculty and students speak about gender. (2001–2002). Retrieved December 15, 2005, from www.yale.edu/ylw

Yoshino, K. (2006). *Covering: The hidden assault on our civil rights.* New York: Random House.

Young, I. M. (1981). Beyond the unhappy marriage: A critique of dual systems theory. In L. Sargent (Ed.), *Women and revolution* (pp. 43–69). Boston: South End Press.

Young, I. M. (1990). *Justice and the politics of difference.* Princeton, NJ: Princeton University Press.

Young, M. (1991). *An inside job: Policing and police culture in Britain.* Oxford, UK: Clarendon Press.

Young, M. H. (1992). Examining keys to success for today's women working in juvenile corrections. *Corrections Today,* August, 106–111.

Young, V., & Reviere, R. (2006). *Women behind bars: Gender and race in US prisons.* Boulder, CO: Lynne Rienner.

Zaretsky, E. (1978). The effects of the economic crisis on the family. In Radical Political Economic Collective (Ed.), *U.S. capitalism in crisis* (pp. 209–218). New York: Union for Radical Political Economics.

Zhao, J., He, N., & Lovrich, N. P. (2003). Community policing: Did it change the basic functions of policing? *Justice Quarterly, 20*(4), 697–724.

Zimmer, L. E. (1986). *Women guarding men.* Chicago: University of Chicago Press.

Zimmer, L. E. (1987). How women reshape the prison guard role. *Gender & Society, 1,* 415–431.

Zimmer, L. E. (1989). Solving women's employment problems in corrections: Shifting the burden to administrators. *Women in Criminal Justice, 1,* 55–79.

Zimmer, M. J. (2004). The new discrimination law: Price Waterhouse is dead, whither McDonnell Douglas? *Emory Law Journal, 53*(4), 1887–1949.

List of Cases Cited

Adarand Constructors, Inc. v. Pena, 515 U.S. 200 (1995).

Antonius v. King County, No. 74759-8 (Supreme Court of the State of Washington 2004).

Barnes v. Train, 13 FEP Cases 123 (D.D.C.) (1974).

Bradwell v. Illinois, 83 U.S. 130 (1872).

Bundy v. Jackson, 641 F.2d 934 (D.C. Cir. 1981).

Burlington Industries v. Ellerath, 118 S.Ct. 2257 (1998).

City of Richmond v. Croson, 488 U.S. 469 (1989).

Cooper v. Pate, 378 U.S. 546 (1964).

Desert Palace v. Costa, 123 S.Ct. 2148, 2155 (2003).

Dothard v. Rawlinson, 433 U.S. 321 (1977).

Ellison v. Brady, 54 FEP 1346 (9th Cir. 1991).

Faragher v. City of Boca Raton, Florida, 524 U.U. 775 (1998).

Forts v. Ward, 471 F. Supp. 1095 (S.D. N.Y. 1978).

Forts v. Ward, 621 F.2d 1210 (2nd Cir. 1980).

Geduldig v. Aiello, 417 U.S. 484 (1974).

General Electric Company v. Gilbert, 429 U.S. 125 (1976).

Gratz v. Bollinger, 539 U.S. 244 (2003).

Griggs v. Duke Power Co., 401 U.S. 424 (1971).

Grummett v. Rushen, 779 F.2d 491 (9th Cir. 1985).

Grutter v. Bollinger, 539 U.S. 306 (2003).

Hardin v. Stinchcomb, 691 F.2d 1364 (11th Cir. 1982).

Harris v. Forklift, Slip Opinion 92-1168 (1993).

Hishon v. King & Spalding, 467 U.S. 69 (1984).

Holloway v. King County, Superior Court of Washington, No. 97-2-23951-6 SEA (1999).

Holloway v. King County, Superior Court of Washington, No. 97-2-23951-6 SEA, Consent Decree (2000).

Johnson v. Transportation Agency, Santa Clara County, 480 U.S. 616 (1987).

Jordan v. Gardner, 953 F.2d 1137 (9th Cir. 1993).

Kohn v. Royall, Koegel & Wells, 59 F.R.D. 515 (S.D.N.Y. 1973), appeal dismissed, 496 F.2d 1094 (2d Cir. 1974).

Meritor Savings Bank FSB v. Vinson, 477 U.S. 57 (1986).

Motion to Admit Goodell, 39 Wis. 232 (1875).

Newport News Shipbuilding and Dry Dock Co. v. EEOC, 462 U.S. 669 (1983).

Price Waterhouse v. Hopkins, 109 S.Ct. 1775 (1989).

Reynolds v. Wise, 375 F. Supp. 145 (N.D. Texas 1974).

Roe v. Wade, 410 U.S. 113 (1973).

South Carolina v. Edwards, 372 U.S. 229 (1963).

Torres v. Wisconsin Department of Health and Social Services, 48 Fair Employment Practices Case 270 (8th Cir. 1988).

Torres v. Wisconsin Department of Health and Social Services, 838 F.2d (7th Cir. 1988).

United States v. Paradise, 480 U.S. 149 (1987).

Index

About the Authors

Susan Ehrlich Martin recently retired from government after 15 years as a program director at the National Institute on Drug Abuse and the National Institute on Alcohol Abuse and Alcoholism. Prior to that, she directed several research studies at the Police Foundation and the National Research Council. Her previous and continuing research interests focus on women's problems as workers, victims, and substance abusers. Her other books include *Breaking and Entering: Police Women on Patrol* (1980) and *On the Move: The Status of Women in Policing* (1990).

Nancy C. Jurik is a sociologist and professor in the School of Justice & Social Inquiry at Arizona State University. She has published research articles in the areas of gender and work, professionalization, changing workplace organizations, self-employment, and economic development programs. She has also published *Bootstrap Dreams: U.S. Microenterprise Development in an Era of Welfare Reform* (2005).